D1429528

THE RHETORIC OF ABRAHAM'S FAITH
IN ROMANS 4

EMORY STUDIES IN EARLY CHRISTIANITY

Number 20

SBL PRESS

THE RHETORIC OF ABRAHAM'S FAITH IN ROMANS 4

Andrew Kimseng Tan

SBL PRESS

 **PRESS**

Atlanta

Publication of this volume was made possible by the generous support of the Pierce Program in Religion of Oxford College of Emory University.

The editors of this series express their sincere gratitude to David E. Orton and Deo Publishing for publication of this series 2009–2013.

Library of Congress Cataloging-in-Publication Data

Names: Tan, Andrew Kim Seng, author.
Title: The rhetoric of Abraham's faith in Romans 4 / by Andrew Kim Seng Tan.
Description: Atlanta : SBL Press, 2018. | Series: Emory studies in early Christianity ;
    Number 20 | Includes bibliographical references and index.
Identifiers: LCCN 2017060320 (print) | LCCN 2018012706 (ebook) | ISBN 9780884142904
    (ebk.) | ISBN 9781628372083 (pbk. : alk. paper) | ISBN 9780884142898 (hbk. : alk.
    paper)
Subjects: LCSH: Bible. Romans, IV—Socio-rhetorical criticism. | Abraham (Biblical
patriarch)
Classification: LCC BS2665.52 (ebook) | LCC BS2665.52 .T36 2018 (print) | DDC
227/.1066—dc23
LC record available at https://lccn.loc.gov/2017060320

Cover design is an adaptation by Bernard Madden of Rick A. Robbins, Mixed Media (19" x 24" pen and ink on paper, 1981). Cover design used by permission of Deo Publishing.

Printed on acid-free paper.

CONTENTS

Acknowledgments vii
Abbreviations ix

Introduction 1
    Statement of the Problem   1
    Literature Review   3
    Thesis Statement   13

1. Approach of Interpretation 15
    Introduction   15
    Textures of a Text   16
    Rhetorolects   22
    Conclusion   29

2. Rhetorical Contextual Framework of Romans 4 31
    Introduction   31
    The Implied Rhetorical Situation of Romans   31
    The Argument of Romans 1:16–4:25   58
    Outworking of Abraham's Trust in Romans 4   72

3. The Rhetoric of Romans 4: Part 1 111
    Introductory Matters   111
    Romans 4:1: A Question of Fatherhood   124
    Romans 4:2–8: Abraham Did Not Earn Righteousness,
        and Hence Fatherhood, by the Mosaic Law   140

4. The Rhetoric of Romans 4: Part 2 201
    Romans 4:9–12: Constructing a Myth of Origins for
        Judean and Gentile Christians   201

Romans 4:13–16: Reliance on the Mosaic Law Abolishes
  the Promise 218
Romans 4:17–25: Trust Realizes Abraham's
  Worldwide Fatherhood 244

5. Summary and Conclusion..271
  Summary 271
  Conclusion 273

6. Bibliography...275

Ancient Sources Index...307
Modern Authors Index...321
Subject Index...327

ACKNOWLEDGEMENTS

I am very grateful to Associate Professor Charles A. Wanamaker, my *Doktorvater*, for his valuable comments on various portions of this book. His many years of Christian friendship and New Testament scholarship have been my encouragement.

I am indebted to Professor Vernon K. Robbins not only for accepting this manuscript into the Emory Studies in Early Christianity series but also for pioneering sociorhetorical interpretation. His interpretive analytic has helped me better understand the rhetoric of Rom 4 by fostering a dialogic relationship with scholars from various disciplines. His numerous suggestions and constant encouragement steered this work toward publication.

I wish to thank the Pierce Program in Religion at Oxford College of Emory University for supporting the production of this book. I want to thank the editorial team at SBL Press.

The members and leaders of Tree of Life Christian Church, Teo Chin Tian, Liu Kerh Li, Koo Sin Kok, and Lawrence Lai, have been my constant encouragement in the course of my research and writing. They have been very patient with their proverbial busy pastor. Edmund Phang has been a good companion for many years in the pursuit of God's Word.

Leong Koon Yoke, to whom I dedicate this book, is a wife of noble character (Prov 31:10–31). She is always encouraging me to do the will of the Lord. My parents, Tan Bah Chek and Seet Lee Wah, and my sons, Shuen Yi and Yan Yi, prayed regularly for me. Their prayers have been my strength. To these people, I owe an unpayable debt.

Μόνῳ σοφῷ θεῷ, διὰ Ἰησοῦ Χριστοῦ, ᾧ ἡ δόξα εἰς τοὺς αἰῶνας, ἀμήν
— Rom 16:27

ABBREVIATIONS

Primary Sources

1 Macc	1 Maccabees
2 Bar.	2 Baruch (Syriac Apocalypse)
2 Macc	1 Maccabees
4 Macc	4 Maccabees
4QFlor	Florilegium
4QpGen	Pesher Genesis
Apoc. Ab.	Apocalypse of Abraham
Abr.	Philo, *De Abrahamo*
Add Esth	Additions to Esther
Ag. Ap.	Josephus, *Against Apion*
Alex.	Plutarch, *Alexander*
Amic.	Cicero, *De amicitia*
Ann.	Tacitus, *Annales*
Ant.	Josephus, *Jewish Antiquities*
Ath. pol.	Aristotle, *Athēnaiōn politeia*
Bar	Baruch
Ben.	Seneca, *De beneficiis*
Bib. hist.	Diodorus, *Bibliotheca historica*
Cal.	Suetonius, *Gaius Caligula*
Cat.	Hesiod, *Catalogue of Women*
CD	Cairo Genizah copy of the Damascus Document
Claud.	Suetonius, *Divus Claudius*
Clem.	Seneca, *De clementia*
Eloc.	Demetrius, *De elocutione*
Ep.	Libanius, *Epistulae*; Martial, *Epigrammata*; Pliny the Younger, *Epistulae*; Seneca, *Epistulae morales*
Ex. con.	Seneca the Elder, *Excerpta controversiae*
Fam.	Cicero, *Epistulae ad familiares*

Frat. amor.	Plutarch, *De fraterno amore*
Gen. an.	Aristotle, *De generatione animalium*
Geogr.	Strabo, *Geographica*
Hist.	Herodotus, *Historiae*; Tacitus, *Historiae*
Hist. rom.	Dio Cassius, *Historia romana*
Inst.	Justinian, *Institutiones*
Inst. orat.	Quintilian, *Institutio oratoria*
Inv.	Cicero, *De inventione rhetorica*
Jos. Asen.	Joseph and Asenath
Jub.	Jubilees
Jul.	Suetonius, *Divus Julius*
Jusj.	Hippocrates, *Jus jurandum* (Ὅρχος)
Legat.	Philo, *Legatio ad Gaium*
Let. Aris.	Letter of Aristeas
LXX	Septuagint
Men.	Plautus, *Menaechmi*
Menex.	Plato, *Menexenus*
Mos.	Philo, *De vita Mosis*
MT	Masoretic Text
Nat.	Pliny the Elder, *Naturalis historia*
Nat. d.	Cicero, *De natura deorum*
Off.	Cicero, *De officiis*
P.Col.	Westermann, W. L., et al., eds. *Columbia Papyri.* 11 vols. New York: Columbia University Press, 1929–1954; Missoula: Scholars Press, 1979–1998
Pol.	Aristotle, *Politica*
Prog.	Aelius Theon, *Progymnasmata*
Pss. Sol.	Psalms of Solomon
Rhet.	Aristotle, *Rhetorica*
Rhet. Her.	Rhetorica ad Herennium
Rhod.	Dio Chrysostom, *Rhodiaca* (*Or.* 31)
Sat.	Juvenal, *Satirae*
Sib. Or.	Sibylline Oracles
Sir	Sirach
T. Jud.	Testament of Judah
T. Reu.	Testament of Reuben
Tib.	Suetonius, *Tiberius*
Tob	Tobit
Top.	Cicero, *Topica*

Virt.	Philo, *De virtutibus*
War	Josephus, *Jewish War*
Wis	Wisdom of Solomon

Secondary Sources

AB	Anchor Bible
ABD	Freedman, David Noel, ed. *Anchor Bible Dictionary.* 6 vols. New York: Doubleday, 1992
ABS	Archaeology and Biblical Studies
AnBib	Analecta Biblica
ANRW	Temporini, Hildegard, and Wolfgang Haase, eds. *Aufstieg und Niedergang der römischen Welt: Geschichte und Kultur Roms im Spiegel der neueren Forschung.* Part 2, *Principat.* Berlin: de Gruyter, 1972–
APOT	Charles, R. H. *The Apocrypha and Pseudepigrapha of the Old Testament.* Oxford: Clarendon, 1913
ASMA	Aarhus Studies in Mediterranean Antiquity
ASORDS	American Schools of Oriental Research Dissertation Series
AUSS	*Andrews University Seminary Studies*
BA	*Biblical Archaeologist*
BDAG	Walter, Bauer, Frederick W. Danker, William F. Arndt, and F. Wilbur Gingrich. *Greek-English Lexicon of the New Testament and Other Early Christian Literature.* 3rd ed. Chicago: University of Chicago Press, 2000
BDB	Brown, Francis, S. R. Driver, and Charles A. Briggs. *A Hebrew Lexicon of the Old Testament.* Oxford: Clarendon Press, 1907
BDF	Blass, Friedrich, and Albert Debrunner, and Robert W. Funk. *A Greek Grammar of the New Testament and Other Early Christian Literature.* Chicago: University of Chicago Press, 1961
BECNT	Baker Exegetical Commentary on the New Testament
Berytus	*Berytus: Archaeological Studies*
BEvT	Beiträge zur evangelischen Theologie

BHT	Beiträge zur historischen Theologie
Bib	*Biblica*
BibInt	Biblical Interpretation Series
BMI	The Bible and Its Modern Interpreters
BNTC	Black's New Testament Commentaries
BTB	*Biblical Theology Bulletin*
BZAW	Beihefte zur Zeitschrift für die alttestamentliche Wissenschaft
CBC	Cambridge Bible Commentary
CBQ	*Catholic Biblical Quarterly*
CBR	*Currents in Biblical Research*
CCT	Classics and Contemporary Thought
CKLR	*Chicago-Kent Law Review*
ConBNT	Coniectanea Biblica: New Testament Series
CovQ	*Covenant Quarterly*
CR	*Classical Review*
CRINT	Compendia Rerum Iudaicarum ad Novum Testamentum
ECL	Early Christianity and Its Literature
ERAW	Edinburgh Readings on the Ancient World
ERS	*Ethnic and Racial Studies*
ERSP	*European Review of Social Psychology*
ESV	English Standard Version
EvQ	*Evangelical Quarterly*
EvT	*Evangelische Theologie*
ExpTim	*The Expository Times*
FAB	Frankfurter Althistorische Beiträge
FB	Forschung zur Bibel
HThKNT	Herders Theologischer Kommentar zum Neuen Testament
HTR	*Harvard Theological Review*
HvTSt	*Hervormde Teologiese Studies*
IBC	Interpretation: A Bible Commentary for Teaching and Preaching
ICC	International Critical Commentary
IG	*Inscriptiones Graecae.* Editio Minor. Berlin: de Gruyter, 1924–
IJPS	*International Journal of Philosophical Studies*
Int	*Interpretation*

JBL	*Journal of Biblical Literature*
JETS	*Journal of the Evangelical Theological Society*
JSJ	*Journal for the Study of Judaism*
JSNT	*Journal for the Study of the New Testament*
JSNTSup	Journal for the Study of the New Testament Supplement Series
JSOT	*Journal for the Study of the Old Testament*
JSOTSup	Journal for the Study of the Old Testament Supplement Series
JTS	*Journal of Theological Studies*
KJV	King James Version
LCL	Loeb Classical Library
LEC	Library of Early Christianity
LNSAS	Leicester-Nottingham Studies in Ancient Society
LNTS	The Library of New Testament Studies
MAAR	*Memoirs of the American Academy in Rome*
MT	Masoretic Text
MTZ	*Münchener theologische Zeitschrift*
NCBC	New Century Bible Commentary
NEB	New English Bible
NICNT	New International Commentary on the New Testament
NICOT	New International Commentary on the Old Testament
NIV	New International Version
NovT	*Novum Testamentum*
NovTSup	NovT Supplements
NRSV	New Revised Standard Version
NTS	*New Testament Studies*
Numen	Numen Book Series
OBO	Orbis Biblicus et Orientalis
OCM	Oxford Classical Monographs
OTP	Charlesworth, James H., ed. *Old Testament Pseudepigrapha.* 2 vols. New York: Doubleday, 1983–1985
Paideia	Paideia: Commentaries on the New Testament
PR	*Philosophy and Rhetoric*
QJS	*Quarterly Journal of Speech*
RBL	*Review of Biblical Literature*
RBS	Resources for Biblical Study

RIG	Michel, Charles. *Recueil des Inscriptions Grecques.* Brussels: Lamertin, 1900. Repr. Hildesheim: Olms, 1976.
RRA	Rhetoric of Religious Antiquity
SBL	Society of Biblical Literature
SBLDS	Society of Biblical Literature Dissertation Series
SBLSBS	Society of Biblical Literature Sources for Biblical Study
SBLTT	Society of Biblical Literature Texts and Translations
SCJR	*Studies in Christian-Jewish Relations*
SEG	*Supplementum epigraphicum graecum.* Amsterdam: Gieben, 1923–
SIG	Dittenberger, Wilhelm. *Sylloge inscriptionum graecarum.* 3rd ed. 4 vols. Leipzig: Hirzel, 1915–1924
SNTSMS	Society for New Testament Studies Monograph Series
SNTW	Studies of the New Testament and Its World
SP	Sacra Pagina
SR	Social Research
SRI	Sociorhetorical Interpretation
StPatr	*Studia Patristisca*
StudNeot	Studia Neotestamentica
SymS	Symposium Series
TBN	Themes in Biblical Narrative
TDNT	Kittel, Gerhard, and Gerhard Friedrich, eds. *Theological Dictionary of the New Testament.* Translated by Geoffrey W. Bromiley. 10 vols. Grand Rapids: Eerdmans, 1964–1976
THKNT	Theologischer Handkommentar zum Neuen Testament
TNTC	Tyndale New Testament Commentary
TOTC	Tyndale Old Testament Commentaries
TU	Texte und Untersuchungen zur Geschichte der altchristlichen Literatur
TynBul	*Tyndale Bulletin*
TZ	*Theologische Zeitschrif*
VT	*Vetus Testamentum*
WBC	Word Biblical Commentary
WGRW	Writings from the Greco-Roman World

WSC	*Western Speech Communication*
WUNT	Wissenschaftliche Untersuchungen zum Neuen Testament
ZNW	*Zeitschrift für die neutestamentliche Wissenschaft und die Kunde der älteren Kirche*

INTRODUCTION

1. Statement of the Problem

Romans 4 treats important themes such as righteousness by faith and the fatherhood of Abraham for Judean Christians and gentile Christians. Thus, interpreters and those interested in Christian theology have rightly engaged this passage when discussing important topics such as salvation history and the nature of the Christian faith.[1] This passage has also been fertile ground for discussing the so-called New Perspective that has become a "reigning paradigm that ... controls contemporary discussion on Paul" and other related themes.[2] Moving the discussion forward, how-

---

1. See, for example, the involved argument between Ulrich Wilckens and Günter Klein, in which Wilckens insists that Paul advocates the continuity of salvation history in Rom 4: Ulrich Wilckens, "Die Rechtfertigung Abrahams nach Römer 4," in *Studien zur Theologie der Alttestamentlichen Überlieferungen: Festschrift für Gerhard von Rad*, ed. Rolf Rendtorff and Klaus Koch (Neukirchen-Vluyn: Neukirchener Verlag, 1961), 111–27; Günter Klein, "Römer 4 und die Idee der Heilsgeschichte," *EvT* 23 (1963): 424–47; Wilckens, "Zu Römer 3,21–4,25: Antwort an G. Klein," *EvT* 24 (1964): 586–610; Klein, "Exegetische Probleme in Römer 3,21–4,25: Antwort an Ulrich Wilckens," *EvT* 24 (1964): 676–83. Leonhard Goppelt interprets Rom 4 as supporting salvation history from the perspective of typology. See Goppelt, *Typos: The Typological Interpretation of the Old Testament in the New*, trans. Donald Madvig (Grand Rapids: Eerdmans, 1982), 137. Klaus Berger takes a mediating position. See Berger, "Abraham in den paulinischen Hauptbriefen," *MTZ* 17 (1966): 47–89. See also the discussion in Halvor Moxnes, *Theology in Conflict: Studies in Paul's Understanding of God in Romans*, NovTSup 53 (Leiden: Brill, 1980), 103–5 and the bibliographic references to scholars (including Ernst Käsemann, Rudolf Bultmann, E. P. Sanders, Peter Stuhlmacher, etc.) who have discussed Rom 4 for various theological interests.

2. Quote from D. A. Carson, introduction to *The Complexities of Second Temple Judaism*, vol. 1 of *Justification and Variegated Nomism*, ed. D. A. Carson, Peter T. O'Brien, and Mark A. Seifrid (Grand Rapids: Baker Academic, 2001), 1. For the New Perspective, see, e.g., E. P. Sanders, *Paul and Palestinian Judaism: A Comparison of*

ever, is difficult, as scholars have yet to come to an agreement on the intent of the passage, and without it, there is no common platform to discuss the significance of the details in this passage for theological issues.[3] Understanding the rhetoric of Rom 4 can help clarify the details and intent of this passage.

Romans 4 also deals extensively with the relationship between Judean and gentile Christians. The term *Judean* is used intentionally in this study. The Greek noun that Paul uses, Ἰουδαῖοι, has been traditionally translated "Jews," the adjective form being "Jewish." As I will explain in detail in chapter 3, Ἰουδαῖοι is primarily a geographical designation, not a religious one; consequently, I and many other scholars prefer the terms *Judeans* and *Judean* to *Jews* and *Jewish*.[4] Because Romans 4 addresses the relationship between Judean and gentile Christians, it has an important "social function" in mediating ethnic issues that are straining the relationship between these two groups.[5] Its social function is accentuated by the fact that it is the first chapter (apart from a brief section in 3:29–30) that addresses, in some length, Judean and gentile Christians as one people (under the father-

---

Patterns of Religion (Philadelphia: Fortress, 1977), 489–91; James D. G. Dunn, *Romans 1–8*, WBC (Waco, TX: Word, 1988), 227; Richard B. Hays, " 'Have We Found Abraham to Be Our Forefather according to the Flesh?' A Reconsideration of Rom 4:1," *NovT* 27 (1985): 76–98.

3. For examples of how different construals of the intent of Rom 4 affect the interpretation of details pertaining to the New Perspective, see N. T. Wright, "Romans and the Theology of Paul," in *Romans*, vol. 3 of *Pauline Theology*, ed. David M. Hay and E. Elizabeth Johnson, SBLSymS 23 (Atlanta: Society of Biblical Literature, 2002), 40–41; Simon J. Gathercole, *Where Is Boasting? Early Jewish Soteriology and Paul's Response in Rom 1–5* (Grand Rapids: Eerdmans, 2002), 233–36.

4. While some scholars use *gentiles* with an uppercase G (e.g., Robert Jewett, *Romans: A Commentary*, Hermeneia [Minneapolis: Fortress, 2007], 113, 117, passim), the group gentiles does not denote an ethnic entity, so it appears in this work with a lowercase g. Although Terence L. Donaldson uses an uppercase G with the word, his comments corroborate my point that gentiles are not an ethnic group: "Left to their own devices and self-definitions, Phrygians, Parthians or Bithynians would no more describe themselves as ἔθνη than they would as βάρβαροι. In each case the term is one imposed by others—Jews in one case, Greeks in the other." See Donaldson, " 'Gentile Christianity' as a Category in the Study of Christian Origins," *HTR* 106 (2013): 451–52. Stanley K. Stowers also uses a lowercase g in *A Rereading of Romans: Justice, Jews, and Gentiles* (New Haven: Yale University Press, 1994), 83, 84, passim.

5. Francis Watson, *Paul, Judaism and the Gentiles*, SNTSMS 56 (Cambridge: Cambridge University Press, 1986), 139.

hood of Abraham). Paul seeks to alleviate the tension in the relationship between Judean and gentile Christians by way of the rhetoric of Rom 4.

Therefore, by investigating and better understanding the rhetoric of Abraham's faith in Rom 4, this book seeks to advance theological discussions and also to understand better how this chapter alleviates the dissension between Judean and gentile Christians in Romans. I shall now provide a literature review of the state of research with regard to the rhetoric of Rom 4 as well as social and cultural studies that shed light onto the meaning of this chapter.

2. Literature Review

Romans 4 is a piece of rhetoric written by Paul to persuade a specific audience, in this case, the Roman Christian audience. This act of communication is only recognizable when read in light of "specific, material and ideological contexts" that involve social and cultural contexts.[6] In other words, the social and cultural contexts that give rise to ideological and persuasive power in Romans need to be investigated. What follows below reviews the state of research on the purpose of persuasion—that is, the rhetorical goal—of Rom 4 and major social and cultural studies done on Rom 4.

2.1. Purpose of Persuasion

Traditionally, this text has been understood as a polemic against righteousness by deeds.[7] Since Abraham is regarded as the model par excellence of obedience to the law of Moses, Paul's interpretation, which shows that

---

6. J. David Hester (Amador), *Academic Constraints in Rhetorical Criticism of the New Testament*, JSNTSup 174 (Shefield: Sheffield Academic, 1999), 19–20, following Mikhail Bakhtin. See Pam Morris, ed., *The Bakhtin Reader: Selected Writings of Bakhtin, Medvedev, and Voloshinov* (London: Arnold, 1994), 26–37. Mikhail M. Bakhtin comments that language must be understood in "all its ideological spheres," as this involves the process of "sociopolitical and cultural centralization." See Bakhtin, *The Dialogic Imagination: Four Essays*, ed. Michael Holquist, trans. Caryl Emerson and Michael Holquist (Austin: University of Texas Press, 1981), 271.

7. E.g., C. E. B. Cranfield, *The Epistle to the Romans*, 2 vols., ICC (Edinburgh: T&T Clark, 1975–1979), 1:224–25; Ernst Käsemann, *Commentary on Romans*, trans. Geoffrey W. Bromiley (Grand Rapids: Eerdmans, 1973), 105; Douglas J. Moo, *The Epistle to the Romans*, NICNT (Grand Rapids: Eerdmans, 1996), 255.

Abraham was made righteous by faith, constitutes a strong polemic against righteousness by means of the Mosaic law.[8] This seems, prima facie, to be the intent, considering that the theme of righteousness by faith is a thread that runs through the chapter. Recently, however, this interpretation has been called into question by proponents of the New Perspective. They claim that Judaism, like Christianity, advocates salvation by grace. Hence, Paul's polemic is not leveled at some form of legalism. Paul's contention, rather, was with the Judeans' perceived privileged ethnic status. Thus, New Perspective scholars argue that Rom 4 revolves around Abraham as the father of Judean and gentile Christians.[9] What follows elaborates on the two views.

2.1.1. Romans 4 as Rhetoric to Establish Righteousness by Faith

The view that the rhetoric of Rom 4 attempts to establish righteousness by faith has several variations. Ernst Käsemann understands the primary purpose of Rom 4 as providing scriptural proof for the thesis in 3:21–26, which is elaborated in 3:27–31, that righteousness comes by faith. This thesis, as Paul explains in Rom 4, is supported by "God's direction of salvation history … as it is documented in the OT."[10] Käsemann further elaborates that Paul chooses Abraham because of "the Jewish tradition which closely connects

---

8. Judeans contemporary with Paul often present Abraham as a model for the devout Judean. E.g., in Jub. 16:25–28, Abraham is said to have obeyed the law although it had yet to be written; see also Jub. 24:11: "And in thy seed shall all the nations of the earth be blessed, because thy father obeyed My voice, and kept My charge and My commandments, and My laws, and My ordinances, and My covenant; and now obey My voice and dwell in this land" (APOT). Similarly, see Bar 57:1–2; CD 3:2.

9. Thus, "Romans is not how a person may find acceptance with God; the problem is to work out an understanding of the relationship in Christ between Jews and Gentiles" (Hays, "Have We Found Abraham," 84). See also Michael Cranford, "Abraham in Romans 4: The Father of All Who Believe," NTS 41 (1995): 71–88; Lloyd Gaston, Paul and the Torah (Vancouver: University of British Columbia Press, 1987), 45–63. Thomas Schreiner subscribes to this view but does not support the New Perspective. See Schreiner, Romans, BECNT (Grand Rapids: Baker, 1998), 209–11; more recently, see John M. G. Barclay, Paul and the Gift (Grand Rapids: Eerdmans, 2015), 481.

10. Käsemann interprets Abraham as "the prototype of faith" (Commentary on Romans, 91, cf. 127). See also Ernst Käsemann, Perspectives on Paul (London: SCM, 1971), 79–101. Similarly, Wilckens interprets Abraham as beginning "election history" ("Die Rechtfertigung Abrahams," 10). Käsemann, however, argues against Wilckens that Paul does not advocate an unbroken continuity in salvation history that "could fit into the theological formula of promise and fulfillment" (Perspectives on Paul, 87).

the covenants with Abraham and Moses."[11] Like Käsemann, Brendan Byrne also regards Abraham in Rom 4 as a scriptural proof of righteousness by faith and sees Abraham being depicted as part of salvation history in Rom 4.[12] He, however, sees Rom 4 as a response to a narrower preceding context, namely, 3:21–22. C. E. B. Cranfield thinks that Rom 4 substantiates the first part of 3:27—that no one has a right to boast. This is achieved by establishing that Abraham has "no right to glory."[13] Paul, as Cranfield understands him, selects Abraham primarily because he is regarded by the Judeans as a model of one who attained righteousness by deeds.[14] In the same vein, Joseph A. Fitzmyer interprets Rom 4 primarily as "an illustration of 3:27" but adds that Rom 4 also responds to 3:31.[15] Douglas J. Moo argues that Paul seeks in Rom 4 to elaborate the key theme of righteousness by faith, as found in 3:27–31, and to draw out its implications, especially that of the "full inclusion of the Gentiles in the people of God."[16] Paul's choice of Abraham stems from several reasons: his pivotal role in the formation of the people of Israel, his position as an exemplar of torah obedience and faith, and his pivotal position in the history of salvation.[17]

Scholars who take the position that Paul in Rom 4 seeks to establish righteousness by faith generally provide first a minimal discussion of how

---

11. Käsemann, *Commentary on Romans*, 105. Scholars who regard Abraham as part of salvation history include Moo, *Epistle to the Romans*, 257, n. 8; Joseph A. Fitzmyer, *Romans: A New Translation with Introduction and Commentary*, AB 33 (New York: Doubleday, 1993), 371.

12. Brendan Byrne does not use the term "salvation history." He implies it, however, when he says that Abraham's "ancestral role continues in a truly representative way ... for his descendants," including "the glorious Israel of the messianic age," and is "a definition of God's eschatological people." See Byrne, *Romans*, SP 6 (Collegeville, MN: Liturgical Press, 1996), 141–42.

13. Cranfield, *Epistle to the Romans*, 1:224; Fitzmyer, *Romans*, 369–71.

14. Cranfield, *Epistle to the Romans*, 1:227. See also, Moo, *Epistle to the Romans*, 256; Byrne, *Romans*, 142; Jewett, *Romans*, 308–9. Contra Hans Conzelmann, who thinks Abraham is chosen as a random example. See Conzelmann, *An Outline of the Theology of the New Testament* (London: SCM, 1969), 169, 190.

15. See also Thomas C. Rhyne, *Faith Establishes the Law*, SBLDS 55 (Chico, CA: Scholars Press, 1981).

16. Moo, *Epistle to the Romans*, 243, quote at 257; Hans Hübner, *Law in Paul's Thought*, ed. John Riches, trans. James C. G. Greig, SNTW (Edinburgh: T&T Clark, 1984), 118. Heinrich Schlier thinks that Rom 4 proves the thesis of 3:28. See Schlier, *Der Römerbrief*, HThKNT 6 (Freiburg: Herder, 1977), 121.

17. Moo, *Epistle to the Romans*, 256–57.

Rom 4 continues the preceding argument before proceeding to demonstrate the logic of Rom 4 based on their preferred position. It is difficult, however, to decide on the correct view from their discussions, as they do not substantiate their positions with sufficient proof. Neither have they interacted sufficiently with the other major position that Rom 4 is a demonstration of Abraham's fatherhood of Judean and gentile Christians.

2.1.2. Romans 4 as Rhetoric to Show That Abraham Is Father of Judean and Gentile Christians

Richard B. Hays claims that Rom 4 attempts to demonstrate that Abraham is the father of Judean and gentile Christians alike. To do this, Hays takes Ἀβραάμ ("Abraham") as the direct object of εὑρηκέναι ("to have found") and its subject, the "we" of ἐροῦμεν ("we shall say"). He then translates 4:1 as follows: "What then shall we say? Have we found Abraham (to be) our forefather according to the flesh?"[18] Most scholars reject this reading, as it is not usual to leave the accusative subject of the infinitive unexpressed.[19] Hays, however, argues that this translation coheres with the preceding and following discussions.[20] James D. G. Dunn disagrees because it weakens the more immediate link between 4:1 and 4:2–8.[21] In response, Michael Cranford asserts that 4:1–3 emphasizes the basis by which righteousness is associated with Abraham and his descendants, and hence supports the theme of Abraham's fatherhood.[22] Similarly, Thomas Schreiner adds that Rom 4 defends the fatherhood of Abraham by confirming the double themes of 3:27–31—righteousness is by faith, and everyone receives it in the same manner.[23]

Hays represents a serious attempt to bolster the position that Rom 4 focuses on Abraham's fatherhood of Judean and gentile Christians. Scholars who subscribe to this position, however, have not explained adequately

---

18. Hays, "Have We Found Abraham," 92, quote at 81.

19. See, e.g., Dunn, *Romans 1–8*, 199; Thomas H. Tobin, "What Shall We Say Abraham Found? The Controversy behind Romans 4," *HTR* 88 (1995): 443; Byrne, *Romans*, 148; Schreiner, *Romans*, 213; Jewett, *Romans*, 307.

20. Hays, "Have We Found Abraham," 83–93.

21. Dunn, *Romans 1–8*, 199.

22. Cranford, "Abraham in Romans 4," 79. So also others, e.g., Byrne, *Romans*, 145; Schreiner, *Romans*, 213.

23. Schreiner, *Romans*, 209.

why Paul describes the content of Abraham's faith in detail and couches it in terms of death and life topoi.

2.2. Social and Cultural Studies on Romans 4

The New Testament is "comprehensible only within a larger constellation of social, economic, political, and cultural currents."[24] Most studies on the social and cultural background of Rom 4 have focused on the influence of Second Temple Judaism. Studies on how Mediterranean culture influences the rhetoric of Rom 4 are needed. The following is a survey of the state of research in this area.

2.2.1. Halvor Moxnes

Halvor Moxnes examines how honor, a value in the Mediterranean culture that "plays a crucial role in establishing a sense of worth," shapes the rhetoric of Romans.[25] Honor "is public esteem, rather than private and individualistic esteem; a culture of this type is public and group-oriented."[26] Moxnes equates righteousness with honor.[27] That honor and its counterpart, shame, play a crucial role in Romans is indicated by related vocabulary found throughout this section of Romans and by the fact that these terms "are more evenly distributed than terms for justification and righteousness."[28] In a setting constrained by this culture of honor and shame, the question arises, according to Moxnes, as to how a crucified Jesus preached by Paul could be powerful or bring honor. This causes a conflict between Judean and gentile Christians who had accepted Paul's gospel. Romans seeks to "bring believing Jews and non-Jews together in one community."[29] To do this, Paul employs "terms which had been used to emphasize the special status of the Jews."[30] At the same time, he also changes the meaning of these terms by sharing "concepts for values

---

24. So John H. Elliott, *What Is Social-Scientific Criticism?* (Minneapolis: Augsburg Fortress, 1993), 9.

25. Halvor Moxnes, "Honour and Righteousness in Romans," *JSNT* 32 (1988): 77.

26. Ibid., 62.

27. Ibid., 71.

28. Ibid., 63.

29. Ibid., 64.

30. Ibid.

with his cultural context" and changing, in many instances, the content of these concepts. Paul's objective is twofold: it alleviates the conflict with the synagogues, and hence the Judean Christians, and it includes "Jews and non-Jews … among those who are made righteous."[31] At the same time, this new community of Judean and gentile Christians can function within Greco-Roman society. In alleviating the conflict with the synagogue, Paul uses two constants. First, God is the "significant other" in whom honor must be sought. Second, Paul argues in Rom 2 that such honor is given by the significant other, God, to those who obey and not to those who merely possess the law.[32] These two points continue to be discussed in Rom 3–4. This discussion on honor is brought out by the boasting of the Judeans in 3:27 and 4:2. This boasting is "linked to the law and to 'works.'"[33] In Rom 4, Paul "retains the concept of the righteous man as the honourable man."[34] According to Moxnes, Paul, however, redefines righteousness in terms of honor as "*father* of a large offspring (4:11–12, 16–18) or *heir* of the world (4:13)."[35] This righteousness is obtained neither by doing good deeds (4:2–4) or observing the Mosaic law (3:27–28; 4:13) nor through circumcision (4:9–10). It is given as a gift and is unconditional (4:13–14).[36] It is given to both Judeans and gentiles so that "this honour is awarded by the one and only 'significant other,' and it is in his eyes, 'before him' [4:2, 17]."[37]

Moxnes has ably demonstrated his major thesis that Paul, in order to reduce conflict between Judean and gentile Christians within an "honour and shame" culture, uses terms that emphasize the special status of Judeans and at the same time reconfigures them so that both Judeans and gentiles can be included as people who are honorable, that is, righteous. How terms that describe a Judean are reconfigured to alleviate the dissension between Judean and gentile Christians can be further explored. Moxnes's argument has, however, several weaknesses. First, it is doubtful that the contention between Judean and gentile Christians in Romans centers on the crucified Jesus.[38] It may be an issue in 1 Corinthians (see 1:23), but this

---

31. Ibid., 64, 71.
32. Ibid., 69.
33. Ibid., 71.
34. Ibid.
35. Ibid., emphasis original.
36. Ibid., 72.
37. Ibid.
38. Ibid., 64.

issue is not explicitly mentioned in Romans. Instead, Paul's gospel and the righteousness it brings are often set in opposition to the law of Moses in Romans. In other words, the controversy in Romans is not about a gospel that preaches a crucified Jesus but about one that preaches a righteousness without the help of the law of Moses.

Second, Moxnes proposes that "the righteous man is the honourable man."[39] This, however, requires a more thorough investigation to prove the equation. He runs roughshod over the argument of Rom 4 when he equates righteousness to the special statuses of Abraham as "father of a large offspring" (4:11–12, 16–18) and "heir of the world" (4:13). These statuses are the results and not the equivalents of becoming a righteous or honorable man. Such an understanding is made more unlikely by the tight nexus between righteousness and holiness in Romans. How righteousness, holiness, and honor are integrated to resolve the dissension between the "weak" and the "strong," which I shall argue to be a major problem facing the Roman Christians, needs to be investigated.[40]

2.2.2. Francis Watson

In *Paul, Judaism and the Gentiles*, Francis Watson utilizes two sociological models to discern Paul's rhetorical strategy. The first model concerns "the transformation of a reform-movement into a sect."[41] This reform movement, while incorporating the content of the old group, also opposes some of the content that defines the old group. If this reform movement, according to Watson, manages to overcome this initial conflict with the old group, it will become a sect. The second model states that to maintain "separation from the religious group from which it originated, it will require an ideology legitimizing its state of separation."[42] In the case of Romans, Watson detects this legitimation taking the form of "denuncia-

---

39. Ibid., 71.

40. See below, chapter 2, §2.6, "Conclusion."

41. Francis Watson, *Paul, Judaism and the Gentiles*, 19. Cf. Philip F. Esler, who opines that a sect is created in the intensity of opposition with the old religion. See Esler, *Community and Gospel in Luke-Acts: The Social and Political Motivations of Lucan Theology*, SNTSMS 57 (Cambridge: Cambridge University Press, 1987), 20.

42. Watson (*Paul, Judaism and the Gentiles*, 19–20) follows the lead of Esler (*Community and Gospel*, 16–18), who modifies the conceptualization of Peter L. Berger and Thomas Luckmann: when the unity and shared history with the old group is broken, "legitimation," which takes the form of explanation and justification, is needed. See

tion" in Rom 2, "antithesis" in Rom 3, and "reinterpretation" in Rom 4.[43] In employing legitimation, Paul contrasts two different views of Abraham in 4:1–8 to stress the incompatibility of membership in the Judean community with "membership in a Pauline congregation."[44] This contrast that seeks to delegitimize the circumcised, in Watson's view, is furthered in 4:9–12, where Paul seeks to communicate that righteousness is not found among the circumcised. Similarly, Watson thinks that Paul is reiterating in 4:14b–15 that "membership of the Jewish community is neither necessary nor desirable."[45] Watson concludes that in all his argument, "Paul's aim was to persuade the Jewish Christians to recognize the legitimacy of the Gentile congregation and to join with it in worship, even though this would inevitably mean a final separation from the synagogue."[46]

Watson offers a plausible application of the use of the social device of legitimation. The Achilles heel of Watson's thesis, however, is brought into sharp focus by Philip F. Esler: "If Watson is correct here, it would mean that Paul was attempting the form of recategorization that social theorists suggest is doomed to failure, namely, one that advocates the abandonment of an existing ethnic identity."[47] Furthermore, as will be demonstrated in my analysis of the argument of Rom 4, Paul appears more to be taking a mediating stance in resolving the dissension between Judean and gentile Christians than to be asking Judean Christians to abandon their ethnic identity as defined by the law of Moses.

2.2.3. Philip F. Esler

Using social-identity theory, Esler argues that Abraham is a prototype of group identity and becomes a common "superordinate" identity that unites the Judean and gentile Christians.[48] As this recategorization does not require the two subgroups to abandon their ethnic identities, it

---

Berger and Luckmann, *The Social Construction of Reality: A Treatise in the Sociology of Knowledge* (London: Penguin, 1967), 110–16.

43. Francis Watson, *Paul, Judaism and the Gentiles*, 109–22 (on denunciation), 124–35 (on antithesis), 135–42 (on reinterpretation).

44. Ibid., 140.

45. Ibid., 141.

46. Ibid., 178.

47. Philip F. Esler, *Conflict and Identity in Romans: The Social Setting of Paul's Letter* (Minneapolis: Fortress, 2003), 178.

48. Ibid., 29, 190.

facilitates unity.[49] According to Esler, Paul promotes this thesis by first explaining "the origin and nature of Abraham's righteousness" (4:1–8).[50] He then demonstrates that the blessing given to Abraham falls upon both the circumcised and the uncircumcised (4:9–12).[51] Paul then proceeds to explain what Abraham's prototypical role is not and the nature of Abraham's faith (4:13–22).[52] Finally, Paul concludes that the identity established above (4:1–22) applies to "those contemporary with Paul."[53] Overall, Esler's main thesis is convincing, and it clarifies Paul's strategy in trying to unite the Judean and gentile Christians. Notwithstanding, some parts of Esler's argument could be strengthened. For instance, Esler, without providing evidence, argues that it is only at 4:9 that Paul takes up the prototypical role of the patriarch and that 4:1–8 is only foundational in that it explains "the cause and character of his [Abraham's] righteousness."[54] Also, to view 4:13–16 as demonstrating from a negative perspective what is not prototypical is not convincing, as it could be argued that 4:9–12 also performs the same function. Neither is it clear that Paul's description of Abraham's faith in 4:17–22 has its main purpose in laying down common grounds for both Judean and non-Judean audiences. Prototypicality may be one of Paul's lines of argumentation, but this needs to be demonstrated from the text. Esler also makes an important observation that Abraham was chosen as a prototype because of the "centrality of kinship in Mediterranean culture."[55] Unfortunately, he only gives passing comments on this. Esler's thesis that Abraham is a "superordinate identity" that unites Judean and gentile Christians represents a convincing attempt at using social identity theory to clarify and reinforce Paul's strategy. Esler also mentions the role of kinship that results in the choice of Abraham as a prototype. These will be used to further explore Rom 4 in this research.

---

49. Ibid., 29, 177–78.
50. Ibid., 184.
51. Ibid., 188.
52. Ibid., 191–93.
53. Ibid., 193–94.
54. Ibid., 184.
55. Ibid., 190.

2.2.4. Robert Jewett

Robert Jewett, in his mammoth commentary on Romans, attempts to incorporate into the study of the letter all methods of historical analysis, including "social scientific reconstruction of the audience situation" and "historical and cultural analysis of the honor, shame, and imperial systems in the Greco-Roman world."[56] He highlights the need to interpret Romans in light of its cultural context and not approach it as "an abstract theological document such as Paul's self-confession or the defense of some modern doctrinal stance."[57] Thus, he correctly reads Rom 4 within the broader scheme of honor and shame culture. For instance, in interpreting 4:6–7, Jewett comments that Paul maintains that God accepts those who are without honor. In dealing with the division between "competitive factions," Jewett interprets the God in whom Abraham believed to be the same as "the father of Jesus Christ who accepts and honors those who have no basis for honor."[58] Jewett regards this act of God "in an honor-shame society ... [as] the ultimate honor one could receive."[59] He is also culturally sensitive in translating terms like χάρις as "favor" in place of the traditional term, "grace."[60] He has, however, only given passing comments without demonstrating how such a Greco-Roman cultural system drives Paul's rhetoric forward in Rom 4. Jewett also interacts extensively with ancient sources.[61] This helps to situate Paul's rhetoric in the ancient social and cultural context. He also utilizes social scientific analysis, namely, social identity theory. For instance, he mentions the contribution of Philip F. Esler and Maria Neubrand in identifying Abraham as a "prototype of group identity" and Abraham's role in sealing the new "in-group identity."[62] In this way, Jewett argues, "whether they are Jews or Gentiles..., they are now Abraham's children and recipients of the righteousness that comes through faith alone." Like his treatment of the honor and shame culture within Rom 4, here, Jewett does not show in substantial depth how social identity theory sheds light on Abraham's role as a prototype of group identity.

---

56. Jewett, *Romans*, 1.
57. Ibid., 46.
58. Ibid., 314.
59. Ibid., 340.
60. Ibid., 313.
61. Ibid., 312, 332: see his comments on 4:4, 17.
62. Ibid., 308–9, 321.

3. Thesis Statement

This book will demonstrate that Paul seeks, by the rhetoric of Rom 4,[63] to ascribe honor to gentile Christians so that Judean Christians will not claim a superior honor status over them for the reason that gentile Christians do not possess the Mosaic law, Judeans' ethnic identity marker.

Honor is ascribed to a person when God, the significant other, regards that person as righteous, that is, when the relationship between God and that person is characterized by righteousness.[64] I shall argue that in Rom 4 Paul contends that gentile Christians are considered righteous by God for a twofold reason. The first has a social basis. Paul crafts a myth of origins for gentile Christians as part of their new Christian identity. In this way, they become descendants of Abraham and so inherit the righteousness that was ascribed to him by God.

The second reason has a religious basis. Death contains religious pollution.[65] Abraham's dead body passes religious pollution onto his descendants, who are present in him in form. This religious pollution results in dead descendants. The reason why Judean and, in particular, gentile Christians can now become Abraham's descendants is because Abraham had faith (πίστις) in—or, more precisely, trusted—his patron, God, to raise to life his dead body and his dead descendants.[66]

---

63. Here, the term *rhetoric* is used in the sense meant by George A. Kennedy, that is, that "quality in discourse by which a speaker or writer seeks to accomplish his purposes." See Kennedy, *New Testament Interpretation through Rhetorical Criticism* (Chapel Hill: University of North Carolina Press, 1984), 3. In this sense, every interpreter, including those who may not have specified his analytical model, is engaged in understanding the rhetoric of a biblical text.

64. Barclay comments that the "label 'righteous' is socially attributed (i.e., dependent on the opinion of others)" (*Paul and the Gift*, 376–77). It does not refer to someone who is saved but who is worthy of receiving gifts from God, in this case, the gift of salvation. Such a notion ties in with Roman patronage where the patron would only give gifts to those he considered worthy (see Barclay, *Paul and the Gift*, 39; see Cicero, *Fam.* 2.6.1–2; Pliny the Younger, *Ep.* 10.51).

65. See below, chapter 4, §3.1, "Death and Pollution."

66. From this point onwards, where appropriate, I shall translate the cognates of πιστ- as "trust" in place of the traditional rendering, "faith," as it coheres better with the usage in the Mediterranean world. As I shall later elaborate (see below, chapter 3, §3.4, "Romans 4:4–5: Deeds and Trust Are Antithetical"), in the preindustrial first-century world of the New Testament, power, property, and wealth were concentrated in the hands of two percent of the people who were the elites of the society. To obtain

This raising to life is made possible by a broker, Jesus Christ, who accomplishes two things. First, he expiates religious pollution, that is, sin. Second, his resurrection life enables gentile Christians to live an ethically righteous life before God. More precisely, they can now satisfy the righteous demand of the Mosaic law and so receive honor that is bestowed by the significant other, namely, God.

I will make use of sociorhetorical interpretation (hereafter, SRI), pioneered by Vernon K. Robbins, to understand the rhetoric of Rom 4, that is, its persuasive goal and its power to persuade. Four textures—the inner texture, intertexture, social and cultural texture, and ideological texture—will be investigated. The rhetorolects (rhetorical dialects) will also be discussed. The above-mentioned elements will not be discussed in turn. Rather, in order to better grasp the rhetoric in its persuasiveness, I shall, generally, discuss these elements in the course of a close reading of the text of Rom 4. Hence, the analysis of Rom 4 and its various paragraphs will proceed verse by verse. Generally, difficulties in the syntax will first be discussed. Only then can SRI be performed.

Chapter 1 will briefly explain the different elements involved in SRI. In chapter 2 I will examine the contextual framework of Rom 4. To do that, I will first ascertain the implied rhetorical situation of Romans, then discuss the preceding argument that leads into Rom 4. This will provide some understanding of the rhetorical strategy of Paul, the implied speaker, when he wrote Rom 4. Chapters 3 and 4 will discuss the rhetoric of Rom 4. Chapter 5 will then summarize how Paul's rhetoric responds to the problem of dissension between Judean and gentile Christians.

---

special goods, the vast majority of the world had to ask favors of these elites. When a patron granted a favor, a long-term patron-client relationship was formed. A patron would grant favors to the client. The appropriate response of the client to the patron was to trust the patron to provide. This trust also included loyalty to the patron. Such an understanding undergirded the relationship between Abraham and God in Rom 4. Similarly, Teresa Morgan comments that "*pistis* and *fides* lexica represent what one might call reifications of trust or of the grounds of trust." See Morgan, *Roman Faith and Christian Faith: Pistis and Fides in the Early Roman Empire and Early Churches* (Oxford: Oxford University Press, 2015), 6.

1

APPROACH OF INTERPRETATION

1. Introduction

Terry Eagleton aptly emphasizes that "literature ... is vitally engaged with the living situations of men and women.... [It] displays life in all its rich variousness, and rejects barren conceptual enquiry for the feel and taste of what it is to be alive."[1] Robbins sharpens the focus when he comments that "texts are performances of language, and language is a part of the inner fabric of society, culture, ideology and religion."[2] Likewise, Romans was written to people who lived in a particular social and cultural setting and sought to bring about social action.[3] Hence, for a text, including the rhetoric of Rom 4, to be properly understood, the insights of "literary critics, linguists, sociologists and anthropologists" need to be considered.[4]

The SRI approach pioneered by Robbins offers an interface for various disciplines to contribute their insights into a text.[5] This approach will be

---

1. Terry Eagleton, *Literary Theory: An Introduction* (Oxford: Blackwell, 1983), 196.

2. Vernon K. Robbins, *The Tapestry of Early Christian Discourse* (London: Routledge, 1996), 1.

3. Maurice Charland emphasizes the need to situate rhetorical analysis within the context of "social formation." See Charland, "Rehabilitating Rhetoric," in *Contemporary Rhetorical Theory: A Reader*, ed. John L. Lucaites, Celeste M. Condit, and Sally Caudill (New York: Guilford, 1999), 465. Similarly, Kenneth Burke, *A Rhetoric of Motives* (New York: Braziller, 1950), 37–39; Karl R. Wallace, "The Substance of Rhetoric: Good Reasons," *QJS* 49 (1963): 239–49.

4. Robbins, *Tapestry of Early Christian Discourse*, 17.

5. Instead of entitling this chapter *methodology*, I have used the word *approach*: Robbins comments that the term methodology presupposes "a limited number of analytical strategies." See Robbins, *The Invention of Christian Discourse*, RRA 1 (Dorset: Deo, 2009), 4. SRI, however, is an interpretive analytic that invites all disciplines to contribute their insights into a text. Vernon K. Robbins, Robert H. von

adopted to investigate the rhetoric of Rom 4. Insights from Robbins's discussion on the textures of texts and rhetorolects will be discussed.[6]

2. Textures of a Text

Robbins describes a text as a "thick tapestry" that contains "multiple textures of meanings, convictions, beliefs, values, emotions and actions."[7] He delineates several textures, including the inner texture, intertexture, social and cultural texture, and ideological texture.[8] The discussion below provides an overview of textures and subtextures that are relevant to Rom 4.[9]

Thaden Jr., and Bart B. Bruehler explain that the advantage of an interpretive analytic over a methodology is that it helps interpreters "learn how a text prompts and influences thinking, emotions, and behaviour." See their introduction to *Foundations for Sociorhetorical Exploration: A Rhetoric of Religious Antiquity Reader*, ed. Robbins, von Thaden, and Bruehler, RRA 4 (Atlanta: SBL Press, 2016), 1. Also, Duane F. Watson remarks that SRI is more comprehensive than rhetorical analysis. See Watson, "Keep Yourselves from Idols: A Socio-rhetorical Analysis of the Exordium and Peroratio of 1 John," in *Fabrics of Discourse: Essays in Honor of Vernon K. Robbins*, ed. David B. Gowler, L. Gregory Bloomquist, and Duane F. Watson (Harrisburg, PA: Trinity Press International, 2003), 281.

6. On textures of texts, see Vernon K. Robbins, *Exploring the Texture of Texts* (Harrisburg, PA: Trinity Press International, 1996); Robbins, *Tapestry of Early Christian Discourse*. On rhetorolects, see Robbins, *Invention of Christian Discourse*.

7. Robbins, *Tapestry of Early Christian Discourse*, 18.

8. Ibid., 21. A fifth texture, "sacred texture," is included in Robbins, *Exploring the Texture of Texts*, 3. This book, however, will not investigate "sacred texture." The reason is that the discussion on rhetorolects (see my analysis of the argument of Rom 4) covers what sacred texture does, namely, "locating the ways the text speaks about Gods or gods, or talks about realms of religious life" (Robbins, *Exploring the Texture of Texts*, 120).

9. Vernon K. Robbins distinguishes "sociorhetorical criticism from historical criticism, social scientific criticism, sociological criticism, social-historical criticism, and the study of social realia and social organization—all of which are historical methods based on data *external* to texts." See Robbins, "Sociorhetorical Criticism: Mary, Elizabeth, and the Magnificat as a Test Case," in Robbins, von Thaden, and Bruehler, *Foundations for Sociorhetorical Exploration*, 29, emphasis added. Likewise, L. Gregory Bloomquist highlights that SRI "asks interpreters to carry forth programmatic analysis, but to do so in light of a hermeneutical sensitivity to the question being asked of the text." See Bloomquist, "Paul's Inclusive Language: The Ideological Texture of Romans 1," in Robbins, von Thaden, and Bruehler, *Foundations for Sociorhetorical Exploration*, 119.

2.1. Inner Texture[10]

For analysis of the inner texture, the interpreter is confined to the environment delimited by the implied speaker and the implied audience.[11] In other words, inner texture analysis does not concern itself with language and information that is outside the text.[12] Several possible subtextures may be present in the inner texture. First, *repetitive texture* is present when the same word occurs more than once. These repetitions provide an overview of the passage, without establishing the precise relationship between the individual units.[13] Second, *progressive texture* arises out of repetitions. By observing the relationship between repetitions or individual clusters of repetitions, one may discern the progression or general scheme of the speaker's rhetorical strategy. Third, *opening-middle-closing* texture is delineated by observing the repetitive and progressive textures. By examining how the closing responds to the opening, and how the middle facilitates the transition from opening to closing, the speaker's overall rhetoric may be discerned.[14] Fourth, *argumentative texture* or *rhetology* investigates the inner reasoning or argumentation within the rhetoric.[15] Declarative statements are not argumentative. When a speaker, however, provides reasons for a declarative statement, he or she is engaging in argumentation that seeks to persuade the audience.[16] Fifth, *sensory-aesthetic texture* can be

---

10. Robbins, *Exploring the Texture of Texts*, 21–29.

11. See Robbins (*Tapestry of Early Christian Discourse*, 28–29), who adapts the narrative-communication situation of Seymour Chatman, *Story and Discourse: Narrative Structure in Fiction and Film* (New York: Cornell University Press, 1978), 151; Shlomith Rimmon-Kenan, *Narrative Fiction: Contemporary Poetics* (London: Methuen, 1983), 86.

12. Robbins, *Tapestry of Early Christian Discourse*, 29.

13. H. J. Bernard Combrink, "Shame on the Hypocritical Leaders in the Church," in Gowler, Bloomquist, and Watson, *Fabrics of Discourse*, 2. David B. Gowler regards the various textures as interacting with one another to "reinforce and build upon each other." See Gowler, "Text, Culture, and Ideology in Luke 7:1–10," in Gowler, Bloomquist, and Watson, *Fabrics of Discourse*, 96.

14. For an example, see below, chapter 3, §3.3.6, "Genesis 15:1–21 LXX."

15. Robbins, *Invention of Christian Discourse*, xxvii.

16. Anders Eriksson, "Enthymemes in Pauline Argumentation: Reading between the Lines in 1 Corinthians," in Eriksson, Olbricht, and Übelacker, *Rhetorical Argumentation in Biblical Texts*, 248. Frans H. van Eemeren posits that the speaker's reasons may include pragmatic and logical considerations. See van Eemeren, "Argumentation Theory: An Overview of Approaches and Research Themes," in *Rhetorical Argumen-*

found in the range of senses to which the text refers. One way of detecting this texture is by identifying *body zones* in the discourse.[17] Humans interact with the environment by means of three zones: "a heart for thinking, along with ears that fill the heart with data; a mouth for speaking, along with ears that collect the speech of others; and hands and feet for acting."[18] By being alert to terms that refer to the above three zones and understanding them in light of Mediterranean culture, how the sensory-aesthetic texture enhances the rhetoric can be better understood.[19]

2.2. Intertexture[20]

Verbal signs (that is, the implied language) in a text sometimes evoke verbal signs in other texts.[21] In addition, the represented world of the text sometimes also evokes the represented world of other texts.[22] Several types of intertexture are possible: oral-scribal, cultural, social, and historical. Occurring frequently in Rom 4 is recitation, a subtexture of oral-scribal intertexture.[23] In this texture, words from another text are either replicated in full or replicated with some words omitted or changed.[24] At other times, the words of the text are completely omitted, but its content is retained. By comparing the recitation and, for instance, the LXX from which the recitation was taken, the author's emphasis may be clarified. Cultural intertexture refers to knowledge of a particular culture learned through the normal process of enculturation by people who are born and live in that culture or knowledge learned through education or direct interaction with people in the culture by those from outside the culture.[25] It refers to *insider*

---

tation in Biblical Texts: Essays from the Lund 2000 Conference, ed. Anders Eriksson, Thomas H. Olbricht, and Walter Übelacker (Harrisburg, PA: Trinity Press International, 2002), 9.

17. Robbins, *Exploring the Texture of Texts*, 30.

18. Ibid.

19. For an example, see below, chapter 3, §1.3, "Inner Texture."

20. Robbins, *Tapestry of Early Christian Discourse*, 96–143.

21. Ibid., 21–22.

22. Ibid., 32.

23. Which includes recitation, recontextualization and reconfiguration; see ibid., 102.

24. Ibid., 106.

25. Robbins differentiates SRI from conventional studies of the social and cultural dimensions of early Christianity (e.g., Wayne A. Meeks, *The First Urban Christians:*

knowledge. Thus, for instance, references to Abraham, David, circumcision, the Passover festival, the messiah, and God are cultural rather than social intertextures. A subtexture of cultural intertexture is reference. This is "the occurrence of a word, phrase, or clause that refers to a personage or tradition known to people in a culture."[26] Although this story or tradition exists in textual form (word, phrase, or clause), the author does not merely intend the reader to recall the text. Rather, the recitation of the text should recall a story or a tradition.[27] Social intertexture refers to knowledge about customs and practices that everyone in a particular region, for instance, in the Roman world and the Hellenistic world, knows.[28] This knowledge is readily available to people through general interaction. It can be obtained simply by observing "the behaviour and public material objects produced by other people."[29] This contrasts with cultural intertexture whose knowledge needs to be taught.[30] Historical intertexture refers to particular events that happened at particular times and places.[31] This intertexture "textualizes" a past experience into a particular event or a particular period of time. It differs from social intertexture, which occurs as regular events in one's life.[32]

In analyzing certain terms—for example, death—for their social intertextures, I will investigate them in light of Roman and Judean cultures. Understanding terms like death in light of particular cultures is reasonable, even necessary, as human beings are shaped by the process of enculturation into the cultures in which they live. Clifford Geertz argues that

---

The Social World of the Apostle Paul [New Haven: Yale University Press, 1983]; Meeks, *The Moral World of the First Christians*, LEC 6 [Philadelphia: Westminster, 1986]) in two aspects: the former focuses on social, cultural, and ideological dimensions, and the context is that of the Mediterranean ("Sociorhetorical Criticism," 33).

26. Robbins, *Tapestry of Early Christian Discourse*, 110.

27. Robbins, *Exploring the Texture of Texts*, 58. For an example, see below, chapter 3, §2.2.2, "Ἀβραάμ: One Who Observes the Mosaic Law."

28. Robbins, *Tapestry of Early Christian Discourse*, 117. For an example, see below, chapter 4, §1.4, "Romans 4:11b: Abraham Is the Father of the Uncircumcised."

29. Robbins, *Exploring the Texture of Texts*, 62.

30. Ibid.

31. Ibid., 63.

32. Robbins, *Tapestry of Early Christian Discourse*, 118. For an example, see below, chapter 2, §4.2, "Romans 6:1–14: Trust in God Enables Christians to Live Righteous Lives."

culture is the fabric of meaning in terms of which human beings interpret their experience and guide their actions; social structure is the form
that actions take, the actually existing network of social relations. Culture and social structures are then but different abstractions from the
same phenomenon.[33]

Robbins disagrees with studies that limit intertextual interpretation of
New Testament literature to the Hebrew Bible and Judean literature.[34] He
insists that "theoretically, the intertexture of any piece of literature may be
with 'every culture in the human world.' It is impossible, however, to study
everything at the same time. For this reason, we establish boundaries."[35]
Robbins limits the boundary of intertextual studies for early Christian texts
to texts, inscriptions, archaeological data, sculpture, paintings, et cetera,
in the Mediterranean world.[36] The dominant culture in Rome would be
Roman culture. Dominant culture is defined as "a system of attitudes,
values, dispositions and norms supported by social structures vested with
power to impose its goals on people in a significantly broad territorial
region. Dominant cultures are either indigenous or conquering cultures."[37]
Roman culture was such a conquering culture, one that asserted influence
over a broad territorial region. Furthermore, as Christianity emerged from
the Judean community, we would also expect Judean culture to influence
Christians—perhaps as a subculture—where people "imitate the attitudes,
values, dispositions and norms of a dominant culture and claim to enact
them better than members of a dominant status. Subcultures are wholistic
entities that affect all of life over a long span of time."[38] Hence, Judean and
gentile Christians in Rome, who lived in the ancient Mediterranean world,
would have been influenced by Roman and Judean cultures and very probably Hellenistic culture to some degree.[39]

---

33. Clifford Geertz, *The Interpretation of Cultures* (New York: Basic Books,
1973), 145.

34. Robbins, *Tapestry of Early Christian Discourse*, 99. The Hebrew Bible here
includes the apocryphal and pseudepigraphical Judean writings.

35. Ibid.

36. Robbins, *Exploring the Texture of Texts*, 63.

37. Robbins, *Tapestry of Early Christian Discourse*, 168.

38. Ibid.

39. Similarly, Morgan contends that as Christianity evolved in a world governed
by Roman rule, "Roman as well as Greek and Jewish ideas may always be in the

2.3. Social and Cultural Texture

Social and cultural texture seeks to answer the question: "What kind of a social and cultural person would anyone be who lives in the 'world' of a particular text."[40] To answer this question, it makes use of anthropological and sociological theories.[41] It explores "the social and cultural nature of the voices in the text under investigation."[42] Social and cultural topoi, including the core value of honor and shame in Mediterranean culture, challenge-riposte, patron-client relations, and purity codes, will be used to shed light on the social and cultural textures in Rom 4. Also, works of sociologists and anthropologists will be utilized to understand aspects of ethnicity related to the dissension between Judeans and gentiles.

2.4. Ideological Texture

L. Gregory Bloomquist provides a description of ideological texture adopted in this book:[43]

> I would suggest that ideological texture is manifest in the rhetorical goal of texts, namely, where authors attempt to get an audience, real or fictive, to do or understand something, and that not just negatively or for reasons of coercive power.

The ideological texture of a text operates within the relationship between the implied reader and the narrator. The particular way the implied reader and the real reader (or audience) receive a message is about ideology.[44] Robbins follows Eagleton's lead in describing ideology as "the ways in

---

background of the thinking of early Christian writers" (*Roman Faith and Christian Faith*, 125).

40. Robbins, *Exploring the Texture of Texts*, 71.

41. Robbins, *Tapestry of Early Christian Discourse*, 144. For an example, see below, chapter 2, §3.3, "Romans 3:21–31: Jesus Atones for the Sins of Both Judeans and Gentiles."

42. Ibid.

43. Bloomquist, "Paul's Inclusive Language," 126. Similarly, Roy R. Jeal insists that the "task of the examination of ideological texture is to come to an understanding of how texts move people to take a point of view." See Jeal, "Clothes Make the (Wo)Man," in Robbins, von Thaden, and Bruehler, *Foundations for Sociorhetorical Exploration*, 402.

44. Robbins, *Tapestry of Early Christian Discourse*, 36–37. For an example, see

which what we say and believe connects with the power-structure and power-relations of the society we live in.... [M]ore particularly, those modes of feeling, valuing, perceiving and believing which have some kind of relation to the maintenance and reproduction of social power."[45]

In other words, in Robbins's and Eagleton's conception, ideology maintains and produces power. Such ideological power is relevant especially in contexts of conflict and can be used to rationalize, legitimize, or delegitimize groups, as in the case of the groups in Paul's letter to the Romans.[46] Charles A. Wanamaker develops Robbins's formulation of ideological texture by drawing on John B. Thompson's conception of how ideology produces social power: "In the sociologically relevant sense of 'power,' however, the power to act must be related to the institutional site from which it derives."[47] In the case of Paul, he mobilizes power by building his ideology on Mediterranean cultural practices such as "imperial and civic politics, kinship, client and patron relationship."[48] This final point sharpens Robbins's conception of how the ideological texture in a New Testament text mobilizes rhetorical power. Thus, detecting the underlying social and cultural intertextures helps to expose the institution from which ideological power is derived.[49]

3. Rhetorolects

Different forms of discourse draw on "distinctive configurations of themes, images, ... topics, reasonings and argumentation."[50] For example, we might speak of political discourse or economic discourse in the modern

---

below, chapter 2, §3.3, "Romans 3:21–31: Jesus Atones for the Sins of Both Judeans and Gentiles."

45. Ibid., 36, quoting Eagleton, *Literary Theory*, 15.

46. John S. Kloppenborg, "Ideological Texture in the Parable of the Tenants," in Gowler, Bloomquist, and Watson, *Fabrics of Discourse*, 67.

47. So John B. Thompson, *Studies in the Theory of Ideology* (Berkeley: University of California Press, 1984), 129; see also Charles A. Wanamaker, "'By the Power of God': Rhetoric and Ideology in 2 Corinthians 10–13," in Gowler, Bloomquist, and Watson, *Fabrics of Discourse*, 199.

48. Wanamaker, "By the Power of God," 199.

49. Russell B. Sisson points out the need to go beyond scriptural intertexture to identify ideological interests. See Sisson, "A Common Agōn," in Gowler, Bloomquist, and Watson, *Fabrics of Discourse*, 256.

50. Robbins, *Invention of Christian Discourse*, xxvii.

world. While these discourses overlap at times, they are nevertheless distinct in their character and are used in different contexts and employ different rhetorics. The term *rhetorolect*, which is Robbins's neologism, refers to just such rhetorical dialects. The term rhetorolect is an elision of *rhetorical dialect*. Robbins postulates that six rhetorolects or rhetorical dialects were crucial in the formation of early Christian discourse. These six are wisdom, prophetic, apocalyptic, precreation, priestly, and miracle rhetorolects. These six rhetorolects blended into one another to create persuasive modes of discourse among early Christians. Christians generated discourses by either blending multiple rhetorolects within an overarching rhetorolect or blending particular rhetorolects in a persuasive manner.

3.1. The Problem of Classical Rhetoric

Interpreting the New Testament using theories of classical rhetoric was led by George A. Kennedy, Hans Dieter Betz, and Wilhelm Wuellner. An advantage of classical rhetorical analysis is that by categorizing the overarching rhetoric as judicial, deliberative, or epideictic, the persuasive goal of the rhetoric can be identified.[51] The present way of doing rhetorical analysis, however, has a fundamental flaw. As Robbins has poignantly pointed out, the setting of early Christian rhetoric does not presuppose the law court, political assembly, or civil ceremony, the traditional settings associated with classical rhetoric.[52] In fact, these social institutions at times caused suffering for early Christians. To counteract the sufferings created by these institutions, early Christians developed rhetorical discourses whose social settings were related to "households, political kingdoms, imperial armies, imperial households, temples, and individual bodies of people."[53] The early Christian discourses around these settings led Robbins to suggest his six rhetorolects of early Christian discourse.

---

51. Charles A. Wanamaker is perceptive when he points out that "rhetorical analysis has the potential to look at the smaller units of meaning as well as the text in terms of their total persuasive effect." See Wanamaker, "Epistolary vs. Rhetorical Analysis: Is a Synthesis Possible?," in *The Thessalonians Debate: Methodological Discord or Methodological Synthesis*, ed. Karl P. Donfried and Johannes Beutler (Grand Rapids: Eerdmans, 2000), 285.

52. Robbins, *Invention of Christian Discourse*, 3.

53. Ibid.

Thus, they can function as a corrective or complement to the use of the traditional rhetorical settings in the analysis of early Christian rhetoric.[54]

3.2. The Nature of Rhetorolects

A rhetorolect is schematized as an idealized cognitive model (abbreviated as ICM). An ICM is a structure by which humans organize knowledge. Robbins formulates his ICM of a rhetorolect according to two theories. The first is critical spatiality theory. This theory relates the geophysical spaces experienced by humans with the mental spaces created by humans in order to give meaning to their experiences in life.[55] The meaning is obtained through metaphorical reasoning whereby "experiential knowledge of places and spaces in the Mediterranean world" is blended with "the cosmos where it is presupposed that God dwells."[56]

The second is conceptual blending theory.[57] This theory concretizes the specifics for metaphorical reasoning to work so as to derive meaning for human experiences. Mark Turner observes that "conceptual blending is a fundamental instrument of the everyday mind, used in our basic construal of all our realities, from the social to the scientific."[58] The construction of how realities are construed is organized in terms of "cultural frames, which George Lakoff calls ICMs and which this book calls rhetorolects."[59] According to Gilles Fauconnier and Mark Turner, conceptual blending

---

54. Robbins astutely observes that "in contrast to an approach that uses worldly rhetoric as a normative standard for real rhetoric, the goal of a rhetorical interpreter must be to use the insight that the New Testament writings blend ... worldly and radical rhetoric, rhetology and rhetography, together." See Robbins, "A New Way of Seeing the Familiar Text," in Robbins, von Thaden, and Bruehler, *Foundations for Sociorhetorical Exploration*, 388. Thus, Robbins's use of rhetorolects builds upon and refines Kennedy's approach to analyzing rhetoric.

55. Robbins, *Invention of Christian Discourse*, 8.

56. Ibid., 107. See also George Lakoff, *Women, Fire, and Dangerous Things: What Categories Reveal about the Mind* (Chicago: University of Chicago Press, 1987), 68–90.

57. Lynn R. Huber notes that, "while conceptual metaphor theory is a relatively recent field of study, its roots are in the classical tradition of Aristotle and Cicero, who assumed a vital connection between thought and language." See Huber, "Knowing Is Seeing: Theories of Metaphor Ancient, Medieval, and Modern," in Robbins, von Thaden, and Bruehler, *Foundations for Sociorhetorical Exploration*, 270.

58. Mark Turner, *The Literary Mind* (New York: Oxford University Press, 1996), 93.

59. Robbins, *Invention of Christian Discourse*, 107.

or integration involves a minimum of four spaces: "two input spaces, a generic space, and a blended space."[60] Robbins conceptualizes rhetorolects in the following way: "Certain words and phrases evoke these [special cultural] memories in a manner that frames the reasoning about topics the discourse introduces to the hearers."[61]

Firstspace is created in the following manner. The human body, when living in various social places in the world—like a household, village, city, synagogue, kingdom, temple, or an empire—has sensory-aesthetic experiences. These experiences will then evoke special firstspace pictures and memories in the minds of those experiencing them.[62] Secondspace is created in the following manner. By means of cognitive and conceptual abilities, the human mind interprets the social places and actions that the human body experiences. This generic space contains processes like part-whole, similar-dissimilar, opposites, and cause-effect to blend firstspace and secondspace. Blending takes place in thirdspace, which is also called the "space of blending." The results of the blend are thirdspace.

These thirdspace results are described by Robbins as "ongoing bodily effects and enactments."[63] By this, Robbins is referring to the effects that a particular rhetoric has on the audience. This outcome may be the audience's response or reaction, a new or renewed motivation, or a mindset, emotion, and so on. For instance, the thirdspace of wisdom rhetorolect is "to create people who produce good, righteous action, thought, will, and speech with the aid of God's wisdom"; apocalyptic rhetorolect seeks to "call

---

60. Gilles Fauconnier and Mark Turner, *The Way We Think: Conceptual Blending and the Mind's Hidden Complexities* (New York: Basic Books, 2002), 279.

61. Robbins, *Invention of Christian Discourse*, 107–8.

62. Ibid., 108. Robert H. von Thaden Jr. underscores that "any means to investigate the production and understanding of meaning by humanity must simply take into account the fact that humans are embodied, social agents." See von Thaden, "A Cognitive Turn: Conceptual Blending within a Sociorhetorical Framework," in Robbins, von Thaden, and Bruehler, *Foundations for Sociorhetorical Exploration*, 287.

63. Robbins, *Invention of Christian Discourse*, 109. The use of rhetorolects in SRI can trace its beginnings to ancient rhetoric, as Huber observes that the first reason Rhetorica and Herennium suggests for using metaphor is "to create a 'vivid mental picture' for the audience (Rhet. Her. 4.34)" and "for making a speech more interesting and possibly more compelling to a speaker's audience" ("Knowing Is Seeing," 244).

people into action and thought guided by perfect holiness" as only perfect holiness and righteousness can admit a person into God's presence.[64]

3.3. Description of the Six Rhetorolects[65]

This section will briefly describe each rhetorolect in order to aid the interpreter in its identification. I shall begin with wisdom rhetorolect.[66] The firstspace of wisdom rhetorolect is related to human experiences of the household. These experiences include household relationships, like parents who take on the role of teaching children God's wisdom. Household experiences also include household activities in gardens, places of vegetation, vineyards, and fields.[67] The secondspace pictures God as the heavenly Father. These two spaces will blend in the thirdspace to produce in the minds of the audience an image of God the Father teaching wisdom to God's children. The result will be an audience who will produce good and righteous action, thought, will, and speech.

The firstspace of prophetic rhetorolect includes a political kingdom and the speech and action of a prophet's body.[68] The prophet's speech confronts a resistant audience. The secondspace conceptualizes the social setting of the firstspace as kingdom of God on earth or in God's cosmos. God functions as heavenly King over his righteous kingdom. The thirdspace blends the firstspace and the secondspace so that the audience conceptualizes God as King transmitting his word through prophetic action and speech. The resulting thirdspace is an audience who lives according to God's righteousness.

The firstspace of apocalyptic rhetorolect is a political empire, the emperor's household, and his imperial army. The human mind concep-

---

64. For the specifics of these "ongoing bodily effects and enactments" of the six rhetorolects, see Robbins, *Exploring the Texture of Texts*, 110–12.

65. Robbins, *Invention of Christian Discourse*, 110–12. The six rhetorolects of SRI develops important concerns in the programmatic essay of Jon L. Berquist, "Theories of Space and Construction of the Ancient World" in Robbins, von Thaden, and Bruehler, *Foundations for Sociorhetorical Exploration*, 176: "Critical spatiality offers an area in which to integrate sociological and philosophical concerns in such a way as to rethink contemporary biblical and religious scholarship and to create new constructions of the ancient world."

66. For an example, see below, chapter 2, §2.4.2, "Romans 1:8–15."

67. Robbins, *Invention of Christian Discourse*, 132.

68. For an example, see below, chapter 2, §2.4.1, "Romans 1:1–7."

tualizes the social setting in the secondspace where God is regarded as a heavenly emperor who commands his heavenly assistants to destroy all evil and enact righteousness. The firstspace and secondspace blends in the thirdspace. The resulting thirdspace causes the audience to think and act according to perfect holiness as "only perfect holiness and righteousness can bring a person into the presence of God, who destroys all evil."[69] This perfect holiness is possible because of the apocalyptic state in which "God's holiness and righteousness are completely and eternally present."[70] This state is also one in which death and sin are overcome.[71]

The firstspace of precreation rhetorolect is the universal emperor, analogous to but beyond the Roman emperor and his household. The secondspace is God's cosmos, where God is a loving heavenly emperor. This status of God is eternal, with Christ as the agency of the created world. The realm of invisible God exists before time and persists continually throughout eternity. People enter into a loving relationship with God by means of worshiping not only God but also his eternal Son. When the firstspace and the secondspace are blended in the thirdspace, it guides the audience towards a "community that is formed through God's love, which reflects the eternal intimacy present in God's precreation household."[72] Love in the ancient Mediterranean world was not necessarily connected with "feelings of affection" but was about "the value of group attachment and group bonding."[73]

Miracle rhetorolect focuses on human bodies that are afflicted with diseases. Human bodies that are sick require an agent of God's power who can heal that diseased body. Thus, the firstspace of miracle rhetorolect is a *space of relation* between an afflicted body and a healer empowered with God's healing power. The secondspace conceptualizes the above space of relation as God who can "function as a miraculous renewer of life." The

---

69. Robbins, *Invention of Christian Discourse*, 110. For an example, see below, chapter 2, §3.4, "Romans 4:1–25: Abraham Is the Father of Judean and Gentile Christians."

70. Ibid., 111.

71. Ibid., 436.

72. Ibid., 111. For an example, see below, chapter 2, §4.1, "Romans 5:1–21: Trust in God Brings Peace between God and Christians."

73. See Bruce J. Malina, "Love," in *Handbook of Biblical Social Values*, ed. John J. Pilch and Bruce J. Malina (Peabody, MA: Hendrickson, 1998), 127. He also notes that Paul views God's love as a concern with "the larger problem of getting those who joined their Christian groups to become attached to each other, their new 'neighbors.'"

thirdspace blends the above-described firstspace and secondspace to produce "renewal within people."[74]

The firstspace of priestly rhetorolect is human experiences in a temple, at an altar, or in a place of worship. The secondspace conceptualizes the firstspace as God dwelling in a heavenly temple. Selected individuals—for example, Jesus—are visualized as priests. People are conceptualized as a holy and pure priestly community. The thirdspace blends the above-mentioned firstspace and secondspace to motivate the audience to be givers of sacrificial offerings and receivers of holiness from God.[75]

3.4. Using Rhetorolects

I will use Robbins's formulation of the six rhetorolects to do several things. First, I will identify the overarching rhetorolect of each section of Rom 4. Robbins has provided a two-dimensional matrix containing the three spaces for the above-mentioned six rhetorolects.[76] By checking against this matrix, the interpreter can identify the rhetorolect used. The presence of a certain rhetorolect can be detected by reading the passage under investigation and checking for elements that may be described in the firstspace, secondspace, or thirdspace of Robbins's matrix.[77] A limitation of this matrix needs to be mentioned. An ICM is a structured mental space, an idealized model of some real life situation. This means that such a model may not fit what is experienced in reality. Rather, the fit ranges from best

---

74. For an example, see below, chapter 4, §3, "Romans 4:17–25: Trust Realizes Abraham's Worldwide Fatherhood."

75. For examples, see below, chapter 2, §3.3, "Romans 3:21–31: Jesus Atones for the Sins of Both Judeans and Gentiles."

76. Robbins (*Invention of Christian Discourse*, 109), through his use of "priestly" rhetorolect, clarifies the interplay of first-, second-, and thirdspaces of Claudia V. Camp, "Storied Space, or Ben Sira 'Tells' a Temple," in Robbins, von Thaden, and Bruehler, *Foundations for Sociorhetorical Exploration*, 187. There she interprets the thirdspace as where ritual worship is experienced "in the Firstspace of power and is, accordingly, mapped onto the Secondspace of royal ideology."

77. Bart B. Bruehler observes that people in the ancient Mediterranean live in a high-context society. Thus, "social-spatial exegesis" is necessary to deduce the implicit author's conceptions of places which the author provides in the text. See Bruehler, "From This Place: A Theoretical Framework for the Social-Spatial Analysis of Luke," in Robbins, von Thaden, and Bruehler, *Foundations for Sociorhetorical Exploration*, 206.

to worst fit.[78] Thus, the interpreter needs to search for a best fit and not an ideal fit of the three mental spaces and then check against the thirdspace to determine the "bodily effects," that is, the desired response from the real audience after hearing a piece of rhetoric. In this way, the persuasive goal of each major section of Rom 4 can be determined. This fills the lacuna left by classical rhetoric due to the fact that the categories of classical rhetoric are not appropriate for determining the persuasive goal of a piece of New Testament rhetoric, as discussed above.

4. Conclusion

SRI contains a two-pronged approach. First, a text is born out of factors that relate to society, culture, ideology, and religion. Hence, disciplines that investigate these various factors should contribute to the meaning of a text. SRI has the advantage of prodding the interpreter to utilize these multiple disciplinary approaches. At the same time, it discourages giving excessive weight to insights derived from any one disciplinary approach. Second, SRI does not yield fragmented analyses. It provides an integrated environment where the multiple textures of a text can be correlated. Thus, this two-pronged approach of SRI facilitates a rich and holistic under-standing of a text.

---

78. Lakoff, *Women, Fire, and Dangerous Things*, 70.

2

RHETORICAL CONTEXTUAL
FRAMEWORK OF ROMANS 4

1. Introduction

This chapter will construct the rhetorical contextual framework of Rom
4 in order to understand the function of Rom 4 in this letter. I shall do
this by first investigating the implied rhetorical situation of Romans. The
implied rhetorical situation is what Dennis L. Stamps describes as "that
situation embedded in the text and created by the text."[1] This book, however, does not seek to provide a definitive answer to the implied rhetorical
situation of Romans, as that alone would easily entail a whole book. Only
details sufficient to construct a working platform to understand the function of Rom 4 will be investigated. Second, I shall trace the argument in
1:16–3:31 to elucidate the issues that precipitate the need for Rom 4. Third,
this chapter will show that the main ideas in Rom 4 are being worked out
in 5:1–15:13. I will identify passages that, in my judgment, contain ideas
central to Rom 4 and provide a brief analysis.

2. The Implied Rhetorical Situation of Romans

To construct the implied rhetorical situation of Romans, I shall discuss
briefly the *exordium* (1:1–15) and *peroratio* (15:1–16:27), as these two sections carry interpretive weight in constructing the rhetorical situation.[2]

---

1. Dennis L. Stamps, "Rethinking the Rhetorical Situation: The Entextualization
of the Situation in the New Testament Epistles," in *Rhetoric and the New Testament:
Essays from the 1992 Heidelberg Conference*, ed. Stanley E. Porter and Thomas H.
Olbricht (Sheffield: JSOT Press, 1993), 199.

2. J. Christiaan Beker views Romans as a situational letter. See Beker, *Paul the*

The intent of my discussion is not to show how Paul the speaker uses the *exordium* to establish rapport with the audience or uses the *peroratio* to recapitulate his main points and stir up the audience's emotion. Neither *ethos* nor *pathos* will be extensively discussed. Rather, as places (in the *exordium* and *peroratio*) that contain *ethos* and *pathos* often betray the speaker's concerns, these places will be examined for their illumination of the rhetorical situation. In constructing the rhetorical situation, I shall also consider selected sections of Romans that, in my judgment, will shed light on the rhetorical situation.

2.1. About Rhetorical Situation

Rhetorical theorists recognize that for a discourse to be intelligible, the rhetorical situation or the social context that generates a discourse needs to be discovered.[3] I shall use Lloyd F. Bitzer's formulation of the rhetorical situation to identify the necessary parameters that generate Paul's rhetoric in Rom 4.[4]

2.1.1. Implied Rhetorical Situation

In discussing how rhetoric in a text is generated, Stamps comments:

> While it may be granted that any text, and an ancient New Testament epistle in particular, stems from certain historical and social contingencies which contribute to the rhetorical situation of the text, it is also true that a text presents a selected, limited and crafted entextualization of the situation. The entextualized situation is not the historical situation which generates the text and/or which the text responds to or addresses; rather,

---

Apostle: The Triumph of God in Life and Thought (Philadelphia: Fortress, 1984), 62. See below, chapter 2, §2.3, "About the *Exordium* and the *Peroratio.*"

3. Mikhail M. Bakhtin refers to the rhetorical situation as a social event that gives rise to utterances. See Bakhtin, "The Problem of Speech Genres," in *Speech Genres and Other Late Essays*, ed. Caryl Emerson and Michael Holquist, trans. Vern W. McGee (Austin: University of Texas Press, 1986), 78–87. Tzvetan Todorov describes the rhetorical situation as a discourse that is generated by "not only linguistic elements but also the circumstances" that include the speaker, time, and place. See Todorov, *Symbolism and Interpretation*, trans. Catherine Porter (Ithaca: Cornell University Press, 1982), 9.

4. Lloyd Bitzer, "The Rhetorical Situation," *PR* 1 (1968): 1–14.

at this level, it is that situation embedded in the text and created by the text, which contributes to the rhetorical effect of the text.[5]

David E. Aune points out that Stamps's "entextualization is an important concept, because the text is all that exists of an ancient communication situation."[6] This means that the text is the only reliable resource from which we can elicit the ancient communication situation. Aligning the term *entextualized situation* with other terms used by many literary critics, such as *implied author* and *implied audience*, Aune relabels *entextualized situation* as *implied rhetorical situation*.[7] The term *rhetorical situation* was first introduced by Bitzer in his landmark discussion on rhetorical situation. Bitzer's method will be utilized to construct the implied rhetorical situation that gives rise to the rhetoric in Romans.

2.1.2. Lloyd F. Bitzer's Rhetorical Situation

Bitzer defines rhetorical situation as follows:

> a complex of persons, events, objects, and relations presenting an actual or potential exigence which can be completely or partially removed if discourse, introduced into the situation, can so constrain human decision or action so as to bring about the significant modification of the exigence.[8]

In this article, he also delineates three constituents of a rhetorical situation. The first is exigence. It is an "imperfection marked by urgency that can be changed only by the intervention of discourse" and is rhetorical "when it is capable of positive modification and when positive modification requires discourse."[9] The second is the audience. It is defined as hearers or readers who can be affected by discourse and become mediators of change. The third constituent is constraints. They consist of persons, events, and

---

5. Stamps, "Rethinking the Rhetorical Situation," 199.

6. David E. Aune, *Westminster Dictionary of New Testament and Early Christian Literature and Rhetoric* (Louisville: Westminster John Knox Press, 2003), s.v. "Rhetorical Situation." Similarly, Lauri Thurén, *The Rhetorical Strategy of 1 Peter with Special Regard to Ambiguous Expressions* (Åbo: Åbo Academy, 1990), 70–75; Wilhelm Wuellner, "Where Is Rhetorical Criticism Taking Us?," *CBQ* 49 (1987): 456.

7. Aune, "Rhetorical Situation."

8. Bitzer, "Rhetorical Situation," 6.

9. Aune, "Rhetorical Situation"; Bitzer, "Rhetorical Situation," 7.

objects that are parts of the situation and have the power to "modify the exigence." These constraints are classified as those that originate from the "rhetor and his method" and constraints generated by the situation. These three constituents, Bitzer contends, define a rhetorical situation.[10]

2.1.3. Validity of Bitzer's Rhetorical Situation

It is not that rhetoricians have not recognized the relevance of the situation that generates a rhetoric. Aristotle, for instance, by categorizing rhetorical discourses into epideictic, judicial, and deliberative, implicitly recognizes the relevance of the situation.[11] Rather, Bitzer has articulated the nature of a rhetorical situation and its key role in generating a rhetorical discourse.[12] He insists that a "rhetorical discourse ... does obtain its character-as-rhetorical from the situation which generates it."[13] The situation "prescribes its fitting response."[14]

Such a depiction of rhetorical situation causes Richard E. Vatz to construe Bitzer as saying that "meaning resides in events."[15] John Patton thinks that Bitzer has been misconstrued.[16] Vatz's (mis)construal of Bitzer's view, however, is understandable, as Bitzer reiterates the almost all-decisive role of the situation in effecting a discourse and does not ascribe any clear role to the speaker in determining the purpose of a discourse.[17] This leads Vatz to formulate an antithesis of Bitzer's theory: "Situations obtain their character from rhetoric that surrounds them or creates them."[18] He argues that Bitzer effectively means that "the nature of the context determines the rhetoric."[19] The problem is that, according to Vatz, "one never runs out of

---

10. Bitzer, "Rhetorical Situation," 8.

11. George A. Kennedy, trans., *Aristotle on Rhetoric: A Theory of Civic Discourse* (Oxford: Oxford University Press, 1991), 15.

12. Bitzer, "Rhetorical Situation," 2.

13. Ibid., 3.

14. Ibid., 11.

15. Richard E. Vatz, "The Myth of the Rhetorical Situation," *PR* 6 (1975): 155.

16. For instance, John H. Patton maintains that Bitzer's position is not that of a "totally objectivist, bound to a realist philosophy meaning." See Patton, "Causation and Creativity in Rhetorical Situations: Distinctions and Implications," *QJS* 65 (1979): 38.

17. Bitzer, "Rhetorical Situation," 8.

18. Vatz, "Myth of the Rhetorical Situation," 159.

19. Ibid., 156.

context [or] runs out of facts to describe a situation."[20] Bitzer's and Vatz's positions create an antinomy.

Arthur B. Miller mediates between these two positions, stating that "the rhetor has creative latitude to interpret the significance of the exigence" within the limits set by the exigence.[21] His description of the process through which the speaker (rhetor) creates a "fitting response" to a rhetorical situation is instructive for understanding how Bitzer's and Vatz's positions can be maintained. Both speaker and hearer will construct their perception of the exigence by combining their own constraints and "perception of an action, phenomenon, or facts."[22] For the intentions of the speaker to agree with the hearer's expectations, however, what Miller terms as *subsidiary constraints* or *value judgments* of the speaker must be aligned with those of the hearer so that they have the same essential constraints.[23]

David M. Hunsaker and Craig R. Smith introduce the term *issue* in their article. It is defined as "*a question occurring in a rhetorical context, in actual or potential form, which is relevant and requires resolution.*"[24] It originates from a privation or exigence.[25] The meaning of issue is effectively Miller's subsidiary constraint or value judgment.[26] But unlike Miller, Hunsaker and Smith, by distinguishing issue from constraint, refine the point of interaction between the speaker and the audience: through rhetorical discourse, the speaker speaks to the audience to resolve an issue that stems from a rhetorical exigency.[27] The issue selected (by the speaker or audience) is affected in turn by two dimensions, namely, motivation,

---

20. Ibid.

21. Arthur B. Miller, "Rhetorical Exigence," *PR* 5 (1972): 111. In a similar vein, Scott Consigny describes the rhetorical situation as one in which the rhetor must "structure so as to formulate and disclose problems." The rhetor, at the same time, is also constrained by the particularities of a "recalcitrant" situation that affects his strategy for resolving the exigence. See Consigny, "Rhetoric and Its Situations," *PR* 7 (1974): 178.

22. Miller, "Rhetorical Exigence," 117.

23. Ibid.

24. David M. Hunsaker and Craig R. Smith, "The Nature of Issues: A Constructive Approach to Situational Rhetoric," *WSC* 40 (1976): 144, emphasis original.

25. Hunsaker and Smith, "Nature of Issues," 146.

26. Miller, "Rhetorical Exigence," 117.

27. Hunsaker and Smith, "Nature of Issues," 154.

which relates to the personal needs or goals, and logic, which is deliberation over matters related to the motivation dimension.[28]

The above discussion qualifies, and hence validates, the use of Bitzer's
understanding of rhetorical situation in this book. The issue is a function of
both the situation and the speaker/audience. Neither holds absolute sway
over the selection of the issue. The process, as described above, through
which the issue is generated, verifies the above observation. Second, to
decide on a rhetorical situation, a speaker has to first sift through a myriad
of facts found in the historical background of the speaker/audience to pick
out those that contribute to forming a rhetorical situation of the *speaker's
choice*. From here, the speaker, in accordance with the motivation and logical dimensions, decides on the issue and the exigence.

2.2. Historical Background

As discussed above, a speaker will pick out facts found in the historical background to form the rhetorical situation of his or her choice. The
question is: What were the facts considered by the speaker Paul? As the
rhetorical situation is that which is "embedded in the text,"[29] only historical details that are required for the text of Romans to make rhetorical
sense would have been considered by Paul. Several observations point in
the direction that the historical situation envisaged by Paul is that the real
audience of Romans comprises both gentile and Judean Christians. Furthermore, the gentile audience is the majority and the Judean audience
the minority.[30]

Christianity in Rome probably started within the Judean community
in the synagogues.[31] This observation is borne out by the evidence of Acts
(11:19–21; 13:5, 14; 14:1; 17:1, 10, 17; 18:4, 19, 26; 19:8).[32] Two references
evince this point. In Acts 18:2, Claudius's edict in 49 CE evicted Judeans,

---

28. Ibid., 148–50.

29. Stamps, "Rethinking the Rhetorical Situation," 199.

30. Dunn, *Romans 1–8*, xlv–liv. See also Peter Lampe, *Christians at Rome in the
First Two Centuries: From Paul to Valentinus*, trans. Michael Steinhauser (Minneapolis: Fortress, 2003), 72; Esler, *Conflict and Identity in Romans*, 113–14; Thomas H.
Tobin, *Paul's Rhetoric in Its Contexts: The Argument of Romans* (Peabody, MA: Hendrickson, 2004), 37–38.

31. As most agree; see, e.g., Lampe, *Christians at Rome*, 11; Dunn, *Romans 1–8*,
xlvi–l; Tobin, *Paul's Rhetoric*, 34; Jewett, *Romans*, 58.

32. Dunn, *Romans 1–8*, xlvii.

among whom were Aquila and Priscilla. According to Suetonius (*Claud.* 25.4) and Acts 18:2, Judeans, who included this couple, were expelled from Rome over a conflict that was related to Christ.[33] If both Priscilla and Aquila were unbaptized Judeans, they presumably would have been opponents of Christ. Offering work and lodging to a Christian missionary, namely Paul (Acts 18:3), would then have been highly improbable. The logical conclusion is that Priscilla and Aquila were already Christians before they left the Judean community and the synagogue in Rome.[34] Converts to Christianity also included gentile Godfearers who worshiped in the synagogue. They were "the main targets of the earliest Gentile Christian mission."[35] After converting to Christianity, Christian Judeans and Christian Godfearers continued to worship in the synagogue with non-Christian Judeans and Godfearers. Peter Lampe notes that, among the gentiles who worshiped in the synagogue, proselytes were to be distinguished from Godfearers, who, "as a rule, were socially better off, even up to the level of the Roman knights. They included fewer slaves than the proselytes did."[36] This would mean that they were highly literate. Such Godfearers would include people like the Roman centurion Cornelius (Acts 10:1–2).[37] According to Luke, these Godfearers had knowledge of the Judean Scriptures (Acts 8:27–35; 13:16–22; 17:1–4). This last observation is also corroborated by Juvenal, who mentions that Godfearers actively studied the Judean Scriptures (*Sat.* 14.96–106).[38] Thus, to assume that these Godfearers had a good knowledge of the Judean Scriptures would not be unreasonable.

The above state of affairs in the synagogue changed with the edict of the emperor Claudius in 49 CE, when he expelled the Judeans from

---

33. Suetonius, *Claud.* 25.4 reads: "Iudaeos impulsore Chresto assidue tumultuantis Roma expulit." Chresto probably refers to "Christus," the Latinized version of the Greek Χριστός. Most scholars take this position: e.g., Dunn, *Romans 1–8,* xlviii; Esler, *Conflict and Identity in Romans,* 100. Lampe correctly explains the discrepancy: "The explanation for the vowel displacement is quite simple: 'Chrestus' was for pagan ears a commonly known personal name; 'Christus' was not" (*Christians at Rome,* 13).

34. Lampe, *Christians at Rome,* 11–12.

35. Ibid., 69.

36. Ibid., 72; A. Andrew Das, *Solving the Romans Debate* (Minneapolis: Fortress, 2007), 262.

37. See Das, *Solving the Romans Debate,* 70–71. Luke describes Cornelius as one φοβούμενος τὸν θεόν (Acts 10:2).

38. Lampe, *Christians at Rome,* 70.

Rome. Acts 18:2 records that "all the Judeans" were forced to leave Rome.[39] The extent of πᾶς in Acts 18:2 is unclear. It is likely that this number included only the agitators and those who led the unrest.[40] Two observations support my point. First, the edict, *Iudaeos impulsore Chresto assidue tumultuantis Roma expulit*, could also be translated: "He expelled from Rome the Jews (who were) constantly making disturbances at the instigation of Chrestus."[41] Second, this limited expulsion provides a plausible explanation for the silence of Josephus and other historiographers about this expulsion.[42] Luke's description of Claudius's edict in Acts 18:2 as an expulsion of "all" (πᾶς) could possibly be a hyperbole.[43] Thus, the scale of this expulsion was probably not massive. Such people who were expelled would have included Priscilla and Aquila since they very likely were advocates for Christ in the Judean synagogues of Rome.

The consequent leadership of the Christian community would have been largely gentile after the expulsion of Judeans.[44] Christians would also have had to worship in house churches after the expulsion.[45] After the

---

39. Except where indicated, all translations from the New Testament, Hebrew Bible, and LXX are my own.

40. Lampe, *Christians at Rome*, 13–14.

41. Bruce N. Fisk, "Synagogue Influence and Scriptural Knowledge among the Christians of Rome," in *As It Is Written: Studying Paul's Use of Scripture*, ed. Stanley E. Porter and Christopher D. Stanley, SymS 50 (Atlanta: Society of Biblical Literature, 2008), 165.

42. Lampe, *Christians at Rome*, 14; Fisk, "Synagogue Influence and Scriptural Knowledge," 165.

43. Fisk, "Synagogue Influence and Scriptural Knowledge," 165. See Luke 1:3; Acts 1:1; 2:5; 3:18; 8:1, etc.

44. Peter Lampe explains that the Christians in Rome met in different house churches in the first two centuries. He observes that "Paul does not call it [the Roman Christian community] *ekklēsia* anywhere in Romans, not even in 1:7 where we would expect it according to the other Pauline letters. Only a part is called *ekklēsia*: the house church around Aquila and Prisca (Rom. 16:5)." See Lampe, "The Roman Christians of Romans 16," in *The Romans Debate*, ed. Karl P. Donfried, rev. and exp. ed. (Peabody, MA: Hendrickson, 1991), 229–30. Furthermore, that Paul sends greetings to various Christian groups in 16:11–14 seems to indicate that these Christians met in different locations. On the composition of the community after the expulsion, see Lampe, *Christians at Rome*, 13–14; Jewett, *Romans*, 61.

45. Mark D. Nanos argues that in the first century CE, Christians could not have met in their homes or in tenement rooms that are not associated with the synagogues, as Julius Caesar had "dissolved all guilds, except those of ancient foundations" (Suetonius, *Jul.* 42.3 [Rolfe, LCL]). See Nanos, "The Jewish Context of the

death of Claudius in 54 CE, Christian Judeans, like Priscilla and Aquila, returned to worship in Christian house churches, which would have been largely gentile in composition.[46]

The above discussion paints a likely historical situation in which the Christian house churches in Rome consisted of a majority of gentile Christians. Some of these gentile Christians were Godfearers who had a good knowledge of the Judean Scriptures. Judean Christians would have formed the minority in the house churches.

That there were Judeans in the audience of the Christian community in Rome is also borne out by Rom 16. Here, Paul sends greetings to a long list of Christians in the Christian community in Rome. Of the twenty-six names listed, most are gentiles. Five to seven of the names, however, are probably of Judean origin, either because of the names themselves or

---

Gentile Audience Addressed in Paul's Letter to the Romans," *CBQ* 61 (1999): 286–88. Esler refutes this objection, as Rom 16 contains Christians who meet in house churches that are independent of the synagogue (*Conflict and Identity in Romans*, 105–6). Furthermore, as George La Piana observes, among freedman and slaves of households, "the *collegia domestica* were very numerous in the time of Augustine, and it is very probable that the law governing associations was not applied to them, and that they were not dissolved." See La Piana, "Foreign Groups in Rome during the First Centuries of the Empire," *HTR* 20 (1927): 275. Similarly, see Das, *Solving the Romans Debate*, 181.

46. The attraction that synagogues and Judeans' places of worship called προσευχαί (see Esler, *Conflict and Identity in Romans*, 88–97; similarly Das, *Solving the Romans Debate*, 190–93) had for gentile Christians reduced after Claudius's edict of 49 CE. This attraction was further diminished by anti-Judean sentiments (see Das, *Solving the Romans Debate*, 193–97). To conclude, however, as Das does, that after Claudius's death in 54 CE "the Jewish Christ-believers were gone" flies in the face of the clear evidence in Rom 16 of the presence of Judean Christians (Das, *Solving the Romans Debate*, 193; see below, 40 n. 47). William S. Campbell paints a situation that is more likely: "There is evidence throughout Romans, and especially in chaps. 14–15, of a form of Christianity that is still attached to the synagogue. Romans, in our view, represents not the final divorce in the 'marriage' between house groups and synagogues but only the beginnings of that separation.... As it is unlikely that up to fifty thousand Jews were expelled from Rome, some form of Jewish community activities would probably continue." See Campbell, "The Rule of Faith in Romans 12:1–15:13: The Obligation of Humble Obedience to Christ as the Only Adequate Response to the Mercies of God," in Hay and Johnson, *Romans*, 265. On the largely gentile profile of house churches, see Dunn, *Romans 1–8*, liii; Lampe, *Christians at Rome*, 70; Moo, *Epistle to the Romans*, 13; Jewett, *Romans*, 42; Tobin, *Paul's Rhetoric*, 37.

because these people could be identified as Judeans.[47] Such a depiction of the historical situation, as will become apparent when I trace the argument of Romans, makes rhetorical sense in relation to the content of Romans and should thus shape the rhetorical situation of Romans.

2.3. About the *Exordium* and the *Peroratio*

Scholars recognize that the *exordium* and *peroratio* shed light on the rhetorical situation of a rhetorical discourse. Esler comments that in order to "discover the apostle's communicative strategy," it is necessary to read 1:1–15 and 15:14–16:27:

> In both of these passages, often referred to as the "frame" of the letter, Paul is speaking expressly of the personal circumstances of himself and his addressees, while he also details his plans for the future. They contain statements in which he offers explicit reasons for writing the letter and

---

47. For a detailed analysis of the names in Rom 16:3–16, see Lampe, *Christians at Rome*, 164–236. Tobin lists five: Priscilla, Aquila, Andronicus, Junia, and Herodion (and possibly Mary; see *Paul's Rhetoric*, 37; contra Lampe, *Christians at Rome*, 176). Esler also identifies the above five names as Judeans for the following reasons (*Conflict and Identity in Romans*, 118). Aquila is a Judean (Acts 18:2), and his wife is probably a Judean too. Paul addresses Andronicus and Junia in 16:7 and Herodian in 16:11 as συγγενής ("kindred"), contra Das, who assigns to συγγενής a metaphorical meaning (*Solving the Romans Debate*, 92–93). David J. Downs correctly refutes this view, as "only three of the twenty-nine receive this unusual designation, which is not found in any other Pauline epistles." See Downs, review of *Solving the Romans Debate*, by Andrew A. Das, *RBL* 10 (2008): 472. If συγγενής means metaphorical kindred, then all twenty-nine individuals in 16:1–16 should be similarly designated. They are probably Judeans, as Paul uses συγγενεῖς in 9:3 to denote fellow Judeans. Esler also adds to the above five names Rufus because Judeans often adopted Rufus as "a sound-equivalent" name of the Hebrew name Reuben. Lastly, Paul mentions a woman who is "his mother—a mother to me also" (16:13). Esler thinks that Paul's closeness to this woman seems to indicate ethnic connection. Das agrees that Priscilla, Aquila, Andronicus, and Junia are likely of Judean origins but dismisses them as members of the Roman congregation because these individuals are addressed in the second person (*Solving the Romans Debate*, 101–2, 262). This, however, as Downs observes, does not cohere with ἀσπάσασθε ἀλλήλους ἐν φιλήματι ἁγίῳ ("greet one another with a holy kiss" [16:16]), which is an injunction Paul gives to the congregations as a whole. Also, B. J. Oropeza, *Jews, Gentiles, and the Opponents of Paul: Apostasy in the New Testament Communities* (Eugene, OR: Cascade, 2012), 136.

which reveal a great deal of information about the identities, ethnicity, and social status of a number of Christ-followers in Rome.[48]

William J. Brandt underscores that the speaker in the *exordium* "must define himself, and he must define the problem."[49] The *exordium* also predisposes the hearers to the rhetoric of the discourse by preparing them to be "well-disposed, attentive, and receptive" (Cicero, *Inv.* 1.15.20 [Hubbell, LCL]). It seeks to establish a favorable *ethos* for the speaker.[50] The *peroratio* has two main objectives: to recapitulate the main arguments of the rhetoric and to move the audience emotionally to assent to the rhetoric.[51] Thus, the *exordium* and *peroratio* carry interpretive weight in constructing the rhetorical situation.[52]

2.4. Romans 1:1–15: The *Exordium*

Several observations converge to indicate that 1:1–15 forms the *exordium* of Romans. First, the unit contains a concentration of self-designating terms: Παῦλος ("Paul" [1:1]), verbs in the first person (1:5, 8, 9 [2x],10, 11, 13 [4x], 14), and first-person pronouns (1:8, 9, 10, 12, 15). Such a concentration coheres with the purpose of an *exordium*: to create a favorable *ethos* for the speaker. This is further reinforced with the observation that "vv. 8–12 reveals the interplay between 'me' and 'you' … and v.12b concludes with 'both yours and mine.'"[53] Second, 1:16–17 is a fitting heading for the

---

48. Esler, *Conflict and Identity in Romans*, 109–11. In a similar vein, Paul S. Minear reminds us that as "the data concerning Paul's personal plans are located at the beginning and at the end of the letter, so too, we may find there the ground for his concern with the Roman brothers." See Minear, *The Obedience of Faith: The Purposes of Paul in the Epistle to the Romans* (London: SCM, 1971), 6–7.

49. William J. Brandt, *The Rhetoric of Argumentation* (Indianapolis: Bobbs-Merrill, 1970), 51.

50. So Brandt, *Rhetoric of Argumentation*, 53.

51. Heinrich Lausberg, *Handbook of Literary Rhetoric: A Foundation for Literary Study*, ed. Davide E. Orton and R. Dean Anderson, trans. Matthew T. Bliss, Annemiek Jansen, and David E. Orton (Leiden: Brill, 1998), §431. For examples, see Lausberg, *Handbook of Literary Rhetoric*, §§434–39; Quintilian, *Inst. orat.* 6.1.1, 6.1.52; Rhet. Her. 2.30.47.

52. Neil Elliott, *The Rhetoric of Romans: Argumentative Constraint and Strategy and Paul's Dialogue with Judaism*, JSNTSup 45 (Sheffield: Sheffield Academic, 1990), 69.

53. So Jewett, *Romans*, 117–18.

exposition of the gospel that follows in 1:18–11:36. Hence, 1:15 should conclude the *exordium*.[54]

2.4.1. Romans 1:1–7

Prophetic rhetorolect dominates 1:1–7. Several related observations demonstrate this. First, 1:1–7 is a description of the gospel. Second, this gospel is described as that which is promised through the prophets. Third, Paul regards himself as a slave and an apostle who is being set apart for this gospel (1:1). Together, these three observations imply that the main rhetorolect of 1:1–7 is prophetic. Also, Paul, by connecting himself to the gospel that was promised through the prophets, would be construed by the implied audience as that "selected" human who takes on the role of prophet (secondspace of prophetic rhetorolect).[55] To mobilize to his letter to the Romans ideological power as a prophet who commands attention, Paul crafts his *ethos* in several ways. First, in the *Familia Caesaris*, slaves and freedmen helped the emperor to discharge his duties.[56] In other words, they formed the imperial bureaucracy. When read in light of the social and cultural intertexture underlying the topos slave, ideological power is mobilized when Paul describes himself as a slave who possesses authority.[57] Also, Christ Jesus takes on the identity of Messiah as he is described as being a descendant of King David. Given that Paul is a slave of Christ Jesus, it implies that he is a slave of the Messiah king prophesied in the Judean Scriptures. The verbal form ἀποστέλλειν ("to send"), related to the noun ἀπόστολος ("apostle"), can refer to people who are sent as "representatives of their monarch and his authority."[58] By describing himself as an apostle, Paul taps into the ideological texture embedded in

---

54. L. Ann Jervis construes 1:14–15 as the end of thanksgiving and 1:16–17 as the body opening. See Jervis, *The Purpose of Romans*, JSNTSup 55 (Sheffield: Sheffield Academic, 1991), 106–7.

55. Robbins, *Invention of Christian Discourse*, 109.

56. Beth Severy, *Augustus and the Family at the Birth of the Roman Empire* (New York: Routledge, 2003), 144–45.

57. Robbins, von Thaden, and Bruehler underscore the need to read a topos in light of cultural concerns (introduction, 10); see also Johan C. Thom, "'The Mind Is Its Own Place': Defining the Topos," in *Early Christianity and Classical Culture: Comparative Studies in Honor of Abraham J. Malherbe*, ed. John T. Fitzgerald, Thomas H. Olbricht, and L. Michael White, NovTSup 110 (Leiden: Brill, 2003), 566.

58. Karl Heinrich Rengstorf, "ἀποστελλω κτλ," *TDNT* 1:398.

the word apostle: Paul, who is sent by the monarch Christ Jesus, possesses royal authority. This enables Paul to project his authority over distances through his letter.

Second, Paul also builds his *ethos* by claiming the authority of the gospel for his apostleship. That the participle ἀφωρισμένος ("having been set apart" [1:1]) describes not just the name "Paul" but also the term *apostle* is evinced by the fact that Paul concludes with a statement of his "apostleship" (1:5). This implies that the description of the gospel (1:2–4) substantiates the authority of Paul's apostleship. First, this apostleship is described in what Moxnes labels as "God language," where God is emphasized. That God language is present is evident from the fact that the phrase τῶν προφητῶν αὐτοῦ ("his prophets") is a rare construction and that the personal pronoun emphasizes "God's personal involvement."[59] In the same way, the prepositional phrase ἐν γραφαῖς ἁγίαις ("in the holy Scriptures") emphasizes God's authority. The intent of God language can be elicited from how Paul describes the gospel: it was that which God "promised beforehand" (1:2). Paul, by using God language, is introducing into the text an ideological texture to forge continuity between the gospel contained in the Judean Scriptures and that which he will later expound in Romans. Paul's likely intent is to gain the attention of Judean Christians who are among the real and implied audience.

The content of the gospel also lends authority to Paul's apostleship and adds to his *ethos* in that this gospel is about Jesus Christ who is Lord.[60] Paul introduces an oral-scribal intertexture that is generally thought to have been a pre-Pauline/extra-Pauline confession.[61] As this confession is

---

59. Dunn, *Romans 1–8*, 10. On the phrase τῶν προφητῶν αὐτοῦ, Jewett observes that it occurs elsewhere only in Luke 1:70 (*Romans*, 103).

60. Ian E. Rock argues that this nature of the gospel "rationalises, legitimises, and even universalises the ideology/theology" of Christians. See Rock, *Paul's Letter to the Romans and Roman Imperialism: An Ideological Analysis of the Exordium (Romans 1:1–17)* (Eugene, OR: Pickwick, 2012), 121.

61. Scholars view differently the origin of the confession in 1:3–4. Robert Jewett sees redactional activities in what he conceives as pre-Pauline or extra-Pauline creedal confession. Archibald M. Hunter and Matthew W. Bates do not detect redaction. Christopher G. Whitsett thinks that 1:3–4 is novel and is Paul's exegesis of Ps 2 and 2 Sam 7, as does Ernest Best. See Jewett, "The Redaction and Use of an Early Christian Confession in Romans 1:3–4," in *The Living Text: Essays in Honor of Ernest W. Saunders*, ed. Robert Jewett and Dennis E. Groh (Washington, DC: University Press of America, 1985), 99–122; Hunter, *Paul and His Predecessors* (Philadelphia: Westmin-

known to the implied audience of Romans, it mobilizes ideological power: Paul's prophet-like call (the secondspace of prophetic rhetorolect) to be the special emissary of Jesus Christ is based on the identity of the son of God as described in the confession. If the Romans accept the validity of Paul's call and position, then an asymmetrical relation of power is created by the introduction to the letter. The identity of Jesus Christ is specific, in that he is the Son of God, who exists in a state of power since the resurrection.[62] The nature of this existence in power is "according to the Spirit of holiness" (1:4). Minimally, this means that Jesus's powerful existence is characterized by the Holy Spirit.[63] Considering that the word holiness (ἁγιωσύνη) used to qualify the Spirit occurs only two other times in the New Testament in the context of ethical obligations (2 Cor 7:1; 1 Thess 3:13), the power of the Spirit emphasized here is in the area of ethical holiness.[64] Thus, Paul the speaker argues that his apostleship is one that preaches a Christ who is endowed with the power of the Holy Spirit. This apostleship enables Paul to produce in the gentiles (ἔθνη) a trust or loyalty that will result in obedience to God.[65]

---

ster, 1961), 28; Matthew W. Bates, "A Christology of Incarnation and Enthronement: Romans 1:3–4 as Unified, Nonadoptionist, and Nonconciliatory," *CBQ* 77 (2015): 109; Whitsett, "Son of God, Seed of David: Paul's Messianic Exegesis in Romans 1:3–4," *JBL* 119 (2000): 661–81; Best, *The Letter of Paul to the Romans*, CBC (Cambridge: Cambridge University Press, 1967), 10–11.

62. Dunn, *Romans 1–8*, 14; Käsemann, *Commentary on Romans*, 12; C. K. Barrett, *The Epistle to the Romans*, BNTC (London: Black, 1957), 20; Cranfield, *Epistle to the Romans*, 1:62. Fitzmyer attaches the prepositional phrase ἐν δυνάμει with υἱοῦ θεοῦ and not the participle ὁρισθέντος (*Romans*, 235). Contra Frederic L. Godet, *Commentary on St. Paul's Epistle to the Romans* (Grand Rapids: Kregel, 1977), 79; Jewett, *Romans*, 107; William Sanday and Arthur C. Headlam, *A Critical and Exegetical Commentary on the Epistle to the Romans*, ICC (Edinburgh: T&T Clark, 1895), 9.

63. Dunn, *Romans 1–8*, 15.

64. Jewett, *Romans*, 106–7: "The qualification of the spirit as the 'spirit of holiness' made clear that the divine power celebrated in the confession entailed moral obligations." Gordon D. Fee, *God's Empowering Presence: The Holy Spirit in the Letters of Paul* (Peabody, MA: Hendrickson, 1994), 483, suggests that the genitive ἁγιωσύνης that qualifies the Spirit should be read as "the Spirit who gives/supplies holiness." L. Ann Jervis similarly construes the main role of the Spirit in Romans as "being characterized by holiness … [and] is capable of making Gentiles into godly people." See Jervis, "The Spirit Brings Christ's Life to Life," in *Reading Paul's Letter to the Romans*, ed. Jerry L. Sumney, RBS 73 (Atlanta: Society of Biblical Literature, 2012), 148.

65. Kathy Ehrensperger comments that "what is expressed in πίστις terminology

Esler understands ἔθνη as referring to non-Judeans. More importantly, he argues that the term ἔθνη also contains a geographical dimension, referring to people who are staying in a geographical region that is outside Judea. Andrew A. Das objects to Esler's interpretation. He argues that Esler "has not provided evidence that ἔθνη is being used in v. 5 in a 'strictly geographical sense.'"[66] Such a (mis)construal glosses over Esler's argument. First, Esler has convincingly demonstrated that the name Ἰουδαῖοι must be connected to a homeland, namely, Judea.[67] Second, Esler emphasizes that the ethnic expression ἔθνη is a term Judeans used to describe the rest of the world and not one that non-Judeans would call themselves:

> First century Judeans divided their world into two realms distinguishable on (what we would describe as) the geographic and religious dimen-

---

has to do with loyalty, trust and faithfulness. This is not merely a 'holding for true or real' state of mind, but something that clearly is only actualized in concrete activities." See Ehrensperger, *Paul at the Crossroads of Cultures: Theologizing in the Space Between*, LNTS 456 (London: Bloomsbury, 2013), 166. Morgan explains that *pistis* and *fides* are action nominals that encompass both active and passive meanings of the verbs from which they are derived and "*fides* means both trust and trustworthiness." For instance, a magistrate is considered *fides* because of his trustworthiness. At the same time, this trustworthiness is founded "on his trust in (or loyalty) to the laws of his city or state, on his trust in (or devotion to) the gods, … on his trust in the people to allow him to govern" (*Roman Faith and Christian Faith*, 31). It is possible that the genitive is epexegetical, that is, "obedience" that is "faith." It is more likely, however, that it is a subjective genitive, that is, a "trust" that produces "obedience" is intended. Two observations evince this. First, since 1:5 is part of the *exordium*, we would expect the ideas of trust and obedience present in 1:5 to be worked out more clearly in the main body of the letter. We find this to be the case; trust and obedience/works are often two distinct terms in the letter. One should not, therefore, collapse the two terms into one. Second, the immediate context also supports a subjective genitive: the Roman Christians form part of those who are called for the ὑπακοὴν πίστεως (1:5). These Christians are those whom Paul longs to see so as to "impart some spiritual gift" εἰς τὸ στηριχθῆναι ὑμᾶς (1:11). Jewett notes that "this verb is used elsewhere in a metaphorical manner to describe Paul's work of 'making firm' the trust of his congregations in spite of afflictions and uncertainties (1 Thess 3:2, 13; 2 Thess 2:17; 3:5)" (*Romans*, 124).

66. Das, *Solving the Romans Debate*, 59. Similarly, Dunn remarks that "(τά) ἔθνη certainly means 'the Gentiles' (and not the 'nations' including Jews)" (*Romans 1–8*, 18), and Moo thinks that construing ἔθνη in a strictly geographical sense does not cohere with the scope of Paul's apostolic work (*Epistle to the Romans*, 53).

67. See below chapter 3, §1.4, "Translation of Ἰουδαῖοι," where I rehearse the salient points of Esler's argument.

sions of ethnic criteria. There was Judea—the sacred homeland of the people and the site of its capital city and the temple of its God—where they were in a preponderant majority and then there was the rest of the Mediterranean region, inhabited by numerous foreign peoples (ἔθνη)…. The peoples so categorized, moreover, did not call themselves in this way [ἔθνη]; they called themselves "Greeks," "Romans," and so on…. Accordingly, Paul's reference at 1:5 to his work "among all the foreigners [ἔθνη]," the first ethnic expression in the letter, immediately characterizes the situation as one seen from a Judean perspective…. It is impossible to exclude a geographic dimension from Paul's mission. His apostleship entailed preaching the gospel outside Judea in the lands inhabited by idolatrous non-Judean peoples (but which also contained minority populations of Judeans).[68]

Thus the ethnic group Ἰουδαῖοι ("Judeans"), including Paul, would construe ἔθνη as referring to a region that is outside Judea. Esler's contention is also supported by Neil Elliot and Terence L. Donaldson, who insist that the term τὰ ἔθνη ("the gentiles") does not refer to gentile individuals but to gentile nations: it should contain an "ethnic-national sense."[69] Paul regards himself as an apostle to the nations, "to the peoples of this earth at large."[70]

Thus when Paul says in 1:5–6 that he seeks to produce obedience in the gentiles (ἔθνη), "among whom are you also," he is referring to the Christians who are living in Rome, a region that is outside Judea. The audience thus includes a majority of gentile Christians and a minority of Judean Christians.[71] By the clause ἐν οἷς ἐστε καὶ ὑμεῖς ("among whom are you

---

68. Esler, *Conflict and Identity in Romans*, 113.

69. Neil Elliott, *The Arrogance of Nations: Reading Romans in the Shadow of Empire* (Minneapolis: Fortress, 2008), 46; Donaldson, "Gentile Christianity," 449–51, quote at 451. Donaldson points out the problem with translating τὰ ἔθνη as "gentiles": "But while 'Gentiles' captures the element of non-Jewishness, the possibility is obscured that (non-Jewish) nations are in view." He adds that even when small groups of individuals are referred to by the term τὰ ἔθνη, these groups represent nations (e.g., Acts 11:1; Rom 15:6).

70. Johannes Munck, *Paul and the Salvation of Mankind*, trans. Frank Clarke (London: SCM, 1959), 52–54. Quote from Dieter Georgi, *Remembering the Poor: The History of Paul's Collection for Jerusalem* (Nashville: Abingdon, 1992), 102 (cited by Neil Elliott, *Arrogance of Nations*, 46).

71. Esler, *Conflict and Identity in Romans*, 114: "Nothing in this excludes the fact that Judeans regularly formed part of this congregation. Nor would any Judean or

also" [1:13b]), Paul asserts his apostolic authority over the Roman Christians.[72] This description of his apostleship to the gentiles in 1:1–5 needs to be applied to the Roman Christians because 1:1–5 prepares for his planned visit mentioned in 1:8–15. In light of the above discussion, the implied audience of Romans is people who dwell in the geographical regions outside Judea, which would likely include Judean and gentile Christians.

2.4.2. Romans 1:8–15

Paul, to stir up *pathos* to further establish rapport with the implied audience, uses wisdom rhetorolect to reason with the implied audience without being confrontational, and hence offensive. That wisdom rhetorolect dominates 1:8–15 is shown by Paul addressing them using a familial term, ἀδελφοί ("brothers" [1:13]), since wisdom is particularly located in the home and in family life. Also, his intention in visiting them is to obtain some καρπός ("fruit"), an agricultural term that correlates with the first-space of wisdom rhetorolect, from amongst them (1:13). By bringing wisdom rhetorolect into the text after the foregoing prophetic rhetorolect, Paul is attempting to first demand respect (1:1–7) before using wisdom rhetorolect to reason with and motivate them. He does this by commending their trust.

Paul's attempt to invoke the *ethos* of the implied audience, in order to increase their level of trust in him, is further heightened by mentioning in 1:9–10 and 1:13 his numerous attempts to visit them. *Pathos* is invoked in 1:13 by addressing the implied audience as ἀδελφοί ("brothers"). This commendation expressed through *pathos* is not a general one but one that has its object in 1:12, the only other place where their trust is mentioned in the *exordium*. Here, Paul seeks to persuade the implied Roman audience that he is eager to be encouraged by their trust in God. He also tells them that he desires to encourage them to trust God by means of his own trust in God. This mutuality heightens *pathos*. Important for helping to identify

---

non-Judean Christ-followers in Rome listening to the letter as it was read deduce from this expression that the Judean members were excluded." See also below, chapter 2, §2.6, "Conclusion," where I demonstrate the presence of Judean Christians in the real audience. In Rom 16, among the people to whom this letter is addressed, at least five are probably Judeans: Aquila, Priscilla, Andronicus, Junia, and Herodion (see chapter 2, §2.2, "Historical Background").

72. Godet, *Commentary on St. Paul's Epistle to the Romans*, 83.

the exigence of Romans (as I will later explain) is the observation that Paul is concerned not just about mutual encouragement. In 1:11–12, Paul's first concern is to strengthen the Roman Christians' trust in God (1:11). This newly strengthened trust will in turn be effective for providing to himself what Paul calls "mutual encouragement." That this order is intentional on Paul's part is corroborated by the use of the phrase τοῦτο δέ ἐστιν ("and that is"). Cranfield remarks that this phrase

> amends the effect of what has been said by expressing a complementary truth.… Paul's desire to see them in order to be the means of their receiving a blessing will only be rightly understood, if it is seen as part of his desire for a mutual παράκλησις between him and them.[73]

In other words, the intention of Paul's future visit to the Roman Christians is twofold. First, Paul will strengthen them when he visits them. This strengthening of their trust in God, as I shall show below, is fulfilled in part by the Letter to the Romans. Second, only after their trust in God has been strengthened will they be able to provide encouragement, including material aid, to Paul for his planned evangelistic expedition to Spain.

I now proceed to show that Paul's objective in strengthening the Roman Christians is fulfilled in part by the Letter to the Romans. Paul's desire to encourage the Roman Christians to trust God is couched in various terms. Paul desires to impart to them a "spiritual gift" so as to strengthen the trust of the implied audience (1:11).[74] That Paul's intention in 1:13 to obtain some "fruit" (1:13) among them continues the same concern of 1:12 is intimated by two observations. For one, the statement "I want you to know" serves to elaborate about what has just preceded.[75] Also, Paul's hope that he will obtain some fruit (1:13) and impart to them some spiritual gift (1:11) is all to be accomplished at his planned visit (1:11).[76] The means Paul uses to achieve the goals mentioned in 1:12–13 are explained

---

73. Cranfield, *Epistle to the Romans*, 1:80.

74. His hope to be mutually encouraged in faith is also equated (τοῦτο ἐστιν) with the preceding imparting of a gift for the purpose of establishing the implied audience.

75. The clause θέλω ὑμᾶς ἀγνοεῖν occurs twice in Romans (1:13; 11:25). As in 1:13, the same clause in 11:25 indicates that what Paul said in 11:24 is being elaborated in 11:25: the "natural branches" that will be "grafted back to their own olive tree" (11:24) is explicated by the event at which "all Israel will be saved" (11:25).

76. Robert L. Foster notes that "the letter to the Romans provides direct evidence that καρπός in 1:13 refers to faithful obedience and not evangelistic fruit"; see, e.g.,

in 1:14–15, as evinced by three observations. First, each pair—"Greeks and barbarians" and "wise and foolish"—is introduced by the pair of particles τε and καί. This pair of particles indicates that each pair of groups described in 1:14 is part of the larger group mentioned in what has just preceded in 1:13, namely, "gentiles."[77] In other words, 1:14 elaborates on how Paul will obtain the fruit discussed in 1:13. Second, Paul's eagerness (πρόθυμον) in 1:15 corresponds to his desire in 1:11, as signified by the verb ἐπιποθῶ. It is reasonable to think that the objects of Paul's eagerness (1:15) and desire (1:11) are the same. Third, Paul's endeavors in 1:11–13 and 1:14–15 are all directed at the Roman Christians. In other words, that which Paul hopes to do amongst the Roman Christians in 1:11–15 is ὑμῖν τοῖς ἐν Ῥώμῃ εὐαγγελίσασθαι ("to preach the gospel to you who are in Rome" [1:15]).[78] That the verb εὐαγγελίσασθαι entails a preaching of the gospel is corroborated by 1:16–17, "for I am not ashamed of the gospel," which serves as the heading for the exposition of the gospel that follows in 1:18–11:36. This implies that what Paul hopes to do when he visits the Roman Christians in the future is actually fulfilled minimally by his letter to the Romans. Elliott shares my view:

> "Evangelizing" the Romans is absent from Paul's future plans, not because that was never really his intention, but because that intention *has been achieved* between chs. 1 and 15, that is, *by the letter itself*. Romans is written as a surrogate for the visit Paul has long desired to make (1.10–15) under the constraint of his obligation as apostle to *all* the Gentiles, including the Roman Christians. The letter *is* Paul's εὐαγγελίσασθαι.[79]

6:21–22; 15:26. See Foster, "The Justice of the Gentiles: Revisiting the Purpose of Romans," *CBQ* 76 (2014): 688.

77. For the same construction and usage, see also 1:16; 2:9, 10; 3:9. Cranfield concurs with my interpretation (*Epistle to the Romans*, 1:83–84).

78. Peter Stuhlmacher thinks that 1:15 refers to plans Paul intended to do in the past. See Stuhlmacher, "The Purpose of Romans," in Donfried, *Romans Debate*, 236–37. Moo refutes this view that "v15 is tied to v14, which uses the present tense" (*Epistle to the Romans*, 63).

79. Elliott, *Rhetoric*, 87, emphasis original; see more recently, Elliott, *Arrogance of Nations*, 45. Similarly, Günter Klein says: "If for Paul the content expressed in Romans and his concrete plans for his intended missionary work in Rome are intimately related, Romans 1:15ff. and 15:5ff. are simply two ways of expressing the very same apostolic task." See Klein, "Paul's Purpose in Writing the Epistle to the Romans," in Donfried, *Romans Debate*, 34. See also A. Roosen, "Le Genre Littéraire de l'Épître Aux Romains," in *Studia Evangelica*, ed. Frank L. Cross, TU 87 (Berlin: Akademie, 1964),

These people whom Paul hopes to visit are a part of the larger group of gentiles (ἐν ὑμῖν καθὼς καὶ ἐν τοῖς λοιποῖς ἔθνεσιν; "among you just as also among the rest of the gentiles") who are described in 1:14–15 as Greeks and barbarians, wise and foolish, and those who are in Rome. This final point indicates once again that a part of the real and implied audience, namely, gentile Christians, is a main focus in this letter.

The above discussion has important bearings on the exigence of Romans. As I shall argue in the discussion on the *peroratio* (see the following section), the above discussion on 1:11–15, when read together with 15:23–24, sheds light on the purpose of Romans: to prepare for Paul's evangelistic expedition to Spain.

2.5. Romans 15:14–16:27: The *Peroratio*

The section 15:14–16:27 constitutes the *peroratio*, as evinced by the observation that elements included in this section are typical of his letter endings.[80] More importantly, as will be shown, this section exhibits the two main functions of a *peroratio*, namely, to recapitulate the main arguments and to influence the emotions of the implied audience.[81] To

---

2:466: "Une équivalence entre cette lettre et la grâce apostolique de l'évangélisation." J. Paul Sampley puts it succinctly: "Romans is not merely or even primarily written 'for the sake of missions': *it is mission* at work" ("Romans in a Different Light: A Response to Robert Jewett," in Hay and Johnson, *Romans*, 115). Such a function of the Letter to the Romans ties in with the observations by Judith M. Lieu that a letter functions as a substitute for the sender's physical presence (Libanius, *Ep.* 2) and is also regarded as a gift (Demetrius, *Eloc.* 224; cf. Rom 1:11, where Paul hopes to bring them a spiritual gift [χάρισμα] when he visits the Roman Christians). She also adds that "the letters of Cicero or Pliny fill the space of the Republic and early Empire with a web of contacts, influence, shared concerns and values, as well as of political manoeuvring or resistance." See Lieu, "Letters and the Topography of Early Christianity," *NTS* 62 (2016): 170–74.

80. Jewett agrees that 15:14–16:24 constitutes the *peroratio*. He construes, however, the sections 16:17–20a and 16:25–27 as non-Pauline interpolations (*Romans*, 900). See also Wilhelm Wuellner, who regards 14:14–16:23 as the *peroratio*. See Wuellner, "Paul's Rhetoric of Argumentation in Romans," *CBQ* 38 (1976): 339–45. James D. G. Dunn regards 15:14–16:27 as the conclusion to the letter and recalls the opening 1:8–15. See Dunn, *Romans 9–16*, 854. For a comparison of the elements present in between 15:14–16:27 and other Pauline letters, see Moo, *Epistle to the Romans*, 884.

81. Aune, *Westminster Dictionary*, s.v. "Peroration." Lausberg, *Handbook of Liter-*

achieve the above-mentioned functions of the *peroratio*, Paul uses wisdom rhetorolect, as it is nonconfrontational. That the dominating rhetorolect is wisdom is demonstrated by Paul addressing them in this section as ἀδελφοί ("brothers" [15:14, 30; 16:14, 17]). I shall now discuss places that contain the two above-mentioned functions to shed light on the rhetorical situation of Romans.

The *peroratio* also exhibits the twofold purpose of Paul's future visit to the Roman Christians mentioned in the *exordium*. First, Paul's intention to strengthen the Roman Christians' trust in God is recapitulated in 15:14–16. Wuellner remarks that Rom 15:14–15 functions to recapitulate a "full statement of his thesis."[82] That this part of the *peroratio* is tied to the *exordium* is shown by Paul's reiteration (1:5–6, 13–14) that he is called to be an apostle to the gentiles and that Romans is written with his apostolic authority. This observation helps to identify the scope of "some points I have written to you" (15:15), namely, the section 1:16–15:13 that intervenes between the *exordium* and *peroratio*. Paul's intent is to minister to the gentile Christians in Rome so that they "may be pleasing, sanctified by the Holy Spirit" (15:16) by means of his letter to the Romans. This corroborates what Paul has reiterated in the *exordium*, namely, that by his visit (the purpose of which, as I have argued above, is fulfilled in part by this letter), he hopes to impart to them "some spiritual gift in order to strengthen them" (1:11) and that he "might have some fruit" among them (1:13). In this way, Paul's objective for his future visit, namely, to encourage them to trust God (1:12), is fulfilled in part by Romans.

Second, the other part of the mutual encouragement mentioned in the *exordium* in 1:12 (συμπαρακληθῆναι διὰ τῆς ἐν ἀλλήλοις πίστεως; "so that we may be mutually encouraged by each other's trust") is fulfilled by 15:23–24 (cf. 15:32): the Roman Christians will encourage Paul.[83] That both passages, 15:23–24 and 1:12, are related is likely. First, the *peroratio*, of which 15:23–24 is a part, often recapitulates the main point(s) of the *exordium*, of which 1:12 is a part. Second, as Jewett notes, Paul being satisfied (ἐμπλησθῶ

---

ary Rhetoric, §434–35. Wuellner asserts that the two basic functions of the *peroratio*, namely, recapitulation and *pathos*, are present in 15:14–15 and 15:16–29, and in 15:30–16:23 ("Paul's Rhetoric of Argumentation," 339–45).

82. Wuellner, "Paul's Rhetoric of Argumentation," 339.

83. Cf. A. J. M. Wedderburn, "The Purpose and Occasion of Romans Again," in Donfried, *Romans Debate*, 199–200.

ὑμῶν) by the Roman Christians echoes the mutual encouragement of trust Paul speaks of in 1:12.[84]

Also important for understanding the purpose of Romans is the relationship between the Roman Christians' trust and that of Paul mentioned in 1:11–12. As I have argued above in my analysis of 1:1–12, the trust that would encourage Paul—the trust in God exhibited by the Roman Christians—is the state that will be attained after they have heard the message of Paul's letter and after he strengthens them with his future visit. This observation leads us to the purpose of Romans: Paul writes to strengthen the trust of the Roman Christians and to obtain their support for his future evangelistic expedition to Spain. This support includes some material help (15:24).[85] That Paul is anxious to receive material support from the Roman Christians is demonstrated by his stirring up *pathos* for his evangelistic expedition. Paul sandwiches between his statements about his intended expedition to Spain (15:23–24, 32) a statement about his approaching visit to Jerusalem (15:25–31), where he will deliver aid to the Judean Christians there. Relevant to our investigation is the fact that Paul spells out the significance of the gift that he is about to deliver to Jerusalem. He explains that the gentiles owe it to the Judean Christians to provide aid to them because the gentile Christians share in τοῖς πνευματικοῖς ("the spiritual gifts" [15:27]). This adjectival substantive is used two other times in Romans, one of which refers to Paul hoping to impart some πνευματικόν ("spiritual") gift (1:11) to the implied audience.[86] Paul's intention in telling the implied audience about his impending visit to Jerusalem is to use the Christians in Macedonia and Achaia as an example. What this means is that just as gentile Christians in Macedonia and Achaia reciprocate the πνευματικόν gift given by the Judean Christians in Jerusalem, the gentile Roman Christians too should reciprocate the πνευματικόν gift (1:11) that Paul, a Judean apostle, will bring when he visits the Roman gentile Christians. This act of reciprocation is built upon a social-cultural texture of friendship.[87] Con-

---

84. Jewett, *Romans*, 926.

85. Ibid., 925; Schlier, *Der Römerbrief*, 872.

86. The adjective πνευματικός occurs a total of three times in Romans: 1:11; 7:14; 15:27.

87. See John T. Fitzgerald, "Paul and Friendship," in *Paul in the Greco-Roman World: A Handbook*, ed. J. Paul Sampley (Harrisburg, PA: Trinity Press International, 2003), 320–27. Fitzgerald, citing Aristotle, makes several observations about friendship that characterize Romans: "friendship … involves mutuality and reciprocity"

sidering, however, that Paul positions himself as someone who possesses apostolic authority and that he asserts this authority on his implied audience, this friendship should be construed as functioning in a patron-client relationship, or what Peter Marshall describes as "patronal friendship."[88] Thus, the Roman Christians are expected to return Paul's favor (or grace) by supporting his evangelistic expedition to Spain, a factor that forms part of the rhetorical situation of the letter. Thus, Achaia evokes *pathos*. Paul's appeal for the Roman Christians' prayer in 15:30 serves two purposes. First, it acts to cement the relationship between the dissenting Judean and gentile Christians by appealing to, as Dunn puts it, the shared "Lordship" of Jesus Christ or, as I argue later, Jesus as the superordinate figure.[89] Paul also appeals to the love of the Spirit as expounded in 5:5. The use of the verb συναγωνίσασθαί ("to strive together"), containing the prefix συν-, serves to "draw them into an alliance over against the potential opposition from Judea and the Jerusalem church."[90] Second, this request for prayer also creates *pathos* and recapitulates Paul's sincere desire mentioned in the *exordium* (1:13) to avoid a repeat of his past failed attempts to visit them. Third, the ultimate aim of this prayer is that he might be "refreshed" or encouraged by the Roman Christians. This recalls 1:12 of the *exordium* and his earlier statement in 15:24. Thus, Paul's purpose in requesting their prayers is to be able to visit them and to have them support his mission to Spain.

(320; cf. Rom 1:12); "of the three forms of friendship, the highest is that which is based on mutual admiration of character" (326; cf. Rom 1:8); "it seeks the good of the friend.... [T]hey help each other morally by not only striving to prevent one another from doing wrong but also by correcting one another when they do err" (327; cf. Rom 1:11). He also comments that Romans contains friendship language (339).

88. Peter Marshall comments that "patronal friendship had the appearance of equality between the two parties but in reality it was an unequal relationship." See Marshall, *Enmity in Corinth: Social Conventions in Paul's*, WUNT 2/23 (Tübingen: Mohr Siebeck, 1987), 144. Fitzgerald observes that "the Greco-Roman world witnessed the emergence of several 'unequal' friendships, that is, friendships between people from different socioeconomic groups" ("Paul," 328). Barclay argues that "the term 'patronage' can be used in a wider or narrower sense, as a broad label for unequal but enduring personal relations involving an exchange of service and favors, or in specific reference to the 'patron-client' relations that were integral to Roman systems of social transactions" (*Paul and the Gift*, 35).

89. See Dunn, *Romans 9–16*, 878; see below, chapter 4, §2.1, "Romans 4:13: Abraham and His Descendants Do Not Inherit the Promise by Means of the Mosaic Law but by Trust in God."

90. Dunn, *Romans 9–16*, 878.

The long list of people in 16:3–16 to whom Paul sends greetings is unusual and indicates that it is purposeful. The recurrence of the second-person plural ἀσπάσασθε ("greet" [16x in 14 verses]) creates a sensory-aesthetic texture that evokes *pathos*. This moves the implied audience to act cordially toward other Christians.

Most scholars either regard 16:17–20 as unrelated to what has preceded or, at best, only loosely related to the content of Rom 16.[91] But as Esler comments,

> If one holds as the fundamental canon of interpretation that the main resource we have for judging the plausibility of the interpretation of any aspect of a Pauline letter, including the context into which it was sent, is the letter itself, it is relatively easy to construe these verses as largely summarizing points that Paul has made earlier in the letter.[92]

This explains why there are common topoi between the earlier parts of the letter and 16:17–20: Paul's appeal to his implied audience to beware of those who cause divisions (16:17) recalls his earlier injunctions not to quarrel but to keep peace (11:17, 20; 12:16; 14:1–5, 10, 13, 19), Paul's attack on those who serve their stomachs (16:18) parallels his rebuke of those who cause others to stumble by the food they eat (14:15), and his description of such people as those who deceive by "smooth talk" and "flattery" recalls his instruction to his implied audience to avoid quarrels over opinions (14:1).[93] Thus, the focus of 16:17–20, that the Roman Christians should avoid dissension, forms part of the rhetorical situation. When viewed contextually, 16:17–20 should form the main part of the rhetorical situation or, more precisely, the exigence of the rhetorical situation.[94] This

---

91. For the passage as unrelated, see Jewett, *Romans*, 986–88; Fitzmyer, *Romans*, 745; Jeffrey A. D. Weima, *Neglected Endings: The Significance of the Pauline Letter Closings*, JSNTSup 101 (Sheffield: Sheffield Academic, 1994), 228. Jewett regards 16:17a–20 as a non-Pauline interpolation. For the passage as loosely related, see Moo, *Epistle to the Romans*, 929; Dunn, *Romans 9–16*, 901; Cranfield, *Epistle to the Romans*, 2:797–98.

92. Esler, *Conflict and Identity in Romans*, 126. Similarly, Karl P. Donfried regards 16:17–20 as concluding the discussion in chapter 14. See Donfried, "A Short Note on Romans 16," in Donfried, *Romans Debate*, 51.

93. Esler, *Conflict and Identity in Romans*, 126–28.

94. Stanley E. Porter agrees that the level of antagonism is muted when compared to other cities. Drawing evidence from other letters (e.g., 2 Cor 3–4; Galatians), he concludes, however, that opponents are present among the Roman Christians. See

is revealed by its location in the letter, in that before Paul ends his letter with his usual greetings from his fellow workers, he reiterates his main concern of this letter.[95]

2.6. Conclusion

For a discourse to be intelligible, the rhetorical situation or the social context that generates a discourse needs to be discovered. Bitzer identifies three constituents that clarify the rhetorical situation: the exigence, the implied audience, and the speaker (the constraint). To understand the rhetorical situation of Romans, I have investigated the *exordium* (1:1–15) and the *peroratio* (15:14–16:27), as they contain information related to the rhetorical situation. This section provides a summary of the above investigation of the *exordium* and *peroratio* in terms of the implied speaker, the exigence, and the implied audience.

2.6.1. The Implied Speaker

The implied speaker is Paul (1:1). His apostolic authority lies in the nature of the gospel that he preaches (περὶ τοῦ υἱοῦ αὐτοῦ; "concerning his son" [1:3]; δι' οὗ ἐλάβομεν ... ἀποστολήν; "through whom we have received apostleship" [1:5]) and that Paul writes about in Romans (1:5). The gospel concerns the nature of Jesus (1:3): specifically, Jesus exists in a state of power that is characterized by holiness (1:4), that is, a life characterized by righteousness. The nature of his apostolic authority allows him to legitimately assert this authority over his implied audience.

Porter, "Did Paul Have Opponents in Rome and What Were They Opposing?," in *Paul and His Opponents*, ed. Stanley E. Porter, Pauline Studies 2 (Leiden: Brill, 2005), 165. That these opponents oppose Paul's status as apostle is possible. His contention, however, is not based on direct evidence from Romans. Oropeza provides a more balanced view: He agrees that Paul is addressing Christians who are causing dissension (*Jews, Gentiles, and the Opponents of Paul*, 135–36). This does not mean, however, that the letter is a "polemic against opponents who may be perverting the gospel" or that there was an "anti-Pauline group in their midst." Even in 16:17, where the tone appears to have changed, Esler argues that Paul's παρακαλῶ δὲ ὑμᾶς, ἀδελφοί ("and I urge you, brothers") is "a gentle imperative" (*Conflict and Identity in Romans*, 127).

95. So Dunn, *Romans 9–16*, 908; Moo, *Epistle to the Romans*, 933.

2.6.2. The Implied Exigence

Paul expresses and reiterates his desire to visit the Roman Christians so as to bring to them some spiritual benefits. This objective is couched variously: Paul hopes to strengthen them (1:11), provide them mutual encouragement (1:12), and have some fruit among them (1:13). What he intends to do during the visit will be fulfilled by preaching to them the gospel (1:15). It is fulfilled in part by Romans itself (1:16–11:36). In the *peroratio* (15:15–16), Paul reiterates the above point that he is an apostle to the gentiles (cf. 1:5) in the "priestly service of the gospel" and hopes to present to God an offering of the gentiles by the gospel that he has just written (15:15). Paul lays the ground for his objective by using what Moxnes calls God language. This emphasizes to the gentile Christians that their trust is in continuity with that which is recorded in the Judean Scriptures. Specifically, this benefit is that which he enunciates at the closing of the letter, which is to enable them to avoid dissension (16:17–20). The *probatio* also hints at a dissension between Judean and gentile Christians: in 11:13–24, gentile Christians are reminded not to boast over Judeans; in 14:1–15:13, "the strong," namely, gentile Christians, are told not to cause the "weak," who probably are Judean Christians, to stumble.[96] Furthermore, in 1:18–3:20, Paul seeks to prove that Judeans do not have a reason to boast over gentiles because of their superior righteousness as no one is righteous (3:9–10).[97] The nature of the gospel, as described in 1:2–3 and 1:16–17, about which Paul writes seems to indicate that the nature of this dissension entails ethical righteousness.[98] The nature of the gospel that Paul brings to the implied audience, as described in 1:2–3, is about Jesus Christ who is empowered by "the Spirit of holiness." The emphasis

---

96. See also William S. Campbell, who contends that in explaining the occasion and purpose of Romans, not only must 1:1–17 and 15:14–16:27 be considered, but the intervening content, 1:18–11:36, must also be factored into the discussion. "A coherence must be established also between 1:18–11:36 and 12–15(16)." See Campbell, "Romans III as Key," in Donfried, *Romans Debate*, 252; see below, chapter 2, §4.7, "Romans 11:17–32: Trust in God Can Make Judeans Holy"; on 14:1–15:13, see below, chapter 2, §4.9, "Romans 14:1–15:13: Trust in God Enables Both the Weak and the Strong to Stand under Judgment."

97. See below, chapter 2, §3.2, "Romans 1:18–3:20: Humankind, Including Judeans, Has Sinned against God."

98. See below, chapter 2, §3.1, "Romans 1:16–17: The Gospel Has the Power to Save Both Judeans and Gentiles."

on the Spirit as that which imparts holiness seems to imply a rhetorical situation that entails ethical righteousness. Furthermore, the description of the gospel as one that brings righteousness in the relationship between Christians as God's clients and God as their patron (1:16–17) again hints at a deficiency of ethical righteousness, which is synonymous with ethical holiness. Paul's ultimate purpose in removing the dissension—or, in the words of the *exordium*, to strengthen their trust in God (1:12)—is to enable them to support him in his evangelistic expedition to Spain.

2.6.3. The Implied Audience

Paul is constructing his *ethos* in the *exordium* when he describes his apostolic authority (1:1–5a). By asserting this authority over gentiles (1:5), he intimates that at least a part of the implied (and real) audience is gentile. This is also corroborated by the fact that they are one part of a larger group of people of whom "the rest of the gentiles" are a part (1:13). Paul also describes the implied audience as "saints" (1:7). Hence, they are gentile Christians. His desire to visit the implied audience stems from his obligation to preach the gospel to Greeks and barbarians, wise and foolish, who together constitute a part of the gentile world. This observation again indicates that the implied audience is gentile Christians. That, however, does not mean that Judean Christians do not form part of the implied audience. Several observations support my view that, besides an implied gentile Christian audience, the implied audience of Romans consists also of Judean Christians.[99] First, as I have argued, the list of names in Rom 16 to whom the letter is addressed contains names of Judean origin.[100] Second,

---

99. See also above, chapter 2, §2.4.1, "Romans 1:1–7," where I argue against construing ἔθνη in 1:5 as constituting evidence for a wholly gentile real audience. Mark D. Nanos insists that the weak are non-Christian Judeans. Mark Reasoner refutes this position as it goes against "14:4–6, 9; 15:5 [that] locate the difference as occurring between parties that identify with Jesus as Lord." See Nanos, *The Mystery of Romans: The Jewish Context of Paul's Letter* (Minneapolis: Fortress, 1996), 110; Reasoner, "The Theology of Romans 12:1–15:13," in Hay and Johnson, *Romans*, 289, 291. Furthermore, the "obedience of faith" (1:5) with faith functioning as a subjective genitive (see above in chapter 2, n. 65), has its outworking in 12:1–15:13. This requires both parties, the "weak" and the "strong," to be Christians. See also Campbell, who notes that "the obedience of faith" determines how faith is worked out in 12:1–15:13 ("Rule of Faith," 275).

100. See above, chapter 2, §2.2, "Historical Background."

I also contended that ἔθνη contains a geographical dimension that refers to people who dwell outside Judea. These people would likely include Judean and gentile Christians. Third, as I will show in my overview of 14:1–15:13, in applying the message of 1:18–11:36, Paul urges reconciliation between the "weak" who are Judean Christians and the "strong" who are gentile Christians.[101] This implies the presence of both groups in the Christian community in Rome.

Although the implied audience is to be distinguished from the real audience, the relation of the implied audience to the real audience needs to be clarified to support the weight of my argument concerning Judean Christians boasting over gentiles. This is necessary as "the rhetorical audience must be capable of serving as mediator of the change that the discourse functions to produce."[102] In Romans, the real audience also comprises Judean and gentile Christians. This is borne out by the historical circumstances that surrounded Claudius's edict in 49 CE, which gave rise to a minority presence of Judean Christians and a majority of gentile Christians.[103] That Judean Christians are in the Roman congregation is evidenced by Rom 16.[104] Furthermore, as I will contend in my analysis of 2:1–29, the Judean interlocutor in 2:17 must represent the views of a real Judean (Christian) audience in order for Paul's rhetoric, which involves honor, the core value of Mediterranean culture, to work.[105]

3. The Argument of Romans 1:16–4:25

As letters were read out to the audience, proceeding from the beginning to the end, the implied audience would naturally understand Rom 4 in light of what precedes it. Hence, to understand the rhetorical goal of Rom 4, I shall trace the argument of 1:16–3:31 and explain how its rhetoric and dominating issues precipitate the need for the rhetoric of Rom 4.

---

101. See chapter 2, §4.9, "Romans 14:1–15:13: Trust in God Enables Both the Weak and the Strong to Stand under Judgment."

102. Bitzer, "Rhetorical Situation," 8.

103. See chapter 2, §2.2, "Historical Background."

104. See chapter 2, §2.2, "Historical Background."

105. See chapter 2, §3.2, "Romans 1:18–3:20: Humankind, Including Judeans, Has Sinned against God."

3.1. Romans 1:16–17: The Gospel Has the Power to Save Both Judeans and Gentiles

The γάρ in 1:16 is causal and introduces the reason in 1:16–17 for Paul's desire to visit the Roman implied audience in 1:8–15: the gospel imparts salvation. That 1:16–17 is connected to 1:1–15 is indicated by common topoi: εὐαγγέλιον ("gospel" [1:9, 16]); the δύναμις ("power" [1:4, 16]) of the gospel; Paul's gospel, which is characterized by the power of the Spirit of holiness (1:4, 16) and is to be preached also to the Greeks (1:14, 16). In other words, Paul's desire to visit the implied audience (1:10–11) and then to impart "some spiritual gift to (them) in order to strengthen (them)" finds its basis in 1:16–17: the power of the gospel to bring salvation to "Judeans first and also to the Greeks."

This comes as a surprise as Paul previously described the implied audience of the gospel as belonging to a group delineated by "Greeks and barbarians" and "wise and foolish" (1:14). The observation that, from this point on, Paul no longer focuses on this group but on issues pertaining to breaking down of barriers between Judeans and Greeks indicates that 1:14 serves to prepare for 1:16–17. This means that the pair "Judeans and Greeks" is somehow related to the pairs "Greeks and barbarians" and "wise and foolish." Dunn comments that Greeks classified the world as comprising Greeks and barbarians or, synonymously, wise and foolish. Both barbarians and foolish are derogatory terms that Greeks used to describe people other than themselves.[106] " 'Jew and Greek' is the Jewish equivalent to the Gentile categorization of the world given in v 14, only here with 'Greek' replacing 'Gentile,' reflecting the all pervasiveness of Greek culture."[107] In the same vein, Kathy Ehrensperger also observes that the pair Ἰουδαῖοι καὶ Ἕλληνες ("Judeans and Greeks"), in particular, are different ways of life based on different traditions of belonging."[108] The term Ἕλληνες ("Greeks") does not refer to an ethnic group but to the Greek παιδεία ("education") that led to a civilized way of life.[109] Greek παιδεία, "combined with Roman values such as *virtutes* and *mores*, provided the means by which to achieve *humanitas*, the way of life most

106. Dunn, *Romans 1–8*, 32–33.
107. Ibid., 40.
108. Ehrensperger, *Paul at the Crossroads of Cultures*, 122.
109. Ibid., 65.

appropriate for civilized peoples in the perception of the Roman elite."[110] The implication is that when Paul says that he has an obligation to preach the gospel to Greeks and barbarians, he implies that the gospel can resolve cultural problems that disrupt relationships between Greeks and barbarians. Furthermore, when Paul describes the gospel as "the power of God that brings salvation" (1:16), the power refers to that which can save Judeans and Greeks from some constraints related to ethical concerns.[111] Whatever the precise concerns are, the above observation indicates that Paul is dealing with a situation where Judeans and Greeks are embroiled in some kind of a competition between one faction and another. This observation is borne out by the content of the letter, where Paul seeks to reconcile these two groups later in his argument. This gospel is capable of effecting salvation for Judeans and Greeks because it reveals the righteousness of God (1:17) that comes through trust, as the expression ἐκ πίστεως εἰς πίστιν ("from trust to trust") indicates.

3.2. Romans 1:18–3:20: Humankind, Including Judeans, Has Sinned against God

The presence of prophetic rhetorolect is indicated by several observations. Romans 1:18–32 begins with the threat of God's wrath (1:18) against those who know the truth and yet suppress the truth. Using diatribe style, Paul indicts the interlocutor of his sins and the punishment that will follow (2:1–29). Paul then rounds off his indictment with further accusations taken from the LXX, including the Psalms and Prophets. By using prophetic rhetorolect and the pointed indictments that accompany this rhetorolect, Paul generates *pathos* in the implied audience in order to convict them of their own state of sinfulness. Also, prophetic rhetorolect allows Paul to take on the role of a prophet. This raises the *ethos* of Paul as the speaker. In this way, the use of prophetic rhetorolect provides Paul access to ideological power that effectively reproves the implied audience of their sins. Following this observation, I shall analyze the details of 1:18–3:20.

It is important to bear in mind the connection of 1:18–3:20 with the preceding context. Paul had expressed his wish to visit the Roman

---

110. Ibid.

111. Jewett observes that Paul "frequently speaks of salvation in terms of preservation from divine wrath in the last judgment" and deliverance "from the present evil age" (*Romans*, 138–39).

Christians earlier in the preceding passage. His objective is described in 1:8–15 by a series of related wishes, which include the desire to impart to them some spiritual gift (1:11), which in turn will bring mutual encouragement (1:12), and the desire to reap some fruit among the Roman Christians. Paul's means for achieving these objectives is through the power of the gospel. This leads to the theme of Romans in 1:16–17 and its elaboration in the main body (1:18–15:13). Thus, the exposition of the gospel has as its objective the reaping of some fruit among the Roman Christians. This fruit is specific. According to 1:16–17, it involves several aspects. It includes salvation, and this salvation is attainable because the gospel creates a righteous relationship between Christians and their patron, God. This righteousness is essential for salvation because 1:18 says that God is angry because of the unrighteousness of humankind. From this point onwards, Paul begins his long rhetorical presentation (1:18–15:13) on how this righteousness—that is, a righteous relationship between God the patron and Christians the clients—can be achieved.

Paul devotes the first section (1:18–3:20) to removing Judeans' reliance on the law of Moses for righteousness. This enables Paul to conclude in 3:20 that Judeans cannot claim that the Mosaic law establishes a righteous relationship between God, who is the patron, and Christians, who are the clients.[112] Paul's main intention in writing this section is not simply to indict the entire human race for having broken that righteous relationship through having sinned against God their patron by deviating from his just requirements. Paul's aim is to divest Judeans of their reliance on observing the law of Moses for establishing this righteous relationship with God.[113] That this is his main concern is demonstrated by several observations.

---

112. Against Seth Schwartz, who describes the Judeans as culturally antireciprocal, Barclay contends that even if the poor are unable to return in kind the gifts given to them by the wealthy, God promises to reciprocate on behalf of the poor by rewarding the wealthy who give (see Deut 14:19; 15:4–5, 10; 24:19; Tob 4:7, 9, 14). Barclay concludes that "Jews were perhaps more likely than non-Jews to give to beggars, not because they did not care about a return, but because they had a stronger ideological reason for expecting one—not of course from the beggars, but from God." See Schwartz, *Were the Jews a Mediterranean Society? Reciprocity and Solidarity in Ancient Judaism* (Princeton: Princeton University Press, 2010), 10; Barclay, *Paul and the Gift*, 44–45.

113. Contra Cranfield, *Epistle to the Romans*, 1:104; Moo, *Epistle to the Romans*, 92; Tobin, *Paul's Rhetoric*, 121–22. Tobin thinks that Paul simply seeks to indict the entire human race.

First, the *inclusio* bracketed by δικαιοσύνη θεοῦ ἀποκαλύπτεται ("the righteousness of God is revealed" [1:17]) and δικαιοσύνη θεοῦ πεφανέρωται ("the righteousness of God has been manifested" [3:21]) delineates a complete unit (1:18–3:20). The change from "the righteousness of God in it is revealed" (1:17) to "but now the righteousness of God that is apart from the law has been manifested" (3:21) indicates that the focus of the intervening section (1:18–3:20) has to do with the law of Moses. This implies that 1:18–3:20 addresses a Judean concern. Second, common among the three sections (1:18–32; 2:1–16; 2:17–29) is the motif that knowledge of the law of God (which includes the general law [cf. 1:14] and the Mosaic law) brings with it also knowledge of sin. Thus, the pericope 1:18–3:20 begins with the programmatic statement in 1:18 that emphasizes that God's anger is revealed against those who suppress the truth, that is, those who know the truth and yet refuse to submit to the truth. The difference among the three sections is a gradual tightening of the proverbial hangman's noose on the Judean interlocutor.

This gradual tightening of the "hangman's noose" starts with 1:18–32, where Paul indicts gentiles who know the truth about God but refuse to acknowledge God. Interpreters have correctly argued that Paul uses Judean apologetic motifs against gentiles (see, e.g., Wis 13:1–9; 14:22–31; Let. Aris. 128–71; Sib. Or. 3.8–45).[114] By this, he seeks to appeal to the Judean Christians who are among the implied audience. Paul does so by a "rhetorical configuration of gentiles (which is done in light of the gentile topos)."[115] By enumerating specific sins gentiles commit, Paul stirs up *pathos* in the implied (Judean Christian) audience, and so generates ideological power "in order to get them on board with him in an overall confirmation of God's righteous judgment against gentiles."[116] Paul's specific intent, however, is to prepare for his indictment of the Judean interlocutor in 2:1, as indicated by the particle of inference διό.[117]

---

114. E.g., Tobin, *Paul's Rhetoric*, 109; Moo, *Epistle to the Romans*, 97; Dunn, *Romans 9–16*, 56–70; Edward Adams, "Abraham's Faith and Gentile Disobedience: Textual Links between Romans 1 and 4," *JSNT* 65 (1997): 49; Moo, *Epistle to the Romans*, 97; Jewett, *Romans*, 150.

115. Bloomquist, "Paul's Inclusive Language," 146.

116. Ibid.

117. Out of its six occurrences in the book of Romans, five (1:24; 4:22; 13:5; 15:7; 15:22) are clearly inferential.

This leads to the next stage of the argument in 2:1–3:30. Scholars recognize that Paul makes use of the diatribe style where he debates with an imaginary interlocutor.[118] Such a mode of rhetoric has the advantage of making the interlocutor take on the identity Paul requires for his rhetoric to work. At the same time, it allows Paul to make "dialogical objections and false conclusions for the purpose of indictment," as seen in this section.[119]

Paul indicts the interlocutor on the basis that the interlocutor condemns the very sins he himself commits. This lively style of debating with an imaginary interlocutor and indicting him of sin heightens *pathos* in emphasizing the gravity of sin. Paul includes the Judeans in his indictment of this interlocutor when he states that God renders retribution for sins to "the Judean first and also the Greek" (2:9). Furthermore, the section beginning with 2:17 simulates the Judeans judging the gentiles.[120] Some interpreters think that the interlocutor referred to in 2:1 cannot be a Judean, as the interlocutor will not agree that he is guilty of idolatry in 1:21–24.[121] The phrase τὰ αὐτά ("the same things"), however, could refer to the nearest list of vices in 1:28–32. Dunn comments that

> a line of argument which accused Jews of idolatry and homosexual practice would be unlikely to commend much support, either from the judgmental Jew or from the God-worshipping Gentile…. But the list of 1:29–31 largely consists of vices into which an individual can slide without being fully aware of it.[122]

This also finds evidence in the fact that the phrase τὰ τοιαῦτα occurs only three times in Romans. In two of these occurrences (2:2, 3), it refers to

---

118. E.g., Stanley K. Stowers, who states that it is characteristic of a diatribe to address the imaginary person "with a vocative of some sort," or typically, "there is a sudden turning to address the fictitious interlocutor." See Stowers, *The Diatribe and Paul's Letter to the Romans*, SBLDS 57 (Chico, CA: Scholars Press, 1981), 87, 93–98; see also Dunn, *Romans 1–8*, 78; Jewett, *Romans*, 196.

119. Aune, *Westminster Dictionary*, s.v. "Diatribe."

120. Dunn observes that "Jew and Greek" is the Judean equivalent of the way gentiles view the world, as in "Greek and barbarians" (1:14). Thus, in Judeans' perspective, "Greeks" equates with "gentiles" (*Romans 1–8*, 40).

121. Esler, *Conflict and Identity in Romans*, 151. Käsemann circumvents the difficulty by regarding the διό as an early marginal gloss and arguing that it is not inferential (*Commentary on Romans*, 54).

122. Dunn, *Romans 1–8*, 80; Moo, *Epistle to the Romans*, 131.

the nearby τὰ αὐτά in 2:1, that is, the sin of judging a person for sins that one also commits. Thus, that the phrase τὰ αὐτά refers to the sins enumerated in the nearby passage 1:28–31 is probable. Also, that a Judean interlocutor is in view in 2:1 explains why Paul, as explained above, casts a critique of gentile sins in 1:18–32 using Judean motifs. Furthermore, Alec J. Lucas observes that the phrase ἤλλαξαν τὴν δόξαν ... ἐν ὁμοιώματι ("they exchanged the glory ... in the likeness") in 1:23 is taken from Ps 105:20 LXX, which recounts Israel's sin of idolatry in the golden calf. This forms the "rhetorical basis on which Paul indicts the Jewish interlocutor of 2:1–11."[123] Simon J. Gathercole adds that identifying the interlocutor in 2:1 as a Judean ties in with the observation that "the designation 'the one who judges' is appropriate to a Jew, not because the Jewish people were more judgmental than others but because they took pride in being able to judge, in the sense of *discern*."[124] This observation is corroborated by 2:17–22. More importantly, Paul, by maintaining that he is dialoguing with the same interlocutor who is a Judean and who "took pride in being able to judge," strengthens his rhetorical question in 3:9, which, as I argue below, is directed especially at Judeans.[125]

The condemnation of the Judean interlocutor in 2:1 is certain because the law that he knowingly violates will condemn him. In a similar way in 2:17–29, the law of Moses that the Judeans know and teach and yet violate will condemn them. Stanley Stowers, who construes a wholly gentile real audience for Romans, regards the Judean in 2:17–29 as a "fictitious interlocutor."[126] Such a conceptualization is untenable, as it divorces Paul's rhetoric from the honor-shame culture, the core value of Mediterranean culture. The purpose of the rhetoric of 2:17–29—and for that matter, the whole of 1:18–3:20—is to lead to the conclusion in 3:19–20: so that "every mouth may be silenced." Specifically, it is to stop Judeans from extracting honor from gentiles through a game of challenge and riposte. This requires real time interaction between Judeans and gentile Christians in the tussle for honor. Hence, Paul uses the motif of knowing the law and

---

123. Alec J. Lucas, "Reorienting the Structural Paradigm and Social Significance of Romans 1:18–32," *JBL* 131 (2012): 136. Similarly, Barclay observes that "a close reading of 1:18–32 suggests that there are echoes here of a biblical rebuke of Israelite idolatry (LXX Ps 105:20 in Rom 1:23)" (*Paul and the Gift*, 463).

124. Gathercole, *Where Is Boasting?*, 198, emphasis original.

125. See below.

126. Stowers, *Rereading of Romans*, 30, quote at 144.

yet breaking it as an indicting device to gradually tighten the proverbial hangman's noose on the Judeans who rely on the law of Moses for acquiring righteousness. Paul's main concern, however, is not just to indict the Judeans who rely on the law of Moses for righteousness (3:20) but to divest them of any reason to feel superior to the gentiles. This is shown by several observations. First, the interlocutor(s) in 2:1–16 and 2:17–29 are characterized as people who have a sense of superiority over gentiles. The Judeans "boast in God" because God has given them the law of Moses. In the honor-shame culture system of the Mediterranean world, it means that the Judeans' honor is received from God, their patron, who has given them the law of Moses. In return, the Judeans (the clients) have an obligation to bring honor to their patron, God. But when they use this to boast toward the gentiles in a bid to increase their share of honor,[127] they are shamed, and this in turn leads to their patron being shamed. That this is the case explains the scenario described in 2:22, where by breaking the law, "they dishonor God" (2:23) and bring shame to God. Furthermore, a riposte by the gentiles is possibly described here in 2:19, when the gentiles instead turn around to judge the Judeans when they (the gentiles) obey the universal moral law. Second, and more importantly, Paul begins his concluding paragraph for this section in 3:9–20 with a rhetorical question: "Therefore what? Are we better off?" (3:9). The self-evident response is that Judeans are no better off in terms of honor that has value before God than the gentiles. Paul does conclude that both Judeans and gentiles are ὑφ' ἁμαρτίαν ("under the power of sin"). Paul's contention, however, is not simply this. Rather, his point is not directed at the gentiles but at *the Judeans:* that they too are ὑφ' ἁμαρτίαν. This is precisely the thrust of 3:9, which introduces the paragraph 3:9–20. Paul also concludes with "every mouth may be silenced" (3:19). The "mouth" probably refers to that of the above interlocutor in 2:1–16 who judges and the interlocutor in 2:17–29 who teaches the gentiles so as to gain honor. That Paul is directing his indictment at Judeans is the reason why he concludes with a statement about the law of Moses upon which Judeans rely: "Therefore, by the deeds required by the (Mosaic) law, no flesh will be made righteous" (3:20). Such an emphasis also accounts for the frequent Judean/Greek refrain (1:16;

---

127. See Moxnes, who also thinks that "in Romans 2:17–24 Paul describes a situation of a competition for honor: Jews claim honor (by boasting) over other people on the basis of status, a claim which is founded both on inheritance and a knowledge of God and law (2:17–20)" ("Honour and Righteousness," 69).

2:9; 2:10; 3:9) that emphasizes that Judeans are no less guilty of sin, which incurs shame, than gentiles.

3.3. Romans 3:21–31: Jesus Atones for the Sins of Both Judeans and Gentiles

Paul has indicted the Judean and also gentile Christians for their sins. This indictment brings shame on them. The consequence is a lack of a righteous relationship with the patron God. At this point, the question that would trouble the minds of the implied audience remains: how can a person establish a righteous relationship with their patron God so as to gain honor that has value before God? At this point, Paul brings in priestly rhetorolect as evinced by the topoi of sin (3:23), blood and atonement (3:24–26), and circumcision (3:30). The shift from the previous prophetic rhetorolect to priestly rhetorolect mobilizes ideological power by motivating them to accept a solution to the condemnation they incur(red) through sin. It motivates them to want to abandon reliance on the Mosaic law and rely on Jesus who provides atonement for sin. The section below explains the details.

Several observations help to pin down the emphasis of 3:21–31. This passage begins with a twofold thesis statement: that righteousness has been manifested "apart from the law" (χωρὶς νόμου) and that it is also "testified by the law [ὑπὸ τοῦ νόμου] and the prophets" (3:21). At the end of the first part of the argument (3:21–26), Paul begins the second (3:27–31) with a rhetorical question whose answer is "the boast" is removed on the basis of trust that comes "apart from the law" (χωρὶς ἔργων νόμου). The addition of ἔργων ("deeds") in the latter expression does not amount to a substantial difference but is introduced for a play of words to contrast the subsequent νόμου πίστεως ("law of trust") of 3:27. This phrase, which recalls the thesis statement in 3:21, implies that the conclusion in 3:27–28 is reached via the argument in 3:22–26 that the expiation by Jesus's blood (3:25) makes the person who trusts Jesus Christ (3:26) as broker righteous with God. Hence, Paul reinforces the thesis statement (3:21) that this righteousness in relationship with God is "apart from the law" (χωρὶς νόμου). Paul, however, does not say (although he obviously implies) in 3:27 that this righteousness is obtained apart from the Mosaic law, as in the thesis statement. What he does say is "the boast" to gain honor is removed by virtue of the fact that this righteousness comes χωρὶς νόμου. In a Mediterranean culture where honor and shame are core values, honor is considered a limited good.[128] In this passage, when Judeans boast because they possess honor, that honor must be obtained at the expense of somebody else, in this case, gentiles.[129] Thus, Paul in 3:27 is saying that Judeans cannot boast toward gentiles and hence gain honor. This conclusion in 3:27 should not be construed as a minor point but one that advances his foregoing rhetoric (1:18–3:20).[130] Paul does this to undermine Judeans' reliance on the law for righteousness in order that they may not "boast" (2:17, 23) against the gentiles.

In the second part of the argument (3:27–31), it is important to note that 3:29–30 does not seek to simply reinforce the point in 3:28 that one is made righteous by trust and not deeds required by the Mosaic law. Rather, 3:29–30 is responding to the entire thesis in 3:27–28; that is, Paul is reinforcing his assertion that Judeans cannot boast toward the gentiles (3:27). When 3:29–30 is read against 3:27–28 and not just 3:28, the reason why Paul uses the idea of "one God" (3:30) becomes intelligible. Esler comments that "Paul appeals to the fundamental Judean belief in monotheism … to legitimate his claim that righteousness through faith comes to Judeans and non-Judeans."[131] Paul's assertion removes the boast of the Judeans toward the gentiles.

The social and cultural texture underlying righteousness gives ideological texture to righteousness. This ideological texture will enable us to understand how Judeans use it to gain honor from gentiles. Judeans construe righteousness as an essential ingredient of their ethnic identity. This causes Judeans to perceive those who are not Judeans—or, in social iden-

---

128. Jerome H. Neyrey comments that limited good is a social construct of the ancient peasants that all good things of this world exist in limited supply. The most precious of goods in antiquity is honor (Neyrey, "Limited Good," in Pilch and Malina, *Handbook of Biblical Social Values*, 122–27).

129. Joseph Plevnik, "Honor/Shame," in Pilch and Malina, *Handbook of Biblical Social Values*, 105–6.

130. Gathercole notes that the boast in 3:27 is a Judean one discussed in 2:17 and 2:23, that God would vindicate Israel against the gentiles (*Where Is Boasting?*, 236). Contra C. E. B. Cranfield, who argues that construing it as a Judean boast is an anticlimax. Cranfield has not adequately captured Paul's preceding rhetoric in 1:18–3:20, which was directed specifically at Judeans who boast in the law against gentiles. See Cranfield, "'The Works of the Law' in the Epistle to the Romans," *JSNT* 43 (1991): 96.

131. Esler, *Conflict and Identity in Romans*, 169. Similarly, Moxnes opines that "God is one" serves "an argument for the inclusion and co-existence of both Jews and non-Jews in the same community, on the basis of faith" (*Theology in Conflict*, 223).

tity terminology, *outgroups*—as unrighteous. Esler's observation, based on Henri Tajfel's understanding of group identity, on how such a perception of righteousness affects Judean-gentile relationship is apt:

> Righteousness: (1) said something to Israelites about the substance of the identity (the cognitive dimension); (2) made them feel good about belonging to it (the emotional dimension); and (3) gave them a criterion against which to make negative judgments concerning outgroups (the evaluative dimension).[132]

The consequence is that gentile Christians were cast in the role of outgroups or outsiders by Judean Christians, and it is this that Paul seeks to correct by creating a unified identity between Judean and gentile Christians.[133] To achieve this, he has to realign the Judean Christians' understanding of righteousness. In 3:27–31, Paul explains that "God is one" (3:30), which implies that he is the God of both Judeans and gentiles. This requires God to ascribe righteousness to both Judeans and gentiles in the same way. Otherwise, it would lead to two classes of Christians, namely, those who had achieved righteousness by means of observing the Mosaic law and those who had to have righteousness bestowed by God directly.

This righteousness, however, is not just a social identity marker. It is also an ethical relational construct as two observations show. First, it is ethical, as evident in how "righteousness" is juxtaposed against 1:18–3:31. Here, the revelation of the δικαιοσύνη ("righteousness") of God in 1:17 is immediately contrasted with the revelation of God against ungodliness and ἀδικίαν ("unrighteousness"), a word belonging to δικ- cognates. This ungodliness and unrighteousness is further described as a refusal to honor God according to what may be known about God and his decrees (1:18–32). It is further described as knowingly violating God's law (2:1–29). In removing the boast of Judeans toward gentiles (3:9), and hence the Judean ethnic identity marker, Paul recites as the reason for this that no one is

---

132. Esler, *Conflict and Identity in Romans*, 167. See Henri Tajfel and John C. Turner, "The Social Identity Theory of Intergroup Behavior," in *Psychology of Intergroup Relations*, ed. Stephen Worchel and William G. Austin (Chicago: Nelson-Hall, 1986), 7–24; Henri Tajfel, M. G. Billig, R. P. Bundy, and C. Flament, "Social Categorization and Intergroup Behavior," *European Journal of Social Psychology* 1 (1971): 149–77.

133. See also Anthony J. Guerra, *Romans and the Apologetic Tradition* (Cambridge: Cambridge University Press, 1995), 109.

δίκαιος ("righteous" [3:10]) and that all have fallen short of God's ethical requirements (3:10–18).

Second, righteousness is also relational, as the above observations show, in that it is couched in terms of what angers or pleases God. It is measured against God's ethical requirements and forms the basis of humankind's relationship with God. This relational aspect becomes clearer when the social and cultural texture, namely, the patron-client relationship that underlies righteousness, is exposed. Paul's description of God as the God of both gentiles and Judeans should be interpreted in light of a patron-client relationship. Righteousness, then, should also be read in light of this patron-client social and cultural texture. Hence, righteousness is a relational construct. In summary, righteousness should be construed as a social, relational, and ethical construct. This righteousness, as explained above, becomes a wedge that disrupts the relationship between Judean and gentile Christians. This takes Paul to the rhetoric of Rom 4.

3.4. Romans 4:1–25: Abraham Is the Father of Judean and Gentile Christians

Before I explain Rom 4, the primary subject of this book, I shall briefly recall the preceding argument. To impart to the implied audience "some spiritual gift" (1:11), that is, to "reap some harvest among" (1:13 NRSV) the gentile and Judean Christians, Paul uses the gospel that he is presently in the midst of writing to them (1:16–15:13). Paul mobilizes ideological power to achieve two related objectives. First, he wants his implied audience to give attention to this gospel, which is about Jesus Christ (1:3–4). Second, by understanding better the gospel about Jesus Christ, he wants to show that Judean Christians should not rely on the Mosaic law. To achieve this twofold objective, Paul begins with apocalyptic rhetorolect to motivate them to desire the eschatological salvation that includes future glory (Rom 8).[134] He then indicts the Judean Christians in the implied audience of sin using prophetic rhetorolect in order to show that they need a solution for their condemnation from God. This brings in priestly rhetorolect that emphasizes that holiness, and hence salvation, comes through trust in

---

134. See Robbins, *Invention of Christian Discourse*, 109. He notes that the speaker of the rhetoric, by use of apocalyptic rhetorolect, seeks to persuade the audience (specifically, in the thirdspace of the minds of the audience) that they will receive eschatological salvation.

Jesus Christ and not the Mosaic law. Up to this point, the subject of how Paul's gospel reconciles the two dissenting parties, namely, Judean and gentile Christians, has not been holistically articulated. At this juncture, Paul uses wisdom rhetorolect to articulate "wisdom" for the purpose of "searching and seeking" for understanding.[135] This wisdom is later further espoused in subsequent chapters (Rom 5–15) using various rhetorolects. Wisdom rhetorolect is especially appropriate in the case of Romans: Paul hopes to produce in the implied audience "righteousness and goodness,"[136] that is, to move the implied audience to respond favorably to his rhetoric while at the same time keeping confrontation with the implied Judean Christian audience to a minimum.[137] He hopes to remove the Judean Christians' boast toward the gentile Christians, a boast resulting from their possession of the Mosaic law and the righteousness that they think it confers. Paul, however, cannot confront the Judean Christians head-on, as the Mosaic law is a key ethnic identity marker for them. This is where wisdom rhetorolect offers an edge over the other rhetorolects like prophetic, apocalyptic, or precreation: wisdom rhetorolect is nonconfrontational. The presence of wisdom rhetorolect in Rom 4 is indicated by the topos of forefather. I shall now discuss pertinent details of Rom 4.

Using a diatribe, Paul engages in an intra-Judean debate with a Judean interlocutor, with the implied audience comprising Judean and gentile Christians listening to the debate. Paul articulates a question posed by the Judean interlocutor: "What shall we say? Have we found Abraham to be our forefather by his own human efforts?"[138] This question is directed at the implied audience, Judean Christians, who think that Abraham by his human efforts, that is, deeds related to the Mosaic law, became the forefather of Judeans.[139] This question is rhetorical in that it expects a negative

---

135. James L. Crenshaw, *Old Testament Wisdom: An Introduction* (Atlanta: John Knox, 1981), 17; George W. E. Nickelsburg, "Response to Sarah Tanzer," in *Conflicted Boundaries in Wisdom and Apocalypticism*, ed. Benjamin G. Wright III and Lawrence M. Wills, SymS 35 (Atlanta: Society of Biblical Literature, 2005), 51–54; Robbins, *Invention of Christian Discourse*, 125.

136. Robbins, *Invention of Christian Discourse*, 109.

137. See the thirdspace of wisdom rhetorolect in ibid.

138. See below, chapter 3, §3.2, "Romans 4:1: A Question of Fatherhood."

139. Stowers notes that " 'works of the law' is explicitly the issue in 3:20, 21, 27–28; 4:2, 4–6.… But 'according to the flesh' is better understood as 'by human efforts' and thus as cohering with the issue of justification by works [of the Mosaic law]" (*Rereading of Romans*, 242). Similarly, Jewett, *Romans*, 308: "κατὰ σάρκα … deals with the

response from the implied audience, comprising Judean and gentile Christians: that Abraham did not become the father of Judean Christians by human efforts. Paul's refutation takes several steps.

First, Paul undermines the deeds required by the Mosaic law in 4:2–8.[140] He recites the Judean sacred Scripture, Gen 15:6 LXX, to show that Abraham became the father of Judean Christians by trust in his patron God and not by deeds of the Mosaic law. The implication of Gen 15:6 is made clear by Rom 4:4–5, where Paul shows that trust precludes deeds required by the Mosaic law. To the same end, Ps 31:1–2a LXX is recited in Rom 4:6–8 to show that blessedness is a result of receiving a righteous relationship with God that precludes deeds of the Mosaic law.

Second, Paul in 4:9–12 undermines circumcision, the epitome of the Mosaic law, by showing that Abraham received righteousness, that is, a righteous relationship with God, his patron, many years before he was circumcised. Paul's purpose, however, is not only to undermine circumcision as a means to obtain righteousness. In 4:2–8, he has removed reliance on the deeds of the Mosaic law and hence proved that righteousness cannot be acquired. Specifically, it cannot be acquired by means of the deeds of the Mosaic law. This implies that righteousness, that is, a righteous relationship with God, must be ascribed. On the basis of 4:2–8, Paul now shows how righteousness can be ascribed, namely, by becoming a descendant of Abraham (4:11b). Gentiles can become Abraham's descendants because he was regarded as righteous (4:10) by God when he was in a state of uncircumcision; Judeans can become Abraham's descendants because his righteousness was affirmed by circumcision (4:11a). In this way, both groups can receive righteousness.

Third, in 4:13–16, Paul undermines the role of the Mosaic law by showing that the law invokes God's wrath, and hence would nullify the promise of Abraham's fatherhood. Hence, to become a descendant of Abraham, one has to trust Abraham's patron, God.

Fourth, having removed the deeds of the Mosaic law (4:2–8), circumcision (4:9–12), and the Mosaic law itself (4:13–16) as means by which a person becomes Abraham's descendant, Paul now explains in 4:17–25 how trust in the patron God achieves the twofold objective of Abraham becoming a father (fatherhood) and the ascription of Judeans and gentiles

---

question of whether Abraham performed works of the [Mosaic] law prior to being set right by God."

140. See below, chapter 3, §3.1.1, "Romans 4:2a."

as Abraham's descendants. Abraham's trust in his patron, God, enables his dead body to have descendants. Specifically, he trusted God to remove religious pollution, that is, sin in his dead body and in the bodies of his future descendants who were present in Abraham's body in seminal form.[141] God removed this pollution by Jesus's death, which expiates this pollution. Furthermore, Jesus's resurrection enables all, including Judean and gentile Christians, to live a righteous life. In this way, Judeans and especially gentiles can now become righteous with God so that Judeans can no longer flaunt their special position toward gentiles. The rhetoric in Rom 4 thus provides a full-circle response to 4:1, namely, that Abraham, and hence his family, Judean Christians, cannot boast vis-à-vis gentile Christians.

4. Outworking of Abraham's Trust in Romans 4

The conclusion of Rom 4 in 4:23–25 is that all who trust God, the one who raised Jesus from the dead, are made righteous in their relationship with their patron, God. As I shall argue in my analysis of 4:23–25, this trust gains the resurrection life of Jesus for both Judean and gentile Christians.[142] This life enables Judean and gentile Christians to live an ethically righteous life that is, minimally, congruous with the requirements of the Mosaic law. In this way, Judean and gentile Christians maintain a righteous relationship with God, their patron. As a result, both groups gain honor in the eyes of the significant other, God. The dissension between the two groups is thus alleviated.

This section will demonstrate that this conclusion is being worked out in greater detail in selected sections of 5:1–15:13, which, in my judgment, contain topoi related to the resurrection life of Jesus Christ.[143] My contention is corroborated by the presence of apocalyptic rhetorolect, which is the overarching rhetorolect of 1:18–15:13. The thirdspace of this rhetorolect, filled with the desired response of the implied audience,

---

141. See below, chapter 4, §3, "Romans 4:17–25: Trust Realizes Abraham's Worldwide Fatherhood."

142. See below, chapter 4, §3.7, "Romans 4:23–25: When We, Like Abraham, Trust God Who Raised Jesus from the Dead, Who Was Delivered over to Death, We Will Also Be Made Righteous."

143. Barclay observes that "the breadth of the patriarchal promise is at the heart of this chapter [Romans 4], and of the letter as a whole" (*Paul and the Gift*, 481).

urges people to pursue resurrection and eternal life in a new realm of well-being.[144]

That the overarching rhetorolect of 1:16–15:13 is apocalyptic is demonstrated by several observations. In 1:16–17, the gospel is described as "the righteousness of God [that] is revealed" (1:17). The verb ἀποκαλύπτεσθαι ("is revealed") has eschatological overtones.[145] Also, the gospel mentioned in 1:16–17 is elaborated in what follows in 1:18–15:13. This observation implies that the overarching rhetorolect of 1:18–15:13 should be the same as that of 1:16–17. Such a viewpoint is corroborated by 1:18, where the revelation of God is mentioned together with "the wrath of God" and is aligned with God's final judgment.[146] This revelation of God's righteousness is further described in 3:21 as that which is recorded in the Judean Scriptures and now finds fulfillment in Jesus Christ. Again, this description of the revelation of God's righteousness contains eschatological overtones and is "the eschatological turning point in the history of salvation."[147] The above observations indicate that in 1:16–17, and hence also in the description of the gospel in 1:18–15:13, Paul is predominantly using apocalyptic rhetorolect.[148] The above contention also finds evidence in how Paul finishes the description of the gospel before he begins to address specific issues of the Roman Christians. In Rom 8, Paul discusses the final (eschatological) glorification of Christians. Furthermore, the ending (15:7–13) of the *peroratio* also contains eschatological language regarding the fact that a time will come when both gentile and Judean Christians will praise the Lord under the kingship of Christ (15:12).[149] This is also a time when the eschatological hope given to Judean and gentile Christians is realized (15:12–13).

The observation that the dominant rhetorolect is apocalyptic has another important implication for this study. Bloomquist states that

---

144. Robbins, *Invention of Christian Discourse*, 109.

145. Dunn, *Romans 1–8*, 43; Moo, *Epistle to the Romans*, 24–25.

146. Dunn, *Romans 1–8*, 54.

147. Ibid., 165.

148. Robbins comments that "the apocalyptic center of Paul's argumentation in Romans is the revelation of the righteousness of God" (*Invention of Christian Discourse*, 432–33). J. Christiaan Beker describes Paul's gospel as "an apocalyptic gospel." See Beker, *Paul's Apocalyptic Gospel: The Coming Triumph of God* (Philadelphia: Fortress, 1982), 13.

149. Dunn, *Romans 9–16*, 845–51; see also Schreiner, *Romans*, 758–59.

one of the things that appears to me to have been clarified in the years-long discussion over rhetorolects (begun among us in earnest in the early 2000s) is the following: rhetorical discourses as defined by Robbins both arise from and create discourse cultures.... [They] create new cultures.[150]

In view of the fact that cultural features demarcate one ethnic group from another, Paul, by using apocalyptic rhetorolect (with other supporting rhetorolects) and the rhetoric in 1:16–8:39, is essentially attempting to reconfigure the ethnic identity of the dissenting groups, the Judean and gentile Christians.[151] The identity he hopes to create is described in Rom 8, as signaled by the eschatological νῦν (8:1).[152] Through the use of apocalyptic rhetorolect, Paul will have constructed, by the end of his rhetoric, an identity that carries with it honor for both Judean and gentile Christians. In this way, dissension between them due to the quest for honor is removed. I shall now discuss how Rom 4, including its conclusion in 4:23–25, is being worked out in selected passages of 5:1–15:13.

4.1. Romans 5:1–21: Trust in God Brings Peace between God and Christians

While Rom 4 concludes the discussion on wisdom about how a person becomes righteous with God as patron, Rom 5 now uses apocalyptic rhetorolect to mobilize ideological power to urge the implied audience to depend on Jesus Christ and receive eternal life. That apocalyptic rhetorolect dominates Rom 5 is shown by the topoi of God's having "raised

---

150. L. Gregory Bloomquist, "Rhetorolects and Critical Rhetoric," email, 2014, emphasis original.

151. On cultural features demarcating ethnic groups, see Fredrik Barth, *Ethnic Groups and Boundaries: The Social Organization of Cultural Difference* (Oslo: Johansen & Nielsen, 1969), 14: "Some cultural differences are used by the actors as signals and emblems of differences, others are ignored." See also Richard Jenkins, *Rethinking Ethnicity: Arguments and Explorations* (London: Sage, 1997), 11: "Ethnic cultural differences are a function of 'groupness.'"

152. Dunn, *Romans 1–8*, 415: "The νῦν is, as usual, eschatological (as in 3:26; 5:9, 11; 6:19, 21; 8:18, 22; 11:5, 30–31; 13:11; 16:26; as also νυνί in 3:21; 6:22; 7:6, 17)." See, similarly, Moo, *Epistle to the Romans*, 472; Jewett, *Romans*, 479. Corroborating this view, see Cranfield, *Epistle to the Romans*, 1:373: "The reference of the νῦν is ... to the gospel events themselves: 'now'—that is, since Christ has died and been raised from the dead"; see also Ulrich Luz, *Das Geschichtsverständnis des Paulus*, BEvT 49 (Munich: Kaiser, 1968), 88.

Jesus our Lord from the dead" in 4:24 (thirdspace), God as king in 5:2 (secondspace), Jesus Christ as broker in 5:1 (thirdspace), and Christians as receivers of eternal life in 5:21 (thirdspace). The details of Rom 5 will now be discussed.

The inferential οὖν indicates that what follows in 5:1–21 draws out the implications of the argument of Rom 4. Christians are made righteous by their patron, God, by trust in him (5:1a). As a result, there is peace between God as their patron and Christians as God's clients. The implied audience now has access to the royal favor or grace of God, the King (5:2a), and hope.[153] This hope is glory, that is, honor that comes from God (5:2b). Thus, all Christians, including gentile Christians, gain honor that has value before the only significant other, God. Both Judean and especially gentile Christians can now rightly boast. This resolves the problem of Judean Christians flaunting their pride toward gentile Christians (3:27–31). This righteousness that gained Christians access to God's favor was brokered by the Lord Jesus Christ (5:2b). Specifically, Jesus's death expiates sin and Jesus's resurrection enables Christians, including gentile Christians, to live a righteous life that gains Christians God's favor (5:2a) and hope.

This hope is attained through θλῖψις ("affliction" [5:3]). The mention of θλῖψις at first reading comes as a surprise, as nothing that preceded it prepares the implied audience for this. Esler's comments are helpful:

> Their membership of the Christ-movement involved them in a loss of honor among outgroups. In an honor-shame culture such as this, the afflictions that Paul has just mentioned would inevitably have been accompanied, perhaps occasionally constituted, by attempts to blacken their name.[154]

These afflictions, in the context of Romans, refer minimally to those tussles for honor exerted on gentile Christians by Judean Christians in Rom 1–3. Here, Paul turns the table around to the advantage of the gentile Christians by arguing that θλῖψις, by the process described in 5:3–4, enables Christians, including gentile Christians, to realize hope (5:4), which entails "sharing the glory of God" (5:2). In this way, Paul denigrates the Judean Christians' boast toward the gentile Christians. In a

---

153. Dunn, *Romans 1–8*, 248; Jewett, *Romans*, 349; Schreiner, *Romans*, 254; Moo, *Epistle to the Romans*, 300.

154. Esler, *Conflict and Identity in Romans*, 198.

bid to further reinforce the certainty of the hope of glory that Christians, including gentile Christians, will receive, Paul draws the implied audience's attention to another facet of Jesus's death (4:24) in expiating sin. The reason why the above-discussed hope does not diminish in the face of affliction (Judean Christians' tussle against gentile Christians for honor) is because of the degree of God's love, that is, God's attachment to his clients as demonstrated by Jesus dying for Christians "while we were still sinners" (5:6–8).[155] God's love stands out when 5:6–8 is read in light of the social and cultural intertexture underlying χάρις ("gift") that "good gifts are given to the worthy, and the costlier the gift the more discriminatingly it is given."[156] This degree of love, together with the twice-repeated phrase πολλῷ μᾶλλον ("much more" [5:9, 10]) and language related to abundance (e.g., 5:15, 17, 20), enhances the essence of the χάρις of God: this gift is made more "perfect" by abundance and incongruity.[157] *Pathos* in the implied audience is invoked. This further persuades the implied audience of the efficacy of Jesus's death in expiating sin (5:10a) and of his resurrection life in enabling Christians to live a righteous life, thereby resulting in salvation (5:10b). In this way, Paul, using the above rhetoric, seeks to convince the implied audience of the conclusion of Rom 4 in 4:23–25 that trust in God brings glory. The boast of the Judean Christians toward the gentile Christians would hence be removed, and likewise the boast of the gentiles who despised them.

By διὰ τοῦτο ("so then"), Paul indicates that what follows in 5:12–21 seeks to draw out the implication of 5:1–11. Specifically, Paul seeks to elaborate on the benefits of the favor that God gives. This favor is granted to those who are made righteous by trust in God who raised Jesus from the dead (5:1–2; 4:24–25). The problem at hand is death as a judgment passed on sin (5:12–14). Paul's *logos* is that the accomplishments of one man, Jesus Christ, counteract the misdeed of one man, Adam. Specifically, the favor from God is more than sufficient to nullify the consequences of Adam's sin and the condemnation that followed (5:15–17).

The last paragraph, 5:18–21, summarizes what has preceded it in 5:12–17. That 5:18–21 is a final summary is evident since the paragraph

---

155. Malina, "Love," 127–30.

156. Barclay, *Paul and the Gift*, 478; see also Seneca, *Ben.* 1.10.5.

157. Ibid., 495: "The perfection of abundance is here at the service of another perfection, the one we have already noted as the Pauline hallmark: God's grace through Christ is marked as extravagant precisely in its incongruity with the human condition."

begins with the connective phrase ἄρα οὖν ("therefore"). Furthermore, the terms that occur in 5:12–17 are found in this final section: κατάκριμα ("condemnation" [5:18, cf. 5:16]); παράπτωμα ("trespass" [5:18, cf. 5:15 (2x), 16, 17]); δικαίωμα ("righteous deed" [5:18, cf. 5:16]); ζωή ("life" [5:17, cf. 5:18]); χάρις ("favor" [5:20, cf. 5:15 (2x), 17]); ἁμαρτία ("sin" [5:20, cf. 5:12 (2x), 13 (2x)]); and βασιλεύειν ("to reign" [5:21, cf. 5:14, 17 (2x)]). This final statement in the concluding pericope emphasizes the result of one act of Jesus Christ, the broker: that Christians can now attain ζωὴν αἰώνιον ("eternal life"), which is a position of honor (cf. 2:7). Hence, trust in God, who raised Jesus from the dead (4:24–25), brings Christians, including gentile Christians, honor and thereby removes Judean Christians' boast toward gentile Christians.

4.2. Romans 6:1–14: Trust in God Enables Christians to Live Righteous Lives

Romans 6:1–23 can be divided into two parts: 6:1–14 and 6:15–23. Two observations point in this direction. First, both 6:1 and 6:15 contain a rhetorical question that begins with τί οὖν ("what then"). Second, 6:1–14 is dominated by the topos of death/life, while 6:15–23 focuses on the topos of bondage/freedom. Romans 6:1–14 will be the center of the discussion, as it builds on the conclusion of Rom 4 in 4:23–25 that Christians are now able to live righteous lives—and, therefore, to be regarded as righteous—because they possess the resurrection life of Jesus.[158] That 6:1–14 and Rom 4 are correlated is, prima facie, shown by the repeated appeal to the fact of Jesus's death and resurrection in Rom 6.

Before examining pertinent details, I shall ascertain the dominant rhetorolect of 6:1–14 in order to shed light on its rhetorical goal. That the rhetorolect is priestly is evident from several observations. Romans 6:1–4 opens with a rhetorical question posed by an interlocutor. It is answered with topoi related to sin, Christ's death, and dying (to sin). Also, the idea that Christians, as recipients of holiness and purity, are now to live a life that is free from bondage to sin (thirdspace) recurs in this section.[159] The

---

158. Moyer V. Hubbard concludes in his analysis of Rom 6:1–11 that "ethical renewal is best expressed by the word 'life' (6:2, 4, 10, 11, 13)." See Hubbard, *New Creation in Paul's Letters and Thought*, SNTSMS 119 (Cambridge: Cambridge University Press, 2002), 103.

159. Robbins, *Invention of Christian Discourse*, 109.

ideological power produced by the use of priestly rhetorolect here responds to the problem raised by Rom 5: if favor (grace) and not the Mosaic law overcomes the problem of sin, does that mean Christians can continue to sin? The use of priestly rhetorolect makes use of the notion of Jesus as "Priest-Messiah."[160] Specifically, the rhetoric of 6:1–14 makes use of the conclusion of Rom 4 that Jesus's death expiates sin and his resurrection enables Christians to live a life that maintains a righteous relationship with God, their patron. This exerts ideological power on the implied audience to arrive at the conclusion that the human body is a "receiver of beneficial exchange of holiness and purity."[161] With this, I shall discuss how the conclusion of Rom 4, namely, 4:23–25, is being worked out in the argument of 6:1–14.

Paul begins 6:1–14 with the rhetorical question posed by an interlocutor: "What shall we say? Shall we remain in sin in order that favor may abound?" (6:1). This question does not seriously imply that Paul thinks that the implied audience believes that sin will produce a level of favor that exceeds the level of sin.[162] The true intent is made clear in what follows in Rom 6: Paul is addressing a mindset that encourages Christians to continue to sin. This thesis is restated in 6:2 by introducing the social intertexture of the Roman master-slave relationship. Christians are metaphorically dead to the master, sin, and thus cannot maintain their relationship with sin. To contend against the erroneous mindset that a Christian can continue in sin, Paul uses the topoi of death and life. Romans 6:4 forms the thesis of Paul's rebuttal in 6:3–14. This thesis, which centers on the death and resurrection of Jesus Christ, is basically the conclusion of Rom 4 in 4:23–25.

In 6:3–5, Paul reminds them of the fact of their baptism.[163] Baptism has a social intertexture wherein the implied audience would construe being

---

160. Ibid.

161. Ibid.

162. Jewett, *Romans*, 395: "By posing the libertinistic option in so ridiculous and insidious a form, Paul effectively opens the issue of the incongruity of persons saved by grace who fail to live the new life." See also Tobin, *Paul's Rhetoric*, 192: "He also asks another rhetorical question [implying] that it is inconceivable that those who have died to sin should continue to live in it."

163. Moo notes that "by the date of Romans, 'baptism' had become almost a technical expression for the rite of Christian initiation by water." In a footnote, he also observes that of Paul's eleven occurrences of the word βαπτίζειν ("to baptize"), all but one denote water baptism (*Epistle to the Romans*, 359 and n. 38). Contra James D. G. Dunn, who interprets it as a metaphor for incorporation into the body of Christ.

baptized according to Paul's explanation: "baptized into his death" (6:3b).[164] This ritual also contains an ideological texture. The ritual of baptism would cause the participant to experience and affirm as real the significance of the rite of baptism: that Christians have died with Christ to sin.[165] This baptism into Christ's death also contains a historical intertexture, in that the death of Christ and his resurrection were conceived as one event. This implies that the rite of baptism also communicates to the Christians that they have been raised with Christ from the dead. On the grounds that they have metaphorically died to the power of sin and received resurrection life, they are able now to "walk in newness of life" (6:4 NRSV). As mentioned previously, 6:4 constitutes the main rebuttal of the rhetorical question in 6:1. What follows in 6:5–14 elaborates on 6:4, as indicated by the causative γάρ in 6:5. The verb περιπατεῖν ("to walk" [6:4]) contains a social intertexture that recalls the Hebrew verb הָלַךְ and denotes a lifestyle. To walk in "newness of life" with its underlying social intertexture of life after death creates an ideological texture that compels Christians to live a lifestyle that has a clear break with sin. This lifestyle conforms to a corporate identity as intimated by the proliferation of first-person plural verbs. These first-person plural verbs assert ideological power on the implied audience, encouraging them to conform to the new corporate identity characterized by the new lifestyle. Thus, by reminding the implied audience of the rite of baptism, Paul exerts ideological power on the implied audience in order to convince them that they have died to sin and have been raised with Christ in some decisive and meaningful way. The twofold reality of the conclusion in 4:23–25 is thus

See Dunn, "Salvation Proclaimed: VI. Romans 6:1–11: Dead and Alive," *ExpTim* 93 (1982): 261.

164. For the possible understandings of Paul's implied audience about baptism, see the discussion in Florence M. Gillman, *A Study of Romans 6:5a: United to a Death like Christ's* (San Francisco: Mellen Research University, 1992), 37–42. She observes the chiasm in 6:3, "We were baptized into Christ, into his death we were baptized," and is probably right to conclude that Paul's implied audience understood the Christian baptism as one that identifies the Christian with Christ's death. Cf. Brook W. R. Pearson, who observes that in the cult of Isis and Osiris, baptism identified the believer with the death of the god Osiris in the Nile. See Pearson, "Baptism and Initiation in the Cult of Isis and Sarapis," in *Baptism, the New Testament and the Church: Historical and Contemporary Studies in Honour of R. E. O. White*, ed. Stanley E. Porter and Anthony R. Cross, JSNTSup 171 (Sheffield: Sheffield Academic, 1999), 51.

165. Émile Durkheim, *The Elementary Forms of the Religious Life*, trans. Joseph Ward Swain (New York: Free Press, 1965), 463–65.

impressed upon Judean and especially gentile Christians: that they are able to live a righteous life without abusing the abundance of favor (5:20–21) that comes with trust in God (4:23–25).

Death is made sure by the fact of the crucifixion in 6:6–10. The social intertexture underlying crucifixion mobilizes ideological power to impress upon the implied audience that the life of sin is over. This social intertexture reinforces the conclusion in 4:23–25 and mobilizes ideological power to assure the implied audience that because Jesus's death on the cross is sure, sin is totally expiated. Thus, the body of sin is destroyed (6:6), and Christians are "freed from sin" (6:7). Paul then applies this twofold reality to the implied audience in 6:11–14. They should not yield to the previous master because they are not ὑπὸ νόμον ("under the [Mosaic] law") that condemns Christians as sinners so as to become its instruments for doing unrighteousness.[166] Instead, they should yield to the new master, God, because they are ὑπὸ χάριν ("under favor"), and thus become his instruments for performing acts of righteousness. The prepositional phrase ὑπὸ χάριν contains a social and cultural intertexture in which clients are expected to reciprocate patrons for their gifts.[167] This also creates an ideological texture that persuades the audience to live a life holy to God in return for his χάρις ("favor"). Thus, a righteous relationship between God the patron and Christians as God's clients is maintained.

4.3. Romans 7:1–6: Trust in God Frees Christians from Condemnation Due to Noncompliance with the Mosaic Law

In 6:15–23, the rhetorical question posed by the interlocutor in 6:15 that asks if Christians are free to sin in the absence of indictment by the Mosaic law is clearly refuted. At this point, Paul returns to where he left off in 6:14.[168] Paul maintains that the power of the Mosaic law has been annulled. That

---

166. Cranfield describes ὑπὸ νόμον as the "law as condemning sinners" (*Epistle to the Romans*, 1:320).

167. Barclay, *Paul and the Gift*, 497–98. See also his comment that "the divine gift in Christ was *unconditioned* (based on no prior conditions) but it is not *unconditional* (carrying no subsequent demands)" (500, emphasis original).

168. Moo thinks that "7:1–6 continues the stress of 6:15–23 on the necessary ethical implications of the believer's transfer into the new realm of grace" (*Epistle to the Romans*, 409–10).

Paul in 7:1–6 is picking up the argument he left off at 6:14 is evinced by the common topos law in 6:14 and 7:1–6.

But before examining the details of the argument of 7:1–6, the sense of the Mosaic law as nonbinding needs to be clarified. Several lines of evidence indicate that it is not in the sense, as some scholars construe, that a Christian no longer needs to obey the moral part of the Mosaic law.[169] That the moral aspect is intended is indicated by Paul's recitation of the tenth commandment of the Decalogue. Rather, Paul means that the Mosaic law no longer has the ability to indict Christians for their sins so as to enslave them to sin. First, the statement in 6:14, which introduces the rhetoric of 7:1–6, explains that sin is able to enslave a person because that person is under the authority of the Mosaic law. This implies that the power of the Mosaic law in 7:1–6 must be read in conjunction with the power of sin and not in isolation from the power of sin. Second, that which the I wishes to perform and agrees that it should perform is the Mosaic law (7:15–22). Third, when Paul says that Christians are discharged from the Mosaic law, they also enter into the new life of the Spirit. This life is discussed immediately after Rom 7 in 8:3, where the requirements of the Mosaic law are said to be fulfilled by those who walk according to the Spirit. Thus, the Mosaic law is not annulled in the sense that Christians no longer have to obey it. The opposite is true. Christians still have to fulfill the requirements of the Mosaic law if they are to maintain a righteous relationship with God.[170] With this introductory note, I turn to discuss 7:1–6.

In 7:1–6, in order to mobilize ideological power to impress upon the implied audience that they have been released from the indictment due to noncompliance with the Mosaic law, Paul introduces into his rhetoric apocalyptic rhetorolect. This rhetorolect creates in the minds (in the third-space) of the implied audience "God Almighty [with] multiple heavenly assistants to God," who will transform the created world into a "totally righteous and holy space."[171] The presence of this rhetorolect is indicated by the centerpiece *law*, which invokes the imperial army to punish those who violate the law. In line with apocalyptic rhetorolect, Paul introduces a social intertexture of Roman law: in Roman society, marriage was monog-

---

169. So Fee, *God's Empowering Presence*, 504; Käsemann, *Commentary on Romans*, 189–90.

170. See E. P. Sanders, *Paul, the Law, and the Jewish People* (Minneapolis: Fortress, 1983), 93–122.

171. Robbins, *Invention of Christian Discourse*, 109, 327.

amous and adultery was punishable by law.[172] Käsemann is probably right to insist that the law referred to in 7:1–3 is unlikely to be the Mosaic law but is instead Roman law.[173] First, a large part of the real audience are gentiles, and they will naturally perceive marriage as a state institution rather than an institution established by the law of Moses. Second, Josephus remarks that Judeans then condoned polygamy: "our ancestral custom that a man may have several wives at the same time" (*Ant.* 17.14 [Marcus and Wikgren, LCL]). In such a culture, the Judean Scriptures are unlikely to constitute evidence for monogamy. Thus, the marriage laws first formulated by Augustus in the *lex Iulia et Papia* are probably referred to here. These laws were later supplemented and complemented by a comitial statute, the *lex Papia Poppaea*, in 9 CE. For instance, a woman guilty of adultery was forbidden to remarry and had to wear the toga as a symbol of her shame.[174] Paul uses this social intertexture to point out that a woman is discharged from the marriage law upon the death of her husband (7:3). Important for understanding the role of Roman law here is the observation that Paul does not claim the marriage law itself is annulled. Rather, it is the *power* of the law *to indict* the woman for the crime of adultery that is annulled. In the same way, when Paul says that Christians "have died to the law," he refers not to the annulment of the Mosaic law but to its power to indict Christians of sin. Relevant for our discussion is the basis of this annulment of the power of the Mosaic law. Paul says in 7:4 that this is possible through (διά) the twofold fact of Christ's death and resurrection (τῷ ἐκ νεκρῶν ἐγερθέντι; "who was raised from the dead"). This basis, together with common vocabulary (νεκρός ["dead"], ἐγείρειν ["to raise"]), recalls 4:23–25. Thus, the conclusion of Rom 4 underlies the argument of 7:1–6. The outworking of 7:4, which is also in essence the conclusion in 4:23–25,

---

172. Lesley Adkins and Roy Adkins, *Handbook to Life in Ancient Rome* (New York: Infobase, 2004), 377.

173. Käsemann, *Commentary on Romans*, 187. See also Sanday and Headlam, who think that "law" here does not refer to the Mosaic law but to "a general principle" of all laws (*Critical and Exegetical Commentary on the Epistle to the Romans*, 172).

174. Thomas A. J. McGinn, *Prostitution, Sexuality, and the Law in Ancient Rome* (New York: Oxford University Press, 2003), 143. The death penalty was also later meted out for adultery, according to sources before the death of Constantine. For an explanation of the Augustan law on marriage, see also Judith E. Grubbs, *Women and the Law in the Roman Empire: A Sourcebook on Marriage, Divorce and Widowhood* (London: Routledge, 2002), 81–83.

is elaborated in 7:5–6. Here, Paul contrasts two kinds of life. An examination of the contrast reveals the similarity of 4:23–25 and 7:4.

These two lives are what the analogy of the Roman marriage law was pointing to, namely, life with the first (and now deceased) husband and life in a new marriage. The first life is analogous to the life described in 7:5 that is lived in sin and empowered by the Mosaic law. This leads to death. Paul says in 7:4 that through the death of Christ, Christians now belong to another (ἕτερος). The question is: to whom or what did Christians belong earlier, before conversion and then later after conversion? Most scholars think the referent from which Christians are set free is the Mosaic law.[175] This interpretation, however, is untenable. For one thing, the marriage analogy (7:1–3) requires three components to work: namely, the first husband, the second husband, and the marriage law. Also, in Romans, the two kinds of life contrasted are almost always one that is lived in the power of the flesh or sin (Rom 1–3, 6–7, 8) and one that is lived for God (Rom 6) or lived in the power of the Spirit (Rom 8). Furthermore, what follows in 7:5 brings into the discussion the component σάρξ (and its attached "sinful desires"). The component σάρξ ("flesh") is characterized as a master in Rom 8. Thus, the other (ἕτερος) in 7:4 should be contrasted not with the Mosaic law but with sin, which Paul later clarifies in 7:5. According to my contention in respect to 4:23–25, the reason why Christians can now belong to another (ἕτερος) through Christ's death is that his death expiates sin. The second kind of life is analogous to the one described in 7:6, where life is lived apart from the power of Mosaic law that indicts a person of sin. This life is one lived "in the new life of the Spirit," which is later explained in 8:2 as a life that fulfills the requirements of the Mosaic law. Here, in 7:4, this new life is characterized by fruit borne for God. According to 7:4, fruitfulness for God is possible because Christ has been raised from the dead. According to the conclusion in 4:23–25, it is the resurrection life

---

175. E.g., Dunn, *Romans 1–8*, 362; Jewett, *Romans*, 435. Cranfield interprets 7:4 as being "set free from the condemnation pronounced by the law" (*Epistle to the Romans*, 1:336), contra Sanday and Headlam, who suggest that ἐν ᾧ ("to that which") in 7:6 is referring to the "old state" or "old man." He observes that "whenever 'death' is spoken of, it is primarily this 'old state' or 'old man' which dies.... It was this sinful old state which brought man under the grip of the Law" (*Critical and Exegetical Commentary on the Epistle to the Romans*, 175). Similarly, see Marie-Joseph Lagrange, *Saint Paul: Épître aux Romains* (Paris: Gabalda, 1916), 164: "Paul remonte plus haut, à la chair au vieil homme; c'est la mort à cet état qui nous a délivrés de la Loi."

of Christ given to Christians that enables them to bear fruit. Ideological power is, thus, mobilized to persuade the implied audience that it is reasonable that Christians too are now "discharged from the (Mosaic) law" in the sense that it can no longer indict them of sin and thereby enslave them to sin (7:6a). Instead, the implied audience, including gentile Christians, are free to live "the new life of the Spirit" (7:6b). The boast of Judean Christians toward gentile Christians is thus removed, and likewise the boast of the gentiles who despised them.

4.4. Romans 7:7–25: Trust in God Frees Christians from Condemnation by Compliance with the Mosaic Law

Before I explain the pertinent details of 7:7–25, several preliminary matters need to be clarified. First, in 7:6, which concludes the pericope 7:1–6, Paul deduces that Christians are discharged from the Mosaic law. Here Paul describes the law as that which holds a person captive. Two observations indicate that Paul expects his implied audience to understand him as implying that the law somehow empowers sin and that it should be viewed negatively. That 7:1–6 continues the argument left off in 6:14 is shown by repetition of the common topos law from 6:14 in 7:1. Here, with the words "sin will not lord over you because you are not under the power of the law," Paul seems to imply that the Mosaic law promotes sin. Similarly, in 7:5, the words "the desires of sin which worked through the (Mosaic) law" seem to be implying that the law is instrumental in creating the desires of sin. This positive correlation between sin and the Mosaic law leads Paul to pose the rhetorical question: "Is the (Mosaic) law sin?" This sets the stage for 7:7–25.

Second, as I will argue in 4:23–25, Christians' trust in Jesus Christ brings them the resurrection life of Jesus.[176] Considering that this point was first discussed at length in Rom 4, it is reasonable to think that the argument that involves the juxtaposition of "body of death" and "Jesus Christ our Lord" as the person who will save the "I" in 7:25 builds upon the argument of Rom 4.

Third, 7:7–25 is a προσωποποιία, that is, speech-in-character discourse.[177] Stowers notes that this form of discourse was made popular by Euripides's

---

176. See below, chapter 4, §3.7, "Romans 4:23–25: When We, Like Abraham, Trust God Who Raised Jesus from the Dead, Who Was Delivered over to Death, We Will Also Be Made Righteous."

177. Stowers, *Rereading of Romans*, 264–84.

Medea, where the figure of Medea gained popularity because she "stood for foreigners who corrupted the purity of the citizen body, and her saying about *akrasia* connoted the moral degeneracy that mixing with foreigners would supposedly bring."[178] This finds an apt application to the gentile implied audience, who do not possess the Mosaic law and whom Judeans regard as unclean, and hence not worthy of honor. In this προσωποποιία, the climax is in the exclamation made by the "I" in Rom 7:24–25 where the I expresses its agony at being unable to fulfill the law. This mode of discourse also invites the implied audience to identify themselves with the I, as the discourse is basically a soliloquy.[179] Thus, *pathos* is created in the implied audience. Understanding that 7:24–25 contains the climax of this cultural discourse also coheres with the dominant rhetorolect used, apocalyptic rhetorolect. Its presence is evinced by the topos law, the centerpiece of 7:7–25, which invokes the imperial army to punish those who violate the law. This creates in the secondspace God and his heavenly assistants who are ready to enforce righteousness and holiness in the world.[180] This use of apocalyptic rhetorolect invokes in the thirdspace of the implied audience an image of those who violate the law being punished. This reinforces the agony felt by the I. With this note, I shall explain the rhetoric of 7:7–25. I shall focus on how 7:7–25 leads to the need for the salvation that Jesus Christ will provide for the I.

To refute the rhetorical question in 7:7a, Paul defends the Mosaic law by arguing that it clarifies the nature of sin in 7:7b. The reason why the Mosaic law empowers sin is because it takes advantage of an "opportunity" (ἀφορμήν). This opportunity refers to what Paul has just explained. The Mosaic commandment in manifesting sin for what it is also creates an "opportunity" for sin to take hold and "produced in me all kinds of covetousness" (7:8). The consequence was that the I died (7:11). Thus, Paul concludes that the Mosaic commandment is good (7:12).

How, then, can the Mosaic law, which is good, result in death (7:13)? Paul's answer is that the problem lies with the inability of the I to obey the Mosaic moral law. The I agrees that the Mosaic law is morally good (7:16). Note that the I also seeks to obey it. This speaks against the annulment of observing the Mosaic law for Christians. The I knows not only that the

---

178. Ibid., 271. In Euripides's *Medea*, Medea contemplated and struggled with the thought of killing her children out of anger and revenge.

179. Ibid.

180. Robbins, *Invention of Christian Discourse*, 109.

commandment is good but also that obeying the commandment is good, as is signified in the clause "for to will good is present with me" (7:18). The word "law" in 7:21 should be construed as the Mosaic law.[181] Similarly, "the law of sin" should also be regarded as referring to the Mosaic law. This understanding is basically that the Mosaic law was exploited or distorted by sin as Paul explained earlier in 7:7–11.[182] The consequence was that the I was convicted of sin and thus died. The I struggles because, on the one hand, it desires to perform the Mosaic law of God (7:22). On the other hand, this same Mosaic law is being exploited by sin to battle against the Mosaic law that is in the mind of the I, a law that the I knows it should obey (7:23a). Consequently, the I comes under the indictment of the Mosaic law because it is being exploited by sin (7:23). The desire to obey the commandment should be used to interpret the cry of agony of the I in 7:24 and the exclamation of victory in 7:25. When the I asks, "who will save me from this body of death," it is referring to its inability to obey the commandments of the Mosaic law that brings death upon the I. At this point, Paul brings into his rhetoric Jesus Christ, who enables the I to obey the Mosaic moral law (7:25a). After its exclamation of victory, however, Paul adds: "Therefore, I myself am serving with the mind the (Mosaic) law of God but with the flesh the law of sin" (7:25b). In essence, this means that the Mosaic law that is being exploited by sin indicts the I of sin and enslaves it to sin.

Scholars view the concluding note in 7:25b as problematic. Jewett, for example, sees this note as "a marginal gloss added by Paul himself that was probably intended to be placed between v. 23 and v. 24."[183] Käsemann perceptively comments that "it would indeed be illogical if after v. 25a there

---

181. Dunn argues that the τὸν νόμος ("the law") should refer to the Mosaic law, as the main thrust of 7:7–25 is to defend the Mosaic law (*Romans 1–8*, 302). Also, 7:10 and 7:21 are structurally similar, which would imply that τὸν νόμος is parallel to ἡ ἐντολή ("the command").

182. Dunn, *Romans 1–8*, 395. Similarly, E. Lohse, "Ὁ νόμος τοῦ πνεύματος τῆς ζωῆς: Exegetische Anmerkungen zu Röm 8,2," in *Neues Testament und christliche Existenz: Festschrift für Herbert Braun zum 70. Geburtstag am 4. Mai 1973*, ed. Hans Dieter Betz, Herbert Braun, and Luise Schottroff (Tübingen: Mohr, 1973), 285–86; Klyne R. Snodgrass, "Spheres of Influence: A Possible Solution to the Problem of Paul and the Law," *JSNT* 32 (1988): 106–7; Bruce W. Longenecker, *Eschatology and the Covenant: A Comparison of 4 Ezra and Romans 1–11*, JSNTSup 57 (Sheffield: JSOT Press, 1991), 240–41; Brice L. Martin, *Christ and the Law in Paul*, NovTSup 62 (Leiden: Brill, 1989), 240–41.

183. Jewett, *Romans*, 473.

were a flashback to the time before the change of aeons."[184] The following explanation unties this conundrum. After being saved by Jesus Christ, the I now serves a new master, the Mosaic law of God. An unresolved problem remains, however. The flesh, that is, the human capacities, continues to be under the authority of the Mosaic law that is exploited by sin.[185] Dunn's interpretation corroborates my view: "The balance of v 25b therefore is not an expression of salvation still to begin, but of the process of salvation under way and still to be completed."[186] Such a state of tension, however, will be resolved at Rom 8. The above analysis shows that the problem the I seeks to resolve is its inability to obey the Mosaic law. Also, the solution to its problem, "Jesus Christ," is that which Paul explained in 4:23–25, the conclusion of Rom 4: namely, that Christ has expiated sin and provides resurrection life for Christians to live a life that minimally fulfills the requirements of the Mosaic law.

4.5. Romans 8:1–39: Christ's Spirit Frees Christians from Sin's Condemnation

I explained above in 7:7–25 that the I's inability to fulfill the requirements of the Mosaic law leads to condemnation, namely, death in the body (7:24). In this section I show that the condemnation is resolved by the rhetoric of Rom 8. This rhetoric, as will be shown, builds on the conclusion of Rom 4, specifically, 4:23–25. Before looking into the details, several preliminaries need clarification.

The dominant rhetorolect in Rom 8 is apocalyptic, as indicated by the presence of the thirdspace of apocalyptic rhetorolect, namely, "resurrection and eternal life in a 'new' realm of well-being."[187] The rhetoric of this chapter utilizes the topos πνεῦμα ("spirit") for its rhetorical invention. This topos introduces a social and cultural intertexture that undergirds the thirdspace of the apocalyptic rhetorolect. Caroline J. Hodge's observations on how Greeks understand πνεῦμα are instructive:

> Medical writers explain that *pneuma* is the vital substance of the body, responsible for sight, hearing, smell and touch. *Pneuma* is also the cru-

---

184. Käsemann, *Commentary on Romans*, 211.
185. Schreiner, *Romans*, 392.
186. Dunn, *Romans 1–8*, 399.
187. Robbins, *Invention of Christian Discourse*, 109.

cial procreative element.... In its finest form, *pneuma* constitutes the very particles which make up the soul and is responsible for the ability to reason.... Particularly interesting is the Stoic theory of *krasis* or blending, in which *pneuma* permeates other objects or beings, effecting change in the matter through which is passes.[188]

In other words, πνεῦμα is regarded as the agent that is able to transform that body, in a fundamental way, into new beings.[189] In this way, this social intertexture underlying πνεῦμα reinforces Paul's use of apocalyptic rhetorolect. This mobilizes ideological power to convince the implied audience that, through the Spirit, Christians can now participate in resurrection and eternal life "in a new realm of well-being."[190] With this note, I shall now enter into my discussion proper.

The I has just expressed its agony of being condemned in 7:24. This prospect of condemnation, says the I, finds resolution in the salvation provided by Jesus Christ (7:25). The question that remains is how Jesus Christ is going to save it. Using apocalyptic rhetorolect, Paul responds to the problem of condemnation raised by the rhetorical question in 7:24 with the claim that "the (Mosaic) law [νόμος] of the Spirit" can set Christians free from "the law of sin and death" (8:2). The word νόμος should not be translated as "principle, rule, or norm."[191] Rather, as explained above, the "law of sin" refers to the Mosaic law that is exploited by sin and consequently indicts a person for sin.[192] Here, in 8:2, the "law of the Spirit" should also be construed in a similar way if Paul's rhetoric is to be relevant in answering to the problem of 7:7–24. Thus, "the law of the Spirit" (8:2) is the Mosaic law that is used by the Spirit to counteract the "law of sin." The result is that the Spirit enables Christians to fulfill the demands of the Mosaic law and sets them free from their previous master, the Mosaic law that is exploited by sin.[193] Hence, Christians are saved from the Mosaic law

---

188. For references of these ancient records, see Caroline J. Hodge, *If Sons, Then Heirs: A Study of Kinship and Ethnicity in the Letters of Paul* (New York: Oxford University Press, 2007), 74–75.

189. Hodge, *If Sons, Then Heirs*, 75.

190. Robbins, *Invention of Christian Discourse*, 109.

191. E.g., Fee, *God's Empowering Presence*, 522. In a similar vein, Cranfield interprets νόμος as "authority and constraint" (*Epistle to the Romans*, 1:376).

192. See above, chapter 2, §4.4, "Romans 7:7–25: Trust in God Frees Christians from Condemnation by Compliance with the Mosaic Law."

193. Scholars who correctly construe "law" not as a "principle" but as the Mosaic

that condemns them to death, and the agony of the I in 7:14–25 is alleviated.[194] Moo incorrectly thinks that "the just demand is fulfilled in Christians not through their own acts of obedience but through their incorporation into Christ."[195] But this goes against what follows. In the statement "we are not walking according to the flesh but according to the Spirit" (8:4), the metaphor "walking" signifies action. Furthermore, it is precisely because the Spirit enables the believer to perform deeds of the Mosaic law that the agony of the I could be removed because the agony of the I in Rom 7 is due to its inability to perform the Mosaic law.[196] In 8:5–8, Paul uses wisdom

---

law include Schreiner, *Romans*, 400: "The Mosaic law is in the realm either of the Holy Spirit or of the powers of sin and death. If the law is appropriated in the realm of the Spirit and by faith, then one is liberated from using the Mosaic law in such a way that it leads to sin and death." In the same vein, see Jewett, *Romans*, 481; see also Snodgrass, who notes that interpreters should view the law as functioning in spheres of influence ("Spheres of Influence," 98–99). In 8:2, the law functions in the realm of the life-giving spirit, and hence frees a person from sin (so Snodgrass, "Spheres of Influence," 107). So also, Ferdinand Hahn, "Das Gesetzesverständnis im Römer- und Galaterbrief," *ZNW* 67 (1976): 47–48; Brendan Byrne, *"Sons of God"—"Seed of Abraham": A Study of the Idea of the Sonship of God of All Christians in Paul against the Jewish Background*, AnBib 83 (Rome: Biblical Institute Press, 1979), 92; Dunn, *Romans 1–8*, 416–17; Hübner, *Law in Paul's Thought*, 144–49; Jervis, "Spirit Brings Christ's Life to Life," 150. This framework of spheres of influence can be refined in terms of the prevailing Mediterranean culture of what John J. Pilch calls "domination orientation," where the party that dominates seeks to gain honor from the person dominated. See Pilch, "Domination Orientation," in Pilch and Malina, *Handbook of Biblical Social Values*, 48–59.

194. Dunn reaches a similar conclusion: "Paul deliberately and provocatively insists on the continuity of God's purpose in the law and through the Spirit" (*Romans 1–8*, 423). So also Cranfield, *Epistle to the Romans*, 1:384; Herman N. Ridderbos, *Paul: Outline of His Theology* (Grand Rapids: Eerdmans, 1975), 278–88. Ridderbos argues that "the work of the Spirit consists precisely in the working out of the law in the life of believers." See also L. Ann Jervis, "Divine Retribution in Romans," *Int* 69 (2015): 331.

195. Moo, *Epistle to the Romans*, 484.

196. Rather than adopting the views of some, e.g., Heikki Räisänen and Michael Goulder, that Paul is inconsistent, it is more reasonable to go along with Lauri Thurén, who proposes an analysis based on a dynamic view of his letters. For instance, some of Paul's "eccentric theological statements" can be read in light of the ancient rhetorical technique of *vituperatio* where the author uses standard labels to denigrate his opponents—in the case of the Letter to the Galatians, Judeans who uphold the law. See Räisänen, *Paul and the Law* (Philadelphia: Fortress, 1986), 11; Goulder, *St. Paul versus St. Peter: A Tale of Two Missions* (Louisville: Westminster John Knox, 1995), 35–37; Thurén, *Derhetorizing Paul: A Dynamic Perspective on Pauline Theology and the Law*, repr. ed. (Harrisburg, PA: Trinity Press International, 2002), 57, 64–65. For the tech-

rhetorolect to explain why those who walk after the Spirit fulfill the Mosaic law: they are resolved to do the things of the Spirit and not the things of the flesh.[197] But why is the Spirit able to help Christians fulfill the Mosaic law? Paul describes the Spirit in two ways. First, the Spirit dwells ἐν Χριστῷ Ἰησου ("in Christ Jesus" [8:2]); that is, the Spirit belongs to Christ Jesus.[198] Second, this Spirit that belongs to the Christ Jesus who "condemned sin in the flesh" (8:3) takes up the theme of 4:23–25, where Paul claims that Jesus's death expiated sin. Thus, the reason why the Spirit that belongs to Christ is able to help Christians live (περιπατεῖν) a life that meets the just requirements of the Mosaic law (8:4) is because of Christ's death. This ability to obey the Mosaic law determines the state of the relationship between Christians and their patron, God, because it shows what the mind, that is, the settled understanding, is intent upon.[199] The mind that is set on the flesh results in condemnation, that is, death (8:6), because it shows that the person refuses to submit to God's Mosaic law (8:7–8).

The above interpretation verifies once again my contention that the role of the Spirit here is to enable Christians to obey the Mosaic law. It is this that will remove condemnation (8:1). Conversely, those who obey the Mosaic law show that they set their minds on the things of the Spirit. The reason why they are able to do this is because they have the Spirit of Christ (8:9). The result of having the Spirit is spelled out in two parallel statements in 8:10a and 8:10b. These two statements lack clarity due to their brevity, as is characteristic of wisdom rhetorolect. Romans 8:10a states that the body produces death because of sin. Romans 8:10b insists that this state of affairs is reversed when the Spirit produces life because of the deeds of righteousness. This means that the Spirit results in Christians receiving life because the Spirit helps maintain a righteous

---

nique of *vituperatio*, see Andreas B. Du Toit, "Vilification as a Pragmatic Device in Early Christian Epistolography," *Bib* 75 (1994): 403–12.

197. That wisdom rhetorolect is present is evinced by the binary structure of positive and negative statements.

198. For a summary of Paul's use of "in Christ Jesus" and its cognates, see Richard N. Longenecker, *The Epistle to the Romans*, NIGTC (Grand Rapids: Eerdmans, 2016), 686–94. He interprets the prepositional phrase as signifying "an intimate, local, and personal" relationship between the Spirit and Christ Jesus. A similar usage occurs also at "6:11, 23; 8:39; 9:1; 14:14; 15:17; and 16:2, 11–13." Cf. Fee, who gives the phrase an instrumental meaning, that is, "by the work of Christ" (*God's Empowering Presence*, 524).

199. Dunn, *Romans 1–8*, 425.

relationship between Christians and their patron God. How this comes about is explained in 8:11, which builds on the conclusion in 4:23–25.

Several observations support my contention. First, not only is the topos about resurrection as in 4:23–25, but the vocabulary used is also the same: ἐγείρειν ("to raise"), νεκρός ("dead"). Second, the two parallel statements of 8:11 make the point that the Spirit is the critical factor for Christians to receive resurrection life: the Spirit gives life; the Spirit belongs to God, who raised Jesus from the dead. In the first statement, Paul underlines the fact that the Spirit must indwell Christians. The second statement views life as being given by the Spirit: ζωοποιήσει ("he will make alive") ... διὰ ("through") ... αὐτοῦ πνεύματος ("his spirit"). This Spirit, however, is described as belonging to God. In other words, the Spirit of God, instead of just simply God, is the critical factor for Jesus to rise from the dead. This construal is due to Paul's focus in Rom 8 on the work of the Spirit. God, however, still features prominently in Jesus's resurrection. Third, both parallel statements of 8:11 describe God, the giver of resurrection life, as the one who raised Jesus from the dead. This description is a clear allusion to 4:24.

In my analysis of 4:23–25, I will argue that Jesus functions as the broker of resurrection life, which enables Christians to live a righteous life in their relationship with God as patron. This point coheres with 7:25 (which leads into the argument of 8:1–11), where the I thanks God for saving it from condemnation due to its inability to fulfill the requirements of the Mosaic law. The salvation for which the I thanks God is brokered by Jesus Christ (χάρις δὲ τῷ θεῷ διὰ Ἰησοῦ Χριστοῦ; "but thanks be to God through Jesus Christ"). The Spirit who gives resurrection life to Christians enables them to live righteous lives. As a result, Christians enter into a state of life (8:10; cf. 2:7), which is a position of honor. These Christians are also people who are "led by the Spirit" (8:14), that is, people who obey the Spirit. As they are now able to live righteous lives, they no longer live in fear of condemnation due to bondage to sin (8:15). This resolves the agony of the I in 7:2. Instead, they are considered "children of God" (8:15–16) and are destined for glorification, which in Mediterranean culture is a position of honor (8:17). Thus, all Christians enter into a position of honor. This removes the boast of Judean Christians toward gentile Christians, and likewise the boast of the gentiles who despised them, and furthers the rhetorical purpose of Rom 4.

The work of the Spirit in 8:1–17 also achieves the final glorification of Christians in 8:18–30. The topos on suffering (πάθημα) that begins the new section in 8:18–39 seems a bit abrupt. Except for a brief mention of affliction (θλῖψις) in 5:3–5, this topos occurs nowhere else in Romans. When suffering in 8:18 is read in light of 8:18–30, however, this word refers to eschatological sufferings.[200] By that, Paul is basically returning to resolve the eschatological tension of the "now/not yet" problem of 7:25b where he speaks of serving "the flesh with the (Mosaic) law of sin." Paul's thesis statement in 8:18 is elaborated as a desire to be set free from the "bondage of corruption," which entails shame, into a state of the "glory of the children of God" (8:19–21), which gains Christians honor.[201] That the Spirit plays a central role in the final glorification is evident. Presently, Christians are in bondage to decay (8:18). This bondage that hinders the final glorification of Christians is being alleviated with the presence of the Spirit as the first fruit of a harvest, namely, the "redemption of our bodies" (8:23). This same Spirit will bring in the full harvest when Christians receive glorified bodies (8:30). How this Spirit assists in the final glorification is explained in 8:26–27, where the Spirit intercedes for Christians.

The result of the Spirit's intercession is spelled out in 8:28. Several observations support this. First, some scholars maintain that πάντα is most naturally understood as the subject of the verb συνεργεῖ ("he works together").[202] This, however, goes against the observation that when πάντα ("all") is the object of a personal verb, it "almost always precedes the verb," as is the case in 8:28.[203] Also, in Pauline usage, πάντα never functions as the subject of an active verb.[204] Furthermore, the verb συνεργεῖν ("to work together") takes on a personal subject in Paul's other two uses.[205] Second,

---

200. Jewett, *Romans*, 508.

201. John Duncan comments that the glory or honor to which Paul refers is the "decisive eschatological manifestation of the divine glory that triumphs over Sin and Death through the appearance of glorified believers in their resurrected bodies." See Duncan, "The Hope of Creation: The Significance of ἐφ᾽ ἐλπίδι (Rom 8.20c) in Context," *NTS* 61 (2015): 414–15.

202. E.g., Dunn, *Romans 1–8*, 481; Käsemann, *Commentary on Romans*, 243; KJV.

203. Fee, *God's Empowering Presence*, 588.

204. So Fee, who also notes the exception of 1 Cor 6:12 and 10:13 (*God's Empowering Presence*, 588). These two exceptions, however, are not real instances of πάντα taking on an active verb since Paul was providing a rhetorical response to the slogan "all things are permitted."

205. Fee, *God's Empowering Presence*, 588. Besides 8:28, Paul uses the verb only in 1 Cor 6:16 and 2 Cor 6:1.

God could possibly be the unexpressed subject of the verb συνεργεῖ.[206] Another possibility, however, is to take the unexpressed subject as the Spirit. This is likely in view of the fact that the Spirit has been taking center stage in what precedes (8:1–27).[207] A social and cultural texture that underlies the providence of God strengthens the plausibility of this view. The Spirit's enablement works in tandem with the providence of God. In the Mediterranean culture of this period, goods were limited, and what one received in life was a matter of fate.[208] More precisely, goods needed to be bestowed by the ultimate patron, God. From Paul's perspective, for these goods to be received, the Spirit needs to broker the deal. Only then will all things, in particular, the sufferings mentioned above in 8:18, work toward the "good" of Christians in 8:28. The above-discussed social and cultural texture also mobilizes ideological power by persuading the implied audience that by depending on the Spirit, Christians—and especially gentile Christians—are able to overcome the eschatological sufferings, which include the agony that the I experiences in Rom 7. In this way, Christians can fulfill the requirements of the Mosaic law and be regarded as righteous in their relationship with God their patron.[209] This gains gentile Christians honor.

---

206. As rendered in RSV, NIV, and Frederick Fyvie Bruce, *The Letter of Paul to the Romans: An Introduction and Commentary*, TNTC 6 (Grand Rapids: Eerdmans, 1985), 166. Similarly, Lagrange insists that God should be the subject of συνεργεῖ, and that "ce doit être une addition, pour la clarté, conforme au sens" (*Saint Paul*, 213–14). Although the reading containing ὁ θεός has the support of P[46] and B, the reading without it has more varied support. This shorter and more difficult reading could also have prompted an Alexandrian editor to insert ὁ θεός for clarification.

207. So Matthew Black, *Romans*, NCBC (Grand Rapids: Eerdmans, 1989), 118; NEB; Fee, *God's Empowering Presence*, 589; Jewett, *Romans*, 527; James P. Wilson, "Romans Viii, 28: Text and Interpretation," *ExpTim* 60 (1948–1949): 110–11.

208. Bruce J. Malina, "Fate," in Pilch and Malina, *Handbook of Biblical Social Values*, 79.

209. My understanding coheres with Paula Fredriksen's in "Paul's Letter to the Romans, the Ten Commandments, and Pagan 'Justification by Faith,'" *JBL* 4 (2014): 804–8, where she explains that Paul's "justification by faith" refers to pagans who were enabled by the Holy Spirit to fulfill the Mosaic law, "specifically, the Law's Second Table, δικαιοσύνη." See also Fredriksen, "Judaizing the Nations: The Ritual Demands of Paul's Gospel," *NTS* 56 (2010): 252: "This insistence that none other than the god of Israel be worshiped ultimately came from the first table of the Law. It was defining; it was non-negotiable; it was uniquely Jewish. For all of the reasons reviewed above, then, but most especially for this one, the last way we should describe Paul's gospel

Thus my argument above shows that the conclusion of Rom 4 in 4:23–25 undergirds the work of the Spirit in 8:1–17 (see especially 8:3 and 8:10–11). This same Spirit also works for the final glorification of Christians in 8:18–30, which in turn brings honor to both Judean and especially gentile Christians. This "good" finds culmination in the series of things that God will do in the eschatological future, namely, the glorification of Christians (8:30), which gains them honor.

With this note, Paul in 8:31–39 is ready to address the problem of 7:25 and the condemnation of 8:1. Paul exclaims that Christians are in a favorable position with God, their patron, and that no one can undermine their well-being (8:31). This well-being refers specifically to being protected from an indictment of unrighteousness (8:33a). The reason why Christians will not be indicted for an unrighteous relationship with God their patron is because "God makes righteous" the relationship between God's self and Christians (8:33b). This righteous relationship is possible because Jesus acts as the broker between God and Christians when he died and rose from the dead (8:34a). That the emphasis is on his role as a broker is corroborated by his intercession on behalf of Christians (8:34b). The role of Jesus as broker recalls the conclusion of Rom 4 in 4:23–25. Owing to Jesus's intercession or his role as broker, Christians are assured

---

to the Gentiles is to say that it was 'Law-free.'" Similarly, N. T. Wright argues that the single theory of justification comprises justification by faith and final justification by works. The latter is made possible by the former: *"Justification by faith in the present truly anticipates the final verdict and thus provides the foundation for the united believing community without the boundary-markers of Jewish life"* because the Spirit who produced faith in Christians "will now complete the task in the present time, not indeed a complete obedience to every jot and tittle of Torah … but a way of life that corresponds to the divine intention of the life-giving Torah." See Wright, "Justification by (Covenantal) Faith to the (Covenantal) Doers: Romans 2 within the Argument of the Letter," *CovQ* 72 (2014): 104–5, emphasis original. Likewise, Kevin W. McFadden contends that the Spirit empowers Christians to fulfill the requirements of the Mosaic law. He also puts up a plausible case that at the resurrection the Spirit liberates a Christian completely from sin so that the law is perfectly fulfilled. See McFadden, "The Fulfillment of the Law's Dikaiōma: Another Look at Rom 8:1–4," *JETS* 52 (2009): 490, 493–94. Cf. James O. Buswell, who maintains that "no one is saved by works but works are considered, in every judgment scene in the New Testament, as an evidence of faith or the lack of faith … Paul makes it clear that the faith through which we are saved is a faith which works. It is 'God who will render to every man according to his deeds' (Romans 2:6)." See Buswell, *A Systematic Theology of the Christian Religion* (Grand Rapids: Zondervan, 1962), 510.

of God's love (8:39). In Mediterranean culture, this love means that God is completely attached or devoted to Christians, and it ensures the final glorification or honoring of Christians.[210] With this note, Paul has completed his demonstration that both Judean Christians and especially gentile Christians are highly honored by God. Thus, the problem, first enunciated in Rom 1–3, that gentile Christians do not possess honor in the eyes of God, their patron, was first foundationally addressed in Rom 4 and fully resolved by the end of Rom 8.

4.6. Romans 9:30–10:13: Judeans Need to Depend on Christ to Broker Righteousness to Them from God

In Rom 4, Paul argues that a righteous relationship between God as patron and Christians as God's clients does not come by the deeds of the Mosaic law. Instead, a righteous relationship between the patron, God, and his clients, Christians, comes by trust. This trust mediates resurrection life to a Christian and thus enables a Christian to live a life of righteousness. Specifically how a Christian is enabled to live a righteous life is elaborated in Rom 5–8. This thesis (first enunciated in the conclusion of Rom 4 in 4:23–25 and then expounded in Rom 5–8) becomes the basis by which Paul removes the boast of Judean Christians, as the possessors of the Mosaic law, over gentile Christians.

In any tussle for honor between parties of social equals, a challenge calls for a riposte.[211] Thus, the arrogance of the Judean Christians to which Paul responds using the rhetoric of Rom 1:18–8:39 will be met with a riposte by gentile Christians. The nature of this riposte can be elicited from how Paul addresses the arrogance of the gentile Christians in Rom 9–11. I shall identify and explain the sections in Rom 9–11 where Paul builds on the conclusion of Rom 4 to speak to this rhetorical exigence: that gentiles should not boast of their superiority to Judeans.

Several observations indicate that 11:13–25 contains the rhetorical exigence: the gentile Christian audience consider Judean Christians to be inferior.[212] First, as Stowers cogently argues, the combined particles

---

210. Malina, "Love," 128.

211. Bruce J. Malina, *The New Testament World: Insights from Cultural Anthropology* (Louisville: Westminster John Knox, 2001), 40.

212. Stowers takes the admonition to the gentile Christians to be "a climactic moment in the letter's rhetoric" (*Rereading of Romans*, 294–95). This implies that the

μὲν οὖν ("then" [11:13]) should be taken together as in 9:20 and 10:18.[213] Together, they indicate that what follows provides an adversative or corrective to what has just preceded. Considering that this is the only place where Paul explicitly addresses his implied audience, it is reasonable to think that 11:13–25 contains the rhetorical exigence of Rom 9–11. Second, the main concerns of Rom 9–11 are also reinforced in 11:13–25: Paul's main goal in 9:1–10:21 is to show that the promise of God to save Israel has not been nullified (9:6). He reiterates this point in 11:1–12. Other supporting themes present in Rom 9–11 are also found in 11:13–25: Israel's unbelief (9:30–33; cf. 11:15, 20) and the need for trust (10:6–17; cf. 11:20, 23). With the contextual framework of 9:1–11:36 set, I shall show how 9:30–10:13 builds upon the conclusion set out in 4:23–25.

Romans 9:30–10:13 seeks to respond to the question: Why did Israel not receive righteousness, that is, a righteous relationship with God the patron, despite the fact that they sought after it? In this section, Paul uses apocalyptic rhetorolect. Its presence is shown by Paul's description of God's destruction-bringing wrath (9:22); the Lord's execution of his sentence on the earth quickly and decisively, with Sodom and Gomorrah as the examples (9:28–29); and God's raising of Christ from the dead (10:7, 9). As a result of resurrection, Christ is one who mediates a righteous relationship between God and humankind (thirdspace), a stone that is part of a physical house (firstspace), and a stone that brings triumphs over the enemies of God, which hints at God as eternal emperor (secondspace).[214] The use of apocalyptic rhetorolect mobilizes ideological power to persuade the gentile implied audience of the need for Christ to broker a righteous relationship for them with God, the divine patron. Thus, the use of apocalyptic rhetorolect correlates with the conclusion in 4:23–25, where Christ functions as a broker.

Paul begins by stating an ironical fact in two almost antithetical statements: "The gentiles, who did not pursue righteousness, obtained righteousness" (9:30), but "Israel, who pursued a law of righteousness

---

letter's rhetoric addresses the issue in 11:13–25. Stower's thesis is plausible but remains to be more thoroughly debated. His thesis, however, supports my point: 11:13–25 is the pressing need of, minimally, Rom 9–11. Johann D. Kim also follows my and Stowers's contention. See Kim, *God, Israel, and the Gentiles: Rhetoric and Situation in Romans 9–11*, SBLDS 176 (Atlanta: Society of Biblical Literature, 2000), 107–14.

213. Stowers, *Rereading of Romans*, 288–89.

214. Robbins, *Invention of Christian Discourse*, 109.

[νόμον δικαιοσύνης], did not arrive at the law" (9:31). Several clarifications are needed. First, the phrase νόμον δικαιοσύνης in 9:31 should be interpreted in light of 9:30: Israel is basically pursuing the same δικαιοσύνη that the gentiles have obtained. Otherwise, Paul's objects of comparison with regard to the gentiles and Israel are not compatible. Paul has phrased it this way to emphasize Israel's rigor in their pursuit of ὁ νόμος. The same reasoning applies to the word νόμος ("law") in εἰς νόμον οὐκ ἔφθασεν ("did not reach the law" [9:31]), which should also refer to righteousness that comes from the Mosaic law. Second, in 9:30–31, Paul contrasts the fact that gentiles have attained righteousness (9:30) with the fact that Israel did not succeed in fulfilling the Mosaic law (9:31). This contrast implies that the requirements of the Mosaic law must be fulfilled for one to obtain righteousness. This point is in line with my contention in 4:23–25 that righteousness is attained when one fulfills the requirements of the Mosaic law.[215]

The reason why Israel did not receive righteousness was because Israel "did not strive for it (righteousness) on the basis of trust (in God)" (9:32b). Important for our discussion is the observation that this trust has God, the patron, as its object. This point is similar to the trust discussed in 4:23–25, whose object of trust is also God. The reason why Judeans refused to enter into a relation of trust with God was because Christ the broker was a stumbling block for them (9:32b–33). To reinforce his point, Paul introduces an oral-scribal intertexture into his rhetoric (9:33).[216] This intertexture not only explains Israel's rejection of Christ, but, more importantly, it exerts ideological power on the implied audience by asserting that Christ is the key if one "will not be put to shame" (9:33).

With the vocative ἀδελφοί ("brothers") to evoke the implied audience's *pathos*, Paul indicates that 10:1–4 continues the discussion started in 9:30–33, albeit in a more emphatic way. He again expresses his desire for his fellow Judeans to be saved (10:1) and gain honor. Israel did not receive salvation because they have not submitted to God's righteousness, that is, Israel has rejected the righteousness that God, their patron, provides. Submission to God's righteousness requires Israel to do two things.

---

215. See my analysis of 7:6 in chapter 2, §4.3, "Romans 7:1–6: Trust in God Frees Christians from Condemnation Due to Noncompliance with the Mosaic Law," where I posit that being discharged from the Mosaic law does not mean that a Christian is no longer obliged to fulfill its requirements.

216. See above, chapter 1, §2.2, "Intertexture."

First, this righteousness is given to "everyone who trusts" God (10:4). Second, this trust in God requires Israel to accept Christ as their broker. The reason why Christ is a worthy broker is because τέλος νόμου Χριστὸς εἰς δικαιοσύνην ("Christ is the fulfillment of the law for righteousness" [10:4]). Some construe the meaning of τέλος as cessation. Romans 10:4 would then mean that Christ is a worthy broker because in some sense he has annulled the Mosaic law.[217] This interpretation is untenable, as, according to the argument in 9:30–33, the Mosaic law needs to be obeyed and not annulled.[218] More likely, the word means "goal" or, as some understand it,

---

217. Räisänen recognizes that "there is no critique of the law here" in 9:30–33 (*Paul and the Law*, 53–56). Thus no negative connotations are attached with the role of the law here. This understanding speaks against the meaning of τέλος as termination in the argument that follows in 10:1–4. That said, however, he argues that since 10:1 begins a new unit of thought, as signaled by the vocative ἀδελφοί, 10:4 should be read in light of the polemical contrast between "righteousness from the law" and "righteousness from faith." This makes construing the meaning of τέλος as termination reasonable. Räisänen's understanding of Paul's argument, however, is flawed. First, the vocative ἀδελφοί does not signal a break in argument. The reverse is true: it is Paul's way of drawing out the *pathos* of his implied audience in order to further his argument in 9:30–33. Second, the focus of 10:1–4 is not to contrast the "righteousness from the law" and the "righteousness from faith." Rather, Paul is contrasting their τὴν ἰδίαν (δικαιοσύνην) ζητοῦντες στῆσαι ("seeking to establish their own [righteousness]") and their need to submit to God's means of attaining righteousness, which is by means of Christ, the broker. Thus, there is nothing negative about the righteousness that comes from fulfilling the Mosaic law. Similarily, Käsemann, *Commentary on Romans*, 283. Dunn thinks both meanings, termination and fulfillment, are present in this word (*Romans 9–16*, 589).

218. See my argument above in chapter 2, §4.6, "Romans 9:30–10:13: Judeans Need to Depend on Christ to Broker Righteousness to Them from God." Stowers observes that "the text [in 9:30–31] gives not the slightest hint of anything negative about the law, Israel's goal. It [the law of righteousness] is parallel to the gentile goal of righteousness without the law" (*Rereading of Romans*, 384). This observation, however, should not be taken to imply that the Mosaic law need not be fulfilled. Rather, the Christian is now enabled by trust in Christ to fulfill the Mosaic law through the help of the Spirit: "Christ reversed the curse on the gentiles, which made their flesh weak, being ... not able to do what the law requires (8:4).... [T]he Spirit gives the gentiles a new mind (8:5–6), allowing them to submit to God's law (8:7).... Now enabled to submit to God's law, gentiles are reconciled to God (8:7)" (pp. 282–83). See also Jewett, who acknowledges that "those set right by faith and thus freed from the law would be involved in fulfilling the Mosaic law seems contradictory, standing in tension with earlier Pauline letters, but this verse is consistent with the effort throughout Romans

"fulfillment."[219] The latter interpretation also coheres with the social and cultural texture that underlies Christ's role as a broker in 9:32–33. As a broker between Christians and God, he needs to stand on a higher plane of honor in order to be a worthy broker. Christ as the broker, described in 10:4, must be able to help both gentiles and Judeans fulfill the requirements of the Mosaic law since this is the problem discussed in 9:30–33. This last point, that Christians must trust God and depend on Christ as broker, is explained in 10:5–13, as the causative γάρ in 10:5 indicates.[220]

By introducing into the text an oral-scribal intertexture, Lev 18:5, Paul emphasizes that if one looks to the Mosaic law for righteousness, that person is also required to do the deeds of the Mosaic law. The "righteousness that comes by trust" in God (10:6), however, does not require impossible deeds, such as ascending to heaven to bring Christ down or descending into the abyss to bring Christ up, before a person can put his trust in God (10:6–7). In fact, righteousness that comes through trust in God requires no deeds at all, as signified by what is involved: the mouth and heart, that is, the mouth confesses and the heart trusts (10:8–11). That God grants a person righteousness by trust and not worthy deeds, and hence by favor (grace), makes Christ a suitable broker: Christ epitomizes favor (grace) that is incongruous with the worth of its recipients.[221] The respective social and cultural textures that underlie "mouth" and "heart" also need to be highlighted if we are to understand how 10:6–9 explains Christ as broker. In Mediterranean culture, the heart refers "to the human capabilities of thinking, judging, evaluating and the like and doing all of these with feelings."[222] Thus, for Paul, heart is where the human capability for trust (here in 10:9, the object of trust is God) is exercised. As for

---

to demonstrate the continuity of God's purpose in the law and through the Spirit" (*Romans*, 485).

219. See Jewett, who argues that τέλος has fulfillment for a meaning in its various occurrences in the LXX, Plutarch, and Josephus (*Romans*, 619).

220. It is possible, as Jewett suggests, that 10:5 begins a Hebrew pesher. His suggestion, however, that Paul intends to show that "the law itself points to faith in Christ and provides no foundation for justification by works" is not borne out by the text (*Romans*, 622–23).

221. Barclay remarks that the value system provided by the Mosaic law is "offensive" to God and that Christ, who is the "unconditioned gift," is the only honor that has value before God (*Paul and the Gift*, 543).

222. Bruce J. Malina, "Eyes-Heart," in Pilch and Malina, *Handbook of Biblical Social Values*, 68.

the social and cultural texture that underlies "mouth," the speech that the mouth utters has great importance. It is the means by which honor, the most sought after limited good in the Mediterranean world, is gained.[223] A social and cultural texture underlies the word κύριος ("lord"). In the ancient Roman setting, clients were to address their patrons as lord or *dominus* (see, e.g., Martial, *Ep.* 6.88).[224] In 10:9, Christians, by addressing with their mouths (στόμα) Jesus as Lord (κύριος), are rendering honor to Christ as a patron-broker.[225] That said, however, Christ's foremost function is that of broker, as 10:1–13 is Paul's response to the Judeans' rejection of Christ's brokerage in 9:30–33. A social and cultural texture underlies the juxtaposition of mouth and heart. Mediterranean culture allows equivocation; that is, one does not have to perform what the mouth utters.[226] For this reason, Paul adds the role of the heart.[227] My point is that these statements about the roles of the mouth and heart in 10:9 should be read in parallel. Thus, Christ's role as patron-broker is closely connected to the Judean Christians' trust in God, as described in 10:9 after the epexegetical ὅτι. Some scholars contend that the verb πιστεύειν ("to trust") refers to belief in a body of knowledge.[228] The emphasis, however, should be on the object of trust, namely, God.[229] Several observations bear this out. First,

---

223. Jerome H. Neyrey, "Equivocation," in Pilch and Malina, *Handbook of Biblical Social Values*, 63.

224. In this satire, written between 95 and 98 CE by the Roman poet Marcus Valerius Martialis (b. 38–41 CE), a client who did not address Caecilianus his patron as *dominus* (lord) forfeited one hundred *quadrantes* (about six sesterces). This money was a *sportula*, a payment (which could take the form of food or money) made by the patron to his client. See Edwin Post, *Selected Epigrams of Martial: Edited, with Introduction and Notes* (Boston: Ginn, 1908), x.

225.. Nelson P. Estrada notes that Jesus, in acting as a broker between Israel and God, also functions as a patron to his (Jesus's) clients. See Estrada, *From Followers to Leaders: The Apostles in the Ritual of Status Transformation in Acts 1–2*, LNTS 255 (London: Bloomsbury, 2004), 58.

226. Neyrey, "Equivocation," 63–68.

227. Neyrey recognizes the prevailing Mediterranean culture of "equivocation" but also adds that what the Mediterranean world is more concerned about is "the intention of doing something or the plan of doing, which can serve as a substitute for achievement" (ibid., 67).

228. So most commentators, e.g., Jewett, *Romans*, 630; Dunn, *Romans 9–16*, 609; Käsemann, *Commentary on Romans*, 290–91.

229. Morgan contends that "propositional belief (secular or religious) is usually marked, in Greek and Latin, by the language of thinking (*dokein, nomizein, putare,*

the emphasis of the rhetoric of 9:30–10:13 is trust as opposed to the deeds of the Mosaic law. In particular, the clause πιστεύεται εἰς δικαιοσύνην ("one trusts so as to become righteous") in 10:10, which explains 10:9, refers to trust in God, as clarified by the recitation of scripture in 10:11: λέγει γὰρ ἡ γραφή πᾶς ὁ πιστεύων ἐπ᾽ αὐτῷ ("for the Scripture says, everyone who trusts in him [God]"). Second, 10:9b resembles 4:24–25, as evinced by the common vocabulary of πιστεύειν ("to trust"), ἐγείρειν ("to raise"), and νεκρός ("dead") and the discussion about Christ's resurrection. My discussion above has shown that Christ's role of brokering righteousness between God and Christians builds upon Christians trusting God based on his raising of Jesus from the dead. This foundational belief is the conclusion in 4:23–25.

4.7. Romans 11:17–32: Trust in God Can Make Judeans Holy

At 11:13, Paul explicitly addresses the gentile Christian implied audience toward whom the rhetoric of Rom 9–11 has been directed all along. Paul enunciates his main thesis in 11:12 that if Israel's failure to be saved means riches for the world of the gentiles, then, when all Israel is saved, the results will be even greater. What this entails is explicated in 11:15: the greater result is ζωὴ ἐκ νεκρῶν ("life from the dead" [11:15]). This may come as a surprise, as what has preceded it apparently does not prepare us for this idea about "life out of the dead." I agree with the view that this refers to the "final resurrection at the end of the age/history."[230] It is, however, difficult to ignore the repeated overtones that come from the preceding passages that talk about resurrection out of the dead and the attached newness of life (Rom 4; 5; 6; 7:24–25; 8). In that sense, the phrase ζωὴ ἐκ νεκρῶν is not a new idea here. Furthermore, the word νεκρός is also used in 4:25. Hence, the implied audience would have remembered this repeated stress. Paul's

---

censere, etc.) rather than that of pistis or fides. An exception in Greek is the phrase pisteuein hoti, 'to believe that,' which occurs occasionally in Greek literature, including the New Testament, in the context of both intra-human and divine relations. Pisteuein hoti, however, in the New Testament and beyond, is much less common than pisteuein with the dative or with prepositions of relationship such as eis or en." She also adds that not only does propositional belief always entail trust and vice versa, but "the focus of both intra-human and divine-human pistis/fides, Graeco-Roman and Christian, is more often than not on relationality" (Roman Faith and Christian Faith, 30).

230. Dunn, Romans 9–16, 658; similarly Moo, Epistle to the Romans, 695–96; Jewett, Romans, 681.

point is that not only is Israel heading for a climactic resurrection from the dead, but more so, Israel is heading for a newness of life in holiness. That this is Paul's emphasis in ζωὴ ἐκ νεκρῶν is evinced by what follows, discussing holiness in terms of the first fruit, lump, root, and branches (11:16). Some commentators see a break between 11:15 and 11:16.[231] This goes against several observations. First, as mentioned above, 11:15 and 11:16 share a common idea about holiness. Second, the structures of both verses are too similar to break them apart: εἰ γὰρ ἡ ἀποβολὴ ("for if the rejection" [11:15]) and εἰ δὲ ἡ ἀπαρχὴ ("and if the first fruit" [11:16]). More importantly, 11:15 and 11:16 both explain Paul's pride in his ministry to the gentiles (11:14). Thus, Paul in 11:13–16 demonstrates to the boasting gentiles that Judean Christians have received a resurrection life that is characterized by holiness, and hence have a righteous relationship with their patron, God. This is the conclusion of Rom 4. In this way, Judean Christians have gained honor in the eyes of the only truly significant other, God. This constitutes for the Judean Christians an appropriate riposte to the boast of the gentile Christians.

With 11:17–32, Paul finally spells out his point: to the gentile Christians, Paul warns them not to boast (11:18). He then follows this up with a warning (11:19–24) and a correction that "all Israel will be saved" (11:25–29). Furthermore, the gentile Christians should not boast over the unsaved Israelites because they have been the instruments through which the salvation of God reached the gentile Christians (11:30–32). With that, Paul's rhetoric breaks forth into a praise for the "riches, wisdom, and knowledge of God" (11:33–35). This praise should be read in light of where Paul started in 9:1: his grief that a majority of Israelites are not saved. What this implies is that the rhetoric of Rom 9–11 has reversed grief into praise.

4.8. Romans 12:1–2: Christians Who Trust in God Must Adopt a Holy Lifestyle

Most scholars agree that the section 12:1–15:13 forms the moral exhortation of the letter, as there is a decided shift from indicative to imperative.[232]

---

231. Incorrectly; see, e.g., Moo, *Epistle to the Romans*, 696. Cf. Jewett, who does not specify a connection with what precedes (*Romans*, 681). Contra Dunn, who sees the connection as Paul attempting to "express the strength of his hope" (*Romans 9–16*, 671).

232. E.g., Moo, who notes that commands are found only in a few places in Rom

This section can be divided into two main sections: general exhortations (12:1–13:14) and specific exhortations (14:1–15:13). That this entire section is dominated by wisdom rhetorolect is apparent from several observations. In 12:1–2, which introduces the moral exhortations that follow, Paul address his implied audience as ἀδελφοί (12:1). This evokes *pathos* in the implied audience so that they will take heed to obey the exhortations. Also, the implied audience addressed belongs to a household, as indicated by the verb προσλαμβάνειν, which means to welcome a person into a household (14:1).[233] Both are familial terms that recall the firstspace of wisdom rhetorolect. Furthermore, the exhortations also often take a binary form, that is, "reasoning and argumentation based on identification and differentiation. Identities and differences are assumed, asserted, or explained by using opposites, contraries, and adversatives."[234] According to the thirdspace of wisdom rhetorolect, Paul seeks by the rhetoric of 14:1–15:13 to produce in the implied audience a body of righteousness, that is, a life characterized by righteous living.[235] This coheres with the intent of the exhortations in 14:1–15:13.

The focus of 12:1–15:13, as most commentators agree, is encapsulated by 12:1–2.[236] I contend that 12:1–2 builds upon the conclusion in 4:23–25. Several observations confirm my point of view. First, the conjunction οὖν is inferential. The question is, however, how far back this conjunction reaches. This brings me to my second observation. The goal of 12:1–15:13, namely, the thirdspace of wisdom rhetorolect, is to persuade the implied audience to perform righteous deeds. Here, in 12:1, the body (σῶμα) is described as θυσίαν ζῶσαν ἁγίαν εὐάρεστον τῷ Θεῷ ("a living sacrifice, holy and pleasing to God" [NIV]). The kind of lifestyle that Paul exhorts the implied audience to demonstrate in 12:1–2 recalls the resurrection life described in Rom 6, which enables Christians to live a holy life. This ability to live a holy life, as I have argued earlier in my discussion on Rom 6, is predicated upon 4:23–25: the resurrection life of

---

1–11: 6:11–13, 19; 11:18–20 (*Epistle to the Romans*, 744). Likewise, Jewett, *Romans*, 724; Cranfield, *Epistle to the Romans*, 2:592; Esler, *Conflict and Identity in Romans*, 308.

233. BDAG, s.v. "προσλαμβανω."

234. Robbins, *Invention of Christian Discourse*, 136.

235. Ibid., 109.

236. E.g., Jewett, *Romans*, 724; Moo, *Epistle to the Romans*, 748; Dunn, *Romans 9–16*, 707.

Jesus enables Christians to live a holy life.[237] The body (σῶμα) that is now alive resolves the body that was dead (τὸ σῶμα τοῦ θανάτου [7:24]) due to the indictment of sin by the Mosaic law in Rom 7. This body (σῶμα) is now saved by the Spirit, as Paul explained in Rom 8 (e.g, 8:10, 11). As I argued earlier in my discussion on Rom 8, the salvation work of the Spirit is predicated upon 4:23–25. Thus, a lifestyle that is characterized by holiness, as described in 14:1–15:13, builds upon the conclusion of Rom 4, specifically 4:23–25.

4.9. Romans 14:1–15:13: Trust in God Enables Both the Weak and the Strong to Stand under Judgment

The problem in 14:1–15:13 involves two groups, the "weak" (14:1) and the "strong" (15:1), who disagree on issues relating to eating and drinking (14:3, 6b, 14–15, 17, 20–23) and observance of certain days (14:5, 6). Some scholars think that 14:1–15:13 is adapted from Paul's earlier discussion in 1 Cor 8–10 and that it is not directed at any specific situation of the Roman congregation.[238] The more widely accepted view today is that Paul was addressing the problems faced by the Christians in Rome.

Scholars who subscribe to this view identify the weak and the strong differently. Some interpret both the weak and strong as gentile Christians. For instance, Stowers argues that the terms strong and weak are concepts

---

237. See above, chapter 2, §4.2, "Romans 6:1–14: Trust in God Enables Christians to Live Righteous Lives."

238. E.g., Sanday and Headlam, *A Critical and Exegetical Commentary on the Epistle to the Romans*, 399–402; Robert T. Karris, "Rom 14:1–15:13 and the Occasion of Romans," *CBQ* 35 (1973); John W. Drane, "Why Did Paul Write Romans?," in *Pauline Studies: Essays Presented to Professor F. F. Bruce on His Seventieth Birthday*, ed. Donald A. Hagner and Murray J. Harris (Grand Rapids: Eerdmans, 1980), 221; Wayne A. Meeks, "Judgment and the Brother: Romans 14:1–15:13," in *Tradition and Interpretation in the New Testament: Essays in Honor of E. Earle Ellis for His Sixtieth Birthday*, ed. Gerald F. Hawthorne and Otto Betz (Grand Rapids: Eerdmans, 1987), 290–300. Contra Mark Reasoner, who shows that the verbal and argumentation similarities between 14:1–15:13 and 1 Cor 8–10 are inconclusive. See Reasoner, *The Strong and the Weak: Romans 14.1–15:13 in Context*, SNTSMS 103 (Cambridge: Cambridge University Press, 1998), 25–37. Likewise, Carl N. Toney critiques Karris's position that it has left unattended the question why "Rom 14–15 adds in the issues of vegetarianism and observance of days while omitting the key terms of 'idol-food.'" See Toney, *Paul's Inclusive Ethic: Resolving Community Conflicts and Promoting Mission in Romans 14–15*, WUNT 2.252 (Tübingen: Mohr Siebeck, 2008), 16–17.

used in Hellenistic philosophies as practiced, for instance, in Epicurean communities.[239] These terms refer to character traits and not ethnic groups: the strong describes those who are able to act according to rational beliefs; the weak are those who are less mature and require psychagogic education. Stower's contextualization as a philosophical school, however, does not match the situation of the congregation in Rome. Carl Toney points out that "the Roman problems are at the community level, yet philosophical education involved personal choices and did not make demands at the community level."[240] Furthermore, the backdrop of the Christian community in Rome is not that of a "philosophically informed friendship," as purported by Stowers,[241] but that of submission or "accountability" to the Lord (14:4–12).[242]

Other scholars regard both groups, the weak and the strong, as each comprising a mix of gentile and Judean Christians. Mark Reasoner, for example, interprets the strong and the weak as terms that denote social status in first-century CE Rome.[243] He contends that these two groups are quarrelling over issues related to a mix of Judean and gentile practices.[244] Several observations, however, indicate that the two groups, the weak and the strong, refer mainly to Judean and gentile Christians respectively. Also, the quarrel is over Judean understanding of purity. First, Joel Marcus makes an important observation that Paul connects the "weak and the strong" in 14:1–15:6 with the Judeans and gentiles in 15:7–13 using a strong connective διό. This link forged by the connective γάρ is further reinforced by Paul's description of Christ as the servant of the circumcision and of the gentiles (15:8–9).[245] Second, Toney provides various threads of

---

239. Stowers, *Rereading of Romans*, 317–23. According to Das, the "strong" and the "weak" do not denote ethnic groups but are gentile Christians. He reasons that Godfearing Christians who were once associated with the synagogues broke away from these Judean institutions after Claudius's edict in 49 CE and started worshiping in house churches. Newer gentile Christian converts who joined these Godfearing gentile Christians were not educated in Judaism. This led to unrest in the Roman Christian community (*Solving the Romans Debate*, 115–48).

240. Toney, *Paul's Inclusive Ethic*, 25.

241. Stowers, *Rereading of Romans*, 321.

242. Toney, *Paul's Inclusive Ethic*, 25.

243. Reasoner, *Strong and the Weak*, 45–63.

244. Ibid., 64–87.

245. See Joel Marcus, "The Circumcision and Uncircumcision in Rome," *NTS* 35 (1989): 68. Esler is perceptive when he emphasizes that this connection is "the

evidence that show that 14:1–15:13 is set against the background of Judean purity concerns. He argues that the contrast between common (κοινός) and clean (καθαρός) is a Hebrew Bible concept (Lev 10:10; Ezek 22:26; 44:23; see also CD 6:17; 12:20).[246] The word κοινός does not mean "unclean" to a Greco-Roman audience. This is evinced by the observation that Mark had to explain the meaning of κοινός as ἄνιπτος ("unwashed") in Mark 7:2. That Paul does not provide a similar commentary in 14:1–15:13 shows that a Judean purity context is assumed so that the audience would construe κοινός as "unclean."[247] C. K. Barrett and Ernst Käsemann do not think that the "weak" abstained from the food and wine because of Judean dietary laws, as the Hebrew Bible does not contain such a prohibition.[248] This is controverted by Second Temple Judaism texts that depict Judeans abstaining from unclean food as a sign of covenant loyalty (1 Macc 1:62–63; 2 Macc 6:18–31; 4 Macc 4–18). Moreover, Romans mocked Judeans who abstained from pork (Philo, *Legat.* 361; Tacitus, *Hist.* 5.4.2). Judeans also abstained from wine that was associated with idols (Dan 1:3–16; 10:3; Add Esth 14:17; T. Reu. 1:10; T. Jud. 15:4; Jos. Asen. 8:5). That Judean dietary laws are in view in 14:1–15:13 also coheres with the interpretation of most scholars who construe the observance of days as that of Judean Sabbaths and sacred days.[249] This view is also in line with William Campbell's

---

best indicator" that links the "weak" and the "strong" with Judean and gentile Christians (*Conflict and Identity in Romans*, 342). Joshua D. Garroway interprets the phrase διάκονον περιτομῆς as a διάκονος who administers the rite of circumcision instead of the usual interpretation of a διάκονος who ministers to the circumcision, namely, the Judeans. The former position is unlikely in view of the observation that in the other two occurrences in the New Testament where a noun that is a person is attached to the genitive substantive, περιτομῆς, the genitive refers to ethnic Judeans (see 4:12; Gal 2:7). Also, according to Garroway, Christ by administering circumcision unites Judeans and gentiles. Such a use of the topic, circumcision, runs contrary to how Paul uses "circumcision" in Rom 4: when Paul attempts to reconcile Judean and gentile Christians under the fatherhood of Abraham, he distinguishes the two groups as the circumcised and the uncircumcised (4:11–12). In other words, the topic, "circumcision," does not unite but distinguishes Judeans and gentiles. See Garroway, "The Circumcision of Christ: 15:7–13," *JSNT* 34 (2012): 306.

246. Toney, *Paul's Inclusive Ethic*, 57. Similarly, Francis Watson, "The Two Roman Congregations," in Donfried, *Romans Debate*, 205.

247. Toney, *Paul's Inclusive Ethic*, 57.

248. See Käsemann, *Commentary on Romans*, 368–69.

249. John M. G. Barclay, "'Do We Undermine the Law?' A Study of Romans 14:1–15:6," in *Paul and the Mosaic Law*, ed. James D. G. Dunn (Tübingen: Mohr Sie-

observation that "there is a growing scholarly consensus that the earliest Christianity to Rome was an intra-Jewish phenomenon."[250] The above clarification on the identities of the weak and the strong further reinforces my perception of the exigency of Romans as a dissension between Judean and gentile Christians. With this, we shall examine how Paul resolves this dissension between the weak, who are the Judeans, and the strong, the gentile Christians.

He urges the strong to welcome the weak, as in welcoming them "into one's household" (14:1).[251] The strong should not be arrogant toward the weak for being weak in faith because they do not eat (14:1–3). This recalls Paul's earlier admonition to the gentiles "not to boast" over the Judeans (11:18). Neither should the weak judge the strong (14:3). In light of 14:4, such judgment by the weak or the strong is tantamount to judging those from the other group as being unable to "stand" (14:4) blamelessly before God as a servant stands before his master. The one who enables him "to stand," however, is the Lord (14:4). When read in light of Rom 4, the Lord enables the "weak" and the "strong" to stand through Jesus, who has expiated sin and given to Christians a righteous life. This life enables both Judean and gentile Christians to live righteous lives. Whether one should eat or not, the guiding principle is: each should act according to how one is persuaded in his or her νοῦς (14:5). The word νοῦς ("mind") recalls the νοῦς in 7:23 that was captivated by the law of sin and that was later set free from the law of sin to serve the law of God (7:25). This liberation is possible

---

beck, 1996), 292; Cranfield, *Epistle to the Romans*, 2:705; Dunn, *Romans 9–16*, 805; Fitzmyer, *Romans*, 690; Moo, *Epistle to the Romans*, 842; Schreiner, *Romans*, 715; Tobin, *Paul's Rhetoric*, 404–5; Toney, *Paul's Inclusive Ethic*, 61. Those who see a mix of Greco-Roman and Judean concerns include Barrett, *Romans*, 257–58; Jewett, *Romans*, 844–45. Norman H. Young is probably right to insist that the "days" to which 14:5 refers are Judean festivals, as early Christians continued to celebrate such days (see also below, chapter 3, §3.5.4, "Secondary Rhetorolects"). Thus, the dissensions in 14:1–15:13 about *kosher* food and observance of days belong to the same issue. See Young, "Romans 14:5–6 in Its Social Setting," *AUSS* 54 (2016): 60–61, 64.

250. Campbell, "Rule of Faith," 265.

251. The interpretation by Fitzmyer (*Romans*, 689) coheres with Paul's use of προσλαμβάνειν: this verb occurs a total of four times in Paul's writings, three of which occur in this passage. Its only other Pauline usage is in Phlm 17. This passage implies that Onesimus was a slave of Philemon, who had absconded from Philemon's household. But Onesimus, under Paul's patronage, was now going to return to the household of Philemon, his master, this time as a brother.

because, as explained in Rom 6–8, the Spirit enables Christians to fulfill
the law. Since Rom 6–8 is premised upon Rom 4, 14:5 also builds on Rom
4.[252] Furthermore, this individual does it for the Lord because one ought
to live for the Lord (14:6–9). This recalls again the previous argument of
Rom 6 that stresses freedom from bondage to sin and a life to be lived for
righteousness. Paul then nullifies all forms of judgment, either of the weak
against the strong or vice versa. The reason is given in 14:10–12. This is not
a new reason but a recasting of the previous argument: both the weak and
the strong should stop judging one another, as no one has a right to do this
because Christians now live their lives to please God and are thus account-
able to God alone.[253] With a pun, ἀλλὰ τοῦτο κρίνατε ("but judge this"
[14:13]), Paul tells the implied audience what it is they should be concerned
"not to put a stumbling block or a hindrance" in their fellow Christian's way
(15:13). Paul is convinced that the food that gentiles eat is not unclean.[254]
That said, however, Paul also contends that, if a Christian is aggrieved as
a result of another Christian eating the food, the Christian who eats is not
showing ἀγάπη ("love") to the aggrieved Christian. Although "our good
act" (14:16), which refers to the act of eating, is not in itself evil, this act
of eating becomes a source of dispute. Such an act is incompatible with
the way Christians ought to live in God's kingdom, a kingdom that should
be characterized by "righteousness and peace and joy in the Holy Spirit"
(14:17). This triad of righteousness, peace, and joy must be read against the
present backdrop where the Judean Christians emphasize the rejection of
certain foods and drinks and the observance of certain days. This means
that the emphasis here is righteousness, and its outworking is described by
εἰρήνη καὶ χαρά ("peace and joy"). The outworking of this righteousness is a
cordial relationship between various parties, in this case Judean and gentile
Christians, and edification (14:19). Seen from this perspective, righteousness is an ethical construct. Fulfilling this requirement is made possible by
what was accomplished in Rom 4:23–25. The opposite is Paul's concern:
the stumbling of the weak (14:20–21). The prepositional phrase ἐν πνεύματι

---

252. See above, chapter 2, §4.2, "Romans 6:1–14: Trust in God Enables Christians
to Live Righteous Lives."

253. Esler, *Conflict and Identity in Romans*, 351; in the same vein, see Moo, *Epistle
to the Romans*, 846.

254. Barclay comments that "this constitutes nothing less than a fundamental
rejection of the Jewish law in one of its most sensitive dimensions" ("Do We Undermine the Law," 300).

ἁγίῳ ("in the Holy Spirit") probably modifies all three elements: δικαιοσύνη, εἰρήνη, and χαρά (14:17). This means that the desired situation of 14:18–21 is the work of the Holy Spirit that fulfills δικαιοσύνη. This again recalls the work of the Holy Spirit in Rom 8, which is premised upon the argument of Rom 4.[255] In this way, the Mosaic law is fulfilled, and Judean and gentile Christians attain righteousness. With 14:22–23, Paul reiterates what he started in 14:1: the strong in trust should strive "not for the purpose of judging over opinions"; that is, the strong are to maintain their trust toward God (14:22) and not impose their views on those weak in trust.

Paul sounds like he is ending the rhetoric he started in 14:1 when he writes 14:22–23. But at 15:1, his attention turns once again to exhorting the strong. This time, however, his objective is different, as the discussion that follows shows. He urges the strong, that is, the gentile Christians, to bear with the weaknesses of the weak, the Judean Christians, just as Christ did (15:1–3). He backs this injunction with a Septuagint recitation and explains that this passage was written to bring to the readers "patience" and "comfort" so they might have "hope" (15:4). Most commentators think that hope (ἐλπίς) refers to salvation and also agree that the mention of hope comes as a surprise.[256] What follows clarifies the content of hope: in 15:5, using the terms patience and hope, Paul indicates that their objective is to unite the Judean and gentile Christians so they may glorify God. When 15:5 is read in parallel with 15:4, the above objective forms the content of ἐλπίς. Hence, Jewett is probably right to say that "the use of the definite article ... indicate[s] a specific hope is in view here. It is the hope in the conversion of the nations which will involve 'the uniting of the church of Jews and Gentiles.'"[257] This hope is achievable because it "derives from a solidly reliable, interpersonal relationship" with God, the patron of Christians, "providing resources for the congregation to overcome their conflicts and reproaches so that they will be able to participate responsibly in the mission to the end of the world."[258]

---

255. See above, chapter 2, §4.2, "Romans 6:1–14: Trust in God Enables Christians to Live Righteous Lives."

256. On ἐλπίς referring to salvation, see, e.g., Moo, *Epistle to the Romans*, 869–71; Cranfield, *Epistle to the Romans*, 2:736; Käsemann, *Commentary on Romans*, 383. Moo opines that "the introduction of hope at this point might also seem to be a detour in Paul's argument" (*Epistle to the Romans*, 869), and Käsemann reads "hope" as a "surprising motif in the context" (*Commentary on Romans*, 383).

257. Jewett, *Romans*, 883.

258. John J. Pilch, "Trust (Personal and Group)," in Pilch and Malina, *Handbook of Biblical Social Values*, 202; Jewett, *Romans*, 883.

With this, Paul concludes with the same word that he began with in 14:1, προσλαμβάνω. This time, however, he addresses both the gentile Christians and the Judean Christians, telling them that they should receive each other for the glory of God, which refers back to what has just been mentioned in 15:4–6. He bolsters his exhortation with the example of Christ, who became a servant of both the "circumcision" and the gentiles (15:7–9). He also urges this unity of Judean and gentile Christians with recitations from the Septuagint (15:10–12).

The discussion above has demonstrated that the conclusion in 4:23–25 forms the basis of the rhetoric that follows in 5:1 to 15:13. Having established this, I will investigate the rhetoric of Rom 4.

3

THE RHETORIC OF ROMANS 4: PART 1

1. Introductory Matters

This chapter and the next will examine the rhetoric of Rom 4. The main discussion will be divided into two parts. In this chapter, I will focus on the issues that frame the rhetoric of Rom 4, following which I shall examine the rhetoric of Rom 4:1–8. The next chapter, chapter 4 of this book, will analyze Rom 4:9–25.

Romans 4 is a diatribe in which Paul engages an imaginary Judean interlocutor with the implied audience comprising Judean and gentile Christians listening to the debate.[1] Paul seeks by the rhetoric of Rom 4 to resolve an exigence created by a twofold factor. First, Judean Christians claim to possess righteousness because they possess the Mosaic law. Second, they use this righteousness to boast against gentile Christians. This creates a rift between Judean and gentile Christians. To heal this rift, Paul responds with the rhetoric of Abraham's faith or trust in God. The opening question (4:1) asks the Judean interlocutor if he is able to argue the case that Abraham received righteousness by his own human efforts, making him (Abraham) the ancestor of the Judeans. Paul then launches a twofold rhetorical strategy (4:2–16; 4:17–25) to refute such a claim.

First, Paul undermines the possibility of gaining righteousness through human efforts (4:2–16). He achieves this rhetorical objective by showing

---

1. On the imaginary Judean interlocutor, see Dunn, *Romans 1–8*, 199; Nancy Calvert-Koyzis, *Paul, Monotheism and the People of God: The Significance of Abraham Traditions for Early Judaism and Christianity*, JSNTSup 273 (London: T&T Clark, 2004), 134; Stowers, *Rereading of Romans*, 231, 234; Stowers, *Diatribe*, 155–84; Jewett, *Romans*, 26; contra Elliott, *Rhetoric of Romans*, 158; Cranfield, *Epistle to the Romans*, 1:227; Ben C. Dunson, *Individual and Community in Paul's Letter to the Romans*, WUNT 332 (Tübingen: Mohr Siebeck, 2012), 131.

the noncongruence between deeds of the Mosaic law and God's favor (4:2–8) and by using the topos "circumcision" (4:9–12). At the same time, Paul also crafts a myth of origins for both Judean and gentile Christians. He argues that the righteousness that gained Abraham his fatherhood came by trust in or loyalty to God as patron.[2] In this way, Abraham becomes the father of gentile Christians so they can inherit righteousness from him (4:11b). Likewise, Judeans who imitate Abraham's trust in or loyalty to God as patron are his descendants and also gain righteousness (4:12). Paul then continues to undermine the role of the Mosaic law in attaining righteousness by framing his rhetoric using the topos "promise" (4:13–16).

Second, after undermining human efforts, Paul introduces the role of trust (4:17–25). Trust in or loyalty to God made Abraham righteous so that God made alive Abraham's dead body. Consequently, he could have descendants. In 4:23, Paul stops engaging the Judean interlocutor and speaks directly to the implied audience, namely, the Judean and gentile Christians. He concludes that as a result of Abraham's trust in—that is, loyalty to—God, both Judean and gentile Christians may gain righteousness (4:23). This righteousness will be realized if they trust God who raised Jesus from the dead. Such a trust in God resolves the problem of trespasses and enables a person to live a righteous life (4:24–25).

My analysis of Rom 4 will proceed as follows. Each paragraph will first be delimited and then, where relevant, analyzed for its various textures and rhetorolects. Generally, analysis will proceed by a close reading of the text. But before we enter into the analysis of each paragraph, several comments are needed.

1.1. The Immediate Context

In the previous section where I traced the argument of Romans to locate the function of Rom 4, I argued that the preceding context, 1:18–3:31, addresses a twofold problem. First, Judeans are relying on the deeds of the Mosaic law to obtain righteousness. Second, Judeans also view the Mosaic law as a Judean identity marker and use it to boast against the gentiles (3:7–31).[3] This adds honor to their family of Judeans. For the rhetoric of Rom 4 to be intelligible, it is important to understand that this boast men-

---

2. Bruce J. Malina, "Faith/Faithfulness," in Pilch and Malina, *Handbook of Biblical Social Values*, 72–75.

3. Räisänen reads the issue of 3:27–30 as "the inclusion of Gentiles in the people

tioned in 3:27 and taken up again in Rom 4 is not individual but familial. This explains why Paul invokes Abraham to construct what constitutes a correct conception of kinship and ethnicity, and it configures his identity as father of both Judean and gentile Christians. Thus, Paul the implied speaker is faced with a twofold exigence. Judeans are depending on the Mosaic law to become righteous. Furthermore, gentiles are considered to be inferior by Judeans because they do not have access to this righteousness. This twofold problem looms in the immediate context that precedes Rom 4 and prompts Paul the implied author to use the rhetoric of Abraham's trust to resolve this exigence.

1.2. The Dominant Rhetorolect

The dominant rhetorolect in Rom 4 is probably Christian wisdom rhetorolect. Several observations demonstrate this. First, the introduction of this paragraph centers on Abraham as προπάτωρ ("forefather"). This fits the firstspace of wisdom rhetorolect, which is the experience of household, whose main figure is the father.[4] Second, several elements indicate that the discourse as a whole is wisdom argumentation. Robbins observes that "one of the basic characteristics of early Christian wisdom rhetorolect is to turn scriptural discourse into proverbial speech. This occurs either by selecting only part of a verse for recitation or by omitting words from the biblical verse to make it shorter."[5]

We observe that Paul recites verses from Gen 15 and 17 LXX and Ps 31 LXX (Rom 4:5, 9, cf. Gen 15:6 LXX; Rom 4:7–8, cf. Ps 31:1–2 LXX; Rom 4:17, cf. Gen 17:5 LXX). Furthermore, Robbins also notes that a "beginning point in wisdom discourse, then, is reasoning and argument based on identification and differentiation. Identities and differences are assumed, asserted by using opposites, contraries and adversatives."[6]

We see such an "identification and differentiation" with assertions of "opposites" in 4:4–5, 9–10, 13–14, 16, 20, 23–24. Furthermore, the tone of these assertions is exhortative. Even when blessing and reckoning of sin are

---

of God," in which "the works of the law are something that separates the Jew from the Gentile" (*Paul and the Law*, 171).

4. See Robbins, *Invention of Christian Discourse*, 133.

5. Ibid., 122.

6. Ibid., 136.

mentioned, the tone remains exhortative and nonconfrontational. If it were confrontational, it would transform the discourse into a prophetic one.[7]

Third, and more importantly, the application in 4:23–25 indicates wisdom rhetorolect. Paul's rhetoric seeks to produce righteousness in the lived space (the thirdspace) of the human body, that is, to move the implied audience to live righteous lives.[8] This fits the thirdspace of wisdom rhetorolect. With this noted, I shall discuss the various paragraphs of Rom 4.

1.3. Inner Texture

A display of the main topoi reveals the subtextures of repetitive, progressive, and opening-middle-closing. This display will facilitate tracing the argument of Rom 4.

Opening	4:1: "What shall we say? Have we found Abraham to be our forefather by his own human efforts?"
Middle	4:2–5: topos related to deed
	4:6–8: topos related to blessing
	4:9–12: topos related to circumcision
	4:13–16 topoi related to promise and law
	4:17–22: topoi related to death and life
Closing	4:23–25: "But the words 'it was reckoned to him' were not written because of him only, but also because of us to whom it (righteousness) is about to be reckoned, who believe on him who raised Jesus our Lord from the dead, who was delivered (to death) because of our transgressions and raised because of our righteousness."

Several observations elucidate Paul's argument. First, the opening question about how the implied audience realizes Abraham as their father meets a response in the closing about Jesus Christ obtaining righteousness for the implied audience. The implication is that the intervening material (4:2–22) bridges the gap between the nature of Abraham's fatherhood and the righteousness obtained for the implied audience by Jesus Christ.

---

7. Ibid., 191.

8. Ibid., xxix–xxx. See below, chapter 4, §3.7.2, "Romans 4:24–25."

Second, the repetitive and progressive texture reveals the main topoi and thus exposes the rhetorolects used in each section.[9] It is important to remember that in SRI, rhetorolects (rhetorical dialects) replace the traditional genres of rhetorical discourse.[10] Paul starts with wisdom rhetorolect in 4:1 and stays within the same rhetorolect in 4:2–8. He then brings in priestly rhetorolect as indicated by the topos "circumcision" in 4:9–12. The topoi of promise and law in 4:13–16 indicate apocalyptic rhetorolect. Paul finishes the rhetoric with miracle rhetorolect in 4:17–25. In my analysis, I shall structure Rom 4 according to the physical setting (firstspace) dictated by New Testament rhetorolects. Hence, these major rhetorolects will delineate the subsections of Rom 4 and provide the framework for analysis. More importantly, by identifying the major rhetorolect that dominates a section, a general idea of the object of the rhetoric can also be narrowed down, as displayed in Robbins's matrix under "Ongoing Bodily Effects and Enactments."[11]

The verb λέγειν ("to say") occurs at 4:1, 3, 6, 9, 18 and forms a repetitive inner texture that drives the argument of Rom 4 forward. This verb contains a sensory-aesthetic inner texture. Human beings are considered to be interacting appropriately with the world outside them and hence satisfying rules of purity.[12] The mouth belongs to the "zone of self-expressive speech." In other words, the mouth serves as a means of "self-revelation through speech."[13] Furthermore, New Testament writers tend to verbalize

---

9. Carolyn R. Miller observes that "the topos is a conceptual space without fully specified or specifiable contents. It is a region of productive uncertainty.… A topos might be thought of as such a point in semantic space that is particularly rich in connectivity to other significant or highly connected points." See Miller, "The Aristotelian Topos: Hunting for Novelty," in Robbins, Thaden, and Bruehler, *Foundations for Sociorhetorical Exploration*, 115. The route connectivity takes, however, is not addressed. SRI fills in the lacuna through rhetorolects that link the propositions invented by the topos to the audience; see Michael C. Leff, "The Uses of Aristotle's Rhetoric in Contemporary American Scholarship," *Argumentation* 7 (1993): 25.

10. Robbins observes that the rhetoric of the New Testament "does not presuppose the rhetorical setting of the law court, political assembly, or civil ceremony" (*Invention of Christian Discourse*, 1–3). Hence, the categories of classical rhetoric are not appropriate for analyzing the New Testament. Instead, Robbins insists on blending "these categories with the inner workings" of rhetorolects.

11. Ibid., 109.

12. Bruce J. Malina, "Communicativeness (Mouth-Ears)," in Pilch and Malina, *Handbook of Biblical Social Values*, 27; Malina, *New Testament World*, 68.

13. Malina, *New Testament World*, 68.

(in this case by means of the mouth) and not engage in introspection.[14] Thus, by using λέγειν, the speaker is not merely articulating something. His entire person is involved. In the case of 4:1, the Judean interlocutor is effectively bringing into the rhetoric his Judean ethnic identity. In addition, the mouth, in the Mediterranean world, was the "key strategy for establishing, maintaining and defending honor."[15] Thus, by using the word λέγειν in 4:1a, the Judean interlocutor is putting forward a challenge. The other occurrences of λέγειν should also be construed as part of the challenge-riposte game set in motion by the Judean interlocutor in 4:1. In what follows, starting with 4:2, Paul is providing a series of major ripostes that build around the statements in 4:3, 6, 9, 18. That a challenge-riposte game frames Rom 4 is evinced by two observations. First, λέγειν connotes the giving of a challenge in 4:1, and the other occurrences are responses that seek to refute 4:1 or are theses related to it. Second, Rom 4 centers on attainment of "righteousness," which is closely related to honor.

1.4. Translation of Ἰουδαῖοι

A section that discusses the translation of Ἰουδαῖοι may at first sight appear unrelated to the rhetoric of Rom 4. A correct translation of Ἰουδαῖοι, however, does affect the persuasiveness of Rom 4. The reason is that Ἰουδαῖοι, as I argue below, is very much an ethnic label. Since Rom 4 is an argument that seeks to resolve issues related to the ethnicity of Ἰουδαῖοι Christians, its translation should indicate that Ἰουδαῖοι denotes an ethnic group. This book translates the term Ἰουδαῖοι as "Judeans." With regard to this translation, David Miller notes that

> although the traditional translation 'Jew' remains dominant, 'Judean' is now common enough that it can be employed without justification—thanks, in part, to the influential arguments of Malina and Rohrbaugh (1992: 32), Danker (2000: 478), Esler (2003), and Mason (2007), who maintain that the religious connotations of 'Jew' are anachronistic, and that *Ioudaios* is best understood solely as an ethnic label.[16]

---

14. Ibid.

15. Malina, "Communicativeness," 28.

16. David M. Miller, "Ethnicity, Religion and the Meaning of Ioudaios in Ancient 'Judaism,'" *CBR* 12 (2014): 216–17.

That said, however, he also acknowledges that this issue is still unresolved. The intent of this section is not to further the scholarly discussion on the translation "Judeans." Rather, it is to provide sufficient evidence to validate translating Ἰουδαῖοι as "Judeans." The following section discusses the salient points of Esler's essay on the translation of Ἰουδαῖοι as "Judeans."[17]

1.4.1. Understanding Ethnicity

Esler follows Fredrik Barth's view of ethnicity as espoused in his *Ethnic Groups and Boundaries* (1969). Barth opines that "a categorical ascription is an ethnic ascription, when it classifies a person in terms of his basic, most general identity, presumptively determined by his origin and background."[18] This view represents a further development of Max Weber's thesis that suggests that members within an ethnic group are naturally attracted to one another with no regard to an objective basis.[19] Barth also refines Everett C. Hughes's construal of ethnicity: "An ethnic group is not one because of the degree of measurable or observable difference from other groups: it is an ethnic group, on the contrary, because the people in it and out of it know that it is one."[20] The distinguishing mark of Barth's understanding of an ethnic group is that cultural features are visible manifestations but not the cause of an ethnic identity.[21] He further clarifies the relationship between the identity of an ethnic group and the cultural features it exhibits. Cultural features may change, but the boundary that

17. Esler adopts this translation in *Conflict and Identity in Romans*, 63–74. For other scholars who think likewise, see Bruce J. Malina and Richard L. Rohrbaugh, *Social-Science Commentary on the Gospel of John* (Minneapolis: Fortress, 1998), 44–46; Bruce J. Malina and John J. Pilch, *Social-Science Commentary on the Book of Revelation* (Minneapolis: Fortress, 2000), 25, 47, 54, 58–67; Richard A. Horsley, *Galilee: History, Politics, People* (Valley Forge, PA: Trinity Press International, 1995); Elliott, *Arrogance of Nations*, 16. Pilch also cites evidence that people in antiquity identified themselves in terms of "their geographical place of origin." See Pilch, "Are There Jews and Christians in the Bible?," *HvTSt* 53 (1997): 119–24.

18. Barth, *Ethnic Groups and Boundaries*, 13.

19. Max Weber, *Economy and Society: An Outline of Interpretive Sociology*, ed. Guenther Roth and Claus Wittich, trans. Ephraim Fischoff (Berkeley: University of California Press, 1978), 389.

20. Everett C. Hughes, *On Work, Race, and the Sociological Imagination*, ed. Lewis A. Coser (Chicago: University of Chicago Press, 1994), 91.

21. Esler, *Conflict and Identity in Romans*, 42.

persists between members and outsiders facilitates the specifying of the ethnic identity.[22]

But what is that most basic identity? Social scientists recognize Barth's (correct) insistence that an ethnic group's self-ascription must be maintained. At the same time, they also recognize the role of *primordialism* in constructing an ethnic identity. Geertz uses the term primordialism for an attachment that results mainly from a common ancestry and is so "overpowering" that it defines an ethnic identity and makes that identity and the ethnic group stable. Geertz insists that primordial attachments create a desire to assert an ethnic group's identity socially.[23] Social scientists recognize the need to mediate between these two seemingly irreconcilable positions.[24]

Jonathan M. Hall develops Barth's viewpoint and offers a way forward: "There is no doubt ... that ethnic identity is a cultural construct, perpetually renewed and renegotiated through discourse and social praxis."[25] John Hutchinson and Anthony D. Smith develop Barth's viewpoint and list six cultural features that are commonly associated with ethnic groups. They are (1) a common proper name to identify the group, (2) a myth of common ancestry, (3) shared historical memories, (4) one or more elements of common culture, (5) a link with a homeland, and (6) a sense of solidarity.[26] This does not mean, however, that these six features constitute an ethnic group. Rather, Esler suggests that

---

22. Barth, *Ethnic Groups and Boundaries*, 9–38.

23. Clifford Geertz, "Primordial Sentiments and Civil Politics in the New States," in *Old Societies and New States*, ed. Clifford Geertz (London: Free Press of Glencoe, 1963), 105–57.

24. See George M. Scott Jr., "A Resynthesis of the Primordial and Circumstantial Approaches to Ethnic Group Solidarity: Towards an Explanatory Model," *ERS* 13 (1990): 147. Scott attempts to provide a synthesis of the primordial and circumstantial approaches to explain ethnic group solidarity. Jenkins concludes that as much as ethnicity is associated with culture, that is, shared meaning, it is also "rooted in, and the outcome of, social interaction" (*Rethinking Ethnicity*, 165).

25. Jonathan M. Hall, *Ethnic Identity in Greek Antiquity* (Cambridge: Cambridge University Press, 1997), 19. See also Barth, *Ethnic Groups and Boundaries*, 14: "The cultural features that signal the boundary may change, and the cultural characteristics may change—yet the fact of continuing dichotomization between members and outsiders allows us to specify the nature of continuity."

26. John Hutchinson and Anthony D. Smith, *Ethnicity* (Oxford: Oxford University Press, 1996), 6–7.

no one feature can be determinative of, or a *sine qua non* for, ethnicity. In each case one needs to observe the nature of the boundaries that the group in question relies on to distinguish itself from other groups, sometimes using some of the above features and sometimes others, thus establishing the patterns of similarity and difference that show its identity to persist.[27]

When, then, does a group use one feature as against other features? This brings us to the concept of "situational ethnicity." Its main idea is that particular contexts, especially in times of conflict, dictate a person's "communal identities or loyalties."[28] Ethnic groups will select cultural features in response to challenges so as to maintain their uniqueness. This applies also to the people known as Ἰουδαῖοι, who had to respond to various challenges during the period starting with the destruction of Solomon's temple in 586/587 BCE and the exile that followed and ending with the sacking of the Second Temple by the Romans in 70 CE. Thus, ethnicity, including that of Ἰουδαῖοι, is a construct of culture. Its features are not static but take on a shape as social circumstances call for them. This understanding of ethnicity as malleable throws light on the context surrounding ancient names. Thus, translation of ancient names should avoid primordial constructs. With this understanding of ethnicity, we shall turn shortly to the task of translating the name Ἰουδαῖοι.

1.4.2. Derivation of the Name Ἕλληνες

Since Paul's world was very much influenced by Greek culture, it will be helpful to understand how this group of people who called themselves Ἕλληνες ("Hellenists") derived their name. We shall see in the discussion below that Greeks, like Ἰουδαῖοι, derived their name from their homeland.

I have argued that ethnicity is not a primordial given. A historical instance, however, may contradict this point: the Greeks invented a myth to connect their name Ἕλληνες to a mythic common ancestor, a king called Hellen (Hesiod, *Cat.* frag. 4). This instance, however, should not be con-

---

27. Esler, *Conflict and Identity in Romans*, 44.

28. Jonathan Okamura, "Situational Ethnicity," *ERS* 4 (1981): 452, citing John Paden, "Urban Pluralism, Integration and Adaptation of Communal Identity in Kano, Nigeria," in *Front Tribe to Nation in Africa: Studies in Incorporation Processes*, ed. R. Cohen and J. Middleton (Scranton, NJ: Chandler Publishing, 1970), 242–70.

strued as primordialism at work. Rather, as Hall states, "ethnicity is not a primordial given but is instead repeatedly and actively structured through discursive strategies."[29] That such a discursive strategy is at work is apparent from the surrounding context: the Athenians were attempting to unite all Greeks against their Persian enemies. This strategy, as Hall notes, was frequently used by the Greeks to garner support from other peoples in the face of the threat of powerful enemies.[30]

Granted, along with Esler and a majority of social scientists, that ethnicity is not a primordial given, the problem remains: How does one decide what constitutes an ethnic identity? Esler's suggestion that one should look for features that the ethnic group concerned uses to differentiate itself from other groups does not help since all descriptions are situational.[31] Lauri Thurén suggests that texts must be derhetorized to elicit the underlying system of thoughts.[32] It is beyond the scope of this book to apply this approach to the Hellenistic literature that we are utilizing here. Minimally, however, we can examine texts that contain names of ethnic groups and whose names are not involved in the main rhetoric of the text. Such texts, noted by Esler, are available.

The term Ἕλληνες, by which Greeks call themselves, is derived from the name of their homeland Ἑλλάς (see Herodotus, *Hist.* 7.150–152). It is also significant that in the *Catalogue of Ships* in book 2 of the *Iliad*, those who sailed to Troy are named in reference to places of origin.[33] Thus, Greeks and ancient people derive their names from their origin of habitation. In *Against Apion*, written in the late first century CE by the Judean historian Josephus, peoples including Hellenists, Egyptians, Chaldeans, Phoenicians, Sicilians, Attikoi (people of Attica), Argolikoi (people of Argolis), Athenians, Arcadians, Babylonians, Galileans, Romans, Ethiopians, Indians, and Cretans are each referred to by the territory they occupy (cf. Acts 2:9–11).[34] The people who call themselves Ἰουδαῖοι do likewise.[35]

---

29. Hall, *Ethnic Identity in Greek Antiquity*, 41.
30. Ibid., 36–38.
31. Esler, *Conflict and Identity in Romans*, 44.
32. Thurén, *Derhetorizing Paul*, 28.
33. Esler, *Conflict and Identity in Romans*, 59.
34. Ibid.
35. Ibid., 63–68.

1.4.3. Derivation of the Name Ἰουδαῖοι

Hecataeus of Abdera describes Ἰουδαῖοι as a people who left Egypt and settled in Ἰουδαῖα ("Judea" [Diodorus, *Bib. hist.* 40.3]). Clearchus of Soli states that the name Ἰουδαῖοι is derived from Ἰουδαῖα, the place they inhabit (Josephus, *Ag. Ap.*1.179). Other Judeans also forged a link between the name and the place Ἰουδαῖα in which they inhabited. An example is found in the *Jewish Antiquities*. Esler observes that Ἐβραῖοι ("Hebrews") is the name used to describe the people during the patriarchal and Egyptian period, while the name Ἰσραηλίτης ("Israelite") is used to describe them during the Egyptian period. Starting from the time when Cyrus permitted them to return to Ἰουδαῖα, they are called by the designation Ἰουδαῖοι on most occasions (*Ant.* 11, passim). Furthermore, the name Ἰουδαῖοι is also often linked to the temple in Jerusalem. For example, Philo mentions that the Ἰουδαῖοι regarded their adopted country as their πατρίς ("fatherland"), whereas they deemed "the holy city where stands the temple of the Most High to be their mother city [μητρόπολις]" (*Legat.* 281 [Colson, LCL]). Thus, inherent in the name Ἰουδαῖοι is a strong geographical dimension. In view of the above discussion, the name Ἰουδαῖοι will be translated as Judeans, as opposed to the usual Jews.

Scholars who object to translating Ἰουδαῖοι as Judeans include Shaye J. D. Cohen, who makes a substantial case and "set the terms for recent debates."[36] His thesis, however, falters on several fronts related to his understanding of ethnicity, as Esler ably shows.[37] I shall not rehearse the details but shall state the salient points. First, Cohen takes a primordial approach over a Barthian one. He defines ethnicity as a belief in a common and distinct origin, especially that of an ancestry. This incorrect understanding has been rejected by the majority of social scientists, including primordialists like Francisco J. Gil-White.[38] Second, he relies on Smith's initial description of what qualifies for ethnic status, which did not include

---

36. Quote from David M. Miller, "Ethnicity, Religion and the Meaning of Ioudaios," 221. See Shaye J. D. Cohen, *The Beginnings of Jewishness: Boundaries, Varieties, Uncertainties* (Berkeley: University of California Press, 1999).

37. For a convincing rebuttal, see Esler, *Conflict and Identity in Romans*, 68–74.

38. Francisco J. Gil-White, "How Thick Is Blood? The Plot Thickens…: If Ethnic Actors Are Primordialists, What Remains of the Circumstantialist/Primordialist Controversy?," *ERS* 22 (1999): 791–92.

a territory.[39] Smith himself later realized his mistake and included "a specific territory" as a feature of ethnicity.[40] Third, Cohen describes "Jewishness" as a religious expression that is independent of kinship, politics, and economics, much like the modern-day understanding of the post-Enlightenment concept of religion. This leads Cohen incorrectly to define ethnicity as being independent of a geographic territory.

Miller thinks, however, that Cohen is right to insist that such a post-Enlightenment concept of religion existed in the ancient world. He cites Cohen's examples that seem to provide evidence for "'conversion' in ancient sources, instances where an individual is described as a *Ioudaios* while being associated with another ethnic group, passages where what we call 'religion' is especially prominent."[41] His refutation, however, has not dealt adequately with Esler or even Smith's revised understanding of ethnicity that understands ethnicity to be associated with a physical territory. Steve Mason also correctly points out that Cohen's example of the conversion of Adiabene's royal family (Josephus, *Ant.* 20.17–96) as an instance of religious conversion fails to take into account the fact that

> the passage in question *brims* with the standard language of *ethnos*, law, and custom, as do Josephus's narratives generally. *Josephus* does not speak of a "religious conversion," but rather of adopting or going over to *foreign laws, customs, and ways*, and that language is precisely what lends the story its force.[42]

Hodge objects to translating Ἰουδαῖοι as Judeans for reasons that I have argued above, even though she did initially prefer the term:

> though "Jew" typically refers to anyone who claims loyalty to the God of Israel or a connection to Judaism, "Judean" refers to someone from the region of Judea.... This double nomenclature stands in contrast to English translations for other ethnic terms such as *Hellēn* or *Aigyptos*. For these we use just one word, "Greek" or "Egyptian," and recognize that

---

39. Anthony D. Smith, *The Ethnic Revival* (Cambridge: Cambridge University Press, 1981).

40. Anthony D. Smith, *The Ethnic Origins of Nations* (Oxford: Blackwell, 1986), 32.

41. David M. Miller, "Ethnicity, Religion and the Meaning of Ioudaios," 222.

42. Steve Mason, "Jews, Judeans, Judaizing, Judaism: Problems of Categorization in Ancient History," *JSJ* 38 (2007): 506, emphasis original.

they stand for various facets of identity, related variously to geography, ancestry, religious practices, and so on.[43]

She also agrees with Esler and Elliott that scholars "should pay close attention to ancient terminology and conceptions of identity ... and whether *Ioudaios* is used by 'insiders' about themselves or by 'outsiders' about others."[44] Hodge, however, changed her position and instead used the transliteration of the Greek, *Ioudaios*.[45] Mason retorts that while this may be a simple solution for academic purposes, it is, however, "of dubious merit in translation projects, and cumbersome in other efforts to make the fruits of scholarship more broadly accessible."[46]

Hodge's change in position is triggered by modern concerns. While agreeing with Elliott's point that the term Jew derives not from the first century but from the third and following centuries, she cautions that many more new terms will have to be invented for traditions that have lasted centuries.[47] Another concern of hers is that the "refusal to use 'Jew' (or *Ioudaios*) to talk about the ancient world ignores the broad cohesion shared by different groups of Jews throughout history."[48] Furthermore, Hodge contends that there is the danger of giving implicit assent to "groups past and present whose explicit goals are to erase Judaism from Christian history."[49] Despite her objections, the above concerns are modern ones that have little or no bearing on how we interpret Paul's rhetoric. The reason is that the immediate real audience was people living in the first century CE. They would hence construe the ethnicity attached with Ἰουδαῖοι like any ancient people: people from the region of Judea. In fact, if Hodge's view that the term Jews should refer to "the broad cohesion shared by different groups of Jews throughout history" is valid, then adopting the term Jews would confuse the rhetoric, since the term Jews would import concerns attached with history beyond the first century CE into a text that belongs to the first century CE.

---

43. Hodge, *If Sons, Then Heirs*, 12.
44. Ibid., 13.
45. Ibid., 15.
46. Mason, "Jews, Judeans, Judaizing, Judaism," 511.
47. Hodge, *If Sons, Then Heirs*, 13.
48. Ibid.
49. Ibid., 14.

2. Romans 4:1: A Question of Fatherhood

As previously mentioned, the rhetorolect used in 4:1 is that of wisdom, as indicated by προπάτωρ ("forefather"), which connotes a household setting. As 4:1 introduces the subject matter of Rom 4, this rhetorolect sets the tone for the entire rhetoric.[50] According to the thirdspace of wisdom rhetorolect, the rhetoric aims to "create people who produce good, righteous action, thought, will, and speech with the aid of God's wisdom."[51] In other words, by means of wisdom rhetorolect, Paul seeks to persuade the implied audience to receive favorably Paul's rhetoric of Rom 4.

The first verse, 4:1, introduces the subject matter of Rom 4 as a whole.[52] Several observations evince this. First, the other five occurrences of τί οὖν ἐροῦμεν in Romans (see 6:1; 7:7; 8:31; 9:14, 30) function in this way.[53] Second, the noun προπάτορα in 4:1 anticipates the discussion of Abraham as father of both Judeans and gentiles in 4:11–22. This makes it reasonable to view 4:1 as introducing the rhetoric of Rom 4. Third, and more importantly, at the conclusion in 4:23–25 of the rhetoric, when Paul applies it to the implied audience, he uses again the first-person plural pronoun. This serves as an appropriate response to the first-person plural verb ἐροῦμεν ("we shall say" [4:1]) that began the rhetoric. This observation suggests that 4:1 introduces the argument of Rom 4 as a whole. I shall now turn to investigate the meaning of 4:1.

---

50. See below.

51. Robbins, *Invention of Christian Discourse*, 110.

52. Contra Moo, who treats 4:2–8 as a response to 4:1 and the other paragraphs as units separate from 4:1–8 (*Epistle to the Romans*, 257–66). Dunn regards Rom 4 as a midrash, with 4:1–2 functioning as an introduction (*Romans 1–8*, 197–98). There he posits that 4:4–8 is an exposition of ἐλογίσθη and 4:9–21 is an exposition of ἐπίστευσεν. This explanation is unconvincing, as it collapses Paul's exposition into an exegesis of secondary details rather than main ideas (see my exegesis). Furthermore, as Moo observes, midrash is a slippery term (*Epistle to the Romans*, 255). For other versions of a midrashic exposition of Rom 4, see Otto Michel, *Der Brief an die Römer* (Göttingen: Vandenhoeck & Ruprecht, 1978), 160. Michel thinks that this might be an pre-Pauline midrash: "Vielleicht war dieser Midrasch ursprünglich selbständig."

53. A similar phrase, τί ἐροῦμεν (3:5), without the connective οὖν, also introduces a short discourse in 3:6–8.

2.1. The Structure of 4:1: What Shall We Say? Have We Found Abraham to Be Our Forefather by His Own Human Efforts?

Romans 4:1, as my discussion below will show, announces the subject matter of Rom 4. A correct translation of this verse is hence important for understanding the rhetoric of this chapter. This book will adopt Stowers's translation: "What shall we say? Have we found Abraham to be our forefather by his own human efforts?"[54] Much of the difficulty in translating 4:1 lies with the relationship of the perfect infinitive εὑρηκέναι ("to have found") to the rest of the sentence. In this section, I shall discuss the two most common translations of 4:1, neither of which is without its difficulties.

2.1.1. Εὑρηκέναι as Introducing Indirect Discourse

The first view construes the infinitive εὑρηκέναι as introducing indirect discourse and the prepositional phrase κατὰ σάρκα ("according to the flesh") as modifying προπάτορα.[55] Romans 4:1 can then be translated as "What then shall we say that Abraham our forefather according to the flesh has found?"[56] The main weakness of this view, as Hays correctly points out, is that the verb εὑρίσκειν ("to find") used with no explicit object finds no precedence in Paul's usage or in the New Testament. The exceptions occur only

> in expressions such as ζητεῖτε καὶ εὑρήσετε (Matt 7:7 = Luke 11:9) or in elliptical constructions where the object is explicitly named in the previous clause (Matt 2:8, 12:43, Acts 11:25–26, etc.). In every case of the latter kind in the NT, εὑρίσκειν is juxtaposed to a verb of seeking in the preceding clause.[57]

---

54. Stowers, *Rereading of Romans*, 242.

55. A variation of this translation construes the prepositional phrase κατὰ σάρκα adverbially as qualifying the infinitive εὑρηκέναι: see Jewett, *Romans*, 304; Peter Stuhlmacher, *Paul's Letter to the Romans: A Commentary* (Louisville: Westminster John Knox, 1994), 71.

56. So most commentators, e.g., Dunn, *Romans 1–8*, 195; Schreiner, *Romans*, 212; Cranfield, *Epistle to the Romans*, 1:225; Käsemann, *Commentary on Romans*, 105.

57. Hays, "Have We Found Abraham," 80. Most commentators similarly acknowledge the weakness; see, e.g., Jewett, *Romans*, 307; Moo, *Epistle to the Romans*, 259; Cranfield, *Epistle to the Romans*, 1:227.

The conditions for 4:1 to be considered an exception as described above clearly are not present. This perhaps explains why the RSV accepts the reading of Codex Vaticanus in dropping the infinitive εὑρηκέναι out of the text so that 4:1 reads: "What then shall we say about Abraham, our forefather according to the flesh?"[58] Most commentators, however, agree that εὑρηκέναι is part of the original text of 4:1.[59]

2.1.2. The Referent of "We" in 4:1

Before ascertaining the structure of 4:1, the referent of "we" needs to be clarified. Several observations help us ascertain the referent of "we" in 4:1. First, when Paul describes Abraham as τὸν προπάτορα ἡμῶν ("our forefather"), προπάτωρ refers to Abraham as the father of Judeans.[60] Except for the occurrences of "Abraham" in the Letter to the Galatians, other occurrences of this name outside Rom 4 (Rom 9:7; 11:1; 2 Cor 11:22 refer to Abraham as the ancestor of Judeans (σπέρμα Ἀβραάμ; "Abraham's descendant"). As for the repeated emphasis in Galatians of Abraham as father of gentiles, this reading must be taken with caution, as Paul was aggressively combating Judean Christians who were coercing gentiles into engaging in Judean ethnic practices of circumcision and the law to enjoy the benefits of the savior. It is hence loaded with much emotionally charged rhetoric.[61] Second, "Abraham is naturally appealed to as father of the [Judean] race, in view of his place within God's salvation-history (Genesis 12–24)."[62] He is accorded first place in his claim as father.[63] Josephus also refers to

---

58. Dunn thinks that the absence of εὑρηκέναι from B "attests the sense of various copyists that the verb was being used somewhat awkwardly here" (*Romans 1–8*, 196).

59. See the discussion of the textual issues in Bruce M. Metzger, *A Textual Commentary On The Greek New Testament*, 2nd ed. (Stuttgart: Deutsche Bibelgesellschaft, 1994), 450; Jewett, *Romans*, 304.

60. Andrew T. Lincoln, "The Stories of Predecessors and Inheritors in Galatians and Romans," in *Narrative Dynamics in Paul*, ed. Bruce W. Longenecker (Louisville: Westminster John Knox, 2002), 185.

61. Thurén cautions interpreters that "many of the difficulties in modern exegetical literature also concerning Paul and the law may be attributed to an unnatural, static view of the Pauline letters as texts.... [Paul] attempts to arouse his addressees' awareness of the theoretical, theological difference, and does so by dramatizing rhetoric" (*Derhetorizing Paul*, 56–57, 63).

62. Dunn, *Romans 1–8*, 199.

63. Gottlob Schrenk, "πατήρ κτλ," *TDNT* 6:697.

Abraham as προπάτωρ (*War* 5.380). Thus, to think of Abraham as being the father of Judeans is only natural for an implied audience who hears this name mentioned for *the first time* in Romans. Furthermore, not even proselytes could address Abraham as "our father." Only ethnic Judeans had this prerogative. More importantly, Paul describes Abraham as the father of Judean and gentile Christians at 4:12 only after a long-drawn debate with the Judean interlocutor. This shows that at 4:1, the implied Judean audience could not have agreed to Paul construing Abraham's fatherhood as including gentile descendants.[64] Third, circumcision is closely associated with Abraham (Rom 4:10–12; Gen 17:9–14). The numerous previous associations of circumcision with Judeans (2:25, 26, 27, 28, 29; 3:1, 30) and the juxtaposition of circumcision with uncircumcision (2:25, 26, 27; 3:30) would tend to imprint on the minds of the implied audience that only the circumcised are Abraham's descendants. Hence, to construe Abraham as the father of both Judean and gentile Christians at an early stage (4:1) of the rhetoric is a non sequitur. It would, however, be reasonable to address Abraham as the father of gentiles after the reconfiguration of Abraham's identity in Rom 4, but not before the reconfiguration. The argument of Rom 4 also bears out my point: Abraham as the father of both Judean and gentile Christians is only made explicit at 4:11–12, that is, after Paul redefines the fatherhood of Abraham through the rhetoric of 4:9–12.

Second, regarding the "we" in 4:1, Dunn similarly remarks that

> when Paul speaks of "*our* forefather" (cf. 9:10—"Isaac our father"), it is not entirely clear whether he was thinking in exclusively Jewish terms (having resumed his dialogue with the Jewish interlocutor of the earlier diatribe—2:1ff.), or intended to include Gentiles as well.... Such transitions in his thought are fairly typical (e.g., Gal 3:10–14; 4:1–5) and indicate the extent to which he both still thought of himself as a Jew and still regarded the debate in which he was involved as intra-Jewish.[65]

---

64. While Longenecker recognizes that addressing Abraham as "our father" is a prerogative of Judeans (*Epistle to the Romans*, 490), he is too quick to extend this right at 4:1 to gentiles who "walk in the footsteps of the faith that our father Abraham had before he was circumcised" (4:12). Similarly, Moo, *Epistle to the Romans*, 259; Jewett, *Romans*, 307.

65. Dunn, *Romans 1–8*, 199. Similarly, Stowers, *Rereading of Romans*, 31: "In 4:1, Paul presents himself in a debate with a Jewish opponent and identifies himself with him as a Jew."

I have argued above that in 4:1 Abraham should be conceived as being the forefather of only Judeans. In light of this, here in 4:1 the "we" that includes both Paul the implied speaker and the Judean interlocutor should indicate, as Dunn suggests, that Paul is involved in an intra-Judean debate. Paul, the implied speaker, takes on a double identity. On the one hand, he articulates the question of the Judean interlocutor. On the other hand, he also refutes the Judean interlocutor. This construal of the "we" in 4:1 makes sense out of the other first-person plural pronouns in 4:23–25. In these closing verses, Paul now dissociates himself from the Judean interlocutor and aligns himself with the implied audience comprising Judean and gentile Christians. He then applies the implications of Rom 4 to both of these groups. Stowers's view is similar to mine, except for the fact that he regards the implied audience as wholly gentile. He correctly identifies the "we" in 4:1 as comprising Paul and the Judean interlocutor. He construes it as a "dialogical 'we' " where Paul is in dialogue with the Judean interlocutor.[66] The identity of this "we," however, changes in 4:23–25:

> Beginning at 4:23, a new element enters the discourse. For the first time since the prescript (1:1–15), the epistolary audience comes explicitly into view. The "we" here is clearly "me, Paul" and "you gentile believers in Rome." The Jewish teacher [the Judean interlocutor] has faded from view.[67]

2.1.3. Unexpressed We as Accusative of εὑρηκέναι

Hays translates 4:1 as: "What shall we say? Have we found Abraham (to be) our forefather according to the flesh?"[68] This book will adopt this trans-

---

66. Stowers, *Rereading of Romans*, 233–34, 236.

67. Ibid., 247; see also 232–33, where Stowers argues (against Hays, "Have We Found Abraham," 79 n. 13) that ancient readers read texts that contained no punctuation, no word division, and nothing to indicate change of speakers. This, however, did not pose a problem to them, as they "read aloud and had ears well trained for the rhythm, rhetoric, and sense of their language." Similarly, Joshua W. Jipp, "Rereading the Story of Abraham, Isaac, and 'Us' in Romans 4," *JSNT* 32 (2009): 229.

68. Hays, "Have We Found Abraham," following the lead of Theodor Zahn, *Der Brief des Paulus an die Römer* (Leipzig: Deichert, 1910), 215. This view is later defended by Cranford, "Abraham in Romans 4." It is also adopted by Maria Neubrand, *Abraham, Vater von Juden und Nichtjuden: Eine exegetische Studie zu Röm 4*, FB 85 (Würzburg: Echter, 1997), 184; J. R. Daniel Kirk, *Unlocking Romans: Resurrection and*

lation with a slight modification: the prepositional phrase κατὰ σάρκα ("according to the flesh") is translated as "by his own human efforts" to yield the translation "What shall we say? Have we found Abraham to be our forefather by his own human efforts?" I shall rehearse briefly the pertinent points of Hays's essay.[69]

2.1.3.1. Τί οὖν ἐροῦμεν as a Complete Sentence and Rhetorical Question
Several scholars correctly recognize the expression τί οὖν ἐροῦμεν ("Therefore, what shall we say?") as a rhetorical question.[70] This expression (apart from 4:1, which is under investigation) occurs only in Romans (6:1; 7:7; 8:31; 9:14, 30–31). The partial expression without the inferential οὖν occurs only in 3:5. Hays makes several pertinent observations regarding the use of the expression τί οὖν ἐροῦμεν.

First, except for 8:31, τί οὖν ἐροῦμεν is a complete sentence. Second, each of these six references (3:5; 6:1; 7:7; 8:31; 9:14; 9:30–31) comprises a pair of questions: the first in each pair is the expression τί ἐροῦμεν. In all six occurrences of τί ἐροῦμεν (not counting 4:1 but including 3:5), this formulation (the first of the pair of rhetorical questions) introduces the second of the pair of rhetorical questions. Third, in these six occurrences of τί ἐροῦμεν, the second of the pair of rhetorical questions "articulates an inference which might be drawn from the foregoing discussion."[71] Fourth, in four of the six references (3:5; 6:1; 7:7; 9:14), the inference is a false one.[72] In

---

the *Justification of God* (Grand Rapids: Eerdmans, 2008), 60; Stephen L. Young, "Paul's Ethnic Discourse on 'Faith': Christ's Faithfulness and Gentile Access to the Judean God in Romans 3:21–5:1," *HTR* 108 (2015): 41. Also, for a slight modification of Hays's translation, see N. T. Wright, *The Kingdom New Testament: A Contemporary Translation of the New Testament* (New York: HarperOne, 2011), 316; cf. a later modification in Richard B. Hays, *The Conversion of the Imagination: Paul as Interpreter of Israel's Scripture* (Grand Rapids: Eerdmans, 2005), 61–84. More recently, see Jipp, "Rereading the Story," 227. Also, with a slight modification, Stowers, *Rereading of Romans*, 242: "What shall we say? Have we found Abraham to be our forefather by his own human efforts?"

69. I.e., Hays, "Have We Found Abraham."

70. Scholars who recognize τί οὖν ἐροῦμεν as a rhetorical question include Hays, who calls it a "rhetorical formulation/question" ("Have We Found Abraham," 78), Jewett, who calls it a "rhetorical question" (*Romans*, 307), and N. T. Wright, "Paul and the Patriarch: The Role of Abraham in Romans 4," *JSNT* 35 (2013): 226–29.

71. Hays, "Have We Found Abraham," 79.

72. Ibid.

other words, the first (τί ἐροῦμεν) of the pair of rhetorical questions in these four cases (3:5; 6:1; 7:7; 9:14), whose specific content is being explicated by the second of the pair of rhetorical questions, contains a false inference. That this inference is false is also obvious from the question that is posed. For instance, the question τί οὖν ἐροῦμεν; ἐπιμένωμεν τῇ ἁμαρτίᾳ, ἵνα ἡ χάρις πλεονάσῃ ("Therefore, what shall we say? Shall we remain in sin in order that favor may abound?") clearly expects to be negated (6:1). Jewett, commenting on the way in which the context requires a negative response from the implied audience in 4:1, notes that "in view of the preceding pericope that proves that no one is made righteous, that is, acceptable to God by 'works of the law,' such a question requires a negative response from Paul's implied audience."[73] Hays makes the same point when he says that "Paul states in the form of a rhetorical question a view which is opposed to his own."[74] This view represents that of one part of the implied audience, the Judean Christians, who are listening to the debate between Paul and the Judean interlocutor. Similarly, N. T. Wright and Robert Jewett agree that Paul poses the rhetorical question in 4:1 "expecting the answer 'no'" from the implied audience.[75]

What is happening in 4:1 is this: Paul the implied speaker is involved in an intra-Judean debate. He voices the question posed by his fellow Judean, a Judean interlocutor. Whether or not this Judean interlocutor is a Christian has no bearing on the argument. He simply functions as someone who articulates the position of a Judean.[76] At the same time, Paul, the implied speaker, also expects the implied audience (Judean and gentile

---

73. Jewett, *Romans*, 308.

74. Hays, "Have We Found Abraham," 79, n. 13.

75. Quote from Wright, "Paul and the Patriarch," 226–27; see also Jewett, *Romans*, 308. Cf. Stowers, who observes that in Arrian's diatribes of Epictetus, "Epictetus emphasizes the use of absurd or unthinkable false propositions or conclusions stated as questions that the interlocutor must strongly reject, that bring to light contradictions in his beliefs, and that lead him to the right conclusion" (*Rereading of Romans*, 136). Such a mode of discourse is at work in 4:1 (see *Rereading of Romans*, 236). Kirk comments that "this rhetorical question [4:1], like so many others in Romans, is intended to be answered in the negative" (*Unlocking Romans*, 60).

76. See Stowers, *Rereading of Romans*, 163: "When a full-scale dialogue occurs and not just occasional objections from an interlocutor, the speaker or writer usually characterizes the imaginary person as a certain type either corresponding to a specific vice or sometimes belonging to a school of thought."

Christians), who are listening to the debate between Paul and the Judean interlocutor, to negate the question, that is, to reply with a "no."[77]

With regard to Hay's fourth observation, it must be emphasized that four rhetorical questions (3:5; 6:1; 7:7; 9:14) expect the implied audience to respond with an immediate "no." All six pairs of the rhetorical questions (3:5; 6:1; 7:7; 8:31; 9:14; 9:30–31) can be immediately answered by the implied audience even without further argumentation. The reason is, as Hays says in his third observation, "the second rhetorical question articulates an inference which might be drawn from the foregoing discussion."[78] In other words, every occurrence (apart from 4:1, which is under investigation) containing the expression τί οὖν ἐροῦμεν (including 3:5, which leaves out οὖν) has in it an implicit but clear statement.

The above observations lead Hays to draw several conclusions. First, that the expression τί οὖν ἐροῦμεν in 4:1 is a complete sentence is not unreasonable. This is consistent with how four out of the total of five occurrences of τί οὖν ἐροῦμεν are used. Romans 4:1 would thus be punctuated as τί οὖν ἐροῦμεν; εὑρηκέναι Ἀβραὰμ τὸν προπάτορα ἡμῶν κατὰ σάρκα; Second, all five occurrences that contain the expression τί οὖν ἐροῦμεν ("Therefore, what shall we say?") in Romans are rhetorical questions. In other words, they are not real questions but statements framed in the form of a question. That being the case, we can reasonably expect the question of 4:1 to function likewise. Thus, in 4:1, Paul the implied speaker poses a (rhetorical) question

---

77. The situation I describe coheres with Alain Gignac, "The Enunciative Device of Romans 1:18–4:25: A Succession of Discourses Attempting to Express the Multiple Dimensions of God's Justice," *CBQ* 77 (2015): 487. Using the methodology of Émile Benveniste (*Problems in General Linguistics*, trans. Mary Elizabeth Meek [Coral Gables: University of Miami Press, 1971]), Gignac views the diatribal dialogues in 1:18–4:25 as an enunciation that is "a speech-act where an *I* or a *we* situated 'here and now' speaks with a *you* (singular or plural) about a third party that can be characterized by the third grammatical person (also singular or plural)" (emphasis original). He regards the "we" in 4:1 as comprising Paul and the Judean interlocutor: "The (secondary) enunciation splits into a feverish dialogue between *I* and its virtual interlocutor.... [L]ike a ventriloquist, the *I* of the primary enunciation lends its voice to objections that he is quick to refute (diatribe). The enunciation, in the form of questions and answers, is in the *we*."

78. Hays, "Have We Found Abraham," 79. See also the section entitled, "God of the Jews only? Rom 4:1 in relation to the foregoing argument" (pp. 83–89), where Hays shows that the argument of Rom 3 would elicit from the implied audience a response of "no" to the second rhetorical question of 4:1 regarding Abraham's fatherhood.

on behalf of the Judean interlocutor. At the same time Paul, the implied speaker also expects his implied audience (Judean and gentile Christians) to respond negatively. That this negation is anticipated is also corroborated by the retort in 4:2: Abraham has no reason to boast before God. This also means that 4:1 is making a statement that introduces the argument of Rom 4 rather than asking a question requiring deliberation.[79]

2.1.3.2. Assuming an Unexpressed We

Despite the attractiveness of this second view, where Hays assumes an unexpressed we, most scholars reject this translation, mainly on the grounds that it assumes an unexpressed first-person plural supplied by ἐροῦμεν.[80] This construction, however, is common in classical Greek,

> where the complement of verbs (perceiving,) believing, (showing,) and saying which indicate the content of the conception or communication, is formed to a great extent by the infinitive. If the subject of the infinitive is the same as that of the governing verb, it is not expressed.[81]

Furthermore, Wright defends the implicit we by arguing, on the basis of 4:16, that this verse—διὰ τοῦτο ἐκ πίστεως ["for this reason of trust"], ἵνα κατὰ χάριν ["so that according to favor"], εἰς τὸ εἶναι βεβαίαν τὴν ἐπαγγελίαν παντὶ τῷ σπέρματι ["in order that the promise certain to all the descendants"]—also lacks finite verbs and subjects.[82]

2.1.3.3. Assuming an Unexpressed εἶναι

Hays supplies an unexpressed εἶναι ("to be") so that 4:1 reads "What shall we say? Have we found Abraham (to be) our forefather?" The construction is legitimate, as is borne out by Paul's usage elsewhere (e.g., 1 Cor 4:2; 15:15; 2 Cor 5:3; 9:4; 12:20; Gal 2:17) where the unexpressed εἶναι connects

---

79. He labels Paul's "Abraham is our forefather according to the flesh" the proposition in the rhetoric of Rom 4 (pp. 83, 86).

80. E.g., Dunn, *Romans 1–8*, 199; Tobin, "What Shall We Say Abraham Found," 443; Jewett, *Romans*, 307.

81. BDF §396; Hays, "Have We Found Abraham," 81.

82. Wright, "Paul and the Patriarch," 228; contra Jan Lambrecht, who in his critique of Wright's article, brushes off in one paragraph Wright's (and Hay's) proposed translation without engaging in any way his evidence. See Lambrecht, "Romans 4: A Critique of N. T. Wright," *JSNT* 36 (2013): 192–93.

the infinitive εὑρίσκειν and a predicate nominative or adjective to yield the expression "to find (someone) to be (something)."[83]

2.1.3.4. Function and Meaning of κατὰ σάρκα

Another grammatical difficulty concerns the relationship of the prepositional phrase κατὰ σάρκα (according to the flesh) to the rest of the sentence. Scholars agree that this expression carries a pejorative sense.[84] This phrase can function adverbially and qualify the infinitive εὑρηκέναι ("to have found") or adjectivally and qualify the noun προπάτορα ("forefather").[85]

Construing the prepositional phrase κατὰ σάρκα as adverbial and translating it as "fleshy capacities" or "human efforts" yields the translation "Have we found according to human efforts ...?"[86] The weakness of this translation is that it does not provide a cogent link to 4:2, which is not about "we" but about Abraham being made righteous by deeds of the Mosaic law. Moo holds to the latter position on the grounds that Abraham's paternity in the flesh (4:1) prepares for Paul's later argument of Abraham's spiritual paternity of all believers.[87] Stowers correctly refutes this position:

> That idea [Abraham is forefather by virtue of physical descent from him], however, is entirely unmotivated. The teacher does not advocate that only those born of Jewish blood can be righteous. He advocates attempting to reform non-Jews. Rather, the issue is whether gentiles can

---

83. Hays, "Have We Found Abraham," 82.

84. Jewett, *Romans*, 308; Moo, *Epistle to the Romans*, 260; Schreiner, *Romans*, 214. Michel thinks that by "unserem Ahnherrn nach dem Fleisch," Paul is thinking of Abraham as "durch den Gehorsam gegen das Gesetz gerecht geworden" (*Der Brief an die Römer*, 161–62). Contra Cranfield, who thinks that the prepositional phrase is to contrast Abraham as having children by a different way (*Epistle to the Romans*, 1:427). This contrast, however, does not escape a pejorative sense as it contrasts with faith, and faith in Rom 4 contrasts with the works of the Mosaic law, in particular, circumcision.

85. The (grammatically incorrect) translation "to have found" highlights the perfect tense of the Greek perfect infinitive.

86. Scholars who construe the prepositional phrase κατὰ σάρκα adverbially include Jewett, *Romans*, 308; Stowers, *Rereading of Romans*, 242. Luz translates 4:1 as: "Hat es unser Vorvater Abraham nach dem Fleische gefunden?" (*Das Geschichtsverständnis des Paulus*, 174). For "fleshy capacities," see Jewett, *Romans*, 308. For "human efforts," see Stowers, *Rereading of Romans*, 242.

87. Moo, *Epistle to the Romans*, 259–60. In a similar vein, Dunn thinks this acts as a "foil" (*Romans 1–8*, 199).

enter into a right relation with God by doing works of the law. "Works of the law" is explicitly the issue in 3:20, 21, 21–28; 4:2, 4–6.[88]

Stowers also construes the prepositional phrase κατὰ σάρκα as qualifying προπάτορα, except that he translates κατὰ σάρκα as "human efforts." This yields the translation adopted in this book: "What shall we say? Have we found Abraham to be our forefather by his own human efforts?"[89]

2.2. The Ideological Texture of 4:1

Underlying this rhetorical question in 4:1 is the social and cultural inter-texture of patrilineal descent in which descendants bear resemblance to their ancestor(s).[90] This social and cultural intertexture can mobilize ideological power in the following ways. If the Judean interlocutor who poses the question in 4:1 has a case that Abraham gained righteousness by deeds of the Mosaic law, then Judeans as descendants of Abraham should also seek righteousness by producing deeds of the Mosaic law.[91] On the other hand, if Paul is right that Abraham did not gain righteousness by observing the Mosaic law but by trusting God, then Judeans and gentiles should do likewise. Thus, in order to refute the interlocutor, Paul needs to reconfigure the nature of Abraham's fatherhood through the rhetoric of Rom 4. This understanding is in line with Campbell's observation:

> Abraham is thus brought into the picture not merely as an example of a believing individual but as the recipient of that grace, promises, etc. which were to make him the first of the faithful, the promise-bearer who as such occupied a unique role in the history of Israel. In Romans the issue concerns Abraham's faith but much more—who are the children of God and how is Israel constituted.[92]

---

88. Stowers, *Rereading of Romans*, 242.

89. Ibid.

90. See below, chapter 4, §3.2, "Patrilineal Descent."

91. See above, chapter 3, §2.1.2, "The Referent of 'We' in 4:1."

92. William S. Campbell, *Paul and the Creation of Christian Identity* (London: T&T Clark, 2008), 63. This does not mean, however, that gentiles become part of Israel. Rather, "Paul does not argue for a single family of Abraham's descendants but for a plurality of families." See William S. Campbell, "Covenant Theology and Participation in Christ: Pauline Perspectives on Transformation," in *Paul and Judaism: Crosscurrents in Pauline Exegesis and the Study of Jewish-Christian Relations*, ed. Reimund

Paul seeks to show that the nature of Abraham's fatherhood was such that he did not gain righteousness by performing the deeds of the Mosaic law but by trust. In this way the social and cultural intertexture of patrilineal descent mobilizes ideological power to persuade the implied audience that they too should imitate Abraham's trust in God. In 4:1, Paul introduces a rhetoric that starts the process of inscribing the nature of the fatherhood of Abraham so as to include gentile Christians as descendants of Abraham. The ideological texture that mobilizes power to persuade resides, first, in the word προπάτωρ and, second, in the name Ἀβραάμ.

2.2.1. Προπάτωρ: Fictive Kinship

Underlying the term προπάτωρ is the social and cultural texture of fictive kinship. This fictive kinship can be constructed by means of rhetoric. Roman families engaged in such a practice of crafting their genealogies when they linked current family members to noble ancestors.[93] Julius Caesar, for instance, linked himself to Venus so as to raise his status to that of a ruler worthy of Rome (Suetonius, *Jul.* 6.1).[94] This social intertexture of fictive kinship assumes that genealogies are malleable and do not need to be a factor of mere physical descent. Instead, the relationship can be attained via mind, soul, or spirit. This is evident in philosophical schools and other schools of learning. For instance, in *De virtutibus*, Philo contends that the factor that decides a noble birth (εὐγένεια) is the gathering of virtues. Conversely, if a person is born physically of noble parents but turns out to be wicked, he is denied that noble birth (εὐγένεια [*Virt.* 189–200 (Colson, LCL)]). Philo continues by saying, τὸ συγγενὲς οὐχ αἵματι μετρεῖται μόνον, πρυτανευούσης ἀληθείας, ἀλλὰ πράξεων ὁμοιότητι ("Kinship is not measured by blood alone, where truth presides, but by a similarity of deeds" [*Virt.* 195 (Colson, LCL)]). Plutarch also cites Alexander, who, in implementing Zeno's "well-ordered and philosophic commonwealth," said that "all good

---

Bieringer and Didier Pollefeyt, LNTS 463 [London: Bloomsbury, 2012], 53; cf. Beker, *Paul the Apostle*, 96–99.

93. Numerous important insights on this subject are drawn from Hodge, *If Sons, Then Heirs*, 19–42.

94. "On her mother's side, my aunt was sprung from kings, and on her father's connected with immortal gods. For the Marcii Reges (that was her mother's name) descend from Ancus Marcius, and the Iulii, to whom my family belongs, descend from Venus" (*Jul.* 6.1 [Rolfe, LCL]).

men are kin [συγγενεῖς] …; the distinguishing mark of being Greek should be virtue, and that of being a barbarian iniquity" (*Alex.* 329 [Perrin, LCL]). Medical schools also describe the relationship between teacher and student as that of father and son. For instance, the medical student takes the Hippocratic oath and promises "to hold my teacher in this art equal to my own parents [γενέτῃσιν ἐμοῖς]" (Hippocrates, *Jusj.* 5–10 [Jones, LCL]).

In 4:1, Paul, by introducing the term προπάτωρ, signals the start of a rhetoric that constructs a myth of origins for gentile Christians to link Judean and gentile Christians to Abraham as a shared forefather.[95] Two observations regarding how ideological power is mobilized when constructing a myth of origins are instructive.[96] First, Burton L. Mack comments that "the alreadiness of social arrangements is accounted for in terms of origin stories in which precedence is established by patriarchs, powers, and authorities not accessible for questioning."[97] In other words, this myth of origins has ideological power because its authority is derived from "authorities not accessible for questioning," and hence is divine and "natural."[98]

Second, kinship and ethnicity are considered "natural" categories as members within the group often share blood ties. At the same time, these two categories are malleable, allowing the narrator to modify them to suit his rhetorical purpose.[99] Such a conception may seem contradictory. Gerd Baumann alleviates the apparent tension by construing ethnic identities as resulting from essentialist (the counterpart of kinship as being natural) and processual (the counterpart of kinship as being malleable) discourses. He observes that "those who preach an essentialist theory of culture rely upon the accuracy of the processual theory of culture."[100] In other words, what is narrated is essentialist in content but the act of articulating the

---

95. Floyd V. Filson postulates that the house church was critical to the early church's development. The fictive kinship construction ties in with how Christians conceived of their relationship with one another. See Filson, "The Significance of the Early House Churches," *JBL* 58 (1939): 105–12.

96. So Bruce Lincoln, who comments that myth is "ideology in narrative form." See Lincoln, *Theorizing Myth: Narrative, Ideology, and Scholarship* (Chicago: University of Chicago Press, 1999), 207.

97. Burton L. Mack, *The Christian Myth: Origins, Logic, and Legacy* (New York: Continuum, 2001), 11.

98. Hodge, *If Sons, Then Heirs*, 5–6.

99. Ibid., 21.

100. Gerd Baumann, *The Multicultural Riddle: Rethinking National, Ethnic, and Religious Identities* (London: Routledge, 1999), 91.

content is processual.[101] This essentialist and processual nature of ethnic identity also entails the social and cultural intertexture that descendants are present in seminal form in their ancestor.[102]

The term προπάτωρ is also a cultural intertextural reference. Paul uses it to mobilize ideological power by leveraging the authority of Abraham in two ways. First, he draws on the authority of a father whose instructions are to be obeyed. For instance, Robbins observes that Mark 10:17–22 emphasizes "doing what your mother and father have taught you."[103] Such a mindset is based probably on Deut 6:6–7.[104] It is also important to bear in mind that in a patriarchal society like Israel, despite the fact that both parents educate a child in the laws of Yahweh, the father is the one who holds the responsibility of imparting such knowledge to his child. Deuteronomy 6:6–9 is instructive. After Moses rehearses the Decalogue to the Israelites and Yahweh responds, Moses exhorts them to obedience in Deut 6:1–5. Moses follows up his exhortation with a charge in Deut 6:6–9 to ensure that following generations of Israelites observe the law of Yahweh. The father is responsible for teaching his children the laws, as intimated by the second-person masculine singular verbs (ושננתם, ודברת, etc.). Furthermore, the obedience of a child to his father and mother is so mandatory that any child who refuses to heed the discipline of his parents is to be stoned to death publicly so as to serve as a warning to the rest of Israel (Deut 21:18–21). This firstspace of a father who imparts wisdom, when blended with God as the progenitor of wisdom, would cause the implied audience to view Abraham as a source of wisdom coming from God, who is the authoritative source of wisdom.

2.2.2. Ἀβραάμ: One Who Observes the Mosaic Law

The name Ἀβραάμ is another reference in the cultural intertexture.[105] Ἀβραάμ (Abraham) is a well-known personage in Judean culture, and

---

101. Ibid.; see also Hodge, *If Sons, Then Heirs*, 21.

102. See below, chapter 4, §3.2, "Patrilineal Descent."

103. Robbins, *The Invention of Christian Discourse*, 152.

104. See William Loader, *The Septuagint, Sexuality, and the New Testament: Case Studies on the Impact of the LXX in Philo and the New Testament* (Grand Rapids: Eerdmans, 2004), 5–9, 15–19. Loader demonstrates the influence of the book of Deuteronomy on Judean and Christian writings.

105. Robbins, *Tapestry of Early Christian Discourse*, 110.

this name presupposes stories in the Judean literature contemporaneous with Paul's time. The significance invoked by the name Ἀβραάμ can
be gleaned from the general perception of the meanings attached to this
name in Judean extrabiblical literature. Nancy Calvert-Koyzis analyzed
the significance of Abraham traditions for early Judaism and Christianity
in the period from 168 BCE to 100 CE. In her assessment, two traditions
frequently occur: that Abraham "rejected idolatry for faith in the one God
and that he was obedient to God especially through observance of the law."[106]
After reading each Judean text in light of its background, she comes to the
following conclusions. The book of Jubilees portrays Abraham as a central
transmitter of the covenant who was obedient to the Mosaic law before it
was even given. He was the first to reject idolatry and embrace monotheism (Jub. 11.16–17).[107] The works of Philo depict Abraham as following
the natural law that is the basis of the Mosaic law (*Abr.* 1.130).[108] In the
Antiquities of Josephus, Abraham obeys the Judean law. For example, in
regard to circumcision and in marriage, he chose to marry a niece rather
than a half-sister (*Ant.* 2.11).[109] Abraham rejects idolatry and worships the
one God as emphasized in the Apocalypse of Abraham (e.g., Apoc. Ab.
2.1–9; 4.3; 6.6–7; 7.7–12).[110] Relevant to the discussion in Rom 4 about
Abraham's trust in God and matters regarding the law, these Judean texts
portray Abraham as one who is faithful to the one God and who obeys the
Mosaic law. In view of the pride of place that Judaism assigns to Abraham
as someone who worships the one God and who keeps the Mosaic law,
Paul leverages Abraham's authority to begin his rhetoric.

The name Ἀβραάμ also contains a social and cultural texture. Esler
employs social-identity theory and self-categorization theory to argue
that Abraham serves as a prototype of common identity.[111] Social-identity
theory is built upon the observation that members within a group tend to

---

106. Calvert-Koyzis, *Paul, Monotheism and the People of God*, 4.

107. Ibid., 16–17.

108. Ibid., 39.

109. Ibid., 68.

110. Ibid., 71–84.

111. Esler, *Conflict and Identity in Romans*, 171–84. Social-identity theory was
first developed by Henri Tajfel and other collaborators, including John C. Turner. See
Henri Tajfel, ed., *Differentiation between Social Groups: Studies in the Social Psychology
of Intergroup Relations* (London: Academic Press, 1978). John C. Turner led the way in
developing self-categorization theory. See Turner, ed., *Rediscovering the Social Group:
A Self-Categorization Theory* (Oxford: Blackwell, 1987).

favor themselves over members of other groups. This identity is a person's self-concept derived from his or her membership in a group and concerned with how a group differentiates itself from another group. Its focus is thus on intergroup relationships. Another theory underlying Esler's approach is self-categorization theory, which is concerned with how a person's self-concept is formulated within a group. Its focus is on intragroup relationships. Self-categorization theory distinguishes between social identity (a person's self-concept with respect to a social group) and personal identity (a person's self-concept with respect to one's personal or idiosyncratic attributes). In this way, personal characteristics or characteristics derived from the group may dominate in different situations. Furthermore, individuals within a group may craft their identities by means of argument, negotiation, and persuasion.[112] The formulation of how such processes lead to a person's self-concept is useful for investigating how the two subgroups of Judean Christians and gentile Christians who belonged to a larger group, the Christian community in Rome, negotiated their identities.

Social-identity theory also identifies three approaches to alleviating conflicts between groups, namely recategorization, decategorization, and crossed categorization. In the case of the situation of conflict between Judean and gentile Christians at Rome, Esler deploys recategorization, which involves "maintaining a common superordinate identity while simultaneously maintaining the salience of subgroup identities…. [This] would be particularly effective because it permits the benefits of a common ingroup identity to operate without arousing countervailing motivations to achieve positive distinctiveness."[113] In Rom 4, Abraham is the superordinate identity that Paul uses to reconcile the two dissenting groups, Judean and gentile Christians.

2.3. Conclusion

I propose that 4:1 should be translated as "What shall we say? Have we found Abraham to be our forefather by his own human efforts?" Paul the

---

112. S. Alexander Haslam et al., "The Group as the Basis for Emergent Stereotype Consensus," *ERSP* 8 (1998): 203–9.

113. Samuel L. Gaertner et al., "The Common Ingroup Identity Model for Reducing Intergroup Bias: Progress and Challenges," in *Social Identity Processes: Trends in Theory and Research*, ed. Dora Capozza and Rupert Brown (Thousand Oaks, CA: Sage, 2000), 143.

implied speaker engages in an intra-Judean debate (which explains the use of "we" in 4:1) with an imaginary Judean interlocutor. Paul, the implied speaker and a Judean, spells out the problem to be investigated in the form of a rhetorical question. He articulates the question of the Judean interlocutor. At the same time, Paul the speaker also expects the implied audience (Judean and gentile Christians) to negate the question of the Judean interlocutor. In essence, this question is asking (in a rhetorical manner) if Judeans are able to say (λέγειν) or argue the case that Abraham becomes their forefather by his own human efforts. Specifically, this refers to Abraham performing deeds of the Mosaic law that in turn validate Judean Christians doing likewise. Such a rhetorical question anticipates a strong negative reply (4:2). Hence, this introduction prepares the implied audience, comprising Judean and gentile Christians, to hear rhetoric in Rom 4 that refutes the suggestion that Abraham became the father of Judean Christians by means of deeds of the Mosaic law. To prepare a receptive implied audience, Paul mobilizes ideological power inherent in the textures of SRI associated with προπάτωρ and the name Ἀβραάμ. The cultural intertexture in προπάτωρ invokes the conception of kinship that Paul uses to begin his reconfiguration of the nature of Abraham's fatherhood from that of being only the forefather of Judean Christians to that of both Judean and gentile Christians. At the same time, Paul draws on cultural intertexture to invoke the authority of a father and a prophet, of someone whom Judeans revere. The name Ἀβραάμ also contains a social and culture texture whereby Abraham serves as a superordinate identity.

3. Romans 4:2–8: Abraham Did Not Earn Righteousness, and Hence Fatherhood, by the Mosaic Law

Wisdom rhetorolect dominates this section as the presence of topoi related to deeds shows.[114] According to the thirdspace of wisdom rhetorolect, Paul aims to persuade the implied audience to receive favorably his rhetoric, as a son would heed his father's instruction on wisdom.[115] This allows Paul

---

114. Robbins observes that the firstspace (experiences of the audience in social places) is that of a household setting (*Invention of Christian Discourse*, 109).

115. Robbins notes that the thirdspace creates a "human body [that is a] producer of goodness and righteousness" (ibid., 109). In other words, the thirdspace is where the mind of the implied audience is persuaded to receive favorably the speaker's rhetoric.

to persuade the implied audience in a nonconfrontational manner, as will be shown in 4:2–8.

Several observations indicate that 4:2–8 is a complete unit. This paragraph is dominated by cognates of ἐργ- (4:2, 4, 5, 6). Also, 4:9 begins a new paragraph, as signaled by a shift of topos to circumcision. The argumentative texture can be displayed as follows:

[Rule₁]	Deeds bring righteousness (assumed)
[Case₁]	Abraham has deeds (assumed)
Result₁/Case₂	εἰ γὰρ Ἀβραὰμ ἐξ ἔργων ἐδικαιώθη ("For if Abraham was made righteous by deeds" [4:2a])
[Rule₂]	Righteousness brings boasting
Result₂	ἔχει καύχημα ("he has something to boast about" [4:2b])
[Rule₃]	Righteousness does not come from deeds
[Case₃]	Abraham has deeds
Result₃	ἀλλ᾽ οὐ πρὸς θεόν ("but not before God" [4:2c])
Result₄	τί γὰρ ἡ γραφὴ λέγει; ἐπίστευσεν δὲ Ἀβραὰμ τῷ θεῷ καὶ ἐλογίσθη αὐτῷ εἰς δικαιοσύνην ("For what does the Scripture say? 'But Abraham trusted God and it was reckoned to him as righteousness'" [4:3]).
[Case₄]	Abraham has trust in God
Rule₄/Rule₅	τῷ δὲ ἐργαζομένῳ ὁ μισθὸς οὐ λογίζεται κατὰ χάριν ἀλλὰ κατὰ ὀφείλημα ("But to the one who works, the wage is not reckoned as a favor but as an obligation" [4:4])
	τῷ δὲ μὴ ἐργαζομένῳ πιστεύοντι δὲ ἐπὶ τὸν δικαιοῦντα τὸν ἀσεβῆ λογίζεται ἡ πίστις αὐτοῦ εἰς δικαιοσύνην ("But to the one who does not work but trusts in the one who makes the ungodly righteous, his trust is reckoned as righteousness" [4:5])
Case₅	καθάπερ καὶ Δαυὶδ λέγει τὸν μακαρισμὸν τοῦ ἀνθρώπου ᾧ ὁ θεὸς λογίζεται δικαιοσύνην χωρὶς ἔργων ("just as David also says: 'Blessed is the man to whom God reckons righteousness apart from deeds'" [4:6])
Result₅	μακάριοι ὧν ἀφέθησαν αἱ ἀνομίαι καὶ ὧν ἐπεκαλύφθησαν αἱ ἁμαρτίαι· μακάριος ἀνὴρ οὗ οὐ μὴ λογίσηται κύριος ἁμαρτίαν ("Blessed are those whose iniquities are forgiven and whose sins are covered. Blessed is the man whom the Lord will not reckon sin" [4:7–8]).

Romans 4:2–8 not only shows that righteousness comes by trust in God; it also refutes the erroneous notion that Abraham had a reason to boast because of his obedience to the Mosaic law (4:2). The word boast invokes a cultural texture that embeds the Mediterranean honor-shame value system. Paul achieves his objective by constructing a right understanding of the nature of honor that provides a legitimate reason for boasting. This serves to undermine the Judeans' wrong basis for boasting. The nature of this honor, which comes from a position of righteousness, is something that is ascribed to Abraham by God.[116] Anyone who wants to receive this righteousness has to inherit it from Abraham by way of kinship relationship, in this case, by becoming a descendant of Abraham by reenacting his trust in—that is, loyalty to—God.[117]

3.1. Romans 4:2: Abraham Could Not Boast by His Deeds of the Mosaic Law

The wisdom rhetorolect used in 4:2 revolves around the topos of deed.[118] The opening statement of 4:2 serves as the introduction for 4:2–8. What follows in 4:3–8 elaborates on it. Construing 4:2 as the introduction to 4:3–8 is reasonable in view of several indications. First, it begins the passage. Second, the next verse, 4:3, begins with a connective γάρ ("for") to indicate that what follows in 4:3–8 serves to support the statement in 4:2 (see above, the argumentative texture).

Enthymematic reasoning in 4:2 leads to two results. First, Abraham has grounds for boasting by means of his obedience to the Mosaic law. The statement spells out the problem to be addressed in 4:3–8. Second, this boast, however, has no value before God. This introduces Paul's refutation in 4:3–8.

---

116. Moxnes describes an honorable man as a righteous man ("Honour and Righteousness," 71).

117. Malina notes that honor is either ascribed or acquired and that ascribed honor can be granted on the basis of birth or given by a notable person of authority (*New Testament World*, 32).

118. See Robbins, who observes that biblical wisdom is evident in the creation work of God (*Invention of Christian Discourse*, 134–50).

3.1.1. Romans 4:2a

The term ἔργα ("deeds") requires clarification. Some scholars construe it narrowly, maintaining that it refers to Judean identity markers such as circumcision and food laws. For instance, Dunn (referring back to the earlier references in 3:20 and 3:27–28) thinks that this refers to the religious practices—in particular, circumcision—that define the Judeans as people of the Mosaic law.[119] Yet others enlarge the semantic domain to mean good deeds in general.[120] Moo takes an intermediate position. Although he rejects Dunn's view, he construes this word as referring to good deeds in general but also sees it as having reference to the Mosaic law. I take a position that is close to Moo's but with an important correction. I agree that ἔργα includes good deeds in general, as made clear in the preceding context, where obedience to the law includes moral behavior mentioned in 2:21–22. Even the rite of circumcision has value only if these moral laws are obeyed (2:24–29). More importantly, in 3:9–20, the conclusion to the argument of 1:18–3:8, Paul, in indicting the Judeans for not having obeyed the law again, couches their disobedience in terms of having broken the law morally (3:13–18). I differ from Moo, however, in construing the emphasis as first the deeds of the Mosaic law, then good deeds in general. This has important ramifications not only for understanding the main problem that is plaguing the Christian community in Rome (a dissension between Judean and gentile Christians over righteousness), but also because it derails the primary focus in Rom 4, which is to divest Judean Christians of their reliance on the Mosaic law as a boast against gentile Christians.[121] The response begins with a first-class conditional sentence

---

119. Dunn, *Romans 1–8*, 154. Peter Stuhlmacher correctly contends that "works of the law" cannot be limited to "boundary markers," that is, "to circumcision, the keeping of kosher laws and of the Sabbath.… Pharisaic καύχησις is illustrated in Luke 18:11–12." See Stuhlmacher, "N. T. Wright's Understanding of Justification and Redemption," in *God and the Faithfulness of Paul: A Critical Examination of the Pauline Theology of N. T. Wright*, ed. Christoph Heilig, J. Thomas Hewitt, and Michael F. Bird, WUNT 2/413 (Tübingen: Mohr Siebeck, 2016), 366.

120. So Barrett, *Epistle to the Romans*, 83. In a similar vein, Jewett extends it to include any human system that competes for honor as in the Mediterranean system of honor and shame (*Romans*, 266).

121. This is one of the main problems between Judean and gentile Christians in the Roman community; see above, chapter 2, §3, "The Argument of Romans 1:16–4:25." Thurén notes that scholars often speak of a liberation from "Lutheran captivity"

where the apodosis assumes a statement that is true for the sake of argument. Whether or not the apodosis contains a fact or a statement that is false but assumed to be true is not apparent from the grammar. Recent commentators reject any possibility for Abraham to boast through deeds.[122] But such an understanding goes against records in Judean writings of the pride that Judeans possess because of Abraham's obedience to the Mosaic law. Furthermore, that this pride exists in the implied rhetorical situation is evident in Paul's rhetoric that Paul levels against the Judeans' boast toward the gentiles, as I have explained earlier.[123] Hence, the apodosis contains not only an assumed truth but also Paul's perception of the rhetorical situation of Romans.

The display of the above argumentative structure in 4:2a reveals a cultural intertexture that Judeans seek righteousness by doing the deeds of the Mosaic law. The social and cultural texture of Mediterranean patron-client culture and rules of purity sheds light on why this righteousness so attained becomes a national marker that excludes the rest of the world, those whom Israel generically calls the gentiles.[124]

First, Israel's relationship with God is that of a client to his patron. In Deut 32:6, when Israel is about to enter and inherit the promised land from God, Moses warns the people about their future rebellion against God. He rebukes them for their future unfaithfulness on the premise that God is

---

(*Derhetorizing Paul*, 9). Krister Stendahl comments that Paul is addressing the role of Torah in the gentile-Judean relationship in God's plan of salvation, rather than "pondering about its [the Torah's] effects upon his conscience." See Stendahl, "The Apostle Paul and the Introspective Conscience of the West," *HTR* 56 (1963): 204. Similarly, see Watson, *Paul, Judaism and the Gentiles*, 179–81.

122. So Moo, *Epistle to the Romans*, 261; Jewett, *Romans*, 310. Similarly, Dunn relegates it to a theoretical possibility that is then totally rejected (*Romans 1–8*, 201). Contra Godet, *Romans*, 170.

123. See above, chapter 2, §3, "The Argument of Romans 1:16–4:25."

124. Donaldson observes with regards to the term τὰ ἔθνη that "no one in the first century whom we might refer to as a Gentile would have naturally thought of himself or herself in these terms. The use of τὰ ἔθνη with reference to non-Jewish nations or individuals was a Jewish construction. Left to their own device and self-definitions, Phrygians, Parthians, or Bithynians would no more describe themselves as ἔθνη than they would as βάρβαροι" ("Gentile Christianity," 451–53). See also Christopher D. Stanley, "'Neither Jew nor Greek': Ethnic Conflict in Graeco-Roman Society," *JSNT* 64 (1996): 105: "The use of the term 'Gentiles' (ἀλλόφυλοι or ἔθνη) to designate all non-Jews represents a 'social construction of reality' developed by a particular people-group (the Jews) in a concrete historical situation."

their father: "Is not he your father, who created you, who made you and established you?" (NRSV). The occasion when God created, made, and established Israel refers to the time when God rescued them out of Egypt and established them in the promised land (Deut 32:6–14). Two points are noteworthy. This father-son relationship started with the creation of the nation of Israel. Ever since, Israel's relationship with God had always been conceived as that of father and son. This father-son relationship is properly the Mediterranean patron-client relationship—the element of reciprocation between God as patron and Israel who must show herself faithful to him (see, e.g., 2 Sam 7:14).[125]

Second, Judeans maintain a relationship of righteousness with God their patron when they obey the Mosaic law: "It will be to our righteousness [צדקה] if we are diligent so as to do this whole commandment before Yahweh our God just as he commanded us" (Deut 6:25). Peter C. Craigie comments that "righteousness in this context describes a true and personal relationship with the covenant God."[126] Paul's contention in 2:17–25 that Judeans are people who observe the Mosaic law is in line with 2 Bar. 48:22–24: "In you we have put our trust, because, behold, your Law is with us, and we know that we do not fall as long as we keep your statutes" (trans. Klijn, OTP 1:636).[127] Related to the Mosaic law is what Bruce Malina calls the "purity rules of the society":

In a limited-good perspective of our first-century foreigners, the main task in life was not symboled by achievement … but rather by the maintenance of one's inherited position in society. This brought prosperity and insured the most harmonious relationship possible in terms of time, place, interpersonal relationships with one's fellows, and relation-

---

125. Bruce J. Malina comments that "in the Bible, anytime anyone is called a "father" who is not a biological father, the title refers to the role and status of a patron" (Malina, "Patronage," in Pilch and Malina, Handbook of Biblical Social Values, 151).

126. Peter C. Craigie, Psalms 1–50, WBC (Waco, TX: Word, 1983), 175. Similarly, Moshe Weinfeld describes righteousness as "moral righteousness and legal innocence … credit or merit" in relation to God. See Weinfeld, Deuteronomy 1–11, AB 5 (New York: Doubleday, 1991), 349.

127. Schreiner notes that the emphasis in this passage that Israel will "not fall as long as we keep your statutes" is in line with Paul's emphasis in 2:17–25 that Judeans are required to observe the law to be regarded as righteous before God (Romans, 129). Dunn glosses over this emphasis by construing the Mosaic law as simply a Judean ethnic marker (Romans 1–8, 110).

ship with God.... The purity rules of the society were intended to foster prosperity by maintaining fitting, harmonious relationships. Thus perfection—the wholeness marked off by purity rules—characterizes God, the people in general, and the individual.[128]

God the patron takes the initiative to give favor to Israel. At the same time, Israel has an obligation to give honor to God. When this happens, Israel is deemed as righteous before God. Put simply, their relationship with God is harmonious. This will cause God the patron to continue to give favor to Israel. The question is: What kind of honor Israel must give to God to become righteous or to maintain a harmonious relationship?

Obeying the "purity rules of the society" is the means by which Judeans honor God.[129] These purity rules are encapsulated in the Mosaic laws and explain the prevailing mindset of Judeans, which is to seek a righteous or a harmonious relationship with God by obeying the Mosaic law (see 3:20; 9:30–33). The essence of the Mosaic law is to differentiate between that which is clean and unclean. The laws of purity are deeply entrenched in the mind of a Judean as seen in the following practices. They categorize Judeans according to genealogical purity and dictate what animals are clean and unclean for consumption and sacrifice.[130] Furthermore, by categorizing both people and animal according to proximity to the temple, they enhance the authority of these categories.[131] The above observations indicate that purity rules that segregate the clean and unclean are a deep-seated concern of Judeans. Thus, Judeans regard their righteous standing with God as exclusive. We will see how the way Judeans regard purity rules, when read together with the statement ("case") that "Abraham has deeds," lends meaning to the result in 4:2a.[132]

Next, we shall examine the unstated rule of the argument, "Abraham has deeds." Abraham is a reference in the cultural intertexture. Gathercole underlines a problem in the use of Judean writings to illumine Abraham as a reference. Considering the wide range of texts that discuss

---

128. Malina, *New Testament World*, 170.

129. Ibid.

130. Joachim Jeremias, *Jerusalem in the Time of Jesus: An Investigation into Economic and Social Conditions during the New Testament Period* (Philadelphia: Fortress, 1969), 271.

131. Malina, *New Testament World*, 136.

132. See the argumentative texture in chapter 3, §3, "Romans 4:2–8: Abraham Did Not Earn Righteousness, and Hence, Fatherhood by the Mosaic Law."

Abraham, which text does Paul have in mind? Several observations by Gathercole narrow down the scope.[133] First, Second Temple Judaism texts that discuss Abraham generally hold the viewpoint that he was a mono-theist and obeyed the Mosaic law. Second, the characters in the narrative of the text concerned must be in a similar situation as Abraham was, that is, they also faced trials. Third, the viewpoint held about Abraham must be attested by various Judean texts. To achieve the last criterion, Gathercole looks at two trajectories of texts. The first trajectory is taken from Sirach and 1 Maccabees:

> Abraham was the great father of a multitude of nations, and no one has been found like him in glory. He kept the law of the Most High, and entered into a covenant with him; he certified the covenant in his flesh, and when was tested he proved faithful. Therefore, the Lord assured him with an oath that the nations would be blessed through his offspring; that he would make him as numerous as the dust of the earth, and exalt his offspring like the stars, and give them an inheritance from sea to sea and from the Euphrates to the ends of the earth. (Sir 44:19–21 NRSV)

> Was not Abraham found faithful when tested and it was reckoned to him as righteousness? (1 Macc 2:52 NRSV)

The second trajectory, which originates from Sirach, is developed in Jubilees and the Damascus Document:

> This is the tenth trial with which Abraham was tried, and he was found faithful, controlled of spirit because he was found faithful and he was recorded as a friend of the Lord in the heavenly tables. (Jub. 19.8–9 [Wintermute, OTP 2:92])

> Abraham did not walk in it [the stubbornness of the heart that follows after the thoughts of the guilty and eyes of lust], and he was accounted a friend of God because he kept the commandments of God and did not choose his own will. (CD 3:2–4 [Vermes])

The above recitations reveal that Judeans perceived Abraham as someone who had obeyed the Mosaic law and won the approval of God, that is, righteousness. Paul's point is that Abraham did nothing to lead God to

---

133. So Gathercole, *Where Is Boasting*, 235.

consider him a worthy or a righteous person so as to begin a patron-client relationship with Abraham.[134] To understand the result in 4:2a, "Abraham was made righteous by deeds," it is important to note that Judeans would have perceived the constrictions imposed by the Mosaic law as thoroughly excluding any gentile from participation in righteousness and restricting access to righteousness solely to Judeans.

3.1.2. Romans 4:2b

In 4:2b, where the result of the enthymeme is expressed, Paul makes explicit the problem he needed to address. This enthymeme comprises a case: Abraham became righteous by deeds (4:2a), followed by an unstated rule: possession of righteousness leads to boasting. It is not immediately obvious as to why righteousness leads to boasting. For this, we need to recall the process through which deeds of the Mosaic law bring righteousness (viewed from the perspective of the Judean interlocutor). As explained in the unstated rule of 4:2a, the rules of purity of the Judean society (as encapsulated in the Mosaic law) generate a righteousness that is exclusive to Judeans. Consequently, Judeans flaunt before the gentiles their pride that they (the Judeans) are the only ones who stand to gain favors from God. The above case and (unstated) rule result in an Abraham who, according to these Judean texts, boasts because he has gained honor, or a position of righteousness, given to him by God. This honor, in light of the Mediterranean culture of honor and shame, is not only an individual achievement; it is first and foremost an honor in the eyes of the public. Furthermore, this honor is also collective.[135] Here, Abraham is viewed as the forefather of the Judeans. This means that the honor he receives is also extended to his descendants, the Judeans. Seen in this light, we can understand why Paul couches honor in terms of boasting. This boasting is not so much Abraham's boast as it is a kinship boast, that is, the boast of the entire family of Abraham, the Judeans, over the gentiles.

---

134. Barclay correctly sets Abraham's relationship with God in the ancient Roman patronage context where patrons tie themselves only to worthy clients (*Paul and the Gift*, 484, cf. 39).

135. Malina, *New Testament World*, 40.

3.1.3. Romans 4:2c

Paul's enthymematic reasoning here includes an unstated rule that righteousness (that is acceptable to God) does not come from deeds. This, together with the unstated case that Abraham has deeds, produces the result in 4:2c, that Abraham by his deeds of the Mosaic law cannot boast before God. The meaning of 4:2c, that Abraham's righteousness has no value before God (οὐ πρὸς θεόν), must be read in light of 4:1: Abraham is considered righteous by the deeds he has performed (at least from the viewpoint of the Judean interlocutor). In other words, this righteousness does not make him the father of many descendants. My point is that the focus of "righteousness" in 4:2c is about Abraham's fatherhood. Two observations support my view. The fatherhood of Abraham has been discussed in 4:1. Furthermore, Judeans would be familiar with the overall story of Gen 15, in which Abraham became a father of many descendants by virtue of his trust in God. Just as the result in 4:2b states the problem to be addressed in 4:2–8, this result in 4:2c lays down the solution that will resolve the problem in 4:2–8. Since 4:2c is the point that provides the solution to the problem in 4:2–8, we would expect Paul to expound the unstated rule that righteousness does not come from deeds of the Mosaic law.

In interpreting 4:2–8, scholars have not given sufficient weight to 4:2c, in particular, the word καύχημα ("boast"), considering that "not before God" constitutes Paul's main refutation in 4:2–8.[136] Instead, by focusing on the term "righteousness," their discussions overtheologize Paul's concern without considering how the Mediterranean culture of honor and shame would understand this passage. Hence, boasting, as a claim to honor, and related concepts must inform our understanding of this passage. By the statement that Abraham "has something to boast about but not before God," Paul intimates that what follows in 4:3–8 is a rhetoric that intends to reconfigure the implied audience's understanding of honor.

---

136. Neil Richardson remarks that this last clause is often neglected. He comments that it is polemical. See Richardson, *Paul's Language about God*, JSNTSup 99 (Sheffield: Sheffield Academic, 1994), 515.

3.2. Romans 4:3: Scripture Says That Abraham Was Reckoned as Righteous by His Trust in God.

With the connective γάρ, Paul begins his refutation of Abraham's possible boast (4:1)—the Judeans' boast toward gentiles. By introducing the term ἡ γραφή ("the Scripture"), Paul leverages its authority. Chaim Perelman and Lucie Olbrechts-Tyteca state that argumentation begins with some presuppositions upon which both the audience and the speaker agree. One of these presuppositions is "values." Such an agreement between the audience and the speaker amounts to

> an admission that an object, a being, or an ideal must have a specific influence on action and on disposition toward action and that one can make use of this influence in an argument, although the point of view represented is not regarded as binding on everybody.[137]

In terms of SRI, this "specific influence" is the power to persuade that comes from the ideological texture. Perelman and Olbrechts-Tyteca distinguish between abstract and concrete values. They contend that in argumentation, the mind cannot avoid relying on both abstract and concrete values. Examples of abstract values are truth or justice, while concrete values include France or the church.[138] A concrete value is attached to a living being, a specific group, or a particular object that is regarded as a unique entity. God would thus be considered a concrete value. At the same time, however, as God could be regarded as the foundation of all values, God is also the absolute abstract value.[139] Such an argument based on an absolute value would, provided that the audience construes that value as absolute, have the potential to appeal to the whole of humankind, or the universal audience. In our case in 4:3, ἡ γραφή ("the Scripture") is a concrete value that is founded upon the abstract value God.[140] This abstract value, God, lends ideological power to ἡ γραφή in order to persuade.

---

137. Chaim Perelman and Lucie Olbrechts-Tyteca, *The New Rhetoric: Treatise on Argumentation*, trans. John Wilkinson and Purcell Weaver (Notre Dame, IN: University of Notre Dame Press, 1969), 65, quote at 74.

138. Ibid, 77.

139. So Burke, who drew up a list of all the abstract values which found their origin in the perfect being (*Rhetoric of Motives*, 229–301).

140. It is unlikely that God is the abstract value upon which γραφή is founded, as

Such Cartesian certitude, however, has been questioned by philosophers.[141] It is more justifiable to think that the ideological power of ἡ γραφή is not only derived from its abstract value but also from its concrete value. J. David Hester (Amador) elaborates on Perelman and Olbrechts-Tyteca's understanding that "particular qualities of 'universality' ... depend not only on the individual perspectives of the rhetor, but on the social, cultural, and historical 'context' in which both rhetor and argumentation are embedded."[142] How this concrete value provides ideological power is our subject of discussion here. To understand the ideological texture inherent in ἡ γραφή, I shall examine its attached social and cultural texture.

Geertz's *The Interpretation of Cultures* represents an important work that conceptualizes culture as being semiotic and seeks to explicate its meaning.[143] Thompson, who construes a semiotic and a symbolic understanding of culture as being synonymous, develops Geertz's thesis. Relevant for our investigation is the refinement that Thompson offers to Geertz's limitation of his conception of culture: cultural phenomena are not only symbolic forms, but these symbolic forms, defined as meaningful actions, objects, and expressions of various kinds, "sustain or disrupt relations of power."[144] This power derives from the social context in which these symbolic forms are embedded.[145] Within this embedding, an individual inscribes value into the symbolic forms.[146] Several concepts help to clarify the value inscribed into the symbolic forms.

First, Thompson utilizes the concept of fields of interaction developed by Pierre Bourdieu. Particular individuals take up a social position and follow a certain course in their lives as determined by three kinds of capital: economic capital, which pertains to material wealth; cultural capital, which includes knowledge and skills; and symbolic capital, which is

---

God is regarded as the originator of what is written in γραφή. See, e.g., Rom 1:2; 9:17; 16:26.

141. Vilfredo Pareto comments that "universal consensus" is often based on sentiments that a person holds. See Pareto, *The Mind and Society* (London: Cape, 1935), 39.

142. Hester (Amador), *Academic Constraints in Rhetorical Criticism*, 70; see also Perelman and Olbrechts-Tyteca, *New Rhetoric*, 33.

143. Geertz, "Primordial Sentiments," 5.

144. John B. Thompson, *Ideology and Modern Culture: Critical Social Theory in the Era of Mass Communication* (Stanford, CA: Stanford University Press, 1990), 134–36.

145. Ibid., 151.

146. Ibid., 146.

related to accumulated praise, prestige, and recognition.[147] Ἡ γραφή (the Scripture) can be regarded as a symbolic form into which different individuals inscribe value through these fields of influence. Individuals, for example, kings, with economic, cultural, and symbolic capitals, are associated with ἡ γραφή, which itself is considered as a single collection that includes the law of Moses (see 9:17; 10:11; 11:2; 15:4; 16:26; cf. Philo, Mos. 2.84; Let. Aris. 158, 168).[148] For instance, in Rom 10:6–8, Paul recites Deut 30:11–14 LXX as ἡ γραφή.[149] Deuteronomy 17:18 is instructive: "When he has taken the throne of his kingdom, he shall have a copy of this law written for him in the presence of the levitical priests" (MT [NRSV]). The kings of Israel are commanded to possess a copy of the Mosaic law. The main purpose of copying the law is expressed by the purpose clause לְמַעַן יִלְמַד ("in order that he might learn [17:19 MT])/ἵνα μάθῃ φοβεῖσθαι ("in order that he might learn to fear" [17:19 LXX]), which in turn is explicated by several infinitive constructs of purpose (MT)/infinitives of purpose (LXX). These infinitive constructs form a pair of contrasts demarcated by the negative particle of purpose בלתי (MT)/particle of negation μή (LXX). The negative counterpart of this contrast is "neither exalting himself above other members of the community." When read in light of the preceding context (Deut 17:8–13), which talks about bringing a case before "levitical priests and the judge who is in office in those days" (Deut 17:9 [NRSV]), the kings replace priests and judges in judicial responsibilities. This means that the law of Moses is to aid the king in his judicial responsibilities. My point coheres with S. Dean McBride Jr.'s observation. He notes that Josephus affirms that the entire book of Deuteronomy (Ant. 4.176–331), including the above passage, is a comprehensive constitution of government (πολιτεία).[150] Commenting on Deut 17:18–20, McBride writes: "The

---

147. Ibid., 147–48.

148. Dunn, Romans 1–8, 202.

149. Sarah Whittle, Covenant Renewal and the Consecration of the Gentiles in Romans, SNTSMS 161 (New York: Cambridge University Press, 2015), 48. Dunn comments that in Rom 10:6–8 Paul recites Deut 30:11–14 LXX as ἡ γραφή (Romans 9–16, 602–3).

150. S. Dean McBride Jr., "Polity of the Covenant People: The Book of Deuteronomy," in Constituting the Community: Studies on the Polity of Ancient Israel in Honor of S. Dean McBride, Jr., ed. John T. Strong and Steven S. Tuell (Winona Lake, IN: Eisenbrauns, 2005), 17. Similarly, Robert R. Wilson, "Deuteronomy, Ethnicity, and Reform: Reflecting on the Social Setting of Deuteronomy," in Strong and Tuell, Constituting the Community, 109.

only positively specified task of the Israelite monarch is to study the written Deuteronomic polity throughout his reign and to serve as a national model of faithful obedience to its stipulations (17:18–20)."[151] The book of Deuteronomy is a "charter for a constitutional theocracy."[152] This form of theocracy also influenced Israel's subsequent history. Kenton L. Sparks's proposal that Deuteronomy was crafted sometime between the reigns of Hezekiah and Josiah to create an ethnic identity is debatable. He has, however, demonstrated that important features of Deuteronomy served to provide the nation of Israel with a distinct ethnic identity.[153] Thus, generations of Israelites would have associated the law of Moses (i.e., Deuteronomy) with the kings of Israel. This adds to the collective memory of Judeans, and hence adds value to ἡ γραφή.[154]

The patron-client culture of the Mediterranean world also lends economic capital to the patrons of Christian house churches. Wealthier Christians host Christian gatherings in their homes at which ἡ γραφή is taught. For instance, Phoebe is probably the patron of the church in Cenchreae.[155] Being a patron to Paul and to many others (16:2) shows that she is wealthy. In writing to Philemon, Paul also ascribes to Philemon the role of patron because he hosts the church in his house (Phlm 1). Philemon is described as someone who refreshes Paul and the hearts of the saints (Phlm 7). These rich patrons of Christian congregations also added value to ἡ γραφή.

Second, the concept of social institutions adds value to ἡ γραφή. They include particular enterprises or organizations. A social institution "gives shape to pre-existing fields of interaction."[156] One feature of these institutions is hierarchical relations between individuals or the positions

---

151. McBride, "Polity of the Covenant People," 30.

152. Ibid., 27; cf. the use of "theocracy" in Josephus, *Ag. Ap.* 9.359.

153. Kenton L. Sparks, *Ethnicity and Identity in Ancient Israel: Prolegomena to the Study of Ethnic Sentiments and Their Expression in the Hebrew Bible* (Winona Lake, IN: Eisenbrauns, 1998), 222–84; see also Wilson, "Deuteronomy, Ethnicity, and Reform," 112.

154. Maurice Halbwachs comments that those who remember are individual members of a group. Sustaining this memory "requires the support of a group delimited in space and time." See Halbwachs, *The Collective Memory*, trans. Francis J. Ditter and Vida Yazdi Ditter (New York: Harper & Row, 1980), 22.

155. Dunn, *Romans 1–8*, 888–89.

156. Thompson, *Ideology and Modern Culture*, 149.

in which they are situated.[157] A Judean family is one such institution in which a hierarchical relationship exists between parent and child. Another social institution is the religious system in house churches, places of prayer, and synagogues, where a formalized hierarchy exists between leaders and followers.[158]

Third, the above two concepts of fields of interaction and social institutions contain a social structure characterized by asymmetries. In the above discussion, the relationship between an Israelite king and his subjects, a rich Christian patron and his Christian client(s), an Israelite parent and his child, and a leader in a religious system and his followers operate in a social context where there are asymmetries in terms of access to resources of various kinds that include authority, opportunities, and more.[159] Where such asymmetries exist, Thompson describes it as one of "domination."[160] In this way Paul, by using the symbolic form ἡ γραφή, takes on a position of dominance over his implied audience. This understanding of domination needs to be modulated. Ehrensperger's essay helps.[161] She agrees with Hannah Arendt that power "is the human ability not just to act but to act in concert" and that a degree of collaboration or interdependence between the author and audience is involved.[162] Along with other scholars, however, Ehrensperger agrees that "the strategic aspect of power"—that is, where the author asserts power over the audience to elicit obedience in response to a command—should not be excluded.[163] At this point, a discussion of Thomas E. Wartenberg's "transformative power" is appropriate.[164] This power operates in an "educational setting ... [that involves a]

---

157. Ibid.

158. See Esler, who cogently argues that "the majority of Judeans of Rome in the mid-first century CE met in buildings specially built or adapted for that purpose—*proseuchai*—and not in the houses of members" (*Conflict and Identity in Romans*, 88–97).

159. Thompson, *Ideology and Modern Culture*, 150.

160. Ibid., 150–52.

161. Kathy Ehrensperger, "Paul and the Authority of Scripture," in Porter and Stanley, *As It Is Written*, 291–319.

162. Hannah Arendt, *On Violence* (London: Lane, 1970), 44, 295, 311 (quote at 44).

163. Ibid., 297–98. Similarly, Amy Allen, "Power, Subjectivity, and Agency: Between Arendt and Foucault," *IJPS* 10 (2002): 131–49; Jürgen Habermas, "Hannah Arendt's Communications Concept of Power," *SR* 44 (1977): 3–24.

164. Thomas E. Wartenberg, *The Forms of Power: From Domination to Transformation* (Philadelphia: Temple University Press, 1990), 27–29.

relationship between student and teacher, or parent and child."[165] Such a relationship is asymmetrical and yet does not take on the extreme form of a "domination-subordination pattern."[166] This mediates between the need for an understanding of power that allows a degree of interdependence between the author and the audience and allows the strategic use of power. Against such a setting of noncoercion and absence of force, "but by care for the other (i.e., the people)," Paul uses Scriptures to elicit obedience from the audience.[167] Although Ehrensperger's essay is directed at Paul's use of power in the context of scriptural quotations, her insistence that "the power of God is perceived as relationality which rules out any form of force, coercion, or domination" does not always accurately depict Paul's use of power.[168] For example, Paul threatens the Corinthian Christians to coerce them into obedience: "What would you prefer? Am I to come to you with a stick, or with love in a spirit of gentleness?" (1 Cor 4:21 NRSV). In fact, here, Paul verges on the side of violence.[169] That said, however, Paul's manner of mobilizing ideological power in a noncoercive way is evident in Rom 4, as my following analysis shows.

Paul assumes this position of dominance not in a direct manner but via a metaphorical use of ἡ γραφή. Here, Paul assumes the role of ἡ γραφή by personifying it with the verb λέγειν ("to say"). Thompson comments that metaphors

> may dissimulate social relations by representing them, or the individuals and groups embedded in them, as endowed with characteristics which they do not literally possess, thereby accentuating certain features at the expense of others and charging them with a positive or negative sense.[170]

In Paul's present situation, he is faced with two difficulties, both of which are circumvented by the metaphorical use of ἡ γραφή. First, the fact that Paul had to devote some space to configure his apostolic authority in the

---

165. Ehrensperger, "Paul and the Authority of Scripture," 298.

166. Ibid.

167. Ibid., 311.

168. Ibid., 164.

169. Anthony C. Thiselton labels this passage as a "warning" and an act of potential "violence." See Thiselton, *The First Epistle to the Corinthians*, NIGTC (Grand Rapids: Eerdmans, 2000), 378, citing C. K. Barrett, *A Commentary on the First Epistle to the Corinthians*, BNTC (London: Black, 1971), 119.

170. Thompson, *Ideology and Modern Culture*, 63.

exordium (1:1–15) before he could assert it over his implied audience indicates that his apostolic authority over the Roman Christians may not be a clear-cut case. The reason could be that he did not found this Christian community, but we are not certain. Left on its own, as Wanamaker aptly puts it, "Paul was only as powerful as his persuasive ability to extract obedience."[171] Paul, by assuming the identity of ἡ γραφή through the mode of ideology that Thompson calls dissimulation, now has access to the full range of its ideological power to extract obedience from his implied audience.[172] Second, in view of the historical intertextual link of this letter to the Letter to the Galatians, Paul would not have wanted to rouse similar unhappy sentiments in Rome as he probably did with the Galatian Christians by his letter to them. Furthermore, considering that Romans seeks to reconcile two dissenting groups, Judean and gentile Christians, muting overtones of opposition is needful. By this metaphorical use of ἡ γραφή, Paul also turns attention away from himself so that if the implied audience refused to heed Paul the speaker's refutation, it would amount to opposing ἡ γραφή of God and not simply Paul.[173] Thus, this metaphorical mode of mobilizing ideological power allows Paul to inherit the full range of the persuasive power of ἡ γραφή without unnecessarily offending his implied and real audience.

This ideological texture inherent in ἡ γραφή also lends ideological power to the rhetoric, as the entire argument of Rom 4 is built on one passage of ἡ γραφή: Gen 15:6 LXX. This is corroborated by the fact that not only is Gen 15:6 LXX recited several times in Rom 4 (4:9, 22, 23), but it also occurs in a critical location within the passage: at the closing where the implication of Rom 4 is applied to the implied audience (Judean and gentile Christians). What that implies is that Rom 4 is a rhetoric based on Gen 15:6 LXX or, more precisely, a rhetoric of Abraham's faith (trust) in God. Before investigating Gen 15:6 LXX, a comment about the nature of the LXX is necessary. Presently, the LXX is represented by the great uncial manuscripts of the fourth and fifth centuries CE. We are not,

---

171. Wanamaker, "By the Power of God," 210.

172. This application of Thompson's use of metaphor is built upon the excellent essay by Wanamaker (ibid.).

173. I am using again the insights of Wanamaker, who observes that in 2 Corinthians Paul "obfuscates the nature of the opposition to him and the nature of his own apostleship by making his opponents enemies of God" (ibid.).

consequently, certain as to the *Vorlage* that Paul used in his recitations.[174] This is a result of the multiple recensions of the LXX. Emmanuel Tov notes that

> as a result of recent finds and studies in early recensions, the heterogeneity of the canon of the LXX has become increasingly evident. It has been recognized that "the LXX" contains translations of different types, early and late, relatively original and significantly revised, official and private, literal and free.[175]

That said, however, Christopher D. Stanley comments that "the evidence seems to suggest the existence of a primary version that enjoyed wide circulation and use throughout the late Second Temple period."[176] We shall now investigate this LXX recitation.

Paul provides an oral-scribal recitation of Gen 15:6 LXX.[177] I contend that this recitation bears the characteristics of a *chreia* as shown by several observations. Aelius Theon describes *chreia* as a "brief saying or action making a point, attributed to some specific person or something corresponding to a person" (*Prog.* 96–97 [Kennedy]).[178] In Rom 4, the brief saying Gen 15:6 is attributed to Abraham. Also, it should probably be classified as an action *chreia*.[179] Furthermore, Paul uses this recita-

---

174. Christopher D. Stanley argues that Paul did not recite the LXX quotations from memory. He suggests, along with Dietrich-Alex Koch, that the majority of these recitations were drawn from some kind of written texts. One such kind of written texts could be a collection of biblical proof texts. See Stanley, *Paul and the Language of Scripture: Citation Technique in the Pauline Epistles and Contemporary Literature*, SNTSMS 74 (Cambridge: Cambridge University Press, 1992), 69–71; Koch, *Die Schrift als Zeuge des Evangeliums: Untersuchungen zur Verwendung und zum Verständnis der Schrift bei Paulus*, BHT 69 (Tübingen: Mohr Siebeck, 1986), 93–99; see also Rendel J. Harris, *Testimonies* (Cambridge: Cambridge University Press, 1916–1920); Stanley, *Did Paul Have Opponents in Rome*, 71–79.

175. Emmanuel Tov, "Jewish Greek Scriptures," in *Early Judaism and Its Modern Interpreters*, ed. Robert A. Kraft and George W. E. Nickelsburg, BMI 2 (Atlanta: Scholars Press, 1986), 225. Similarly, Stanley, *Paul and the Language of Scripture*, 42.

176. Stanley, *Paul and the Language of Scripture*, 48.

177. Robbins, *Tapestry of Early Christian Discourse*, 103.

178. See also Ronald F. Hock and Edward N. O'Neil, eds., *The Progymnasmata*, vol. 1 of *The Chreia in Ancient Rhetoric*, SBLTT 27 (Atlanta: Scholars Press, 1986), 26.

179. Vernon K. Robbins notes that "Theon's discussion of this class calls attention to the chreia's potential for action either in the situation or response." See Robbins,

tion to develop an argument by elaboration.[180] This construal also fits the dominant wisdom rhetorolect of Rom 4 since a *chreia* belongs to wisdom speech genres.[181] There are two significant differences between Paul's recitation and the present tradition of the LXX at Gen 15:6. First, δέ replaces καί of the LXX. Stanley thinks that the presence of δέ could have come from the wording of his *Vorlage* in Rom 4:3. That Paul could have been in possession of such a *Vorlage*, so he contends, is shown by the reading containing δέ in Jas 2:23.[182] This line of evidence can be controverted by the fact that in the Letter to the Galatians, a letter whose content is closely related to that of Romans, Paul recited Gen 15:6 LXX without the particle δέ (Gal 3:6).[183] In the final analysis, perhaps Stanley is right to conclude that the evidence does not point us in either direction. That said, however, the location of δέ within the recitation is awkward. This implies strongly that this particle has a purpose. The particle δέ is probably adversative, as it functions in this way in what follows (it occurs a total of three times in 4:4–5). Also, the conjunction καί denotes the result in Gen 15:6 LXX.[184] This explains why Paul did not include καί in the recitation, as such a resultative use does not fit the present need of 4:3–5. But Paul could have simply not included any connective. In fact, having begun the recitation with a causative γάρ, discarding δέ would be smoother grammatically, as in Gal 3:6.[185] The fact that he replaces καί with δέ hints that this change is intended to contrast with the preceding statement ἔχει καύχημα ("He has something to boast about" [4:2 NRSV]).[186] Also, this contrast is a pronounced one, considering that δέ

"The Chreia," in *Greco-Roman Literature and the New Testament: Selected Forms and Genres*, ed. David E. Aune, SBLSBS 21 (Atlanta: Scholars Press, 1988), 8. In the case of Rom 4, the potential lies in the situation where Abraham demonstrates trust in God.

180. Ibid., 19–20.

181. Amos N. Wilder, *Early Christian Rhetoric: The Language of the Gospel* (Cambridge: Harvard University Press, 1964), 1–54, 71–88.

182. Stanley, *Did Paul Have Opponents in Rome*, 100.

183. Benjamin Schliesser, *Abraham's Faith in Romans 4: Paul's Concept of Faith in Light of the History of Reception of Genesis 15:6*, WUNT 2/224 (Tubingen: Mohr Siebeck, 2007), 334.

184. BDAG, s.v. "καί."

185. In Gal 3:6, Paul inserts Gen 15:6 LXX immediately after the connective: καθὼς Ἀβραὰμ ἐπίστευσεν τῷ θεῷ, καὶ ἐλογίσθη αὐτῷ εἰς δικαιοσύνην ("just as Abraham trusted God and it was reckoned to him as righteousness").

186. Moo thinks that the recitation of Gen 15:6 explains ἀλλ᾽ οὐ πρὸς θεόν ("but

subsequently occurs another three times in the subsequent verses (4:4–5). This observation sharpens the focus of 4:3–8: to *refute* the contention of the Judean interlocutor that Abraham has a reason to boast over gentiles by his deeds (of the Mosaic law).

Second, Ἀβραάμ ("Abraham") replaces Αβραμ ("Abram") of the LXX. Paul could have chosen the name Ἀβραάμ over Αβραμ, as the former is the prevailing address given to the forefather of Judeans. When read against the fact that Αβραμ is the name used throughout Gen 15 LXX, Paul's choice of Ἀβραάμ should be viewed as intentional. When understood in light of the above discussion, at this stage, Paul is highlighting the name Ἀβραάμ, which means "father of a multitude." He is arguing that Abraham became the father of Judeans not by doing the deeds of Mosaic law but by trust in God.[187]

The emphasis of 4:3 is clear: Abraham obtained righteousness by trusting God.[188] Several details, however, cloud how Gen 15:6 LXX substantiates Paul's thesis that Abraham has no grounds to boast against the gentiles and that such a boast has no value before God (4:2). For one, it is not clear as to how Abraham's trust in God removes any possibility for him to boast about his deeds (of the Mosaic law). Hence, it is premature at this point in 4:3, as some commentators would like, to draw out the implications of Gen 15:6 LXX for Paul's argument.[189] That Paul's point is not immediately clear explains why he elaborates on Gen 15:6 LXX in Rom

---

not before God") (*Epistle to the Romans*, 261). Although he is right in the sense that Paul is trying to refute the thesis that Abraham has a boast before God, Moo's interpretation removes the focus from the word καύχημα, which carries a pejorative sense of boasting against gentiles.

187. Jewett, *Romans*, 311; Dunn, *Romans 1–8*, 202. This also casts doubt on the view that the rhetoric of Rom 4 is primarily to prove justification by faith, as much as it is an important and valid doctrine of the Christian faith.

188. Herman C. Waetjen denies imputation of righteousness by citing as evidence Abraham's ongoing trust in God, where Abraham demonstrated trust in Gen 12 and continued to do so in Gen 15:6. His exegesis collapses the contexts of the various Genesis accounts. In particular, he has glossed over the clear fact that God reckoned Abraham as righteous because of his response in Gen 15:5. The trust involved was not something that was ongoing, although Abraham did continue to trust God. He also claims that the trust involved is a mutual relationship between God and Abraham. This claim is not borne out by sound exegesis. See Waetjen, *The Letter to the Romans: Salvation as Justice and the Deconstruction of Law*, New Testament Monographs 32 (Sheffield: Sheffield Phoenix, 2011), 121–23.

189. E.g., Moo, *Epistle to the Romans*, 261–62; Jewett, *Romans*, 310–12. Contra

4:4–5. Genesis 15:6 LXX, at this juncture in 4:3, serves as a key text that he will later use in his argument. I shall now examine Gen 15:6 LXX.

3.3. Genesis 15:6 LXX

One of the questions investigated in the six-year course of the SBL seminar on Paul and his use of Scripture is: "How do Paul's references to the Jewish Scriptures relate to their original context?"[190] Opinions are divided into basically two camps. One camp believes that Paul factors into his rhetoric the literary and theological contexts of the passages to which he refers.[191] The other insists that tensions and discrepancies exist in the way Paul applies these texts. Stanley acknowledges that this question remains unresolved. The role of the implied audience forms a main part of this impasse.

3.3.1. The Role of the Implied Audience

Scholars agree that the speaker must adapt his rhetoric to his real audience.[192] This implies that Paul would have considered the extent of the

---

Cranfield, who confines his commentary mainly to its function (*Epistle to the Romans*, 1:228–30; cf. Barrett, *Epistle to the Romans*, 88).

190. Christopher D. Stanley, "What We Learned and What We Didn't," in *Paul and Scripture: Extending the Conversation*, ed. Christopher D. Stanley, ECL 9 (Atlanta: Society of Biblical Literature, 2012), 325. See also David M. Allen, "Introduction: The Study of the Use of the Old Testament in the New," *JSNT* 38 (2015): 7–9.

191. For a comprehensive treatment of this position, see Gregory K. Beale, *Handbook on the New Testament Use of the Old Testament: Exegesis and Interpretation* (Grand Rapids: Baker Academic, 2012), 41–54. Against those who think that New Testament writers, when citing the LXX, sometimes fail to respect the related contexts of the Hebrew Bible, C. H. Dodd asks, first, why the same verse was often not recited in identical ways and, second, why different verses of a LXX section were recited. See Dodd, *According to the Scriptures: The Sub-structure of New Testament Theology* (London: Nisbet, 1952), 110, 126–27. Dodd concludes that these observations show that the New Testament writers were aware of the larger context from which they recited. See, e.g., Robert Rendall, "Quotation in Scripture as an Index of Wider Reference," *EvQ* 36 (1964): 214–21; Richard T. France, "The Formula-Quotations of Matthew 2 and the Problem of Communications," *NTS* 27 (1980): 233–51. For examples that demonstrate that New Testament writers recited LXX passages in context, see Walter C. Kaiser, *The Uses of the Old Testament in the New* (Chicago: Moody Press, 1985).

192. So Bitzer, "Rhetorical Situation," 8: "The rhetorical audience must be capable of serving as mediator of the change which the discourse functions to produce." See

knowledge his real audience had of any quotation of the LXX. Although scholars agree that a large part of Paul's real audience is illiterate, both camps differ on how this data should be used. Those who oppose the view that Paul is faithful to the Hebrew Bible contexts of his quotations argue that he does not expect his real audience to look up the context of his quotations. The other camp thinks that Paul is faithful to the Hebrew Bible contexts of the texts to which he refers and contends that Paul expects his real audience to continue to study his letters under the guidance of more knowledgeable members.[193] Stanley mediates between these two camps by suggesting that Paul requires his real audience to go no further than just to hear what is being quoted and accept the authority of the Hebrew Bible. Stanley's rationale is that should more information be provided than what is given in the words of the quotation, Paul's real audience might interpret the assumed data and turn it against him. Furthermore, he contends that Paul has provided sufficient "snippets of information" to enable his real audience to follow his argument.[194] In response, first, whether or not the real audience will use the additional information against Paul is moot, as the reverse can also be true: too little information may create a misunderstanding. Second, that Paul has provided enough "snippets of information" is based on the assumption that Paul's rhetoric can be effective just by a minimal use of a LXX recitation. This point is debatable, as there are no objective criteria to gauge the persuasiveness of a rhetoric. Thus, the strongest argument leveled against the position that a wider context of the Hebrew Bible recitation is invoked is the low literacy rate of the ancient real audience. I shall argue, however, that the real audience was likely to have known the wider context of the LXX quotations.

---

also Perelman and Olbrechts-Tyteca, who underscore that a rhetor must be both *persuasive* by adaptive to the views of his particular audience and *convincing* to a universal audience by appealing to a universal set of facts and truths possessed by a normal or a rational being (*New Rhetoric*, 26–31). See also Eugene E. White, who lists six factors for an effective rhetoric. Among these are "the capacity of the readers/listeners to alter the urgency" and "the readiness of the readers/listeners to be influenced." See White, *The Context of Human Discourse: A Configurational Criticism of Rhetoric* (Columbia: University of South Carolina Press, 1992), 38–39.

193. Stanley, "What We Learned," 327.

194. For his summary of what Paul's audience could have inferred about Abraham solely from the way Paul describes him in Rom 4, see Christopher D. Stanley, *Arguing with Scripture: The Rhetoric of Quotations in the Letters of Paul* (New York: T&T Clark International, 2004), 154.

3.3.2. The Influence of the Synagogue

Gentile Christians, including gentile Godfearers who formed part of the real audience of Romans, were likely to have been familiar with the Mosaic law due to the influence of synagogues where the law was read, taught, and studied. Bruce Fisk lists several factors that support this contention.[195] In view of the possibility that Claudius's edict to evict Judeans in 49 CE was narrow in scope and of limited impact, the ties between Roman Christians and the synagogues were probably maintained a few more years beyond 49 CE.[196] Furthermore, historical studies indicate that synagogue service before 70 CE included as some of its most important activities sermons and public readings of the Hebrew Bible.[197] Josephus, Philo, the New Testament, and rabbinic literature support the observation that "scriptural readings constituted the core of contemporary Jewish worship in the synagogue."[198] When the need arose, Greek and/or Aramaic translations were provided.[199] Fisk correctly cautions us that "it is precarious to make claims solely on evidence within Romans about the competence of Paul's actual first readers ... given the lack of evidence that Rome's Christian community had uniformly severed its ties with the synagogue."[200]

3.3.3. Tertius and Phoebe

Jewett is probably right to conclude that "Tertius and Phoebe were engaged in the creation, the delivery, the public reading, and the explanation of

---

195. Fisk lists seven considerations that argue for the plausibility of the fact that gentile Christians may have been educated in the Torah ("Synagogue Influence and Scriptural Knowledge," 184–85).

196. Fisk, "Synagogue Influence and Scriptural Knowledge," 177; see also above, chapter 2, §2.2, "Historical Background."

197. Lee I. Levine, "The Second Temple Synagogue: The Formative Years," in *The Synagogue in Late Antiquity*, ed. Lee I. Levine (Philadelphia: American Schools of Oriental Research, 1987), 7–31; James F. Strange, "Ancient Texts, Archaeology as Text, and the Problem of the First-Century Synagogue," in *Evolution of the Synagogue: Problems and Progress*, ed. Howard Clark Kee and Lynn H. Cohick (Harrisburg: Trinity Press International, 1999), 27–45.

198. Lee I. Levine, *The Ancient Synagogue: The First Thousand Years*, 2nd ed. (New Haven: Yale University Press, 2005), 150.

199. Ibid., 159.

200. Fisk, "Synagogue Influence and Scriptural Knowledge," 184–85.

the letter."[201] Several observations evince the above comment. In his study of the role of the secretary in the writing of ancient letters, E. Randolph Richards explains that an ancient letter was carried by hand and brought directly to the recipient. The carrier of the letter provided the personal connection between the sender and the recipient. "The carrier was then expected to elaborate all the details for the recipient."[202] There are many such examples. Richards cites two of them.[203] In one case, the son of a woman was being mistreated. This mother then sought the help of Zenon through a letter. She added in her letter: "The rest please learn from the man who brings you this letter. He is no stranger to us" (P.Col. 3.6). In another case, Cicero complained that the carrier did not bring the letter to him personally and provide the missing details:

> I received your letter.... Having read it, I apprehend that Philotimus has not acted very sensibly in forwarding the letter to me instead of coming in person, when he had, as you say, a message from you covering all points. I realized that your letter would have been longer if you had not expected him to carry it to its destination. (*Fam.* 4.2.1 [Bailey, LCL])[204]

Cicero's point was that the letter was shorter than he had expected. Thus, he thought that the carrier would provide the details. Richards comments that "the sender did not usually state that the carrier had additional news; it was expected."[205] In other words, the sender did not just communicate in writing. He also provided additional information through the carrier of the letter. The carrier of the letter was also competent to provide clarification of the content of the letter. Ancient letters were read aloud. James D.

---

201. Jewett, *Romans*, 23. Allan Chapple thinks that Tertius was unlikely to have delivered the letter to Rome in view of the way he included his greeting in 16:2. See Chapple, "Getting Romans to the Right Romans: Phoebe and the Delivery of Paul's Letter," *TynBul* 62 (2011): 213. But that Tertius accompanied his owner, Phoebe, is likely. Moreover, the note in 16:2 serves to assure the audience that "as the amanuensis of this letter, he was in the best position to present this complicated text orally, taking advantage of each stylistic nuance" (Jewett, *Romans*, 979).

202. E. Randolph Richards, *The Secretary in the Letters of Paul*, WUNT 2/42 (Tübingen: Mohr Siebeck, 1991), 9.

203. E. Randolph Richards, *Paul and First-Century Letter Writing: Secretaries, Composition and Collection* (Downers Grove, IL: InterVarsity Press, 2004), 183–84.

204. For other examples, see *Fam.* 1.8.1; 3.1.1; 3.5.1; 10.7.1.

205. Richards, *Paul and First-Century Letter Writing*, 183.

Hester remarks that "one had better begin to take seriously the possibility that Paul saw his letters as speeches."[206] Pieter J. J. Botha comments that "reading in antiquity ... was a performative, vocal, oral-aural happening."[207] As such, Paul, when dictating his letter to the secretary, would have also coached and explained the letter to the carrier and the eventual reader.[208] Similarly, Lee Johnson militates against the view that Paul's letters, upon delivery, were unfurled and then read verbatim to the church. The low literacy rate makes it imperative that letters were not only read but also performed.[209] Johnson observes that Aristotle and later Cicero both emphasize the importance of performance, without which speeches and their speakers lose their "esteem" (Aristotle, *Rhet.* 3.12.1–3; Cicero, *Inv.* 3.54).[210] These performers of the letters also needed to be trained, as ancient manuscripts were not easily sight-read due to a lack of punctuation, headings, paragraphs, capitalization, and spaces between words.[211]

In the case of the Letter to the Romans, Tertius was the secretary of the letter (see Rom 16:22).[212] The writing of the letter was probably funded by Phoebe, whom Paul says was "a patron to many and to myself as well" (16:2). Tertius was probably Phoebe's slave or employee. Jewett is likely correct to think that although Phoebe delivered the letter, a person of her social class, as patron, would have her scribe or slave read the letter. "Phoebe and Tertius would then be in the position to negotiate the complex issue advanced by the letter in a manner typical of the ancient world."[213]

John L. White's observations corroborate the above point that the letter bearer would serve "both as interpreter of the letter's content and as letter

---

206. James D. Hester, "The Use and Influence of Rhetoric in Galatians 2:1–14," *TZ* 42 (1986): 389.

207. Pieter J. J. Botha, "The Verbal Art of the Pauline Letters: Rhetoric, Performance and Presence," in *Rhetoric and the New Testament: Essays from the 1992 Heidelberg Conference*, ed. Stanley E. Porter and Thomas H. Olbricht, JSNTSup 90 (Sheffield: Sheffield Academic, 1993), 413–14.

208. Ibid., 417. Similarly, Richards, *Paul and First-Century Letter Writing*, 202.

209. Lee A. Johnson, "Paul's Letter Reheard: A Performance-Critical Examination of the Preparation, Transportation, and Delivery of Paul's Correspondence," *CBQ* 79 (2017): 64.

210. Ibid., 67.

211. Ibid. 64.

212. E. Randolph Richards ranks Romans as a letter certainly written with secretarial assistance (*Secretary in the Letters of Paul*, 189–90). See also Jewett, *Romans*, 22.

213. Jewett, *Romans*, 23.

carrier." He also adds that "in the case of the messengers of the wealthy and eminent, we may assume the couriers tended to be more conversant with the letter's contents and capable of adding supplementary news by word of mouth."[214]

Hence, although the literacy rate was likely low in the ancient real audience of Romans, in line with ancient letter practices, Tertius and Phoebe were present to shed light, where necessary, on the wider Hebrew Bible context.

3.3.4. The Role of the Wider Context in Romans 4

In spite of the evidence presented in my previous point, I am not insisting that we should always assume that the implied audience invokes the wider context of the LXX recitations. Rather, whether or not a Hebrew Bible context is factored into analysis should be judged on an individual basis. In the case of the use of Gen 15:6 LXX in Rom 4, several observations indicate that Paul intends the implied audience to invoke the surrounding context of Gen 15.

First, Wright makes the observation that in citing Gen 15:6 LXX, Paul considered the chapter as a whole. This is evident in that besides citing Gen 15:6 LXX in several places in Rom 4, he also recites Gen 15:5 LXX in Rom 4:18. Paul also makes use of the fact that certain events in Gen 15 precede the events in Gen 17. Furthermore, Paul alludes to Gen 18 and 22. Wright, however, does not delve more deeply into the argument of Gen 15, which yields substantial dividends for understanding Rom 4.

Second, as argued above, Gen 15:6 LXX should be viewed as a *chreia* and Rom 4:4–5 as a commentary on it. This poses a problem, as Gen 15:6 does not contain the idea of someone being an ungodly person. The suggestion that Abraham is the referent for this ungodly person is not borne out by Rom 4.[215] In fact, the reverse is true: Gen 15 and Rom 4 portray Abraham as a man of great trust in, or more precisely, loyalty to his patron, God. God justifying the ungodly (4:5), as Wright contends, recalls Gen 15:13–16, where the future descendants of Abraham are discussed.[216]

---

214. John L. White, *Light from Ancient Letters* (Philadelphia: Fortress, 1986), 216–17.

215. So most commentators, e.g., Dunn, *Romans 1–8*, 205; Godet, *Commentary on St. Paul's Epistle to the Romans*, 175; Moo, *Epistle to the Romans*, 265.

216. Wright, "Paul and the Patriarch," 218, 223. Wright remarks that "it is no

Third, in the seminar mentioned above on Paul and Scripture, Stephen Fowl suggests a way forward for detecting the presence of the larger context of a Hebrew Bible recitation. He suggests that in the absence of a direct indicator that Paul is engaging a LXX reference, one can rely on distinctive vocabulary to make the case.[217] Here, righteousness and trust in God are concepts emphasized in both Rom 4 and Gen 15. That Gen 14 is in view is corroborated by the tight nexus between Gen 14 and Gen 15: Abraham receives the promise of descendants that was catalyzed by a prior patron-client relationship between Abraham and God (Gen 14:17–21). Without this prior relationship of Abraham's trust in God, the promise of a descendant that finds its inception at Gen 15:1 would not have been possible. Thus, Rom 4:4–5 requires one to read the larger context of Gen 15:6 in Gen 14–15. Fowl also suggests that if Paul intends for the implied audience to dig deeper than just the LXX quotation, the interpreter should demonstrate that such a use of the larger context of the Hebrew Bible quotation enhances or advances the argument.[218] In the case of Rom 4, as I shall show in my analysis below, the larger context of Gen 15:6 enhances our understanding of "righteousness" as a relational term between a patron and a client or as the state of a relationship in a covenant.

Having made this introduction, I shall now show that the righteousness in Gen 15:6 refers to a relationship where Abraham finds favor with God. Abraham's position of favor causes God to grant to him the promise of numerous descendants who will possess the land. Thus, my analysis seeks to demonstrate two points: first, that righteousness involves a relationship, and second, that the result of Abraham's righteousness is that he is promised descendants and a land for these descendants. My analysis will proceed as follows. I will first analyze briefly the narrative in Gen 14:17–24 that forms the backdrop of Gen 15. Then the narrative in Gen 15:1–21 will be examined to shed light on the meaning of Gen 15:6. This analysis of the narratives of Gen 14–15 is not intended to be an exhaustive commentary. Only details that help to explain the focus of Gen 15:6 will be discussed.

---

objection to this to point out that τὸν ἀσεβῆ in Rom. 4.5 is singular, 'the ungodly one'; as BDAG 141 points out, citing the parallel 1 Pet. 4.18, this is an example of the 'collective singular,' as indeed in Gen. 18" (218 n. 33).

217. Stephen Fowl, "The Use of Scripture in Philippians," in Stanley, *Paul and Scripture*, 180–81.

218. Ibid., 180.

3.3.5. Genesis 14:17–24 LXX

The war that takes place in Gen 14 is one waged between King Chedor-laomer and the kings of his client states, one of whom is the king of Sodom. The relationship between the king of Sodom and King Chedorlaomer is likely a Hittite vassal-suzerainty type, but one that could also be subsumed under a patronage system, as I shall explain below.

George E. Mendenhall suggests that the Hittite suzerainty treaty by which a king bound his vassal states to faithfulness and obedience was in existence during the beginning of the Israelite people.[219] The Hittites, however, probably did not create this type of treaty, as it was already in use during the second millennium BCE by any number of peoples and states.[220] A similar treaty pact probably governed the relationship between King Chedorlaomer and his vassal states. According to Niels P. Lemche, treaties that bound vassals in Syria or Asia Minor to their Hittite overlord should be viewed as expressions of basic notions related to the system of patron-age.[221] Lemche points out that, despite the amount of material found in the archives of the Bronze Age Syrian states of Ugarit and Alalakh, extensive written laws that govern societies have not been discovered. Lemche is probably correct to suggest that justice was meted out by means of the patron-client system.[222] He also observes that during the Late Bronze Age, a king of a higher standing and one in a lower class would address each other metaphorically as father and son, respectively. These observations point to the existence of a patron-client system. That such patron-client relationships were in operation by the Late Bronze Age is also demonstrated by the letters discovered in the archive of Tell el-Amarna. This correspondence indicates that the local Palestinian kings regarded the relationship between themselves and their overlord Pharaoh to be a patronage system. A misunderstanding arose where the dependents had expected their overlords to protect them as a form of recompense, since they had

---

219. George E. Mendenhall, "Covenant Forms in Israelite Tradition," *BA* 17.3 (1954): 52.

220. Ibid., 54.

221. Niels P. Lemche, "Kings and Clients: On Loyalty between the Ruler and the Ruled in Ancient Israel," *Semeia* 66 (1995): 127.

222. Niels P. Lemche recites Deut 16:18–20 as an example. See Lemche, "Justice in Western Asia in Antiquity, or: Why No Laws Were Needed!," *CKLR* 70 (1995): 1708–16.

paid tribute to the Pharaoh of Egypt. These Palestinian states thought of themselves as clients of their Egyptian patron. The ruler of Egypt, however, regarded these dependents as mere employees who had an obligation to pay dues.[223] Such an existing patron-client system, as mentioned above, was probably in operation in the Middle Bronze Period, that is, during the time of Abraham. Genesis 14 should be read against such a backdrop of existing patronage systems. Within this framework, I shall examine Gen 14:17–24.

The narrational texture, a subtexture of inner texture, "resides in voices" as spoken by the narrator.[224] The narrational pattern of Gen 14:17–24 can be discerned by observing the sequence in which the narrator introduces characters and in which the characters speak. In Gen 14, after Abraham rescues his nephew Lot from the hands of the patron King Chedorlaomer—and, inadvertently, the king of Sodom—the voice of the narrator introduces two characters, first the king of Sodom and then King Melchizedek. These two persons come to see Abraham. What is interesting is the sequence in which these two characters approach Abraham. Whether or not both kings met Abraham at the same time is moot. The voice of the narrator introduces two characters who speak, who again are the same two characters mentioned above. By correlating the identities of the two characters who are introduced without making any speech and the same two characters who speak, it appears that the author of this passage has deliberately juxtaposed both characters, possibly in a chiastic manner.[225] This helps explain why the king of Sodom, who arrives at Gen

---

223. See Mario Liverani analysis of key ideas and words that gave rise to the misunderstanding between the patron Pharoah and his Palestinian state clients in "Political Lexicon and Political Ideologies in the Amarna Letters," *Berytus* 31 (1983): 41–56; see also Liverani, "Pharoah's Letters to Rib-Adda," in *Three Amarna Essays* (Malibu, CA: Undena, 1979), 3–13.

224. I am drawing on the insights of Robbins, "Sociorhetorical Criticism: Mary, Elizabeth, and the Magnificat," 41–45.

225. This answers the observation of Gordon J. Wenham that "it is admittedly strange that the king of Sodom having been introduced to Abram in v 17, Melchizedek should suddenly appear ... and the king of Sodom say nothing until v 21." See Wenham, *Genesis 1–15*, WBC (Dallas: Word, 1987), 304–5. Melchizedek's abrupt appearance has caused some scholars to view Gen 14:18–24 as a later insertion. For example, J. A. Emerton views the framework of Gen 14 as original but verses 18–20 as insertions. See Emerton, "The Riddle of Gen XIV," *VT* 21 (1971): 408–12. Similarly,

14:17, should wait until Gen 14:21 to speak. This narrational pattern aims to compare and contrast these two characters:[226]

14:17   Arrival of king of Sodom
    14:18   Arrival of king of Salem
    14:19–20   Speech by king of Salem
14:21   Speech by king of Sodom

The LXX has Melchizedek, in pronouncing blessings (εὐλογημένος) from the most high God, attach to the proper noun Αβραμ the dative substantive τῷ θεῷ τῷ ὑψίστῳ.[227] What is in question is the relationship between the proper noun and the dative substantive. Construing the dative as instrumental is possible. This would yield the translation "Blessed be Abram by the most high God."[228] Such a translation of Gen 14:19 LXX, however, is strange, as the verb is not expressed. Translating it as a dative of possession is better:[229] "Blessed be Abram of the most high God" (trans.

Gerhard von Rad views the king of Sodom as a "sharp contrast" with Melchizedek (*Genesis*, trans. John H. Marks [Philadelphia: Westminster, 1955], 176).

226. Wenham seems to imply a juxtaposition of these two kings when he writes that such an abrupt insertion about Melchizedek's enthusiasm heightens the reader's sense of the king of Sodom's "surliness towards Abram" (*Genesis 1–15*, 307).

227. G. Levi Della Vida notes that the Hebrew equivalent אֵל עֶלְיוֹן where 'Elyon is preceded by El occurs only here and in Ps 78:35. In this psalm, the expression parallels Elohim, and hence refers to Yahweh. See Vida, "El 'Elyon in Gen 14:18–20," *JBL* 63 (1944): 1–2. Similarly, Norman C. Habel, "Yahweh, Maker of Heaven and Earth," *JBL* 91 (1972): 321–24.

228. So NIV, NRSV, and ESV translate Gen 14:19 MT.

229. See Daniel B. Wallace, *Greek Grammar Beyond the Basics: An Exegetical Syntax of the New Testament* (Grand Rapids: Zondervan, 1996), 149. BDF §495 explains the difference between the dative of possession and genitive of possession, that "the genitive is used when the acquisition is recent or the emphasis is on the possessor … and the dative [is used] when the object possessed is to be stressed." Gen 14:19 LXX is a case in point. Josef Scharbert, based on analogies from Aramaic and Phoenician inscriptions, interprets ל as "in front of." The phrase ברוך אברם לאל עליון would then be translated as "blessed be Abram in front of El Elyon." See Scharbert, "'Gesegnet sei Abraham vom Höchsten Gott'? Zu Gen 14,19 und ähnlichen Stellen im Alten Testament,'" in *Text, Methode und Grammatik: Wolfgang Richter zum 65. Geburtstag*, ed. Walter Gross, Hubert Irsigler, and Theodor Seidl (St. Ottilien: EOS, 1991), 387–401. This possible translation, however, fails to shed light on the context whose emphasis, as I argue, is on Abram as Yahweh's client.

Brenton). Such a construal has two advantages. First, this understanding coheres with the Hebrew Bible, where the preposition לְ in the expression אברם לאל עליון indicates possession. This yields the translation "Abram of El Elyon," which emphasizes Abraham as belonging somehow to God. Second, this translation fits the emphasis of Gen 14:17–24 on Abraham as a client of the patron God, Yahweh. Melchizedek praises the most high God for delivering Abraham's enemies into his power. Considering that the incident about Abraham giving tithes to Melchizedek follows closely on the heels of Melchizedek's pronouncement of a blessing on Abraham, the tithe should be read as a response of gratitude that a client shows toward his patron. This ties in with the custom in this milieu of giving tithes to sanctuaries and kings.[230] As this tithe is probably a part of the booty that is rightfully Abraham's, by giving it to Yahweh, Abraham indicates that he acknowledges this booty was won by the help of Yahweh.[231] Thus, Abraham, by presenting a tithe to Melchizedek, indicates that he is a client of אל עליון, or as the LXX translates it, τῷ θεῷ τῷ ὑψίστῳ. The intent of the king of Sodom's speech in Gen 14:20 LXX should be read in light of Abraham's rejection in Gen 14:22 LXX: the king of Sodom is offering Abraham a part of the booty won during the war.[232] This offer must be read in light of the patron-client setting of Gen 14, where King Chedorlaomer acts as the patron of the vassal state kings, including the king of Sodom.[233] This setting sheds light on the speech made by the last character who speaks, as introduced by the "voice" of the narrator. Considering that this final character who speaks breaks away from the chiasm of Gen 14:17–21, it is reasonable to construe what Abraham says in Gen 14:22–24

---

230. So Wenham, *Genesis 1–15*, 317. Von Rad views Abraham's tithe as a sign of submission to the blessing from Melchizedek (*Genesis*, 175).

231. Wenham comments that the tithe, that is, a tenth of all (כל), must be taken from the booty since he was on his way home (*Genesis 1–15*, 317); so also Victor P. Hamilton, *The Book of Genesis: Chapters 1–17*, NICOT (Grand Rapids: Eerdmans, 1990), 413.

232. Wenham misses the point of this juxtaposition when he regards the king of Sodom as making "a short, almost rude demand" (*Genesis 1–15*, 318). In fact, the opposite is true: the king of Sodom was offering something (a part of the booty) to Abram.

233. Gary Stansell agrees with my view that "this is not about Abraham's generosity ... but about his refusal to enter into a patron-client relationship with the king." See Stansell, "Wealth: How Abraham Became Rich," in *Ancient Israel: The Old Testament in Its Social Context*, ed. Philip F. Esler (Minneapolis: Fortress, 2006), 100.

as constituting the main point of the narrative. Furthermore, Abraham's voice should also be construed as the dominant voice that carries with it ideological power to subvert the voice of the king of Sodom, and hence persuade the audience to assent to Abraham's voice.[234] Abraham's rejection resembles legal texts that renounce property rights.[235] This implies that he (Abraham) is formally rejecting the king of Sodom's offer of patronage. Thus, Gen 14:17–24 emphasizes Abraham's rejection of the king of Sodom's patronage and his acknowledgement of the patronage of Yahweh, the most high God.

3.3.6. Genesis 15:1–21 LXX

The opening-middle-closing subtexture of the inner texture of Gen 15 can be displayed as follows:

Opening (15:12): Abraham laments that he has no descendant
Middle (15:13–17): God resolves Abraham's lament
Closing (15:18–21): Abraham's descendants will inherit the land
Significant for our analysis is the observation that Abraham's lament about not having descendants in the opening is apparently resolved in the closing by God's promise that Abraham's descendants will inherit the land. It appears, as my analysis below will verify, that Abraham's concern about having descendants is closely related to his descendants inheriting the land. My analysis will proceed according to the above-delineated sections of opening, middle, and closing: Gen 15:1–2; 15:3–17; 15:18–21.

3.3.6.1. Genesis 15:1–2 LXX

Genesis 15 LXX begins with the prepositional phrase μετὰ δὲ τὰ ῥήματα ταῦτα ("and after these things"), which ties the events in Gen 15 to Gen 14. The prepositional phrase אחר הדברים in the Hebrew Bible also signals a clear tie to the events in Gen 14.[236] The phrase τὰ ῥήματα ταῦτα refers to

---

234. I am again using the insights of Robbins, "Sociorhetorical Criticism: Mary, Elizabeth, and the Magnificat," 66.

235. So Wenham, *Genesis 1–15*, 318.

236. Bruce K. Waltke and M. O'Connor construe the function of this preposition as temporal. See Waltke and O'Connor, *An Introduction to Biblical Hebrew Syntax* (Winona Lake, IN: Eisenbrauns, 1990), 192–93. Bruce K. Waltke and Cathi J. Fredricks comment that, "although 'after this' may refer to all the scenes of Genesis 12–14,

events that could have made Abraham afraid. One event to which it likely refers is that of Gen 14:17–24 LXX.

Seen from this perspective, we would be able to understand why Yahweh gives to Abraham a word of assurance: "Fear not, Abram. I am shielding you and your reward is exceedingly great" (Gen 15:1 LXX). The fear is a consequence of rejecting the patronage of the king of Sodom. The reward is a result of Abraham remaining under the patronage of Yahweh. What this implies is that Gen 15 must be read in light of Gen 14:17–21, that is, with a view to the formation of a patron-client relationship.

At the outset in Gen 15:1–2, Abraham is concerned with having not only a descendant but a descendant who will inherit his inheritance. After Yahweh promises to reward Abraham for acknowledging him as patron, Abraham responds immediately with a rhetorical question. Scholars agree this is not a real question but rather a complaint. Victor Hamilton comments on the meaning of Abraham's reply: "What useful purpose would be served by a reward that could not be transmitted?"[237] The subject matter that follows concerns having a descendant who comes from Abraham's own physical body. The question is rhetorical, as intimated by the clause that connects (by way of the light adversative δέ) this question to its explanation: he is childless and his slave will be his heir. Abraham is essentially lamenting that there is nothing that he desires from Yahweh since what he desires most—a son—cannot be fulfilled at a time when his death draws

---

it is most closely connected to chapter 14." See Waltke and Fredricks, *Genesis: A Commentary* (Grand Rapids: Zondervan, 2001), 240. Many scholars view Gen 14:18–24 as a late addition, and various conjectures have been postulated on the compositional history of Gen 14. This does not mean, however, that Gen 14 cannot be analyzed as a consistent literary unit. Gard Granerød argues that chapter 14 is a "unified and internally consistent narrative." See Granerød, *Abraham and Melchizedek: Scribal Activity of Second Temple Times in Genesis 14 and Psalm 110*, BZAW 406 (Berlin: de Gruyter, 2010), 16. Robert Alter suggests that "the editorial combination of different literary sources might usefully be conceived as the final stage in the process of artistic creation which produced biblical narratives." See *The Art of Biblical Narrative* (New York: Basic Books, 1981), 133. Thomas D. Alexander notes the conjunction that connects Gen 14 and 15. He also detects common ideas in these two chapters. Unfortunately, he does not explore the connection but instead links Gen 15 with Gen 11:27–12:9.

237. See Thomas D. Alexander, "A Literary Analysis of the Abraham Narrative in Genesis" (PhD diss., Queen's University of Belfast, 1982), 43. See also Hamilton, *Genesis 1–17*, 420. Similarly, Wenham, *Genesis 1–15*, 328; Waltke and Fredricks, *Genesis*, 241.

near.[238] Instead, Abraham continues his lament that Eliezer, his slave, will be his heir. How Abraham's lament will be alleviated is narrated in Gen 15:3–17.

3.3.6.2. Genesis 15:3–17 LXX

I shall begin by tracing the flow of the narrative in Gen 15:3–17 while highlighting certain details along the way. After that, I will explain how those details demonstrate my contention that Yahweh's promises to Abraham of descendants and land are basically different facets of the same promise. I will also show that righteousness is relational, specifically, a favorable relationship between God as the patron and Abraham as the client.

Construing the dialogue in 15:3–6 as a normal conversation is possible. More likely, however, this dialogue is Abraham's strategy of requesting a gift from Yahweh. Using dialogue to secure a promise from Yahweh is not unusual for Abraham, as he later utilizes this mode to secure the safety of Lot in Gen 18:16–33. Specifically, this gift is a descendant who will become Abraham's natural heir.

Abraham begins by lamenting and suggesting that "a slave in my house, he will inherit [יוֹרֵשׁ] me (a metonym for 'my inheritance')" (Gen 15:3 MT) or "A slave in my house will inherit [κληρονομήσει] me (a metonym for "my inheritance")" (Gen 15:3 LXX). Yahweh, however, rejects Abraham's suggestion: "This man will not inherit [יִירָשְׁךָ] you (your inheritance) ... but he who comes out from your own belly will inherit [יִירָשְׁךָ] you (your inheritance)" (Gen 15:4 MT) or "he who will come out from you will inherit [κληρονομήσει] you (your inheritance)" (Gen 15:4 LXX). In Gen 15:5, Yahweh grants to Abraham many descendants.

When Abraham הֶאֱמִן/ἐπίστευσεν ("trusted") Yahweh in Gen 15:6, Abraham was regarded as righteous. Important for a right interpretation of this verse is determining the time when Abraham acknowledged Yahweh as his patron, that is, trusted Yahweh. Abraham had already trusted Yahweh *as patron* as early as Gen 15:1. When Abraham trusted Yahweh at Gen 15:6, it was not to begin a patron-client relationship but to trust Yahweh for some provision, in this case, a descendant. Abraham's trust was demonstrated when he rejected the king of Sodom as patron and

---

238. Robert Alter interprets the Hebrew text as a euphemism for dying; the verb ἀπολύομαι (LXX) is used sometimes to denote death (e.g., Num 20:29; Tob 3:6). See Alter, *The Five Books of Moses: A Translation with Commentary* (London: Norton, 2004), 73.

gave a tithe to Melchizedek. This observation has implications for how we construe "righteousness" in Gen 15:6. The verbs אמן/πιστεύειν must be understood in light of the patronage backdrop of Gen 14:17–21, with which Gen 15 is tightly linked. This implies that the patron-client relationship of Gen 14 forms the framework for the grant of descendants in Gen 15. In other words, this righteousness refers to covenant faithfulness or loyalty that makes Yahweh favorably disposed to rewarding Abraham with numerous descendants. In this respect, I am following Hermann Cremer's interpretation of צדקה/צדק as a concept of relationship (*Verhältnisbegriff*). People bring their own claims to a relationship. When these claims are mutually fulfilled, they are considered righteous.[239] In other words, both parties demonstrate covenant faithfulness. This understanding is a corrective to the long-held view that construes "righteousness" as merely conformity to the norm of distributive justice.[240] As far as Gen 15:6 is concerned, the righteousness that is immediately in view refers not to conformity to an absolute norm—the holiness of God—but to Abraham having fulfilled his role by trust in Yahweh or loyalty in his covenant relationship with Yahweh.[241] This conceptualization of righteousness also coheres with Greco-Roman usage:

The idea of justice [δίκη/*iustitia*], which acknowledges that there is such a thing as a social group, that all its members of the group have value (if

---

239. Hermann Cremer, *Die Paulinische Rechtfertigungslehre* (Gütersloh: Bertelsmann, 1899), 33–38.

240. E.g., after David spared the life of his enemy Saul, Saul spoke to David saying: "You are more righteous [צדיק] than I; for you have repaid me good, whereas I have repaid you evil" (1 Sam 24:17 LXX [24:18 MT]). John Piper cites Ps 143:1, 2 as an example that shows "righteousness" to denote God fulfilling covenant faithfulness. Here, the psalmist requests God to save him on the basis of God's righteousness in spite of the fact that he is not a righteous man. See Piper, *The Justification of God: An Exegetical and Theological Study of Romans 9:1–23* (Grand Rapids: Baker, 1993), 107–8. That said, righteousness as conformity to a norm of distributive justice exists in the Greco-Roman world. For references that indicate that the Greco-Roman world acknowledged the existence of natural law, see Morgan, *Roman Faith and Christian Faith*, 490–98. For example, Cicero recognizes the universe as a household shared by gods and humans who live according to justice and law (*Nat. d.* 2.154); laws of justice are legislated by Isis (*IG* 12 Suppl. 14).

241. See Gerhard von Rad, *Old Testament Theology*, trans. D. M. G. Stalker, 2 vols. (New York: Harper, 1962), 1:371. This implies also that the post-Reformation concept of forensic justification, as much as it is valid, is not immediately in view here.

not necessarily equal value), and that the group cannot hold together or pursue individual or collective interests unless all its members' interests are in some degree served.[242]

When God promises Abraham and his descendants a land, Abraham asks in Gen 15:7 for an assurance: "By what will I know that I will possess [אירשנה] it (the land)?" (Gen 15:8 MT); "How will I know that I will inherit [κληρονομήσω] it (the land)?" (Gen 15:8 LXX). Yahweh gives him the assurance by instituting a Hittite-type treaty (Gen 15:9–17). Yahweh, however, not only assures Abraham of land; his reply in Gen 15:9–21 also states that a distant future generation of Abraham's descendants will inherit the land.

The above discussion shows that, despite the seeming difference in concerns, whereas Gen 15:1–6 focuses on descendants and Gen 15:7–21 is about the land, both passages are closely related.[243] First, the same verbs, ירש/κληρονομεῖν, are used to talk about who will possess Abraham's inheritance. Thus, a verbal link exists between Gen 15:1–6 and 15:7–21. Second, in Gen 15:1–6, Abraham desires not only a descendant, but a descendant who will inherit his inheritance. In other words, the concern that Abraham's descendant will inherit Abraham's inheritance dominates both Gen 15:1–6 and 15:7–21. After all, without descendants, land is worthless.[244] I also contend that the inheritance in Gen 15:1 and the land that Yahweh will give Abraham are basically the same thing. This is corroborated by the fact that in an agrarian society, both terms refer to the land and its produce. The difference is that what Abraham possesses now is a much smaller subset of the future land that he, through his descendants, will possess.

---

242. Morgan notes that Greek and Roman writers use the lexica of δίκη/iustitia to refer to that which is "legally sanctioned, divinely sanctioned, and customary or socially normative" (*Roman Faith*, 487).

243. E.g., Wenham focuses his discussion of Gen 15:7–21 on the land without giving attention to the land's relationship to descendants (*Genesis 1–15*, 335). Similarly, Alter, *Five Books of Moses*, 74; Hamilton, *Genesis 1–17*, 429.

244. Paul R. Williamson opines that without descendants, land was worthless. See Williamson, *Abraham, Israel, and the Nations: The Patriarchal Promise and Its Covenantal Development in Genesis*, JSOTSup 315 (Sheffield: Sheffield Academic, 2000), 133; see also Walter Brueggemann, *Genesis*, IBC (Atlanta: John Knox, 1982), 142.

3.3.6.3. Genesis 15:18–21 LXX

The argument above has shown that Abraham's desire was not merely to have a descendant but to have a descendant who would inherit the land promised to him along with its produce. When this is understood, we are able to see that the closing section, Gen 15:18–21, constitutes a closing to the opening in Gen 15:1–2. In Gen 15:18–21 Yahweh concludes the Hittite covenant ceremony by declaring that Abraham's descendants will inherit the land. This has come to fruition because Abraham in Gen 15:6 acted righteously by trusting Yahweh as patron to provide descendants for him (Abraham). This act of trusting Yahweh, and not someone else, is also an act of loyalty. Paul will later (in 4:4–5) explain that this act of trust is in contrast to deeds. Furthermore, Yahweh also acted righteously by promising to provide for Abraham. Consequently, the relationship between Abraham and Yahweh, his patron, is considered a righteous relationship.

3.3.7. Relationship between Trust and Righteousness

A social and cultural texture underlies the relationship between trust and righteousness. Teresa Morgan's discussion helps. First, Romans honor Jupiter and Fides as the guardians of oaths, treaties, and contracts.[245] Fides is also thought to support all aspects of the well-being of the society, from agriculture to politics, and in times of war and peace.[246] Romans, thus, regard Jupiter and Fides as the significant others with regard to what constitutes a righteous treaty or contract. Second, in both the Greek and Roman world, πίστις/fides and δίκη/iustitia are closely related. This relationship is founded upon the relationship between Zeus or Jupiter, who are both closely associated with righteousness, and the goddess Fides. The goddess Fides is thought to be the hypostasis of Jupiter.[247] The relationship between righteousness and trust, "mirroring that between Jupiter, Fides, and divine Iustitia, is so intimate that each can be seen as giving rise to the other or the two together forming the foundation of civil society."[248] Romans thus understand that trust is essential for a relationship to be considered as righteous. This social intertexture creates an ideological

---

245. Morgan, *Roman Faith and Christian Faith*, 129.

246. Ibid., 130.

247. Ibid., 128–29. See Georg Wissowa, *Religion und Kultus der Römer* (Munich: Beck, 1912), 52–53.

248. Morgan, *Roman Faith and Christian Faith*, 130.

texture to persuade the audience that Abraham obtained righteousness by trust.

3.4. Romans 4:4–5: Deeds and Trust Are Antithetical

How 4:4–5 explains the significance of Gen 15:6 LXX is debated. Barrett thinks that the use of 4:4–5 hinges on the word λογίζεσθαι ("to be reckoned"), that the implication of righteousness having been reckoned to Abraham means that Abraham did not do deeds. The conclusion that ensues is that Abraham is made righteous by divine favor ("grace"). Moreover, trust and favor, so Barrett presumes, correlate to one another and so lead to the conclusion that deeds and trust are opposites.[249] This view falters on several observations. First, Cranfield retorts that λογίζεται ("is reckoned") is associated with both φείλημα ("obligation") and χάρις ("favor").[250] Second, how trust correlates with favor needs to be explained in view of the fact that Judean interpretation of Gen 15:6 understands Abraham's trust in God to refer to faithfulness when he was tempted.[251] Jewett interprets the weight of 4:4–5 as resting on two words. First, he thinks that the word λογίζεσθαι is a commercial term that denotes charging a bill, calculating a debt, or counting out wages for work done. Second, he argues that the term πιστεύοντι ("trusting") is a theological term whose meaning has been expounded in the preceding chapter, and hence is already clear to the audience. Jewett's view is refuted by Cranfield (see above). Also, this view ignores the contemporary use of πίστις ("trust"). As I will argue below, since 4:4–5 should be construed as expounding Gen 15:6 LXX, the immediate context of 4:4–5 should be Gen 15:6 LXX. To properly understand 4:4–5, we will need to investigate the cultural contexts of the terms χάρις, ἔργα, and πίστις and their relationship with one another.

As argued above, Paul's recitation of Gen 15:6 LXX constitutes a *chreia*.[252] Hermogenes of Tarsus explains that a *chreia* is elaborated in several

---

249. Barrett, *Epistle to the Romans*, 88.

250. Cranfield, *Epistle to the Romans*, 1:230.

251. "Remember the deeds of the ancestors, which they did in their generations; and you will receive great honor and an everlasting name. Was not Abraham found faithful when tested, and it was reckoned to him as righteousness?" (1 Macc 2:51–52).

252. See above, §3.2, "Romans 4:3: Scripture Says that Abraham Was Reckoned as Righteous by His Trust in God."

ways, one of which is by means of comparison and contrast.[253] The above observation means that the significance of Paul's recitation of Gen 15:6 LXX is encapsulated by Rom 4:4–5. In addition, the meaning of Rom 4:4–5 should be read in light of Gen 15:6 LXX. I will now analyze Rom 4:4–5 for how this passage substantiates Gen 15:6 LXX.

Romans 4:4–5 basically comprises a pair of parallel lines as the common vocabulary τῷ δὲ ἐργαζομένῳ ("but to the one who works") and λογίζεται indicates. The particle of negation μή makes them a pair of contrasting parallel lines. They do not, however, correspond exactly to one another. By observing elements that disrupt the parallelism, we can gain insights into the significance of this passage. To keep the parallelism, the second line should read "but to the one who does not work, the wages are reckoned according to favor and not due." Instead, Paul writes "But to the one who does not work, but trusts...." This observation exposes a twofold social intertexture.

First, the above comparison and contrast shows that ἔργα and χάρις operate in opposite ways. As Paul explains, a μισθός ("wage") that is derived from ἔργα is not a result of χάρις. This becomes clearer when χάρις is read in light of the patron-client culture. We have established that the *chreia*, Gen 15:6 LXX, should be read against a patron-client backdrop. As Gen 15:6 is set during the Middle Bronze Age, it seems anachronistic for Paul to use a first century CE analogy to elaborate on Gen 15:6 LXX. But this does not appear to be an issue with Paul, probably because the basic parameters underlying the patron-client culture in both the Hebrew Bible and New Testament times did not change: the relationship between a patron and a client is asymmetrical and requires "reciprocity not by balanced exchange or by a return of equal or greater value but by the giving of honor, gratitude, and loyalty."[254]

In the preindustrial, first-century world of the New Testament, power, property, and wealth were concentrated in the hands of two percent of the people.[255] They were the elite of the ancient society, specifically, the Roman senatorial families and the Roman emperor, who could gain for the rest of

---

253. George A. Kennedy, trans. and ed., *Progymnasmata: Greek Textbooks of Prose Composition and Rhetoric*, WGRW 10 (Atlanta: Society of Biblical Literature, 2003), 77.

254. Zeba A. Crook, "Reciprocity: Covenantal Exchange," in Esler, *Ancient Israel*, 82–83.

255. Malina, *New Testament World*, 89.

the people access to the resources of the Roman state.[256] Necessary goods could be purchased from the market. For special goods, which included "legal advocacy, financial aid, political influence, and in general, access to the lever of powers,"[257] the vast majority of the world had to ask favors of these elites. When a patron granted a favor, an enduring and personal patron-client relationship was formed.[258] John M. G. Barclay reiterates the importance of patronage: "In a city without a strong, independent, or impartial bureaucracy, whom one was connected to, and what favors one could ask or call upon, were the crucial mechanisms for success."[259]

James Harrison argues that Paul's use of χάρις should not be read against an aristocratic literary backdrop. Rather, the patronage system should inform the use of this word.[260] Several observations support this. Harrison ascribes priority to the public inscriptions (200 BCE–200 CE) as they were readily accessible to the Greco-Roman public for several reasons. For one, patrons engraved these inscriptions so that posterity could read them.[261] Also, these eulogistic inscriptions were widespread

---

256. Barclay, *Paul and the Gift*, 36.

257. Ibid., 37.

258. David A. deSilva, *Honor, Patronage, Kinship and Purity: Unlocking New Testament Culture* (Downers Grove, IL: InterVarsity Press, 2000), 96–97.

259. Barclay, *Paul and the Gift*, 37.

260. James R. Harrison, *Paul's Language of Grace in Its Graeco-Roman Context*, WUNT 2/172 (Tübingen: Mohr Siebeck, 2003), 26–27.

261. Harrison construes χάρις against the backdrop of the Hellenistic benefactor-beneficiary reciprocity system (ibid., 1). He argues that this was the prevailing system in the eastern Mediterranean basin, the area where Paul founded his house churches. He prefers this construal over the Roman patronage system, espoused in Richard P. Saller, *Personal Patronage under the Early Empire* (Cambridge: Cambridge University Press, 1982). The problem with Saller's research, some felt, was that it glossed over differences in the various asymmetrical relationships that involve exchange (e.g., marriage and slavery). See, e.g., Claude Eilers, *Roman Patrons of Greek Cities* (Oxford: Oxford University Press, 2002), 6–7; A. N. Sherwin-White, review of *Personal Patronage under the Early Empire*, by Richard P. Saller, *CR* 33 (1983): 271–73. In this book I have chosen to use the terminology of the Roman patronage system not because every asymmetrical relationship is the same but because, as Bruce A. Lowe comments: "What this case study shows, though, is how difficult it is to choose terms—more difficult than those opposing Saller have often acknowledged, with their failure to properly distinguish the synchronic from the diachronic as well as the signified from the signifier. What is more important in all this is finding a word that means something to a modern implied audience and yet still captures the sense of intention in terms of the things originally signified." Lowe adds that "with Saller's work acting as a paradigmatic

throughout the eastern Mediterranean basin. In the Latin West, *gratia* and its cognates were also widespread in honorific inscriptions. This ensured familiarity with Paul's use of patronage terminology. Moreover, decrees erected by small clubs or associations made patronage terminology pervasive in Greco-Roman culture.[262] Several inscriptions indicate that χάρις may refer to a favor bestowed on the client by the patron. In 71 BCE, the Roman patrons of Gytheion, Numerius, and Marcus Cloatius demonstrated their favor (χάρις) by releasing the city Gytheion from a repayment of two loans (*SIG* 3.748). In the late second century BCE, Xenocleas of Akraeoguae "had performed not a few favors [χάριτας οὐκ ὀλίγας] for the people" of Akraephiae (*RIG* 236). Harrison concludes that these numerous inscriptions demonstrate that χάρις functions as the central term for favors bestowed by patrons on clients.[263] This term can also refer to the return of a favor by the client. During the first century CE, the people of Busiris set up a stone stela to praise General Gnaius Pompeius so as "to reciprocate with favors" (ἀμείβεσθαι χά[ρισιν]) for building dikes and the fair distribution of the crop (*SEG* 8.527). In an honorific first-century CE decree in which the people of the city of Cardamylae praise their patron Poseidippos (*SEG* 11.948), terminology of exchange— ἀμοιβή ("recompense"), ἀντί ("in exchange for"), καθιστάναι ("reinstate"), and ἀποδιδόναι ("to repay")—is used in conjunction with χάρις.[264] In this inscription, the favor rendered to the patron by the client is described as the lesser favor (ἐλάττονος χάριτος). This implies that χάρις is used to denote both the favor dispensed by the patron and the client. Reciprocity in gifts and favors governed relations in the Greek social world.[265] In Roman culture, a client was also obliged to return gifts (χάρις) to the client in both senatorial and imperial patronage (see, e.g., Pliny the Younger, *Ep.* 2.13; cf. Cicero, *Off.* 1.47).[266] However, χάρις should not be construed

---

starting point for so much of New Testament studies, it would be a backwards step to insist upon a different word, or some clumsy expression like *reciprocity system.*" See Lowe, "Paul, Patronage and Benefaction: A 'Semiotic' Reconsideration," in *Paul and His Social Relations*, ed. Stanley E. Porter and Christopher D. Land, Pauline Studies 7 (Leiden: Brill, 2013), 84 and 79, respectively, emphasis original.

262. Harrison, *Paul's Language of Grace*, 27–29.

263. Ibid., 47.

264. Ibid., 51.

265. See the Greek literature cited in Barclay, *Paul and the Gift*, 24–35.

266. Ibid., 38–39. Barclay also notes that Romans were explicit about the obligation to reciprocate a favor, and that "the language of 'binding' (*obstringere*; *obligare*)

as services or goods dispensed that expected or served as repayments. Rather, χάρις should be regarded as a gift. Barclay contends that

> what distinguishes the sphere of gifts is [that] it expresses a social bond, a mutual recognition of the value of the *person*. It is filled with sentiment because it invites a personal, enduring, and reciprocal relationship—an ethos very often signaled by the use of the term χάρις.[267]

This above contention is corroborated by Seneca's exposition of the *ethos* of gift giving.[268] Seneca advocates that gifts must be reciprocated (see, e.g., *Ben.* 2.17.3; 2.32.1; 4.18.1–4; 7.18.1).[269] At the same time, giving is done for the sake of friendship between the involved parties: gift giving is about "sociality (*res socialis*, 5.11.5), tying people together in bonds of debt or obligation."[270] What is foremost in the gift is not the *res* ("the thing")—specifically, the object and its worth—but the *animus* (*Ben.* 2.34–35), which refers to how the gift is given (1.5.3). In other words, reciprocal giving demonstrated a personal relationship, that is, a friendship, between the giver and receiver, and it did not serve as a repayment. This same reasoning undergirds my contention that righteousness in Rom 4 has ethical implications: Christians are expected to live ethically righteous lives not as a repayment for God's favor (4:4) in regarding Christians as righteous; rather, ethical living is evidence of an existing cordial or righteous relationship between God as patron and Christians as the client.

In the above example, the phrase "lesser favor" emphasizes that the favor the people of the city of Cardamylae received was *unpayable*. Furthermore, a patron—as in the case of the city of Cardamylae's praise for its patron, Poseidippos—does not intend the favor to be repaid in kind.

---

is ubiquitous in such contexts" (p. 39). Cicero describes the return of χάρις as more necessary (*magis necessarium*) than all other obligations.

267. Ibid., 31, emphasis original. Similarly, Troels Engberg-Pedersen, "Gift-Giving and Friendship: Seneca and Paul in Romans 1–8 on the Logic of God's Χάρις and Its Human Response," *HTR* 101 (2008): 20.

268. Barclay, *Paul and the Gift*, 45–51.

269. In 7.18.1, he describes gift giving as a ball that is being circulated back and forth. Barclay observes that Seneca "*never* idealizes the one-way, unreciprocated gift" (*Paul and the Gift*, 50 [emphasis original]).

270. Ibid., 46.

This finds evidence in φιλοτιμία ("love of honor") as motivation.[271] Thus, Poseidippos receives favor (χάρις) in return for his love of honor, which was considered "the main form of return that the socially inferior can give to the superiors."[272] This "love of honor" was considered to be positive in ancient culture. In other words, the favor returned by the city of Cardamylae to Poseidippos is honor. In another example, a corporation of merchants erected an honorific decree from Delos in praise of its patron who dispensed favors out of love of honor. A first-century honorific decree (41/42 CE) makes the same point, although the word αἰμιτολιφ is not used: Phainios, son of Aromatios, left a sum of eight thousand denarii to city magistrates in order that the needy might take loans (*SEG* 13.258). His generosity is also demonstrated in allowing slaves to share in Phainios's gift of oil for six days a year. He also makes explicit his intent in dispensing these favors, which is "to achieve immortality in making such a just and kindly disposal (of my property)."[273] Read in light of the inscriptions, the antithesis of χάρις and ἔργα becomes pronounced.

The contrast between χάρις and ἔργα is also accentuated when ἔργα is read in light of the social and cultural intertexture of wage laborers. The per-capita income was invariably low. The minimum annual cost of average subsistence is estimated to be 115 sesterces and the wage of an ordinary Roman citizen is about one-and-a-half times subsistence.[274] Furthermore, wage laborers (*mercennarii*), whom the upper-class authors regarded as almost slaves,[275] were often employed only seasonally for haymaking, harvesting, or work in the vineyard.[276] Aristotle locates them in the lowest class of wage laborers (*Pol.* 4.11), dependent labor who comprise mostly

---

271. See also *RIG* 998, where a corporation of merchants erected an honorific decree during the early second century BCE.

272. Barclay, *Paul and the Gift*, 29.

273. See Harrison, *Paul's Language of Grace*, 60–61.

274. Keith Hopkins, "Rome, Taxes, Rents, and Trade," in *The Ancient Economy*, ed. Walter Scheidel and Sitta von Reden, ERAW (Edinburgh: Edinburgh University Press, 2002), 190–230.

275. For evidence of the similarity between a wage laborer and a slave laborer, see G. E. M. de Ste. Croix, *The Class Struggle in the Ancient Greek World: From the Archaic Age to the Arab Conquests* (Ithaca: Cornell University Press, 1981), 179–204.

276. William V. Harris, "The Late Republic," in *The Cambridge Economic History of the Greco-Roman World*, ed. Walter Scheidel, Ian Morris, and Richard Saller (Cambridge: Cambridge University Press, 2007), 528.

slaves.[277] Living conditions for them were harsh.[278] Viewed in light of the above-described Greco-Roman social setting, paying a worker for work done is imperative. There is no place for χάρις where ἔργα is present. This brings out the antithesis between χάρις and ἔργα.

Another social and cultural intertexture also underlies the antithesis between χάρις and ἔργα. The Mediterranean culture developed from an "overlay of Roman political power onto 'Greek' traditions."[279] Hence, to understand gift reciprocity in Roman patronage, assumptions underlying Greek gift reciprocity need to be highlighted. Barclay argues that reciprocity in gifts pervaded Greek social relations. This makes life pleasant and more secure. At the same time, gift giving had its inherent problems. It could function like modern-day bribery in legal disputes, as judges were obligated to return the gifts given them by their benefactors. In response, the Athenian Constitution provides payment (μισθοφρά) to the citizen-jurors so as to distance them from the influence of reciprocal giving, which can turn into a form of bribery (Aristotle, *Ath. pol.* 27.2). Another area where reciprocal giving became in reality bribery was trading. An instance was when Menelaus received gifts from kings in the Arab trade (Strabo, *Geogr.* 1.2.32).[280] When χάρις is read against its abuse in bribery,

> a subtle change comes over the meaning of such words as μισθός…. [W] ithin the domain of commodity exchange or work-for-pay, it gains the meaning of "wage" or "hire," with a commercial sense outside of (and morally inferior to) the domain of gift.[281]

Underlying the term χάρις is the social and cultural intertexture that a gift must be given to a worthy client. When it is given to an unworthy client, it becomes "an incongruous gift."[282] In such a circumstance Barclay

---

277. William V. Harris convincingly argues for the relevance of the concept of class in application to Roman society. See Harris, "The Concept of Class in Roman History," in *Forms of Control and Subordination in Antiquity*, ed. Toru Yuge and Masa-oki Doi (Leiden: Brill, 1988), 598–605.

278. Although Harris may be overstating his case when he argues that the economic factor defines a social class, one's economic standing is certainly one of the defining characteristics ("Concept of Class in Roman History," 604).

279. Barclay, *Paul and the Gift*, 24.

280. Ibid., 30–31.

281. Ibid., 31–32.

282. Barclay recognizes that χάρις ("grace" or "gift") is polyvalent and suggests

regards such a gift as "perfect." This observation further contrasts χάρις and ἔργα.

The second social intertexture exposed by the pair of contrasting statements in 4:4–5 is a close nexus between trust and favor (grace). The above discussion has shown that a favor dispensed by patrons must be returned with a favor. The returned favor took the form of honor. If a favor was not returned, that client was considered ungrateful. The question is what constitutes a legitimate mode of showing gratitude. Several observations indicate that demonstrating trust (*fides*/πίστις) in the patron is the main mode.[283] Ehrensperger maintains that

> *fides* was not only important in the relation between Rome and conquered nations, it permeated all aspects of Roman society. The patronage system depended on *fides* in that the client was granted protection and certain favours by the patron and in turn owed the patron unconditional *fides*. Loyalty and trust in these relationships were neither an affair of mutuality nor merely voluntarily as most free non-elite people depended on patronage relationships as a matter of survival.[284]

Trust constitutes the main component that cements the relationship between the patron and the client. Morgan contends that "when one partner in a commercial transaction gives credit to another, he or she expresses his or her trust and belief that the debtor is trustworthy; at the same time, the transaction becomes a legal entity with enforceable properties recognized by both parties."[285] *Fides*/πίστις also sustains and extends a business

---

six ways in which it can become the ideal or "perfect" gift (ibid., 66–78). The modern notion of a perfect gift is when it is given without expecting reciprocation in any form is one of them. That, however, is not the only way to perfect a gift. Here, the gift is perfect because it is given to an unworthy client.

283. Ehrensperger, *Paul at the Crossroads of Cultures*, 171. Regarding the terms *pistis* and *fides* and their cognates, Morgan observes that "after a period in which their differences were stressed, it is now widely accepted that they share almost all their meanings. 'Trust,' 'trustworthiness,' 'honesty,' 'credibility,' 'faithfulness,' 'good faith,' 'confidence,' 'assurance,' 'pledge,' 'guarantee,' 'credit,' 'proof,' 'credence,' 'belief,' 'position of trust/trusteeship,' 'legal trust,' 'protection,' 'security,' are all widely attested as meanings of both lexica" (*Roman Faith and Christian Faith*, 7). See also the discussion in Salvatore Calderone, *Pistis-Fides: Ricerche di storia e diritto internazionale nell'antichità* (Messina: Università degli studi, 1964), 61–98.

284. Ehrensperger, *Paul at the Crossroads of Cultures*, 171.

285. Morgan, *Roman Faith and Christian Faith*, 6; similarly, deSilva, *Honor*, 115.

patron-client relationship (see, e.g., Pliny the Younger, *Ep.* 2.13.5; 3.2.1–3; 10.4.3–4).[286] In the Greek play *Menaechmi*, written by Plautus (ca. 254–184 BCE) and translated into Latin, the hero Menaechmus, after attending to the legal problems of his clients, returns frustrated. He laments that the elites want clients (*clientes*) as long as they are wealthy. What is noteworthy is that despite the fact that his rich clients are likely to be able to repay the help Menaechmus has given them, he complains of the absence of trustworthiness (*fides*) in such clients (*Men.* 571–572). This indicates the importance Roman patrons placed on *fides*.[287] Cicero, in comparing rendering help to the poor and to the wealthy, remarks that helping the poor is a better investment than helping the wealthy. Cicero explains by drawing on the following analogy: "A man has not repaid money if he still has it; if he has repaid it, he has ceased to have it. But a man still has the sense of favor, if he has returned the favor, and if he has the sense of favor, he has repaid it" (*Off.* 2.69 [Miller, LCL]). In other words, the poor repays with a mindset of repaying a favor and not with money. In this way, the poor feels indebted, and hence remains loyal to the patron.[288] Cicero draws a contrast with a wealthy person—they dislike as "death" to accept a patron (*patrocinio*) or become clients (*clientes*). The point of contrast is that a poor man would tend to remain loyal to the patron when compared to a wealthy person (*Off.* 2.69–71). Cicero thus commends *fides* or loyalty in a patron-client relationship. In the same vein, Seneca says that "if you wish to make return for a favor [*referre vis gratiam*], you must be willing to go into exile, or to pour forth your blood, or to undergo poverty" (*Ep.* 81.27 [Gummere, LCL]). The meaning of πίστις read in light of 4 Macc 16:18–22 is instructive. Here, when faced with the threat of punishment from King Antiochus IV, the mother of seven Judean brothers begins by

---

Morgan also insists that the language of *fides*/πίστις should be read in light of the early principate, with its related social and cultural complexities.

286. Morgan, *Roman Faith and Christian Faith*, 62.

287. Andrew Wallace-Hadrill comments that the "client should be marked by dependability, one for whom the patron can pledge his faith (*fides*)." See Wallace-Hadrill, "Patronage in Roman Society," in *Patronage in Ancient Society*, ed. Andrew Wallace-Hadrill, LNSAS 1 (London: Routledge, 1989), 82.

288. My interpretation concurs with Phebe Lowell Bowditch, who states that "Cicero quotes this dictum to point out that patronage of the poor who are unable to repay the service in kind leads to a lasting emotional gratitude that cultivation of the rich may not yield." See Bowditch, *Horace and the Gift Economy of Patronage*, CCT (Berkeley: University of California Press, 2001), 52.

reminding them of the benefits they have received from God: that they had a share of this world and received life. She then urges them to endure suffering for God's sake (διὰ τὸν θεόν). What that entails is enumerated by various examples of men who endured for God's sake (διὰ τὸν θεόν/δι' ὃν [16:20–21]). She then returns to exhort them to emulate their trust toward God (τὴν αὐτὴν πίστιν πρὸς τὸν θεόν [16:22]). The author of 4 Maccabees then reformulates such a demonstration of trust or loyalty as "to die rather than violate God's commandments" (16:24). In other words, trust equates to not violating God's commandments, or faithfulness to God's commandments. Morgan makes a similar point that "(sometimes contrary to initial appearances) the two ends of a trust relationship are not only complementary and different: they are simultaneously complementary and the same."[289]

The term πίστις can mean at the same time both "loyalty" and "trust in the ability of the patron." Such a meaning is evident in the speech by King Antiochus IV when he threatens the seven Judean youths (4 Macc 8:5–7). In his attempt to win their allegiance, he urges them to trust (πιστεύσατε) him. That this trust involves King Antiochus's ability to provide is evident. First, that which follows explains the object of this trust: the ability to bestow on them positions of authority. Second, he expressed earlier that just as he is able (δυναίμην) to punish the seven youths, he is able also to be a patron (εὐεργετεῖν) to them. Thus, loyalty is also present in the word trust (πιστεύσατε) since King Antiochus's main intent is to urge them to transfer their allegiance from God and his commandments to himself (2 Macc 16:24). This understanding of πίστις is also reasonable. That which motivates a client to trust his future patron is driven first by the dependent's need and later develops into loyalty. Similarly, Cicero and Pliny the Elder also recognize that people place *fides* in those who are capable (Cicero, *Top.* 74; Pliny the Elder, *Nat.* 29.17).[290] These two facets, loyalty and trust in a patron's ability, are present in Abraham's trust in Rom 4. The element of trust in the patron's ability is evident when Abraham trusts that God can give him descendants despite "his own body, which was already dead" (Rom 4:19–20). Abraham's trust includes also a demonstration of

---

289. Morgan, *Roman Faith and Christian Faith*, 53. She does, however, acknowledge that Greek and Latin texts "seem to shy away from marking the reciprocal nature of their relationships," as that "might in some contexts mitigate or complicate too much the relationship's hierarchical structure."

290. See ibid., 64–65.

loyalty toward God.[291] At this point in Rom 4:4–5, the implied audience would be clear that Abraham's act of trust in God in the recitation of Gen 15:6 LXX implies trust as a response to favor, and hence does not constitute deeds.

I shall now continue to explain the remaining parts of Rom 4:4–5. The object of πίστις is the one who makes righteous τὸν ἀσεβῆ ("the ungodly"). Since 4:4–5 is an elaboration on Gen 15:6 LXX (which I take to be functioning here as a *chreia*), the meaning of ἀσεβής should be read in light of its immediate context in Gen 15:6. As I have argued above, Abraham's state of being righteous is set within a patronage matrix. This righteousness is a result of Abraham trusting in God that he (God) will give him innumerable descendants and is not primarily about the sixteenth-century forensic justification from sin, valid as it is. Scholars who interpret Abraham from the perspective of a polytheistic pagan, as one who needs justification from sin, have read this into Rom 4.[292] That means ὁ ἀσεβής does not refer to Abraham. Wright identifies ὁ ἀσεβής as referring to the future descendants that God will give Abraham.[293] Such an understanding coheres with how Paul describes Abraham's trust in the other two occurrences (Rom 4:3, cf. Gen 15:6; Rom 4:18), where Abraham's trust is in what God will do for his descendants rather than for Abraham himself. Abraham's trust in 4:5 is specifically believing that "somehow God will bring into this family people from all sorts of ethnic and moral backgrounds, i.e., the 'ungodly.'"[294] This interpretation makes sense as it responds to the wider concern enunciated in 4:1, where the issue is about whether or not the Judean interlocutor (or the implied audience, Judean Christians) can have Abraham as their ancestor on the basis of human efforts.

This observation about Abraham's trust in God is critical for a correct understanding of the rhetoric of Abraham's trust, which will repair the deteriorating ties between Judean and gentile Christians in the Roman Christian community. Paul utilizes the aspect of Abraham's trust that believes in a God who receives the ungodly to reconcile the two dissenting groups—the Judean and gentile Christians.

---

291. See my analysis of Gen 15:6 LXX in chapter 3, §3.3, "Genesis 15:6 LXX."

292. E.g., Käsemann, *Perspectives on Paul*, 71; Käsemann, *Commentary on Romans*, 110–12.

293. Wright, "Paul and the Patriarch," 218–19. See also chapter 3, n. 215, above.

294. Ibid., 218.

To maintain contrasting parallelism with ὁ μισθὸς οὐ λογίζεται ("The wages are not reckoned"), we would have expected ὁ μισθὸς λογίζεται. Instead, Paul writes λογίζεται ἡ πίστις αὐτοῦ εἰς δικαιοσύνην ("His trust is reckoned as righteousness"). In place of ὁ μισθός ("the wages"), Paul has inserted ἡ πίστις αὐτοῦ ("his trust"). It appears that Paul construes ἡ πίστις αὐτοῦ as some form of a reward from God that comes as a result of Abraham's act of trusting what God said about having innumerable descendants. Ἡ πίστις αὐτοῦ ("his trust") is a status granted by God to Abraham for his act of trusting in God's promises. That πίστις is a status coheres with Cicero's understanding that "the support and stay of that unswerving *constancy*, which we look for in friendship, is" *fides* (*Amic.* 65 [Falconer, LCL], emphasis mine).[295] Morgan also observes that "in funerary inscriptions *pistis/fides* is not usually attached to any particular activity, though it is often attached to a particular relationship. It becomes a virtue which the dead person possessed over time and now has forever."[296] In Mediterranean culture, this trust, as Malina describes it, is "personal loyalty, personal commitment to another person."[297] This status leads (εἰς) to the position of being righteous before God. Here, Paul accentuates the role of πίστις by couching it in terms of μισθός. Furthermore, by using wisdom rhetorolect to frame Rom 4:4–5 in the form of contrasting parallel lines, Paul seeks to elicit from the implied audience a demonstration of πίστις.[298]

3.5. Romans 4:6–8: David Says That Trust, Not Deeds, Brings Blessedness.

Wisdom rhetorolect dominates 4:6–8. This is shown by the name David and the genre of this recitation, poetry, in which proverbial wisdom is usually couched.[299] Although the name David belongs to the story line of Christian prophetic rhetorolect, Ps 31 LXX is nonconfrontational, and hence should not be classified as prophetic rhetorolect (which is

---

295. Morgan, *Roman Faith and Christian Faith*, 57.

296. Ibid.

297. Malina, "Faith," 74.

298. See the thirdspace in Robbins, *Invention of Christian Discourse*, 109: wisdom rhetorolect seeks to produce in the human body goodness and righteousness, that is, to persuade the audience to respond favorably to Paul's rhetoric.

299. See below, chapter 3, §3.5.1, "Δαυὶδ Λέγει." Robbins cites Sir 45:25–26, 47:2–11, a "deutero-biblical" wisdom literature in the Mediterranean world (*Invention of Christian Discourse*, 180). There, David is listed as one of the people who produce righteousness and goodness. This fits the thirdspace of wisdom rhetorolect.

sometimes transformed from wisdom rhetorolect).[300] Furthermore, the fact that μακάριος occurs frequently in wisdom literature (e.g., Pss 1:1; 2:12; 31:1 LXX; Sir 14:1, 2, 20; 25:8, 9; 48:11; 50:28) and that it frames Paul's recitation in Rom 4:6–8 indicates that 4:6–8 should be classified as wisdom rhetorolect.

Romans 4:6–8 functions to support 4:4–5. The presence of wisdom rhetorolect is indicated by Paul's rhetorical question couched in terms of "righteousness apart from deeds." This recalls the topic of 4:4–5. Thus, as in 4:4–5, Paul uses wisdom rhetorolect in 4:6–8 to coax the implied audience to seek a righteousness that is obtained apart from the deeds of the law. Paul does this in several ways.

3.5.1. Δαυὶδ λέγει

Just as personified Scripture λέγει ("speaks") in 4:3, serving as a riposte to the challenge that the Judean interlocutor asks (λέγει) in 4:1, so now David also λέγει, serving as a riposte to the Judean interlocutor's challenge in 4:1.[301] At the same time, this riposte in 4:3 supports Paul's contention in 4:4–5.

The name David in 4:6 is a cultural reference in the intertexture of SRI. Its significance can be elicited from two of its four occurrences in Romans (1:3; 15:12).[302] Romans 1:3 describes Jesus as a descendant of David (ἐκ σπέρματος Δαυίδ). This description represents a prophetic hope long awaited by the nation of Israel that the Messiah will come from the seed of David (Isa 11; Jer 23:5–6; Ezek 34:23–31; 37:24–28; Pss. Sol. 17.23–51; 4QFlor 1:10–13; 4QpGen 49; Shemoneh Esreh 14–15). Similarly, the description "root of Jesse" in 15:12 refers to the Messiah as David's descendant (Isa 11:1; Sir 47:22; Rev 5:5; 22:16). The Hebrew Bible corroborates the above contention, as kings who rule Israel in the united kingdom are often described as the house (בית) of David, which is kinship terminology.[303] In other words, David is to be construed not

---

300. Robbins, *Invention of Christian Discourse*, 222, 229, 248–49.

301. As discussed above in chapter 3, §2.1.2, "The Referent of 'We' in 4:1," Paul is involved in an intra-Judean debate with a Judean interlocutor. Thus, Paul is articulating the question posed by the Judean interlocutor.

302. The contexts of the other two occurrences, 4:6 and 11:9, do not reveal clearly how one should understand David as a reference in SRI.

303. E.g., 2 Sam 2:4, 7, 10; 3:1; 5:11, 16; 2 Kgs 12:19, 20; 14:18; 17:21.

only as the first king in the Davidic dynasty but as the patriarch of the Davidic dynasty.

The above conclusion that David is a father figure is borne out by the social organization of the nation of Israel, which was ruled by kinship. Several comments are needed to elucidate this social organization. First, Robert Coote posits that "in the biblical world, tribal organization was nearly always embedded in monarchic settings, and therefore nearly always took shape in relation to monarchic court policy and discourse."[304] This finds evidence in the relationship between monarchy and tribe in the Mari kingdom as recorded in the Middle Bronze Age Mari texts.[305] In biblical history, David was made king over the whole of Israel by the tribes of Israel (2 Sam 2:4; 5:1–3). Ernst A. Knauf-Belleri remarks that "tribal organization usually is the political response of a non-state population to a state expanding into their territory."[306] Thus, tribalism is embedded into a political system. James W. Flanagan also convincingly shows that between the reigns of Saul and David, an intermediate rule by tribal chiefdom intervenes. This rule "provided leadership for family-based, but non-egalitarian, social groups."[307] This transition from chiefdom to monarchy was only completed during the reign of Solomon.[308]

Second, Norman Gottwald provides a much needed corrective to how biblical scholars understand the social organization of Israel:

---

304. Robert B. Coote, "Tribalism—Social Organization in the Biblical Israels," in Esler, *Ancient Israel*, 38–39. He also critiques studies in biblical tribalism that erroneously tend to view village and field organization as not being influenced by the political court in all periods.

305. See Victor H. Matthews, *Pastoral Nomadism in the Mari Kingdom (ca. 1830–1760 B.C.)*, ASORDS 3 (Cambridge: American Schools of Oriental Research, 1978). Also, Moshé Anbar, after studying the Mari documents, concludes that there is interaction between tribal groups and the governing body: "Dans les documents se reflètent à la couche gouvernante ainsi que des simples citoyens." See Anbar, *Les Tribus Amurrites de Mari*, OBO 108 (Fribourg: Universitätsverlag; Göttingen: Vandenhoeck & Ruprecht, 1991), 9.

306. Ernst A. Knauf-Belleri, "Edom: The Social and Economic History," in *You Shall Not Abhor an Edomite for He Is Your Brother: Edom and Seir in History and Tradition*, ed. Diana V. Edelman, ABS 3 (Atlanta: Scholars Press, 1995), 108.

307. Paula M. McNutt, *Reconstructing the Society of Ancient Israel* (Louisville: Westminster John Knox, 1999), 115.

308. James W. Flanagan, "Chiefs in Israel," *JSOT* 20 (1981): 66–67.

> Biblical scholars generally assume that Israel was internally articulated into "tribes," and that these tribes were subdivided into "clans," which were further divided into "families" or "fathers' houses."... Yet as soon as one turns to the wider social-scientific literature, it emerges that "family," "clan," and "tribe" are terms that have been applied to an amazingly varied array of kinship and sociopolitical arrangements.[309]

A tribe, real or putative (fictive), is basically "a social extension of household kinship conceptions."[310] This conceptualization is evident in what the rest of the Israelite tribes (Benjamin and the other northern tribes) said in making David their king: "We are your bone and flesh" (2 Sam 5:1).[311] After the main body of Israelites had punished the tribe of Benjamin, Judg 21:6 records that "the sons of Israel had compassion on אחיו (his brother)." This construct noun takes on a masculine singular suffix that refers to the plural "the sons of Israel." In other words, the relationship between the tribe of Benjamin and the other tribes of Israel is regarded as (putative) kinship.

In Mediterranean honor-shame culture, the patriarch (or matriarch) of a family, tribe, or clan is responsible for maintaining the honor of the family's social standing. Paying honor to the patriarch (or matriarch) is the duty of children. Paul, by attributing Ps 31:1–2 LXX to David, emphasizes that he (David) possesses royal patriarchal authority. But David is not just any patriarch. His authority, measured by the level of honor, is absolute because David's honor was ascribed by God to him for his faithfulness (Sir 47:1–11; 1 Macc 2:57; 1 Sam 13:14; cf. 2 Sam 7:1–17). As in Rom 4:3, where Paul uses the dissimulation mode of ideology to tap into the authority of the Judean sacred Scriptures by the clause ἡ γραφὴ λέγει ("the Scripture says"), here Paul again employs dissimulation by the clause Δαυὶδ λέγει ("David says") to assume the authority of the royal patriarch David to persuade his implied audience to pursue a righteousness that is derived apart from deeds.

---

309. Norman K. Gottwald, *The Tribes of Yahweh: A Sociology of the Religion of Liberated Israel, 1250–1050 B.C.E.* (Maryknoll, NY: Orbis Books, 1979), 257–84.

310. Coote, "Tribalism," 39.

311. Joyce G. Baldwin notes that one reason why the northern tribes approached David to be their king was because of strong kinship ties. See Baldwin, *1 and 2 Samuel: An Introduction and Commentary*, TOTC (Leicester: Inter-Varsity Press, 1988), 194.

3.5.2. Μακάριοι

Ideological power is mobilized in the use of the cognates containing μακαρ- (blessedness/blessed) in several ways. Although the term μακαρισμός ("blessedness") is a new term at this point of the argument, it is in essence another expression related to honor, and hence is not abruptly introduced. That it carries the meaning of honor is apparent in Gal 4:15, a text that is intertextually related to Romans. In Gal 4:15, μακαρισμός is correlated to Gal 4:13–14, when the Galatians accepted Paul despite his "physical infirmity" (Gal 4:13), which could have caused the Galatians to be ashamed of Paul. But they regarded the reception of Paul an honor because he preached to them the gospel. Hence, μακαρισμός is another word for honor, a claim for boasting.

This word also generates ideological power in other ways. In Perelman and Olbrechts-Tyteca's terminology, Paul adopts a "pragmatic" approach where an act or event is evaluated by its favorable or unfavorable consequences. Here, the value of the consequent blessedness is easily transferred from the consequence to the cause that is the state of righteousness acquired apart from deeds. No justification is required since acceptance of that act (in this case, righteousness apart from deeds) is a matter of common sense.[312] The value placed upon the cause, righteousness apart from deeds, is derived from the consequence blessedness. The question is from where blessedness derives its value. Underlying the word blessedness is the premise that it carries performative power from God when spoken by a person of divine authority.[313] Moreover, blessedness is related to the concept of favor and, therefore, can be associated with client-patron relations that God establishes with God's people. Thus, this blessing is given by the divine patron. The thrice-repeated cognates of μακαρ- frame 4:6–8 and weave the sensory-aesthetic texture, a subtexture of inner texture, so that the conception that blessing comes with trust in God would be ringing in the ears of the implied audience, and hence sustained in their minds.[314] The pronouncement of blessing also contains another aspect

---

312. Perelman and Olbrechts-Tyteca, *New Rhetoric*, 266–67.

313. Kent H. Richards, "Bless/Blessing," *ABD* 1:756; cf. J. L. Austin, *How to Do Things with Words*, 2nd ed. (Cambridge: Harvard University Press, 1962).

314. Robbins, *Exploring the Texture of Texts*, 29–30.

of the sensory-aesthetic texture. As discussed above,[315] the mouth, in the Mediterranean world, is a "key strategy for establishing, maintaining and defending honor."[316] By reciting Ps 31:1–2a LXX, Paul is ascribing honor (one of the two available means of acquiring Mediterranean honor) to the person whose transgressions are forgiven and who does not rely on deeds of the Mosaic law. But that which results in blessing is not just righteousness, but righteousness that comes apart from deeds of the Mosaic law that Paul's recitation of Ps 31:1–2 LXX seeks to prove. I shall discuss below how this recitation bolsters Paul's thesis.

3.5.3. Psalm 31:1–2a LXX

Paul recites only Ps 31:1–2a LXX and omits the second half of the second colon: "in whose spirit there is no guile" (Ps 31:2b LXX). The reason is that Ps 31:2b, as perceived by the implied audience, appears to contradict Paul's intent. At the same time, however, by citing just Ps 31:1–2a LXX, Paul is able to include the essence of the entire psalm without highlighting the parts of the psalm that would seemingly contradict his (Paul's) intent.[317] This is shown by two observations. First, 31:1–2 is the prologue to the entire psalm. Several observations support my point. Psalm 31:3 LXX begins with the particle ὅτι.[318] This particle should be construed as causal, since 31:3 describes a state that is opposite to that of the blessedness mentioned in 31:1–2: in his unrepentant state, the psalmist says that "my body wasted away through my groaning all day long"; "your hand was heavy upon me"; "my strength was dried up." The flow of the argument also corroborates the centrality of blessedness in 31:1–2. The psalm begins with the section 31:1–2, which functions as a pronouncement of blessedness. This is followed by 31:3–5, which recounts the process that led up to this

---

315. See above, chapter 2, §4.6, "Romans 9:30–10:13: Judeans Need to Depend on Christ to Broker Righteousness to Them from God."

316. Malina, "Communicativeness," 28.

317. Christopher G. Norden observes that when Paul recites the Psalms in Romans, Paul's "attention to detail, the originality of his exegesis, his introductory phrases, and his sensitivity to features of the original contexts, all support Hay's argument that Paul grapples and dialogues seriously with the texts." See Norden, "Paul's Use of the Psalms in Romans: A Critical Analysis," *EvQ* 88 (2016): 86.

318. This Greek particle translates the Hebrew כִּי, which can take on a causal meaning (BDB, 473). Contra Robert G. Bratcher and William D. Reyburn, *A Handbook on Psalms* (New York: United Bible Societies, 1993), 3; Craigie, *Psalms 1–50*, 263.

state of blessedness. This state of blessedness is then elaborated in 31:6–7. That the section 31:8–11 constitutes the psalmist's exhortation directed at his implied audience is demonstrated by two observations. The section 31:8–9 is sandwiched between 31:3–7 and 31:10–11. Since the speakers of 31:3–7 and 31:10–11 are clearly the psalmist, construing the speaker of 31:8–9 as the psalmist is reasonable. Furthermore, since 31:10–11 contains instructions given by the psalmist to his implied audience, that the immediately preceding 31:8–9 is of the same nature is reasonable.[319]

Second, Paul introduces 4:6–8 with 4:6, which contains the recitation of Ps 31:1–2a LXX and the noun δικαιοσύνη ("righteousness"). In Ps 31:8–11 LXX, where the psalmist applies the psalm to his (the psalmist's) implied audience, he describes the recipient of Yahweh's blessing as a δίκαιος ("righteous") man (31:11 LXX). This is the *only* occurrence in the psalm that contains the δικ- cognate. This intimates that when Paul recites Ps 31:1–2a LXX, he has an eye on not only the start of the psalm but also its conclusion (31:11 LXX).

Having established my point that Paul uses the entire psalm, I shall explain how the recitation of Ps 31:1–2a LXX bolsters Paul's point that righteousness does not come by deeds of the Mosaic law. Psalm 31:1–2 LXX consists of a pair of synonymous couplets:

Blessed are those whose transgression is forgiven, (A)
 whose sin is covered. (B)
Blessed are those to whom the Lord imputes no iniquity (A′)
 and in whose mouth there is no deceit. (B′)

This structural layout implies that colon A is parallel to colon A′, and colon B is (purportedly but not exactly semantically) parallel to B′. The similarity sets the background against which we can interpret the differences between the two cola.[320] To properly interpret the significance of the differences, how the parallel cola are related to one another needs to

---

319. Contra Bratcher and Reyburn, who incorrectly attributes the speech in Ps 32:8–9 to Yahweh (*Handbook on Psalms*, 308). Likewise, Mitchell S. J. Dahood, *Psalms 1–50*, AB 16 (New York: Doubleday, 1966), 196.

320. Jan P. Fokkelman, *Reading Biblical Poetry: An Introductory Guide*, trans. Ineke Smit (Louisville: Westminster John Knox, 2001), 78–79.

be investigated as poetry tends to be elliptical in nature.[321] James L. Kugel argues that the second colon in Semitic parallelism accentuates the first colon.[322] This implies that the emphasis of the couplet in Ps 31:1–2 LXX is on the Lord's imputation of righteousness to a person. Paul's recitation of Ps 31:1–2a LXX is thus apropos in reinforcing the need for a righteousness that has value in God's estimate (Rom 4:2; cf. Gen 15:6). The psalmist, by placing them in parallel, seems to imply that the result of having sins covered up requires the fulfillment of colon B′. This understanding is borne out by what follows, that is, the meaning of colon B′, "in whose spirit there is no deceit," is explicated by what follows in Ps 31:3–5 LXX, where the psalmist acknowledges his sin.[323] The verbal recitation of an incomplete couplet in Ps 31:1–2a LXX is poetically jarring as it gives the implied audience a sense of incompleteness. As mentioned above, the reason why Paul recites only Ps 1:1–2a is to avoid a possible misunderstanding that the psalmist's transgression has obtained forgiveness because his mouth contains no deceit (Ps 31:2b LXX). At the same time, by creating in the implied audience a sense of an incomplete reading of the psalm, Paul was probably making use of the elliptical nature of poetry to prompt the implied audience to fill in the gap left by the missing second half of colon B′.[324] That which is to be filled in by the implied audience would naturally be the missing half colon: "in whose mouth there is no deceit." But since this missing half colon serves as the heading for what follows in Ps 31:3–5 LXX, where repentance from sin is stressed, the desired effect would be to bring to the mind of the implied audience the point that forgiveness of iniquities was achieved not by deeds of the Mosaic law but by repentance.

3.5.4. Secondary Rhetorolects

In order to mobilize ideological power to coax the implied audience into pursuing a state of "blessedness," Paul, as discussed above, uses the

---

321. Bruce K. Waltke, *The Book of Proverbs*, NICOT (Grand Rapids: Eerdmans, 2004), 45.

322. James L. Kugel, *The Idea of Biblical Poetry: Parallelism and Its History* (New Haven: Yale University Press, 1981), 51–58.

323. Craigie has a similar interpretation as mine when he says that "the fourth line of the parallel structure (v 2b) refers to the absence of *deceit* ... by which forgiveness is granted" (*Psalms 1–50*, 266, emphasis original).

324. Fokkelman describes this technique as "gapping" (*Reading Biblical Poetry*, 73).

dominant rhetorolect of the passage, wisdom rhetorolect. At the same time he introduces prophetic rhetorolect into this overarching wisdom rhetorolect. Its presence is indicated by the words ἀνομία (Ps 31:1 LXX) and ἁμαρτία (Ps 31:1, 2 LXX). These two words are important vocabulary in the prophetic discourses of the Hebrew Bible, since they are used to indict the sinning of ancient Israelites. These words in the firstspace conjure up in the secondspace images of God as King and David as a prophet sent by God to highlight sin and the threat that is attached to unforgiven sins. Fauconnier and Turner explain the resulting effect on the audience: "There is nothing more basic in human life than cause and effect."[325] One outworking of cause and effect is "stimulus-response conditioning."[326] In this case, since Paul has proven in 4:2–5 that Abraham did not and the implied audience, too, does not become righteous by deeds, the threat brought on the implied audience by a prophet for unforgiven sins is real. This will urge the implied audience to search for a way to resolve this threat. In this way, priestly rhetorolect is introduced into the rhetoric. That priestly rhetorolect is invoked is indicated by the use of Ps 32 (Ps 31 LXX), which was frequently recited during the Day of Atonement. Furthermore, the focus on "iniquities are forgiven" and "sins are covered" recalls the secondspace of priestly rhetorolect.[327] At this point of the argument, Ps 31 LXX offers Paul a ready-made text in several ways.

First, Ps 31 LXX was frequently recited during the Day of Atonement.[328] It is probable that the real audience of Romans, Judean Christians and gentile Christians, the latter of whom were probably also Godfearers, knew Ps 31 LXX because it was recited as part of the liturgy associated with the Day of Atonement. Several observations support my point. This day was observed by Godfearers. Philo and Josephus boast that many Godfearers observed the Day of Atonement (Philo, *Mos.* 2.20–25; Josephus, *Ag. Ap.* 2.282). Furthermore, Daniel Stökl Ben Ezra is probably right to argue that

---

325. Fauconnier and Turner, *Way We Think*, 75.

326. Ibid., 76.

327. See Robbins's description of the thirdspace of priestly rhetorolect, which specifies that the objective of a rhetoric that uses priestly rhetorolect is to persuade the audience to become "a receiver of beneficial exchange of holiness and purity between God and humans" (Robbins, *Invention of Christian Discourse*, 109).

328. Dunn, *Romans 1–8*, 207; see Hermann L. Strack and Paul Billerbeck, *Kommentar zum Neuen Testament aus Talmud und Midrasch*, 6 vols. (Munich: Beck, 1922–1961), 3:202–3.

the Day of Atonement was observed by first-century CE Christians. His point finds evidence in Acts 27:9, where ἡ νηστεία refers to the fast conducted during the Day of Atonement. He comments that, in the context of Acts 27:9, this word

> appears with complete neutrality in the context, without polemical or pejorative accretions. In the same way, a modern Jew would understand a friend saying in late summer that he will return "after the holidays" as meaning "at the end of Sukkot." We can therefore assume that the attitude of Luke and his addressees to the fast of the Day of Atonement was to that of a revered and observed festival.[329]

Stökl Ben Ezra acknowledges the possibility that ἡ νηστεία in Acts 27:9 was simply "a common reference to the time of the year."[330] The problem with such a possibility, as he correctly retorts, is that there is no instance of "another non-Jewish source using 'the fast' as common chronological reference in a non-polemical or exegetical context."[331] That Luke should use a Judean calendrical reference to address a secular problem indicates that Luke and his implied readers observed the Day of Atonement.[332] There are

---

329. Daniel Stökl Ben Ezra, *The Impact of Yom Kippur on Early Christianity: The Day of Atonement from Second Temple Judaism to the Fifth Century*, WUNT 163 (Tübingen: Mohr Siebeck, 2003), 215. Similarly, Joseph A. Fitzmyer, *The Acts of the Apostles: A New Translation with Introduction and Commentary*, AB 31 (New York: Doubleday, 1998), 775; I. Howard Marshall, *The Acts of the Apostles*, TNTC (Leicester: Inter-Varsity Press, 1980), 406; Ben Witherington III, *The Acts of the Apostles* (Grand Rapids: Eerdmans, 1998), 762; James M. Beresford, "The Significance of the Fast in Acts 27:9," *NovT* 58 (2016): 160.

330. Daniel Stökl Ben Ezra, "Fasting with Jews, Thinking with Scapegoats: Some Remarks on Yom Kippur in Early Judaism and Christianity, in Particular 4Q541, *Barnabus* 7, Matthew 27 and Acts 27," in *The Day of Atonement: Its Interpretations in Early Jewish and Christian Traditions*, ed. Thomas Hieke and Tobias Nicklas, TBN 15 (Leiden: Brill, 2012), 172, citing Dmitrij F. Bumazhnov, "Review of Daniel Stökl Ben Ezra, The Impact of Yom Kippur," *SCJR* 1 (2006): R16–17, https://tinyurl.com/SBL4822a.

331. Stökl Ben Ezra, "Fasting with Jews," 173. Similarly, Markus Tiwald, "Christ as Hilasterion (Rom 3:25): Pauline Theology on the Day of Atonement in the Mirror of Early Jewish Thought," in Hieke and Nicklas, *Day of Atonement*, 196.

332. Daniel Stökl Ben Ezra, " 'Christians' Observing 'Jewish' Festivals of Autumn," in *The Image of the Judaeo-Christians in Ancient Jewish and Christian Literature*, ed. Peter J. Tomson and Doris Lambers-Petry, WUNT 158 (Tübingen: Mohr Siebeck, 2003), 62.

also other instances in the New Testament that indicate that early Judean Christians attended temple services. Acts 2:46, 3:1, and 5:20 show the original apostles attending the temple, day after day, while in Acts 21:26, Paul is depicted as observing temple worship. Judean festivals are also regularly mentioned in the Acts of the Apostles. These included Pentecost (Acts 2:1; cf. 1 Cor 16:8), Passover (Acts 12:3), and the Feast of Unleavened Bread (Acts 20:6).[333] Furthermore, the fact that Paul in Rom 14:5–6 allows the Christians in Rome the freedom to observe Judean festivals shows that first-century CE Christians were likely still observing Judean festivals.[334] One of these festivals would be the Day of Atonement in view of its importance to Judeans. In fact, Paul thinks that Christians who observe such Judean festivals can honor God.[335]

The above discussion shows that first-century CE Christians, which include gentile Godfearers, observed the festival of the Day of Atonement. For gentile Godfearers to properly observe this important Judean festival, however, it is reasonable to expect that the various parts of the festival should be made intelligible to them. This would include the recitation of Ps 32 (Ps 31 LXX), which could have been read out in Hebrew, Aramaic, or even Greek.[336] Lee I. Levine's comments are helpful:

> There can be little question that Jews of the Diaspora worshiped in the vernacular, although evidence in this regard is largely inferential. We know of some prayers with an apparently Jewish orientation that have been preserved in early church documents, although we cannot be certain that the source was synagogue liturgy. Clear cut evidence for the use of Greek is preserved in Justinian's famous *Novella* 156 of 553 C.E., wherein it is stated that Jews read the Torah in Greek.[337]

Thus, when Paul recites Ps 32:1–2a LXX, the implied audience would recall the Day of Atonement and thereby the temple, altar, or some place

---

333. G. Rouwhorst, "The Origins and Evolution of Early Christian Pentecost," *StPatr* 35 (2001): 309–11.

334. Stökl Ben Ezra, *Impact of Yom Kippur*, 215–16. See also Beresford, who concurs that the first-century Christian community was "very possibly actively participating in festivals such as the Yom Kippur" ("Significance of the Fast," 160).

335. Stökl Ben Ezra, " 'Christians' Observing 'Jewish' Festivals," 60–61.

336. Lee I. Levine, *Judaism and Hellenism in Antiquity: Conflict or Confluence?* (Seattle: University of Washington Press, 1998), 158.

337. Ibid., 160.

of worship. Furthermore, the verb ἀφιέναι is frequently used with regard to sin and guilt offerings (Lev 4; 5 LXX). These factors create the firstspace consisting of the altar and the temple or some place of worship that conjures in the secondspace the image of God as holy and pure. Regarding this secondspace, the image of God as holy and pure is also made more persuasive to the implied audience by purity rules: as discussed above, rules of purity, which mark off clean and unclean food and demarcate the temple precincts, are deeply entrenched in the mind of a Judean. These purity rules thus form the intangible institution from which Paul derives ideological power to persuade the implied audience of God's holiness.[338] This legitimizes God's demand for holiness.[339] The implied audience is therefore persuaded to maintain a relationship of holiness between God and humans.[340] This desire for holiness will cause the implied audience to agree with David, and hence Paul's assessment that a person whose transgressions are forgiven is blessed.

Second, Ps 31:1–2a LXX is historical intertexture that recalls the Day of Atonement. Several aspects of this day would probably be obvious to the implied audience.[341] The implied audience would understand the significance of this day as summarized in Lev 16, an important text that is closely related to the observance of the Day of Atonement: the priest "shall make atonement for the sanctuary, and he shall make atonement for the tent of meeting and for the altar, and he shall make atonement for the priests and for all the people of the assembly" (Lev 16:33 [NRSV]). This truth is clearly communicated by means of a "powerful visual aid" to the public when a goat was dispatched into the wilderness.[342] This goat was the one on which Aaron laid his hands and confessed "over it all the iniquities of the people of Israel and all their transgressions, all their sins, putting them on the head of the goat ... [which] shall bear on itself all their iniquities" (Lev

---

338. For how ideological power is mobilized, see Thompson, *Studies in the Theory of Ideology*, 129. He argues that "the power to act must be related to the institutional site from which it derives."

339. Thompson calls it a misrecognition of cultural arbitrariness so as to legitimize the cultural arbitrariness (*Studies in the Theory of Ideology*, 57).

340. See above, chapter 3, n. 326.

341. Robbins describes a historical intertexture as one that "'textualizes' past experience into a 'particular event' or 'a particular period of time'" (*Tapestry of Early Christian Discourse*, 118–20).

342. Gordon J. Wenham, *The Book of Leviticus*, NICOT (Grand Rapids: Eerdmans, 1979), 236–37.

16:21–22 [NRSV]). Such an object lesson constitutes rhetography, where a goat that bears the sins of the people communicates in clear terms the "forgiveness of iniquities" apart from deeds. Furthermore, in view of the tight nexus between Rom 4 and 3:21–31, the implied audience would possibly recall the mercy seat (ἱλαστήριον), which signifies Christ as atonement for sins (3:25).

Thus the recitation of Ps 31 LXX, on the one hand, impresses upon the audience the threat of unforgiven sins and, on the other hand, offers the implied audience relief from the forgiveness of sins. Fauconnier and Turner emphasize that the cause (here, the threat) and effect (here, forgiveness of sins) "have to be brought together in one mental space."[343] In other words, the audience visualizes the threat and the effect as one. The resulting thirdspace is that the implied audience regards their sins as having been resolved. This would lead the implied audience to give mental assent that a person whose sins are forgiven is indeed blessed, and hence agree that to be regarded as righteous apart from deeds is blessed.

The "righteousness" that results in blessedness should not be read simply as a contrast to the person described in the psalm whose transgressions have not been forgiven or whose sins are not covered. Rather, in keeping with how the term righteousness is used in what precedes, righteousness here is essentially relational. It refers to David's status in his covenant relationship with God where David is regarded as righteous by God. This relationship is maintained when David's transgressions are forgiven. Also noteworthy is the common stress on both Abraham's and David's righteousness, righteousness obtained through trust in God, their patron.

---

343. Fauconnier and Turner, *Way We Think*, 76.

4
The Rhetoric of Romans 4: Part 2

1. Romans 4:9–12: Constructing a Myth of Origins for Judean and Gentile Christians

The topos circumcision dominates this section and suggests priestly rhetorolect as the overarching rhetorolect of this section. Several observations demonstrate my point. During circumcision, blood is shed. This invokes the firstspace (temple or some place of worship and afflicted body) of priestly rhetorolect. Also, the rite of circumcision is performed in formal religious settings.[1] This belongs to the firstspace of priestly rhetorolect. Romans 4:9–12 discusses whether or not circumcision can take on a mediating role of communicating righteousness to Christians. This fits into the thirdspace of priestly rhetorolect that seeks to move the implied audience to seek after "holiness and purity between God and humans."[2] Thus, priestly rhetorolect fits into the discussion of circumcision here. In this

---

1. Shmuel Safrai comments that various traditions from the Second Temple period record that on the eighth day of circumcision, many people gathered for celebration and feasting. Moreover, "although only the later [Tannaitic] sources mention a quorum of ten men for circumcision and the accompanying blessings, it seems that in actual practice, this was the ancient rule as well." See Safrai, "Home and Family," in *The Jewish People in the First Century*, ed. Shmuel Safrai and Menachem Stern, CRINT 1.2 (Philadelphia: Fortress, 1976), 767. Lawrence A. Hoffman observes that by the first century CE, two institutions, the *chavurah* and the synagogue, had emerged. Circumcision was performed in these two institutions. See Hoffman, *Covenant of Blood: Circumcision and Gender in Rabbinic Judaism* (Chicago: University of Chicago Press, 1996), 59. Levine comments that by the first century CE, the synagogue had become a "universal Jewish institution" (*Judaism and Hellenism in Antiquity*, 139). Considering that circumcision is central to Judaism, it is reasonable to think that this important rite would be performed in the synagogue.

2. Robbins, *Invention of Christian Discourse*, 109.

section, Paul rejects the mediating role of circumcision and investigates who or what can take the role of mediating righteousness. In response, Paul constructs a myth of origins that instates Abraham as father. Through Abraham's fatherhood and not circumcision, Paul contends, Judeans and gentiles inherit righteousness.

1.1. Romans 4:9: Is the Blessedness of Righteousness Given to the Circumcised or the Uncircumcised?

Paul, representing the Judean interlocutor, introduces 4:9–12 with a rhetorical question in 4:9.[3] The inferential οὖν and the word μακαρισμός, which recalls 4:6–8, pick up the preceding argument and move the argument forward. The question is: how? Commentators think that Paul takes up the topic on circumcision to address a common misconception that this blessing is available only to Judeans. Paul aims, so they say, to shed light on the implication of Ps 31 LXX.[4] As much as this is part of Paul's objective, however, this position does not take seriously the inferential force of οὖν. Rather, it tends to reduce it to a resumptive particle, as if Paul is taking up the subject of blessing without much regard for the argument of 4:6–8.[5]

More likely, the demonstrative pronoun οὗτος points not only to the blessedness that he has just constructed by his exposition of Ps 31 LXX but also to the whole point that Paul has just established in 4:2–8, namely, that Abraham is promised descendants by trust in God and not by deeds of the Mosaic law.[6] In other words, the whole argument of 4:2–8, and not just 4:6–8, leads to the argument in 4:9–12. This is shown by the fact that 4:2–5 is closely linked to 4:6–8 through the discussion on blessedness. More precisely, 4:2–8 discusses the nature of a kinship honor that has value before God. This lays the premise for Paul to challenge and refute the Judean

---

3. As discussed above in chapter 3, §2.1.2, "The Referent of 'We' in 4:1," Paul is involved in an intra-Judean debate with a Judean interlocutor. Thus, Paul is articulating the question posed by the Judean interlocutor. Similarly, Jipp, "Rereading the Story," 225; Jewett, *Romans*, 317.

4. So Käsemann, *Commentary on Romans*, 114; Schreiner, *Romans*, 224; Moo, *Epistle to the Romans*, 267; Jewett, *Romans*, 317.

5. For example, Moo thinks that 4:9 seeks to add a "further dimension" to Ps 32:1–2 (*Epistle to the Romans*, 267). Jewett, while recognizing that 4:9 is tied to the preceding context by both οὖν and the mention of "blessing," does not explore how 4:9–12 develops 4:2–8 (*Romans*, 317).

6. See above, chapter 3, §2.1.2, "The Referent of 'We' in 4:1."

mindset contained in the rhetorical question of 4:9 that this blessedness is given only to the circumcised, that is, Judeans. This implies that 4:2–8 lays the foundation for the construction of a myth of origins for gentile Christians that is later made explicit in 4:11–12.

By recalling the word blessedness (4:9), Paul applies the blessedness constructed in the preceding verses (4:2–8) to the groups *circumcised* and *uncircumcised*. This intimates that Paul has begun to address the social dissension between Judean and gentile Christians. The referent of ὁ μακαρισμός is basically the righteousness of 4:6. Paul, however, has chosen to couch it in terms of blessedness. Fauconnier and Turner's insights on conceptual blending help. By the end of the rhetoric of 4:6–8, Paul, by blending in the thirdspace of the implied audience's mind, seeks to persuade the implied audience (comprising both Judean and gentile Christians) that they are blessed.[7] This thirdspace, as discussed above, was produced by cause and effect and by compression in the generic space. That being said, the individual inputs can also be distinguished to achieve what Fauconnier and Turner call "global insight" that gives a sense of deep understanding.[8] In other words, although this blessedness is compressed, it can also be decompressed into its individual input spaces. Thus, the topos blessedness carries with it the input space that blessedness is a result of forgiveness of sins and not deeds of the Mosaic law. Paul, by juxtaposing blessedness and circumcision as a mediator of righteousness, the aim of priestly rhetorolect, creates a disanalogy that is jarring for the implied audience.[9] In other words, at the onset, Paul is casting circumcision in a bad light by juxtaposing blessedness and circumcision. With this, Paul probably could have drawn out the conclusion that he later does in 4:11–12. Instead, however, attention is shifted to the topos circumcision. Why Paul chooses to delay the conclusion has to do with the role circumcision plays in the dissension between Judeans and gentiles.

---

7. For a description of the thirdspace of "wisdom rhetorolect," see Robbins, *Invention of Christian Discourse*, 109. The thirdspace creates a "human body as producer of goodness and righteousness." This means that the implied audience is persuaded to "produce good, righteous action, thought, will, and speech with the aid of God's wisdom" (p. 110).

8. See Fauconnier and Turner, who stress that understanding requires one to grasp the parts and the whole (*Way We Think*, 119, 78–78).

9. Ibid., 99.

Περιτομή ("circumcision"), by its widespread adherence among Judeans, has become a metonym that refers to Judeans. Ἀκροβυστία ("uncircumcision"), on the other hand, is a term Judeans use to refer to gentiles (see, e.g., 1 Macc 1:15).[10] Reading these two terms against the backdrop of a dissension between Judean and gentile Christians indicates that Paul is here addressing a cultural intertexture in which Judeans reject gentiles because they are uncircumcised. The severity of this rejection can be gleaned from the role circumcision plays in the preceding passages. The fact that a section (2:25–29) is devoted to putting circumcision into perspective indicates that Judeans regard circumcision as important. Furthermore, it appears that Judeans regard circumcision as being more important than keeping the moral law of Moses (2:25). Judeans also view circumcision as that which defines their ethnicity (2:28–29). The immediately preceding context (3:29–30) also corroborates the latter point: "Or is God the God of Judeans only? Is he not the God of gentiles also…, since God is one? And he will make righteous the circumcised on the ground of trust (in God) and the uncircumcised through the same trust (in God)" (3:29–30 NRSV modified). This passage must be read in light of the social and cultural texture in which every nation has a patron god. By saying that "God is one," Paul implies that circumcision does not determine whether or not a nation or an ethnic group belongs to God. Thus, Paul needs to address this main obstacle that is impeding reconciliation between Judean and gentile Christians before he can take the final step in crafting a myth of origins for gentile Christians. Paul begins by refuting the notion that "this blessedness" is extended only to the circumcised. He does this by citing again Gen 15:6: "Trust was reckoned to Abraham as righteousness." This recitation aims to do two things.

First, it reiterates the previous conclusion (4:5) reached by the rhetoric in 4:2–8. Several observations show this. Although 4:9 is a recitation of Gen 15:6 LXX, it follows 4:5 more closely.[11] This is demonstrated by the initial position of the verb λογίζεσθαι ("to be reckoned") and the use of the verb πιστεύειν ("to trust") instead of the noun πίστις ("trust"). The display below clarifies my point:

---

10. In 1 Macc 1:15, this term is used to refer to Judeans who become uncircumcised and abandon the "holy covenant" and join the gentiles (ἔθνη).

11. Richard N. Longenecker insists that 4:9 should not be construed as a direct recitation of Gen 15:6 but "Paul's own summation" (*Epistle to the Romans*, 503).

- Gen 15:6 LXX: ἐπίστευσεν Ἀβραμ τῷ θεῷ καὶ ἐλογίσθη αὐτῷ εἰς δικαιοσύνην ("Abram trusted God and it was reckoned to him as righteousness")
- Rom 4:5: λογίζεται ἡ πίστις αὐτοῦ εἰς δικαιοσύνην ("His trust was reckoned as righteousness")
- Rom 4:9: ἐλογίσθη τῷ Ἀβραὰμ ἡ πίστις εἰς δικαιοσύνην ("Trust was reckoned to Abraham as righteousness")

An observation about the repetitive-progressive texture, a subtexture of the inner texture of SRI, also corroborates my point. In 4:1, Paul, who represents the Judean interlocutor, introduces with "we say" (λέγειν) a rhetorical question that expects to be negated by the implied audience comprising Judean and gentile Christians. The refutation in 4:3 is introduced with "the Scripture says [λέγει]" where Paul recites Gen 15:6 LXX. Similarly, in 4:9a, Paul, representing the Judean interlocutor, asks a rhetorical question that expects to be negated by the implied audience. The refutation in 4:9b, which is also taken from Gen 15:6 LXX, however, is introduced not with "the Scripture says" but with "we say" (λέγομεν). To maintain a repetitive-argumentative structure that is structured around the verb λέγειν, we would expect Paul to say in 4:9 that "the Scripture says," as in 4:3. Paul, however, here introduces the recitation of Gen 15:6 LXX with "we say" to signify that the Judean interlocutor's rhetorical question in 4:1, which implies that Judeans received Abraham as forefather by his (Abraham's) human efforts, has been modified by the rhetoric in 4:2–8. In other words, in Paul's intra-Judean debate, the Judean interlocutor, together with Paul, now agrees with the conclusion that "trust (in God) was reckoned to Abraham as righteousness." This reinforces my earlier point that 4:2–8 lays the foundation for the myth of origins of the gentile Christians in 4:11–12. What Paul intends in 4:9 is to reiterate the foundational nature of this myth of origins: that Abraham became the father of many descendants by trust in God before he addressed the obstacle posed by the rite of circumcision.

Second, this recitation also sets the stage for 4:10–11.[12] Paul will now seek to remove the rite of circumcision as a prerequisite to becoming Abraham's descendant before he completes his construction of a myth of origins for gentile Christians.

---

12. So Moo, *Epistle to the Romans*, 267.

1.2. Romans 4:10: Abraham Was Reckoned as Righteous before Circumcision

The preceding argument has established that the blessedness that results in Abraham's fatherhood of many descendants is an ascribed honor. With the connective οὖν and ἐλογίσθη, which recall the argument in 4:4–5, Paul indicates that he is ready to take the argument to the next stage with what he has established in the preceding argument (4:2–8) as a springboard. He seeks to answer the following question: was the ascribed honor that led to Abraham's fatherhood obtained ἐν περιτομῇ ὄντι ἢ ἐν ἀκροβυστίᾳ ("while he was in a state of circumcision or in a state of uncircumcision" [4:10])? Here, Paul focuses not only on the rite of circumcision but the states of circumcision or uncircumcision as signified by the present participle ὄντι ("being") and the temporal dative.[13] This participle emphasizes circumcision or uncircumcision as a settled state of affairs and not merely as an act.[14] Such a construction is a fitting response to 4:4–5, where Paul construes trust as not merely an act but a settled state that results from his act of trusting God in Gen 15. Specifically, the emphasis on a settled state by the use of the present participle ὄντι sharpens the focus on how Abraham established a favorable patron-client relationship with God—that it was by trust in God, as argued earlier in 4:2–8 and reiterated in 4:9, and not by circumcision. To do that, Paul uses the fact that in the Genesis narrative, Abraham was reckoned as being righteous in Gen 15 before he was circumcised in Gen 17.[15] That makes it self-evident that Abraham was uncircumcised when he was regarded as righteous in his relationship with his patron, God. This paves the way for Paul to conclude his construction of the nature of Abraham's fatherhood in 4:11.

1.3. Romans 4:11a: Circumcision Affirmed Abraham's Righteousness That Came by Trust in God

Most commentators construe 4:11a as a digression from Paul's main objective of constructing a myth of origins. They think that in order to undermine

---

13. BDF §107.

14. BDAG, s.v. "εἰμί." The present participle ὄντι occurs two other times (7:23; 12:3), both of which denote a settled state of affairs.

15. The Genesis chronology of these two event spans over a minimum of thirteen years (cf. Gen 16:16; 17:24).

circumcision as a means of attaining righteousness, Paul explains the right use of circumcision, namely, that it is a seal of righteousness.[16] The weakness of this interpretation is that Paul does not directly refute circumcision as a means to obtain righteousness. As commentators agree, Paul only implies that circumcision is not a means to obtaining righteousness.[17] A better interpretation is that 4:11a does not merely clarify the meaning of circumcision but leads into or supports the myth of origins for Judean Christians. Since 4:11b–12 describes Abraham as being the father of both gentile and Judean Christians, we would expect Paul to construct a myth of origins for both groups. This is precisely what Paul does here. He contends that just as the fact that Abraham was regarded as righteous when he was uncircumcised suits him for the role of father of gentile Christians, Abraham receiving the sign of circumcision fits him for the role of father of Judean Christians. That this is Paul's meaning is clear when one reads 4:11a for what it says and not for what it might be thought to imply. Paul says that Abraham received a sign (σημεῖον) whose content is signified by the genitive of apposition περιτομῆς ("circumcision"). Σφραγῖδα ("seal") is the complement in the object-complement construction and describes the object σημεῖον. Thus, the emphasis of 4:11a is that circumcision is a σφραγίς, that is, a seal that affirms the reality of righteousness that comes by trust (τῆς δικαιοσύνης τῆς πίστεως).[18] This implies that Paul regards circumcision in 4:11 as advancing his argument rather than, against most commentators, as something to be attacked. Construing a constructive role for circumcision in Paul's rhetoric ties in with Esler's contention that in Rom 4, Paul is not attempting to persuade the implied and real audience to abandon their Judean ethnic identity, which is connected to circumcision. In other words, by constructing a myth of origins for Judean Christians in terms of circumcision, Paul is preserving the Judeans' sense of ethnic identity.[19] To do otherwise, that is, to undermine the meaning of

---

16. E.g., Moo, *Epistle to the Romans*, 268; Jewett, *Romans*, 318.

17. Dunn thinks that Paul's implication is clear (*Romans 1–8*, 209); similarly, Cranfield, *Epistle to the Romans*, 1:236.

18. BDAG, s.v. "σφραγίς."

19. Rom 2:17–29 does not contradict my point that Paul seeks to preserve the Judean ethnic identity denoted by circumcision. Rom 2:25 puts circumcision in the right perspective: "Circumcision indeed is of value if you obey the law." In other words, Paul is not opposing circumcision but circumcision that is not accompanied by obedience to the Mosaic law.

circumcision as one that marks out a Judean, would be viewed by Judeans as an attack on their ethnic identity. Paul needs to defend circumcision in view of the quarrel in 14:1–15:13 where the strong (gentile Christians) are somehow regarding the weak (Judean Christians) as inferior for observing certain rituals of Judaism.[20] But Paul, by stating that circumcision is a seal, is not merely defending the ethnic identity of Judeans; he is also strengthening the fact that Abraham was made righteous on account of his trust in God. This move reinforces the myth of origins he constructs for gentile Christians. How circumcision further advances his argument will be explained below.

Romans 4:11 contains an oral-scribal intertexture recitation: the words σημεῖον ("sign") and περιτομῆς ("circumcision") recall similar terms in Gen 17:11 LXX; Paul probably recited σημεῖον διαθήκης ("sign of the covenant" [Gen 17:11 LXX]) as σημεῖον ... τῆς δικαιοσύνης ("sign ... of righteousness"). This is probable in view of the following observation. The clause ἐλογίσθη αὐτῷ εἰς δικαιοσύνην ("It was reckoned to him as righteousness"), other than the reference to Abraham, is only used one other time in the LXX, in Ps 105:31, where it refers to Phinehas, who punished his fellow Israelites for indulging in sexual immorality: ἐλογίσθη αὐτῷ εἰς δικαιοσύνην εἰς γενεὰν καὶ γενεὰν ἕως τοῦ αἰῶνος ("It was counted to him for righteousness, to all generations forever" [Brenton]).[21] What is entailed in this righteousness is described in Num 25:10–13 LXX, where Yahweh enacted a διαθήκη εἰρήνης ("covenant of peace" [25:12]) with Phinehas and his descendants. Paul's intent is to garner support from a LXX text (Gen 17:11) that talks about circumcision as a mark of Abraham's descendants that the implied audience would have understood as referring to Judeans. He replaces the word διαθήκη ("covenant") of Gen 17:11 LXX, however, with "righteousness that comes from trust (in God)." In this way, Paul leverages the authority of Gen 17:11 with its stress on circumcision. At the same time, he brings to the fore a righteousness that comes from trust in Yahweh. This recitation thus reconfigures the initial identity of Abraham's descendants from one marked by circumcision to one based on trust and paves the way for Paul to craft a myth of origins for both gentile and Judean Christians.

---

20. See above, chapter 2, §4.9, "Romans 14:1–15:13: Trust in God Enables Both the Weak and the Strong to Stand under Judgment."

21. Wright, "Paul and the Patriarch," 220; Richard N. Longenecker, *Epistle to the Romans*, 494.

To understand why the fact of circumcision carries such ideological power, we shall examine the social and cultural texture of circumcision as a ritual.[22] Catherine Bell comments that ritualization is a strategy for exercising power in relationships within a particular social organization.[23] Her observations about rituals explain how ideological power is derived. I shall discuss some salient points of her essay in what follows.[24]

First, "beliefs could exist without rituals; rituals, however, could not exist without beliefs."[25] Émile Durkheim sharpens this point in his discussion of cults, stating that ritual allows the participating community to experience and affirm as real their ideas and beliefs.[26] Geertz's view is similar. He maintains that "in ritual, the world as lived and the world as imagined fused as under the agency of a single set of symbolic forms, turns out to be the same world." In Geertz's formulation, the imagined world is the culture of the people, which he defines "as an ordered system of meaning and symbols, in terms of which social interaction takes place." The lived world refers to the social system that contains "the pattern of social interaction."[27] The fusion of the world as lived and the world as imagined is critical for a successful ritual. Second, a successful ritual will be one in which the culture and social system and their associated forces are integrated.[28] Where a ritual is successful, it facilitates changes. For instance, grief resulting from death is resolved by means of funeral rites.[29]

---

22. Hodge points out that circumcision is a ritual that "marks the baby as a member of the lineage of Abraham" (*If Sons, Then Heirs*, 28). To understand how rituals negotiate ideological power, she refers to Catherine Bell, *Ritual Theory, Ritual Practice* (New York: Oxford University Press, 1992), 99.

23. Bell, *Ritual Theory, Ritual Practice*, 197; see also Crystal Lane, *The Rites of Rulers: Ritual in Industrial Society—the Soviet Case* (Cambridge: Cambridge University Press, 1981), 14. Lane construes ritual form as an acting out of social relationships so as to express and alter these relationships.

24. Bell, *Ritual Theory, Ritual Practice*, 30–117.

25. Edward Shils, "Ritual and Crisis," in *The Religious Situation*, ed. Donald R. Cutler (Boston: Beacon, 1968), 736.

26. Durkheim, *Elementary Forms*, 463–65.

27. Geertz, *Interpretation of Cultures*, 112–13, 144.

28. See ibid., 146, where Geertz analyzes a failed ritual of a Javanese funeral ceremony as a case where the people's practice of their culture (the social system) does not fit with the local officiant's perception of the culture. The result was that instead of helping the community to accept the fact of the death of a young boy, the rites produced distress.

29. Bell, *Ritual Theory, Ritual Practice*, 34–35.

Rituals, however, sometimes fail. Ronald L. Grimes identifies several types of ritual failure.[30] Relevant for the discussion on the ritual of circumcision in Rom 4 is *misframing*. It is described as a misconstrual of the genre of a ritual, the result of which "is akin to missing the point of a joke."[31] Here, in Rom 4, Paul speaks to the Judean implied audience on circumcision probably because some Judeans are resorting to circumcision to establish a righteous relationship with God. On the one hand, whether or not a ritual performed is successful is subjective, as it depends on the evaluator's "perspective and expectations."[32] On the other hand, "ritual specialists" hold the authority to evaluate the success of a ritual.[33] One source of authority is that of a "certain sets of values which might stem from canons" or "tradition(s)."[34] In Rom 4, Paul holds the authority to evaluate the success of the ritual of circumcision performed by the Judeans. This authority taps into his earlier configuration of apostolic authority in 1:1–5. Furthermore, Paul's construal of the intent of circumcision is different from that of his Judean contemporaries. They think that circumcision achieves for them a righteous relationship with God (e.g., Jub. 15.26, 27; Add. Esth. 14:15; Josephus, *Ant.* 13.257; CD 16:4–6). This leads Paul to buttress his authority in evaluating how Judeans performed circumcision with traditions. He uses the narrative about Abraham as recorded in the Judean Scriptures to argue that Abraham could not have been regarded as righteous by God through circumcision, as Abraham received righteousness before being circumcised (4:10). But Paul's evaluation of the ritual of circumcision as having failed inadvertently diminishes the importance of circumcision, and hence threatens the ethnic identity of Judeans. A means of coping with ritual failure is thus needed. According to Ute Hüsken, one way of coping with ritual failure is "frequently [done] under the pretext of 'returning to older (severer) rules.'"[35] Furthermore, deviations from estab-

---

30. Ronald L. Grimes, *Ritual Criticism: Case Studies in Its Practice, Essays on Its Theory* (Waterloo, ON: Ritual Studies International, 2010), 183–200. For a concise summary of Grimes's list of ritual failures, see also Peter-Ben Smit, "Ritual Failure in Romans 6," *HvTSt* 72 (2016): art. 3237, p. 5. https://doi.org/10.4102/hts.v72i4.3237.

31. Grimes, *Ritual Criticism*, 195.

32. Smit, "Ritual Failure," 5.

33. Ute Hüsken, "Ritual Dynamics and Ritual Failure," in *When Rituals Go Wrong: Mistakes, Failure and the Dynamics of Ritual*, ed. Ute Hüsken, Numen 115 (Leiden: Brill, 2007), 344–46. Also, Smit, "Ritual Failure," 6.

34. Hüsken, "Ritual Dynamics," 339, 340.

35. Ibid., 346.

lished rules can serve as a creative process of renovating a ritual system.[36] Through this process of coping with the failure of the ritual of circumcision, without obliterating the importance of circumcision, the Judean ethnic identity is preserved. Paul copes with ritual failure by spelling out the correct meaning of circumcision (4:11–12). This point requires explanation.

Performance theorists deny a distinct dichotomy between the act of the ritual and the concepts that underlie it. They think that such a dichotomy impedes our understanding of how ritual activities are generated and experienced.[37] Instead, drawing on two points made by Milton Singer, they think that people regard "their culture as encapsulated within discrete performances, which they can exhibit to outsiders as well as to themselves."[38] Also, "the most concrete observable units of the cultural structure" are communicated via ritual performances. In other words, meaning is to be found in the act of rituals rather than in the concepts underlying these rituals. The difficulty with this construal, that meaning is to be found in the performance of the ritual, is that it meets with the hermeneutical impasse that meaning cannot be objectivized.[39] Bell is thus right to conclude that performance theory, despite its advantages, still needs to fall back on the conceptual ideas and values that underlie ritual activity if the meaning of a ritual is to be properly communicated.[40] We find this to be the case in Romans, where Paul, in communicating the meaning of circumcision, relies on the meaning he constructs through rhetoric. There, he explained the conceptual ideas underlying this ritual earlier in 2:25–29, and now he elaborates them in 4:9–11.

The ideological power of rituals lies not merely in the conceptual ideas but in how ritual effectively communicates these conceptual ideas. Ritual is

---

36. Ibid.

37. Ronald L. Grimes thinks that the result of dichotomizing an act of a ritual and its concepts is to make the ritual "foreign." See Grimes, *Beginnings in Ritual Studies* (Washington, DC: University Press of America, 1982), 246. Victor W. Turner cites D. H. Lawrence's remarks that such an "analysis presupposes a corpse." See Turner, *From Ritual to Theater: The Human Seriousness of Play* (New York: Performing Arts Journal Publications, 1982), 89.

38. Milton Singer, *Traditional India: Structure and Change* (Philadelphia: American Folklore Society, 1959), xiii.

39. Hans-Georg Gadamer, *Truth and Method*, trans. Garret Barden and John Cumming, 2nd ed. (London: Sheed & Ward, 1975).

40. Bell, *Ritual Theory, Ritual Practice*, 43.

defined by difference and adopts strategies to differentiate itself from other acts so that they appear to be sacred.[41] This endows them with authority to mobilize ideological power. There is also a degree of ambiguity that makes rituals mysterious and impresses upon those present that they carry an authority "from well beyond the immediate human community itself."[42]

Paul also employs wisdom, priestly, and prophetic rhetorolects to mobilize ideological power. Besides priestly rhetorolect, circumcision also invokes wisdom rhetorolect since it is performed in the presence of the father whose son is to be circumcised. Prophetic rhetorolect is also used: σφραγίς probably refers to the seal of a king when read against the backdrop of the patron-client relationship, or more specifically, a vassal suzerainty Hittite treaty between God and Abraham. This fits the firstspace of political kingdom, prophetic rhetorolect. The language of "righteousness" also corroborates the above observation. Thus, Paul seeks to persuade the implied audience amicably through an overarching wisdom rhetorolect. At the same time, by describing circumcision as a seal, Paul exerts the authority of a prophet (secondspace) to strengthen the priority of trust in God. By this, Paul hopes to elicit obedience from the implied audience (thirdspace), that is, the assent of the implied audience.

1.4. Romans 4:11b: Abraham Is the Father of the Uncircumcised

With that, Paul is now ready to craft a myth of origins for the gentile Christians. He does that with εἰς plus an articular infinitive, which should be construed as denoting result. This coheres with Paul's intent. By emphasizing a present reality, as is the force of a result clause, the result clause enables Paul to better influence the divided Judean and gentile Christians toward reconciliation.[43] Paul describes the gentile Christians as those who believe δι' ἀκροβυστίας ("during uncircumcision"). This construction is

---

41. Ibid., 90. Claude Lévi-Strauss notes that rituals centre on how they differ from similar activities in daily life. See Lévi-Strauss, *The Naked Man: Introduction to a Science of Mythology*, trans. John Weightman and Doreen Weightman (New York: Harper & Row, 1981), 671; cf. Mary Douglas, *Natural Symbols* (New York: Random House, 1973), 11; Stanley J. Tambiah, "The Magical Words of Power," *Man* 3 (1968): 198; Pierre Bourdieu, *Outline of a Theory of Practice*, trans. Richard Nice (Cambridge: Cambridge University Press, 1977), 5.

42. Bell, *Ritual Theory, Ritual Practice*, 109–10. See also David I. Kertzer, *Ritual Politics and Power* (New Haven: Yale University Press, 1988), 69–75.

43. Contra the NRSV and most commentators: e.g., Cranfield, *Epistle to the*

unusual in that Paul could have used his usual construction ἐν ἀκροβυστίᾳ ("in uncircumcision" [4:10, 11, 12]) to denote a state of uncircumcision. Hence, to translate the prepositional phrase as denoting attendant circumstances does not bring out the intended force. A correct construal should take on its usual emphasis, that of a marker of extension in time. Thus, δι' ἀκροβυστίας qualifies the present substantive participle τῶν πιστευόντων ("those who trust") and emphasizes that gentile Christians' trust in God was exercised when they were in a settled state of uncircumcision. In this way, Paul accentuates the uncircumcision of those who trust in God.[44]

Paul then adds another result clause, εἰς τὸ λογισθῆναι αὐτοῖς δικαιοσύνην ("so that it might be reckoned to them as righteousness"). The intent of this clause is debated. Some construe it as parenthetical, in that Paul, while positing Abraham becoming the father of the uncircumcised, seizes the opportunity to make a secondary point that gentiles become righteous on the basis of Abraham's example.[45] Dunn makes a similar point:

> It is just this point which he wants to make (hence the addition of this clause [εἰς τὸ λογισθῆναι αὐτοῖς δικαιοσύνην] to give the point emphasis); that God always intended to reckon righteousness to Gentiles without reference to whether they became proselytes and accepted the obligations (works) of the law.[46]

More likely, this result clause should be viewed as pointing toward where Paul is finally heading, which is to posit that this is how gentile Christians attain righteousness, namely, by becoming descendants of Abraham. Scholars who hold to the former position have glossed over how these two result clauses—that Abraham becomes the father of gentile Christians and that gentile Christians obtain righteousness—relate to each other.[47] Their interpretations do not address the following observation. Earlier, Paul had said that Abraham was regarded as righteous with the result that he received

---

Romans, 1:236–37; Moo, *Epistle to the Romans*, 269; Jewett, *Romans*, 319; Schreiner, *Romans*, 225.

44. BDAG, s.v. "διά."

45. So Moo, *Epistle to the Romans*, 270; Jewett, *Romans*, 319. See Dunn, *Romans 1–8*, 210: "in order that it might be clear that God accepted the uncircumcised as circumcised." Similarly, some, like Cranfield and Käsemann view it as "consecutive" (Cranfield, *Epistle to the Romans*, 1:237; Käsemann, *Commentary on Romans*, 116).

46. Dunn, *Romans 1–8*, 210.

47. Barrett, *Epistle to the Romans*, 90; Michel, *Der Brief an die Römer*, 120.

the promise of becoming a father. Here, however, righteousness follows on the heels of Abraham becoming a father. In other words, 4:2–8 argues that Abraham's trust leads to his attaining righteousness that eventually leads to fatherhood. Here, in 4:11, Abraham's trust leads to fatherhood that eventually leads to gentile Christians obtaining righteousness. The difference in order of fatherhood and righteousness has to do with the point I made in my discussion of 4:2–8. There, I argued that righteousness is ascribed and is to be inherited via becoming a descendant of Abraham.[48] We need to note that the δικαιοσύνη that is reckoned to the gentile Christians must be read in light of the subject discussed here, which is about Abraham and his descendants. In other words, this righteousness describes a relationship in which God the patron is favorably disposed toward gentile Christians. The second result clause should be construed as what Paul is trying to finally derive and is not merely parenthetical or consecutive. This is also borne out by the fact that it responds directly to the main concern of Rom 4, which is to remove the boast of Judean Christians, on the basis that they alone possess righteousness, toward gentile Christians.

The role of πιστεύειν ("to trust") also needs to be explained in the equation between Abraham's fatherhood and gentile Christians' righteousness. The social intertexture that Paul is employing is the idea that a son will resemble his father. Several ancient sources evince the prevalence of such an assumption.[49] For example, in 4 Macc 13, when the seven brothers were undergoing torture, they urged each other to remain loyal (faithful) to God (13:13). They said to the brothers who were dragged away, "Do not put us to shame … or betray the brothers who have died before us" (13:18 NRSV). Such love for one another, the author of 4 Maccabees explains, is a result of what "the divine and all wise Providence has bequeathed through the fathers to their descendants and which was implanted in the mother's womb" (13:19 NRSV). Another example is the *Iliad*, which was still influential and well known in Paul's day. When the character Diomedes questions the worth of Glaucus on the battlefield, Glaucus traces his lineage by going back ten generations. Diomedes discovered through Glaucus's recounting that their forefathers had been

---

48. My interpretation is corroborated by the observation in Stowers, *Rereading of Romans*, 243–44: "The Greek indicates a relation of purpose or result between Abraham's faithfulness signified in the covenant and his fatherhood, which in turn results in the justification of gentiles (11c) and fatherhood of Jews (12)."

49. Cited by Hodge, *If Sons, Then Heirs*, 23–26.

friends and even guests in each other's homes. On the basis of this realization, Diomedes responds, saying, "You are my guest friend from far in the time of our fathers" (*Iliad* 6.215 [Lattimore]). This incident implies that descendants should manifest the behavior of their ancestors.[50] In other words, gentile Christians, by trusting God, show their resemblance to Abraham, and hence prove themselves to be Abraham's descendants. The result, as indicated by the infinitival result clause, is that gentiles inherit Abraham's righteousness so that they become Abraham's descendants. Thus, Abraham becomes a superordinate figure. This mobilizes ideological power to unite Judean and gentile Christians on the basis that they have a common ancestor. More importantly, gentile Christians can thus be ascribed righteousness. Consequently, gentile Christians should not be considered inferior by Judean Christians.

1.5. Romans 4:12: Abraham Is the Father of the Circumcised

The εἰς-plus-articular infinitive construction that denotes result has a second part to it: καὶ πατέρα περιτομῆς τοῖς οὐκ ἐκ περιτομῆς μόνον ("and the father of circumcision to those who are not only of the circumcision"). This infinitival result clause indicates that what follows is the second part of the construction of a myth of origins—this time, for Judean Christians. The syntax here poses some difficulties. Scholars debate the identities denoted by the metonym περιτομή ("circumcision") and the dative substantive participle τοῖς στοιχοῦσιν ("who follow"). Some commentators think that both belong to the same group denoted by περιτομή, with the second τοῖς στοιχοῦσιν qualifying the first term περιτομή. A variation of this position views this group as referring to Judean Christians.[51] This construal accounts for Paul subsuming both groups (the first περιτομή and the second τοῖς στοιχοῦσιν) under the description πατέρα περιτομῆς ("father of circumcision"). These two groups, however, are more likely to be two

---

50. Ibid., 24–25.

51. So Moo, *Epistle to the Romans*, 270–71. So also Cranfield, who does not interpret this statement in 4:12 as implying, therefore, that Paul wishes to deny the physical kinship between Judeans and Abraham (*Epistle to the Romans*, 1:238). Jules Cambier incorrectly thinks that περιτομή takes on a spiritual meaning that refers also to gentile Christians. This understanding collapses the repeated distinction made between Judeans and gentiles in Romans. See Cambier, *L'Évangile de Dieu selon l'Épître aux Romains: Exégèse et théologie biblique*, StudNeot 3 (Bruges: de Brouwer, 1967), 170–71.

separate groups. This view is borne out by the fact that the combination containing οὐ μόνον ("not only") followed by ἀλλὰ καί ("but also") is never used in such a way that the second group qualifies the first.[52] However, to conclude, as Jewett does, that when οὐ μόνον is followed by ἀλλὰ καί, it refers indiscriminately to two groups with opposing characteristics (gentiles and Judeans) overstretches the evidence.[53] The above analysis leads to the interpretation that the expression ἐκ περιτομῆς ("of the circumcision") refers to Judeans as an ethnic group, while the group denoted by τοῖς στοιχοῦσιν τοῖς ἴχνεσιν ("those who walk in the footsteps") refers to Christian Judeans. In other words, Paul in crafting a myth of origins that includes people who become descendants of Abraham by means of trust in God has purposefully included ethnic Judeans in this group. He could have omitted this fact since he had already achieved his objective of constructing a common ancestor for both Judean and gentile Christians. But Paul does so probably because he does not wish to be mistaken that he is obliterating the Judeans' ethnic identity as children of Abraham who are recipients of God's covenantal promises.[54] This social and cultural texture underlies Paul's rhetorical strategy of constructing a viable superordinate prototype to unite dissenting groups. Such a strategy requires that ingroups be allowed to maintain their individual ethnic status. Paul, by saying that Abraham is the father of ethnic Judeans, does not, however, mean that trust in God is not necessary for ethnic Judeans. For now, he is content to leave his point at that since he has achieved the rhetorical objective of constructing a common ancestry for Judean and gentile Christians while

---

52. Neubrand, *Abraham*, 234–36. James Swetnam argues that Paul by placing τοῖς ("the") before οὐ ("not"), indicates that the two groups are the same group. He cites the construction in 4:16 as evidence. See Swetnam, "The Curious Crux at Romans 4,12," *Bib* 61 (1980): 113–15. Rom 4:4, however, where the article is placed before the particle of negation, οὐ, counters his evidence.

53. See Jewett, *Romans*, 320. In the many occurrences of this construction, the two elements are clearly not opposing: e.g., in 1:32, "those who do" (ποιοῦσιν) and "those who approve" (συνευδοκοῦσιν) are certainly not opposites. Rather, the latter is an accentuation of the former. Similarly, 5:10–11; 8:32; etc.

54. This concern surfaces frequently in Romans: 3:1–4; 9:1–7, 30–32, where Paul emphasizes that God does not forsake Israel; see also 11:1 (cf. 3:21; 1:1–4), where Paul stresses continuity between the Christian faith and Judaism. This conception agrees with the observation of Rodney Stark that "people are more willing to adopt a new religion(s) with which they are familiar" (*The Rise of Christianity: A Sociologist Reconsiders History* [Princeton: Princeton University Press, 1996], 55).

keeping intact the ethnic identity of Judeans. But he will revisit this topic in Rom 9–11.[55] Such a construal explains why Paul uses the construction οὐ μόμον followed by ἀλλὰ καί in 4:12, which has the effect of accentuating the first group by the description of the second group without collapsing these two groups into one. In this case, the second group denoted by τοῖς ἐκ περιτομῆς ("those who are of the circumcision") is qualified by the description of the second group as τοῖς στοιχοῦσιν τοῖς ἴχνεσιν ("those who walk in the footsteps").[56] At the same time, Paul, by using this construction of οὐ μόμον followed by ἀλλὰ καί, also keeps intact the ethnic identity of Judeans as descendants of Abraham.

The second group is described as "those who walk in the footsteps of the trust (in God) of our father Abraham while he was in the state of uncircumcision." The footsteps (ἴχνεσιν) are qualified by the emphatic attributive genitive τῆς πίστεως ("of trust").[57] Thus, the emphasis of this second group is on their trust in God. But Paul, by embedding the temporal dative ἐν ἀκροβυστίᾳ ("in the state of uncircumcision") within the emphatic term τῆς πίστεως, brings the nature of this trust in God to the fore. He emphasizes that it is a trust in God that Abraham exercised while he was in a state of uncircumcision. In this way, Paul gathers together his twofold emphasis, that Abraham exercised trust in God and that he was in a state of uncircumcision when he was regarded by God as righteous. He uses this twofold emphasis to make an explicit statement about the nature of Abraham's fatherhood: that it was a fatherhood founded upon trust in God and did not come via circumcision. The ideological power underlying the claim that those who walk in the footsteps of Abraham are his descendants is built upon the social and cultural intertexture of patrilineal descent, which states that descendants bear resemblance to

---

55. Contra Esler, who incorrectly thinks that Paul does not answer "the status of Judeans who have not come to righteousness by faith in respect of Abraham" (*Conflict and Identity in Romans*, 191). More correctly, Paul did provide a response to that question, although he does not provide a complete answer.

56. For explicating the identity of the group denoted by the expression τοῖς ἐκ περιτομῆς (4:12), Paul could not possibly be referring to people who belonged to the "true circumcision" in Rom 2:28–29. The reason is that 2:25–29 defines "true circumcision" (2:28) as those who obey the Mosaic law (2:25). If Paul was referring to 2:28–29, he would be undermining his own rhetoric as the emphasis of 4:9–12 is on the need for trust in making a Judean Abraham's descendant.

57. Wallace provides an example to clarify the emphasis: that "body of sin" is more emphatic than "sinful body" (*Greek Grammar*, 87).

their ancestor. Thus, when gentiles imitate Abraham, they demonstrate that they are his descendants.[58]

The above discussion allows us now to better discern Paul's rhetorical strategy. Describing Abraham as πατὴρ περιτομῆς ("father of circumcision") indicates that the overarching rhetorolect used in 4:12 is that of wisdom. This is evident since both groups are subsumed under the description of Abraham as being a father. The term father belongs to the firstspace (household) of wisdom rhetorolect. Likewise, circumcision invokes wisdom rhetorolect and also priestly rhetorolect.[59] The main (wisdom) and secondary (priestly) rhetorolects have the ideological power to persuade the implied audience to accept Abraham not just as the father of Judeans but of Judeans who trust God. To achieve the latter objective, Paul uses priestly rhetorolect embedded in the conception of circumcision to reinforce the fact that the trust that Judeans (who are circumcised) place in God has gained them the status of Abraham's descendants. That being said, however, Paul does not (as discussed above in the section on 4:12) mean that circumcision is essential for becoming Abraham's descendant. By using the construction οὐ μόνον ("not only") followed by ἀλλὰ καί ("but also"), Paul cleverly qualifies circumcision as marking out Judeans as Abraham's descendants while relegating it to a position of nonessentiality.

2. Romans 4:13–16: Reliance on the Mosaic Law Abolishes the Promise

Apocalyptic rhetorolect dominates 4:13–16. Its presence is indicated by the topos ἐπαγγελία ("promise" [4:13, 14, 16]). The promise that Abraham will inherit the world (4:13a) positions him as *pater patriae* (4:13a) when both Judeans and gentiles become descendants of Abraham (see the discussion below). Thus, the experienced firstspace is a political empire. This input fits the firstspace of apocalyptic rhetorolect.[60] Furthermore, Abraham inheriting the world hints at the eschatological age and fits the thirdspace of apocalyptic rhetorolect. Also, the recurring topos νόμος ("law" [4:13, 14, 15 (2x), 16]), when read against a backdrop of the Roman Empire,

---

58. See below, chapter 4, §3.2, "Patrilineal Descent."

59. See above, chapter 4, §1.3, "Romans 4:11a: Circumcision Affirmed Abraham's Righteousness that Came by Trust in God."

60. For the definition of "firstspace," which refers to the physical setting that is experienced by the audience, and for the firstspace of apocalyptic rhetorolect, see Robbins, *Invention of Christian Discourse*, 108 and 109, respectively.

contains a social intertexture to the Roman army.[61] This experienced first-space of the implied audience is a political empire and an imperial army. These inputs again fit the firstspace of apocalyptic rhetorolect. Thus, in line with the dominant rhetorolect of 4:13–16, the goal of 4:13–16 is to persuade the implied audience to agree with its rhetoric so as to receive the eschatological "promise" (4:16). This also fits the thirdspace of apocalyptic rhetorolect, which is described as "eternal life and resurrection in a new well-being in the eschatological age."[62]

2.1. Romans 4:13: Abraham and His Descendants Do Not Inherit the Promise by Means of the Mosaic Law but by Trust in God

Romans 4:13 begins with γάρ, which most scholars construe to be causal. They have not, however, discussed the implication of its connection with what precedes in 4:9–12.[63] Jewett contends that construing the causal particle as substantiating the preceding argument is overly simplistic. He thinks that the connection reaches back to 3:27–31 and that Paul is trying to "cut the nexus between promise and obedience."[64] Such a construal of γάρ, however, not only ignores the consistent force of this particle in Rom 4 but also obscures clear conceptual links between 4:9–12 and 4:13–16.[65]

More likely, 4:13–16 provides a reason for what has preceded, most probably to validate, from the perspective of the law, Paul's final construc-tion of Abraham's fatherhood in 4:9–12. In other words, Paul seeks to

---

61. See below, chapter 4, §2.2, "Romans 4:14–15a: Reliance on the Mosaic Law Nullifies Trust and Abolishes the Promise," where I argue that the Roman emperor is subject to Roman law, whose power lies with the Roman populace. Moreover, for him to ascend to the throne, he is also subject to the law in the sense that he needs the sup-port of the Roman populace.

62. Vernon K. Robbins, "Conceptual Blending and Early Christian Imagination," in *Explaining Christian Origins and Early Judaism: Contributions from Cognitive and Social Science*, ed. Petri Luomanen and Ilkka Pyysiainen Uro, BibInt 89 (Leiden: Brill, 2007), 109.

63. For example, Dunn translates γάρ with a causal "for" but totally ignores the connection with what precedes it (*Romans 1–8*, 212). Similarly, Byrne, *Romans*, 151–52; Käsemann, *Commentary on Romans*, 118; Barrett, *Epistle to the Romans*, 94; Cran-field, *Epistle to the Romans*, 1:238.

64. Jewett, *Romans*, 325. Quote from Byrne, *Romans*, 152; contra Gaston, who rejects this position (*Paul and the Torah*, 45–63).

65. This is consistent with its other occurrences in Rom 4 (4:2, 3, 9, 14, 15).

give further proofs that Abraham is the father of both Judean and gentile Christians without the need to undergo circumcision. This is borne out by the fact that the topoi "law" and "circumcision" are tightly linked in 2:25–27. What the connection between 4:9–12 and 4:13–16 implies is that Paul still has in view his recently constructed myth of origins. Exactly what he is doing here is the concern of this section.

Why does Paul use the topos law to provide further refutation of the nonessentiality of circumcision? First, by the end of 4:9–12, Paul has established that by trust, Judeans and gentiles can inherit Abraham's righteousness so that they become his descendants. At 4:13–16, Paul couches this promise in terms of Abraham inheriting the world in the eschatological age. In this way he introduces apocalyptic rhetorolect. Although the content of the promises of Abraham's fatherhood in 4:9–12 and 4:13–16 are essentially the same, they differ in time frame. The former is operative in time contemporaneous with the implied audience, while the latter is operative in the eschatological age. Paul, however, in Fauconnier and Turner's terminology, compressed the intervening time so that both promises are identical although they can be distinguished.[66] His rhetorical strategy is to allow the law to come into play in the rhetoric. The social setting has changed from that of a temple (the firstspace of priestly rhetorolect) to that of the apocalyptic kingdom of God. The resulting secondspace in the implied audience's mind is an image of "multiple heavenly assistants" who enforce the law of God.[67] This terror of God's army will dissuade the implied audience from relying on the law of Moses to realize the promise.

Second, the preceding verses (2:25–27) make a connection between the Mosaic law and circumcision. This reveals the cultural intertexture underlying νόμος ("law"). Dunn observes that

> the argument has narrowed from a vaguely defined "doing good,"
> through the more specific "doing the law," and now to the single issue
> of circumcision, in a progression the devout Jewish interlocutor would
> have appreciated. For such a one ... the point of the law, the privilege of

---

66. Fauconnier and Turner, *Way We Think*, 96, 125–26.

67. Robbins explains that the experiences of the audience in a social space (first-space), in this case, the Roman political kingdom, will generate in the secondspace of the audience's mind "cultural, religious, and ideological places," in this case, "God as Almighty ... [with] multiple heavenly assistants to God" (*Invention of Christian Discourse*, 108–9).

the Jew—could quite properly and fittingly be focused on the one question of circumcision.[68]

The tight nexus Paul forges between circumcision and the Mosaic law reflects the prevailing cultural view that the practice of circumcision is the epitome of performing the Mosaic law. Thus, Paul defines a Judean as one who relies on the Mosaic law (2:17) and also as someone who is circumcised (2:28). Furthermore, obeying the Mosaic moral law is essential for circumcision to have value (2:25–27).[69] This implies that when Paul brings in the topos law, as the causal γάρ indicates, his focus is not merely on the law. Rather, he is using the discussion on the Mosaic law to bolster his claims about the nonessentiality of circumcision. Why Paul brings in the topos law has to do with circumcision being a part of the law and the law being the whole. What this means is that since the whole includes the part, the law, which is the whole, is consequently more important, and hence carries the weight of the argument.[70] This reasoning, however, does not assume an argument that resorts to a locus of quantity.[71] Rather, law is ascribed greater importance because it is also a locus of quality; that is, the law is that element whose violation invokes divine wrath and that results in a client of God running out of favor with his patron (4:15).[72]

Third, the Mosaic law enters the discussion because it is the main factor that is disrupting the relationship between Judean and gentile Christians. This point has been discussed in my overview of the argument of Rom 1–3.[73]

---

68. Dunn, *Romans 1–8*, 119.

69. See also the historical incident in Josephus, *Ant.* 13.257–258, in which the Hasmoneans required the conquered Idumeans and Itureans to be circumcised before they could be permitted to stay together with the people of the covenant (ἐπέτρεψεν αὐτοῖς μένειν ἐν τῇ χώρᾳ εἰ περιτέμνοιντο τὰ αἰδοῖα; "He permitted them to stay in the country if they would circumcise their genitals"). These people who are circumcised, as denoted by the anaphoric τοῖς ("the") in καὶ τοῖς Ἰουδαίων νόμοις χρήσασθαι θέλοιεν ("and if they would make use of the laws of the Judeans"), would then be allowed the use of the laws of the Judeans. Here again, there is a tight nexus between circumcision and obeying the law of Moses.

70. Perelman and Olbrechts-Tyteca, *New Rhetoric*, 233.

71. Perelman and Olbrechts-Tyteca describe this as a *locus* of quantity, where importance is ascribed to something that is greater in quantity (ibid., 85–89).

72. Perelman and Olbrechts-Tyteca qualify the use of the "loci of quantity" by "loci of quality" to prevent "the part and the whole from being considered as homogenous" (ibid., 233)

73. See above, chapter 2, §3, "The Argument of Romans 1:16–4:25."

I demonstrated that Paul was tightening the proverbial hangman's noose on a Judean interlocutor who took pride in possessing the Mosaic law. The Mosaic law, or more specifically, the boast of possessing the Mosaic law, is a bone of contention that drives the argument that precedes Rom 4. But why Paul discusses the Mosaic law immediately after his note on circumcision requires explanation. The Mosaic law, specifically, that which disrupts the relationship between Judean and gentile Christians discussed in Rom 1–3, polarizes over circumcision because it epitomizes observance of the Mosaic law. This polarization accentuates the extent to which Judeans are called the circumcised and circumcision becomes an ethnic marker that differentiates Judeans from gentiles. Thus, the discussion of the law at this point in 4:13 is timely. I shall now explain how Paul puts the Mosaic law into the right perspective.

Scholars interpret the referent of ἡ ἐπαγγελία ("the promise") variously: the promises delineated in Gen 12–22 can include a combination of descendants, land, and blessings for the world or restoring humankind to the original Adamic status of being a steward of creation.[74] These interpretations basically look into the Genesis account or look forward to the later chapters of Romans for support. They are not, however, substantiated by any clear evidence within the immediate context of Rom 4. For one, Paul clearly states that the content of ἡ ἐπαγγελία is Abraham becoming the heir of the world (κόσμος). I wish to argue that κόσμος refers to all Christians, specifically, Judean and gentile Christians.[75] Several observations

---

74. For promise as descendants, land, and blessings on the world, see Esler, *Conflict and Identity in Romans*, 191; Moo, *Epistle to the Romans*, 274; cf. Byrne, who identifies the promise as that of the "land" (*Romans*, 152). For promise as restoration of humankind, see Dunn, *Romans 1–8*, 213; in a similar vein, see Käsemann, *Commentary on Romans*, 120; Cranfield, *Epistle to the Romans*, 1:240.

75. Interestingly, Esler comes close to my interpretation when he says that "it is not impossible that having the world as one's inheritance could be another way of saying that Abraham's seed would be as numerous as the stars in heaven (Gen 15:5), but this may be pushing the latter promise too far" (*Conflict and Identity in Romans*, 191). Unfortunately, he was too quick to dismiss this understanding. The veil that prevented Esler and other interpreters from seeing the (obvious) solution appears to be their recourse to the Genesis account rather than the immediate context of Rom 4 for a solution. Richard N. Longenecker lends support to my view when he observes that the promises given to Abraham in Genesis include his descendants becoming a great nation, the land of Canaan, the blessing that will come on the nations through Abraham, etc. "Here in Rom 4:13 (and continuing on throughout 4:14–24), however,

indicate this. If we take the force of the causal γάρ seriously, the promise referred to here must relate to the preceding context, and hence minimally includes Abraham becoming the father of both Judean and gentile Christians (4:9–12). This understanding is also borne out by the use of the word κόσμος in Romans. This word occurs a total of nine times (Rom 1:8, 20; 3:6, 19; 4:13; 5:12, 13; 11:12, 15). Significant for our discussion is the fact that, not counting 4:13, in all except for 1:8, the word in this letter invariably refers to the animate world of human beings. This observation, prima facie, throws doubt on the physical land as a referent for κόσμος.

The meaning of Abraham inheriting the world can be discovered by exposing the cultural intertextures of κληρονόμος ("heir") and πατήρ ("father"). Roman family law was founded upon the basis that each family had its *pater familias*, the head of a Roman household. This household included relatives and slaves.[76] The oldest living male in the family possessed *potestas*, the authority of the *pater familias*.[77] This authority was almost absolute. It included the right of the *pater familias* to put to death his own children.[78] Such unlimited power was only curtailed to inflicting reasonable punishment around the reign of Emperor Justinian (527–565 CE).[79] When a *pater familias* died, Roman law sought out an heir who would assume all the rights and obligations of the deceased *pater familias*.

Paul speaks in a generic fashion of only the promise that God gave to Abraham about his becoming 'the heir of the world'—which is a locution for both (1) the new status and life credited to him by God *and* (2) the widespread and significant presence of Abraham and his progeny in the then-known world" (*Epistle to the Romans*, 509–10, emphasis original). Cf. William D. Davies, who observes that "Paul ignores completely the territorial aspect of the promise. The land is not within his purview" (*The Gospel and the Land: Early Christianity and Jewish Territorial Doctrine* [Los Angeles: University of California Press, 1974], 178).

76. So James C. Walters, "Paul, Adoption, and Inheritance," in Sampley, *Paul in the Greco-Roman World*, 52–53.

77. Carolyn Osiek and David L. Balch note that the family included the ancestors as well as the extended family, slaves, and assets of a household. See Osiek and Balch, *Families in the New Testament World: Households and House Churches* (Louisville: Westminster John Knox, 1997), 216.

78. Yehiel Kaplan, "The Changing Profile of the Parent-Child Relationship in Jewish Law," in *The Jewish Law Annual*, vol. 18, ed. Berachyahu Lifshitz (London: Routledge, 2009), 29–30.

79. Jane F. Gardner, *Family and Familia in Roman Law and Life* (Oxford: Clarendon, 1998), 121–23; Andrew Borkowski, *Textbook on Roman Law* (London: Blackstone, 1994), 103, 107.

All descendants of all ages of the deceased *pater familias* were to come under the *postestas* of the new *pater familias*. These descendants were now considered his property. Hence, they could not own any property until they were released from the new *potestas*. That this was the case is evident from the fact that the *pater familias* held the right to sell even his own child into slavery or civil bondage.[80] In light of the above discussion, Abraham inheriting the world becomes intelligible: it refers to him becoming the *pater familias* of both Judean and gentile Christians. Construing the κόσμος that Abraham inherits in 4:13–15 as comprising Judean and gentile Christians provides a connection with the preceding and succeeding arguments: in what precedes, 4:11–12 emphasizes the result of Abraham's trust in God (4:9b) as becoming the father of both Judean and gentile Christians. The same point is also emphasized in what follows: Abraham's trust in God made him the "father of many nations" (4:18).

A possible objection to construing Abraham as *pater familias* must be dealt with. Did Judeans conceptualize Abraham's fatherhood in terms of the Roman *pater familias*? This is possible because the institution of the *pater familias* was part of the larger patron-client system that pervaded every stratum of the Roman Empire. Furthermore, these two systems are congruous, as is shown by the fact that the patron-client relation is modeled on the dominance and subordination of the father-son relationship. The client, like a son in relation to his father, is dependent on the patron for benefactions.

Abraham, however, is not only *pater familias*; he also takes on the role of *pater patriae*, a title attributed to the Roman emperor Augustus and the emperors who followed. In 2 BCE, Augustus Caesar was proclaimed *pater patriae* ("father of the fatherland"). Earlier, Cicero and Julius Caesar were called *parens patriae* and *pater patriae* respectively (Dio Cassius, *Hist. rom.* 44.4.4; Suetonius, *Jul.* 76). Augustus, however, not only took on the honorific title but also fulfilled the role of *pater patriae*.[81] His authentic role as *pater patriae* can be seen in him using his own money to provide public services (*pecunia sua*).[82] Family slaves and freed staff were also assigned

---

80. Kaplan, "Changing Profile of the Parent-Child Relationship," 29–30. This right or the *potestas* of the *pater familias* ends when the child becomes a legally independent child (*sui iuris*) by requesting legal independence when he comes of age.

81. Clifford Ando, *Imperial Ideology and Provincial Loyalty in the Roman Empire* (Berkeley: University of California Press, 2000), 400–1.

82. Severy, *Augustus and the Family*, 140–41. Donald Dudley notes that all emper-

to manage his accounts, including money from the *aerarium stabulum* ("treasure house"), which was used to fund public service projects. This reflects the expansion of the imperial *familia* into public service.[83] Augustus's wife, Livia, together with his daughters and nieces, managed foreign relations.[84] That such an authentic role of *patria patriae* also extended beyond Augustus is corroborated by later Latin writers who accorded such a duty to later *patres patriae* (e.g., Seneca, *Clem.* 1.14; Tacitus, *Ann.* 1.12).[85] My point is that Augustus and subsequent Roman emperors, in taking on the role of *pater patriae*, are essentially functioning as the patron of the Roman Empire in the patron-client system.[86] Considering that Abraham inherits the world comprising minimally all peoples in the Roman Empire, Paul's positioning of Abraham as *pater patriae*, the Roman emperor, is not an overstatement. Such a construal is in line with Elliott's comments that

> the observation is now commonplace that some of Paul's most theologically significant phrases would have resonated with imperial overtones. His titles for Christ ("lord," *kyrios*, and "son of God," *huios tou theou*), for example, were titles that the Caesars also claimed. The terms normally translated "gospel" or "good news" (*euangelion*) and "preach the gospel"

---

ors after Augustus "had to undertake these expensive obligations, which showed that the populace of Rome was in some sense the *clientela* of the Emperor." See Dudley, *The Romans* (London: Hutchinson, 1970), 148.

83. Severy, *Augustus and the Family*, 144–45.

84. Ibid., 148–49.

85. In *Clem.* 1.14, Seneca exhorts the young Nero, who has inherited the role of a *pater patriae*, to care for the interests of his children: "This is the duty of a father, and it is also the duty of a prince, whom not in empty flattery we have been led to call 'the Father of his Country' [Patrem Patriae] ... we have given the name in order that he may know that he has been entrusted with a father's power, which is most forbearing in its care for the interests of his children" (Winterbottom, LCL). Ando comments that since this was addressed to a young Nero, Seneca was not dwelling on the characteristics of a bad prince but what was expected of a *princeps* of Rome. Ando notes that in Tacitus, *Ann.* 1.12, Tiberius, upon succeeding the throne, also promised to take up the role of the *patria patriae* to the Roman people (*Imperial Ideology*, 402).

86. Barclay notes that Augustus succeeded in curbing the exercise of senatorial patronage of powerful individuals in Rome. His universal patronage, however, was not "a monopoly of patronal power. Rather, by making the senatorial families, together with his 'friends' and *familia*, the brokers of his own power, the emperor enhanced their patronal networks in extension of his interests" (*Paul and the Gift*, 37–38).

(*euangelizesthai*) were readily employed in Paul's world as an element of imperial propaganda.[87]

Hence, Elliott correctly points out that Romans "is itself Paul's effective proclamation of an alternative lordship at work as the Romans hear it." In other words, this letter challenges the lordship of Caesar. Paul, however, conceals this political overtone behind the note of "inheriting the world" because he has in mind the eschatological age to which he will refer in Rom 8 and not the immediate hegemony of the Roman Empire.

This Roman emperor cult, besides being part of the cultural intertexture of Romans, also relates to social and cultural texture. Clifford Ando argues that the emperors and the governing class unite the cultural scripts of their subjects by providing Rome with a system of concepts. These concepts are concentrated in the figure of the Roman emperor or, more specifically, the Roman emperor cult.[88] Ando follows Bourdieu, who investigated breakdowns in social orders by going beyond the (reductionist) level of politics and economics that characterize Marxist ideologies. Instead, Bourdieu, following Victor Turner, situates an individual within the grids of *habitus*, the world of every day experiences, and *doxa*, social memories.[89] The Roman emperor cult is one such system that generates a *habitus* and *doxa*. This social texture contributed to a part of the ideology in the Roman Empire that united the cultural scripts of the subjects of the Roman emperor and the governing class.[90] By positioning Abraham as *pater patriae*, Paul mobilizes ideological power to unite the dissenting

---

87. Elliott, *Arrogance of Nations*, 44, 45. See also Dieter Georgi, who asks provocatively: "Paul's use of terminology drawn from the law of royal succession in Rom 1:3–4 shows that he is making more than a religious claim.... Is Paul using the traditional formula in order to support an alternative theory concerning true rulership and the legitimate *princeps*? Is he offering an alternative to the social utopia of Caesarism, with its promise of universal reconciliation and peace as the prerequisite for undreamed achievements resulting in unimagined prosperity?" See Georgi, *Theocracy in Paul's Praxis and Theology*, trans. David E. Green (Minneapolis: Fortress, 1991), 86–87. Similarly, Sylvia C. Keesmaat construes Romans as challenging the "imperial story" in the context of the Pax Romana ("Reading Romans in the Capital of the Empire," in Sumney, *Reading Paul's Letter to the Romans*, 52–53).

88. Ando, *Imperial Ideology*, 27.

89. Pierre Bourdieu, *The Logic of Practice*, trans. Richard Nice (Stanford: Stanford University Press, 1990), 54–55; Bourdieu, *Outline of a Theory of Practice*, 20–21, 78.

90. Ando, *Imperial Ideology*, 23.

Judean and gentile Christians. This construal refines Esler's conceptualization of Abraham as a superordinate figure by situating Abraham within the ancient context of the Roman Empire.

The above understanding also coheres with the meaning of ὁ κόσμος ("the world"). The term κόσμος is used consistently in its other occurrences in Romans to connote the totality of humankind, including minimally the world of the Roman Empire.[91] Quite clearly, a sociopolitical dimension underlies the idea of inheriting the world.[92] When this sociopolitical aspect of the world is read in light of my contention that Abraham is *pater familias*, Abraham takes on the role of *pater patriae* of the Roman Empire.[93] This promise that Abraham will inherit the world is also promised to his descendants (4:13). Jewett agrees with Klaus Haacker that this promise refers to Abraham and his descendants' rule over the entire world.[94] It is a "nonpolitical and at any event nonmilitary" form of imperial rule.[95] By emphasizing Abraham as patron of the world, Paul positions him as a superordinate figure to unite the dissenting Christian factions, namely, Judean and gentile Christians. With the preliminaries in place, we are now in a position to understand the rhetoric of 4:13.

Romans 4:13 serves as the thesis statement for 4:14–16. Paul's thesis is that Abraham and his descendants did not inherit the promise by means of the Mosaic law. As opposed to inheriting the promise by observing the Mosaic law, Paul argues that righteousness comes by trust in God. Again,

---

91. For instance, in 1:8, Paul, when praising the Roman Christians, says hyperbolically that their faith is being reported ὅλῳ τῷ κόσμῳ ("in the whole world"); in Paul's conclusion in 3:19, in indicting all of humankind (both Judeans and gentiles) for sin, he refers to humankind as πᾶς ὁ κόσμος ("all the world").

92. See Mark Forman, *The Politics of Inheritance in Romans*, SNTSMS 18 (Cambridge: Cambridge University Press, 2011), 58–101. Forman there shows that κληρονόμος ("heir") and נחל word groups are often associated with national territory. To say, however, that "Paul indicates that the *how* of the inheritance also subverts the hegemonic and militaristic approach of Rome" is probably stretching Paul's emphasis. His point, however, is valid: hegemonic and militaristic overtones are present.

93. John H. Elliott thinks that Mark's rhetoric, with its stress on believers as a household, is directed at the Roman emperor's title of *pater patriae*. See Elliott, "Household/Family in the Gospel of Mark as a Core Symbol of Community," in Gowler, Bloomquist, and Watson, *Fabrics of Discourse*, 63.

94. Jewett, *Romans*, 325.

95. Klaus Haacker, *Der Brief des Paulus an die Römer*, THKNT 6 (Leipzig: Evangelische Verlagsanstalt, 1999), 106.

righteousness here refers to a favorable relationship between God and his clients, namely, Judean and gentile Christians. This thesis is substantiated by the argument that follows in 4:14–16.

2.2. Romans 4:14–15a: Reliance on the Mosaic Law Nullifies Trust and Abolishes the Promise

Below is a display of the argumentative structure of 4:14–15a:

Case	εἰ γὰρ οἱ ἐκ νόμου κληρονόμοι ("For if those who are of the law are heirs" [4:14a])
Result	κεκένωται ἡ πίστις ("trust has been nullified") καὶ κατήργηται ἡ ἐπαγγελία ("and the promised has been abolished" [4:14b])
	[Case₁] (Judean and gentiles fail to keep the moral law of God)
	[Rule₁] (wrath comes from not keeping the moral law of God)
Rule/Result₁	ὁ γὰρ νόμος ὀργὴν κατεργάζεται ("for the (Mosaic) law works wrath" [4:15a])

This paragraph responds to the twofold thesis of 4:13: that the promise of Abraham inheriting the world comes, first, not by the Mosaic law but, second, by trust in God.

2.2.1. Romans 4:14

Assuming for the sake of argument that those who rely on the Mosaic law are heirs, two results, with the perfect tense signifying the resulting state of affairs, follow: trust in God has been nullified (κεκένωται) and the promise has been abolished (κατήργηται).[96] Paul is essentially utilizing the classic strategy of evaluating an act or event in terms of its favorable or unfavorable consequences. In this case, the act of relying on the law is undesirable because of the consequence faced, namely, the promise is abolished. What is unusual here is that Paul inserts in between the cause (a reliance on the

---

96. This is a first-class conditional statement that assumes the protasis to be true for the sake of argument. See BDF §189; Wallace, *Greek Grammar*, 690–94.

Mosaic law) and its unfavorable consequence (promise abolished) another consequence: trust in God is nullified. Perelman and Olbrechts-Tyteca's conception of value transfer in what they call the "pragmatic argument" helps to explain the function of trust here.[97] The value attached to the second consequence of the abolishment of the promise gets transferred not only to the act of relying on the law but also to the nullification of trust in God. In this way, Paul not only denigrates the role of the law in securing the promise but also accentuates the importance of trust in God. How a reliance on the law leads to the twin consequences of a nullification of trust in God and an abolishment of the promise is explained in 4:15.[98]

2.2.2. Romans 4:15a

Commentators argue over the specific context for understanding how wrath is invoked. Some think that the universality of the law provokes God's wrath on all humankind.[99] Others think that the law, as made explicit in the Mosaic law, makes sin more grievous so as to provoke God to anger.[100] Both positions, however, dwell on questions about which Paul is not concerned here. First, the law alluded to here must be the Mosaic law because the argument continues the contentious issue of 4:9–12, namely, circumcision. Second, whether or not the Mosaic law aggravates the seriousness of sin is superfluous. The fact is that in 4:15a, Paul does not explain how the Mosaic law provokes God's wrath. He simply states it because the point that the Mosaic law provokes God's wrath has already been established earlier in 1:18–3:20. The discussion below explains my point.

---

97. Perelman and Olbrechts-Tyteca, *New Rhetoric*, 266.

98. Moo thinks that Paul makes this statement on the basis of the preceding argument in Rom 1–3 and 4:15 (*Epistle to the Romans*, 275); so also Frank J. Matera, *Romans*, Paideia (Grand Rapids: Baker Academic, 2010), 139; Barrett, *Epistle to the Romans*, 94–95; Schreiner, *Romans*, 229. Dunn seems to imply that Paul bases his conclusion about the nullification of faith on Gen 15:6 (*Romans 1–8*, 214). This search for a proof is unnecessary since Paul immediately, with an inferential γάρ, indicates that he is about to substantiate his claim. More correctly, Godet states that the proofs are spelled out in what follows (*Commentary on St. Paul's Epistle to the Romans*, 176–77).

99. E.g., John Murray, *The Epistle to the Romans* (Grand Rapids: Eerdmans, 1997), 143–44; R. C. H. Lenski, *The Interpretation of St. Paul's Epistle to the Romans* (Minneapolis: Augsburg, 1936), 312.

100. E.g., Godet, *Commentary on St. Paul's Epistle to the Romans*, 177; Barrett, *Epistle to the Romans*, 95; Cranfield, *Epistle to the Romans*, 1:241.

Why does a reliance on the Mosaic law provoke God's wrath and, consequently, abolish the promise? To properly understand the reason, we need to discern the social intertexture of law in general. In the honor-shame system of the Mediterranean agonistic culture, honor, if not ascribed, needs to be acquired. A means of acquiring this honor is by being virtuous in one's dealings.[101] For a person living in Roman society, virtuous behavior must conform to the behavioral standards or laws as dictated by community consensus. In other words, the community is the significant other.[102] This gains a person honor. In Rom 4, the significant other is God since he alone can grant honor by making a person a descendant of Abraham. As the Mosaic law encapsulates God's moral requirements, the standard by which God grants honor to his clients is the Mosaic law. This law also includes the conception of moral law held in part by the gentiles (2:14–15). One way of acquiring (or losing) this honor is to enter into a game of challenge and riposte with Paul, who, as an apostle (see 1:1), represents God.

With the above understanding of how the Mosaic law functions within the honor-shame system, we are in a position to understand how relying on the Mosaic law provokes the wrath of God according to the argument in 1:18–3:20. According to 2:14–15, Paul contends that the gentiles know, to a certain degree, the Mosaic law: "When gentiles, who do not possess the (Mosaic) law, do instinctively what the law requires, these, though not having the law, are a law to themselves. They show that what the (Mosaic) law requires is written on their hearts" (NRSV). The unstated result ($Result_1$) that the Mosaic law produces wrath is a product of the unstated case ($Case_1$) that humankind (both Judeans and gentiles) has failed to obey the law and the unstated rule ($Rule_1$) that wrath comes from not keeping the moral law of God. This wrath of God leads to a loss of honor for the interlocutor in the challenge-riposte tussle as demonstrated

---

101. See deSilva, *Honor, Patronage, Kinship and Purity*, 28.

102. Richard L. Rohrbaugh, "Honor: Core Value in the Biblical World," in *Understanding the Social World of the New Testament*, ed. Dietmar Neufeld and Richard E. DeMaris (London: Routledge, 2010), 119; see also Plutarch, *Frat. amor.* 1 (478b): "For as to the exhortations this essay contains, since you are already putting them into practice, you will seem to be giving your testimony in their favor rather than to be encouraged to perform them; and the pleasure you will take in acts which are right will make the perseverance of your judgment more firm, inasmuch as your acts will win approval before spectators, so to speak, who are honorable and devoted to virtue" (Helmbold, LCL])

by the argument of 1:18–3:20. The unstated case (Case₁) has been established in Rom 1–3, as the discussion that follows explains.

First, Paul indicts the gentiles in 1:18–32 who know God (and hence, his moral law) but fail to glorify God. That the gentiles have failed to make the necessary riposte in the challenge initiated by Paul (representing God) is shown by the fact that they enter a state of dishonor. There, God gives the gentiles over to dishonor (ἀτιμάζεσθαι [1:24]) of their physical bodies and to a depraved mind (εἰς ἀδόκιμον νοῦν [1:28]). Second, Paul turns his attention to the implied Judean audience. Having obtained the assent of the Judean interlocutor of the guilt of the gentiles, Paul (representing God) challenges the Judeans. They, like the gentiles, have failed to keep the law despite knowing the law. The Judean interlocutor makes several ripostes (2:2, 17–23; 3:5), but Paul counters these ripostes that the Judean interlocutor fails to ward off. This signifies that Paul (and hence God) has shown that Judeans and gentiles have sinned against God. Consequently, God's wrath is provoked. Paul (and thus God) has won the challenge. As a result, Judeans and gentiles incur a loss of honor. This leads to the unstated result, namely, the abolition of the promise as initially articulated by Paul in his opening statement in 4:14b.

The term *law* should not be considered just in light of Judean culture as encapsulated in the Mosaic law. It also contains another social intertexture that involves Roman culture. Such a construal, as I have argued above, is reasonable, as Roman culture was the dominant culture in Rome.[103] Furthermore, it played a major role in Corinth as a Roman colony governed on the model of the Roman republic.[104] As the dominant culture, Roman culture "is vested with power to impose its goals on people in a significantly broad territorial region."[105] In other words, the term "law" in Rom 4 references not only Judean law but also Roman law.

A social intertexture underlies the relationship between Roman law and *fides*. Patrons and clients relate to one another on the basis of *fides*. However, Cicero, for instance, acknowledges that *fides* cannot be guaranteed in practice (*Off.* 3.69–70). This explains in part how terms like *mala fides*, *fraus*, *dolus*, and *dolus malus* arise. In response, the law is used to reify trust. The term *bona fides* reflects such a function of the law. For instance,

---

103. See above, chapter 1, §2.2, "Intertexture."

104. Jerome Murphy-O'Connor, "Corinth," *ABD* 1:1135–39. See also Murphy-O'Connor, *St. Paul's Corinth: Texts and Archaeology* (Wilmington: Glazier, 1983), 5–7.

105. Robbins, *Tapestry of Early Christian Discourse*, 168.

Augustus encoded in law *fideicommissum*, the mechanism whereby property was entrusted to a person for the benefit of a third party. Effectively, *fides* in this relationship is guaranteed by a third party, the emperor (see Justinian, *Inst.* 1.2.23.1).[106] In this way, when *fides* is not demonstrated in a patron and client relationship, the dishonest party is liable to being prosecuted by and incurs the wrath of Roman law. Using the law to enforce trust, however, creates tension "between *fides* as an intrinsic quality of good people and *fides* as something guaranteed by a third party in which two principals share trust."[107] This tension is pronounced when the involved parties demonstrate *fides* only when threatened by the law. In such a situation, the law, and no longer *fides*, effectively governs the patron and client relationship. Thus, law and *fides* are opposing entities. This underlying social intertexture explains why Paul in 4:14–15 says that the law nullifies trust, and the law, in the absence of trust, also brings wrath.

The Roman law under consideration involves the role of the Roman emperor. The presence of this social intertexture can be detected when law is considered in light of Abraham inheriting the world, which is tantamount to him attaining the role of the Roman emperor. The Roman emperor was considered a *princeps* (leader of the Senate). From Augustus until the period before the reign of Diocletian (284 CE), the Roman Empire was a principate and an *imperium legitimum* in which the emperor was not above the law.[108] Authority rested with the people of Rome, whose power was expressed via the Senate and the *princeps*.[109] The legislative power of the emperors was largely an extension of the Roman Republic's *ius edicendi* (the right of the higher magistrates to proclaim edicts to the people). The emperors did not possess the authority to create, change, or abrogate a law. Thus, popular election was the basis of the office of the principate.[110] That said, the emperor was never elected by the people but

---

106. Morgan, *Roman Faith and Christian Faith*, 113–14.

107. Ibid., 114.

108. Starting with the reign of Diocletian, the Roman Empire was *princeps legibus solutus*, that is, a period when the king was above the law. Mason Hammond, *The Augustan Principate in Theory and Practice during the Julio-Claudian Period* (Cambridge: Harvard University Press, 1933), 159.

109. So Theodor Mommsen, *A History of Rome under the Emperors*, trans. Clare Krojzl (London: Routledge, 1996), 82.

110. Mommsen also comments that this popular vote was never realized through an election but rather "by a spontaneous seizure of power by the ruler on the strength of the will of the people" (*History of Rome*, 83).

"was proclaimed by the soldiers."[111] Nonetheless, this seizure was seen as an act of the will of the Roman populace.[112] Hence, any attempt to allow the heir of an emperor to take the office of the principate without respect for the authority of the Roman populace and the Senate risked invoking the wrath of the army.

The Augustan and post-Augustan eras demonstrate that the military was the mainstay of the Roman emperor's throne. Although the army in theory had no role in the choice of the ruler, its power was almost always decisive in the choice of a new Roman emperor.[113] This is shown by the following observations. Augustus was an army general when he established himself as the supreme ruler of Rome, the *princeps civitatis*.[114] Tiberius accepted the help of the military to establish his rule upon the death of Augustus (Suetonius, *Tib.* 24.1). The Praetorians' support for Caligula, Claudius, and Nero made possible their reigns.[115] Emperors Galba, Otho, Vitellius, and Vespasian, who reigned in the period after the death of Nero in 68 CE, also claimed the throne with the support of the military.

This shows that the social and cultural intertexture that underlies law is connected with the installation of a Roman emperor. Why Paul, in discussing Abraham's fatherhood as inheriting the world, brings the topos law into his discussion becomes comprehensible. The reason is that both law and emperor were common topoi.[116] Thus, a Roman emperor could suffer the wrath of the law. Hence, to ascend the position of emperor, a person needed to be loyal to (trust) his patron, the Roman populace, whose power in practice was vested in the Roman army.

The above-discussed social intertexture informs the reading of 4:15a and mobilizes ideological power. How it does this requires clarification. Robbins emphasizes the need "to interpret reasoning in argumentation but also to interpret picturing of people and the environments in which

---

111. Ibid.

112. Ibid.

113. Hammond, *Augustan Principate*, 149; see also Michael Peppard, *The Son of God in the Roman World: Divine Sonship in Its Social and Political Context* (Oxford: Oxford University Press, 2011), 67.

114. Mommsen, *History of Rome*, 83.

115. Hammond, *Augustan Principate*, 151–52; Mommsen, *History of Rome*, 133. For Claudius, the Praetorian Guards opposed the Senate in favor of their chosen candidate.

116. See Kennedy, *New Testament Interpretation*, 20.

they are interacting," or what he calls "rhetography."[117] This second aspect
of the social intertexture lends itself to rhetography. Davina C. Lopez
refines Robbins's rhetography by pointing out several inhibitions to reading or hearing Paul's letter when they were read out loud. For a start, the
literacy rate was low. Also, even if a select few were literate, we cannot
assume that they received it in terms of abstract concepts. Rather, the
ancient people may have heard the letter by envisioning images while
reading the letter.[118] Along this line of analysis, Paul's implied audience
would probably have recalled images of the army and their attached sig-
nification when they heard of the association of wrath and law read out in
Romans. A source of such images is found on Roman coins. For instance,
figure 1 shows Claudius being pronounced as emperor by the Praetorian
Guard. Figure 2 shows the victory of Octavianus (Augustus) and Agrippa
at Actium in 31 BCE over Marcus Antonius and Cleopatra. Figure 3 shows
Caligula giving a speech to the Praetorian Guard, who supported him after
Emperor Tiberius died.

These coins, however, do not just constantly recall for the implied
audience vivid images of the wrath of the Roman army. An example of the
Roman army's wrath that would have been well known to the Roman populace was when the Praetorian Guard (fig. 1) helped to secure the throne for
Claudius by murdering his predecessor, Caligula, and Caligula's wife and
child at the imperial palace. The social cultural texture underlying coins
is that they contain a locus of quality of being useful, and hence contain
value.[119] By inscribing on the coins memories of the strength (and wrath)
of the army, the value of the coin and the image of the army are somehow

---

117. Robbins, *Invention of Christian Discourse*, 16. The use of rhetography and
rhetorolects builds upon and improves on Aristotle's understanding of rhetoric. See
George A. Kennedy, "Reworking Aristotle's *Rhetoric*," in Robbins, von Thaden, and
Bruehler, *Foundations for Sociorhetorical Exploration*, 78: "Rhetoric also is given its
spatial visualization and actualization by Aristotle. A striking instance occurs in his
famous definition of rhetoric as an ability or faculty of *seeing* [his emphasis] the available means of persuasion in each case [*Rhet.* 1.2.1]." Cf. Bloomquist, who reinterprets
Aristotle's understanding of rhetoric in sociorhetorical terms as "pictorial-narrative
elaboration (rhetography)" and "enthymematic-syllogistic elaboration (rhetology)"
("Paul's Inclusive Language," 129).

118. Davina C. Lopez, "Visual Perspectives: Imag(in)Ing the Big Pauline Picture," in *Studying Paul's Letters: Contemporary Perspectives and Methods*, ed. Joseph A.
Marchal (Minneapolis: Fortress, 2012), 102.

119. Perelman and Olbrechts-Tyteca, *New Rhetoric*, 89–93.

Fig. 1. Claudius. Aureus. Rome mint. Struck 46–47 CE. Obverse: Laureate head of Claudius right; Reverse: IMPER RECEPT along top of circular wall enclosing the Praetorian camp. RIC 36 (R4); BMCRE 37; Calicó 362. Courtesy of Heritage Auctions.

Fig. 2. Augustus. Denarius. Lugdunum mint. Struck 15–13 BCE. Obverse: Head of Augustus, bare, right; Reverse: Apollo standing left, holding plectrum in right hand and lyre in left hand. RIC I 171A. Courtesy of Münzkabinett der Universität Göttingen, Archäologisches Institut, Photo Stephan Eckardt.

Fig. 3. Caligula. Sestertius. Roman mint. Struck 37–38 CE. Obverse: Laureate head of Caligula left. Reverse: Caligula standing left atop platform. RIC 32; MCRE 33; BN 45; Cohen 1. Courtesy of Heritage Auctions.

mystically linked together "at the level of the divine vision of reality."[120] In terms of conceptual blending, there is a "compression of vital relations" where the coin (the part) contains the power of the Roman army (the whole).[121] In this way the value of the coin gets transferred to the image as well. The Roman coin that contains a compression of vital relations, namely, that of the power of the Roman army and the Roman law, provides input for the firstspace of apocalyptic rhetorolect. This firstspace creates in the secondspace of the implied audience's mind an image of God as almighty and enlisting his multiple heavenly assistants to enforce justice.[122] Apocalyptic rhetorolect thus mobilizes ideological power to dissuade the implied audience from relying on the law for realizing the promise.

2.3. Romans 4:15b–16: Wrath Is Removed So That the Promise Is Fulfilled Because Abraham Trusted in God

The argumentative structure of Rom 4:15b–16 can be presented as below:

Case	οὗ δὲ οὐκ ἔστιν νόμος οὐδὲ παράβασι ("but where there is no law, there is no transgression" [4:15b])
[Rule]	(law is antithetical to trust)
Result	διὰ τοῦτο ἐκ πίστεως, ἵνα κατὰ χάριν, εἰς τὸ εἶναι βεβαίαν τὴν ἐπαγγελίαν παντὶ τῷ σπέρματι, οὐ τῷ ἐκ τοῦ νόμου μόνον ἀλλὰ καὶ τῷ ἐκ πίστεως Ἀβραάμ, ὅς ἐστιν πατὴρ πάντων ἡμῶν ("For this reason it is by trust, so that it may be according to favor, with the result that the promise may be certain to all his descendants, not to the one who is of the law only but also to the one who is of the trust of Abraham, who is the father of us all" [4:16])

2.3.1. Romans 4:15b

The emphasis of 4:15b is that only when the law is absent can there be no transgression that will destroy the promise. But Paul's intent is not to denigrate the law. His objective is to displace the law so as to pave the way for trust to be restored to its rightful place. Trust should be deemed

---

120. Ibid., 331–32.

121. Fauconnier and Turner, *Way We Think*, 97.

122. Robbins, *Invention of Christian Discourse*, 109.

as the means to secure the promise of inheriting the world and becoming a descendant of Abraham. Thus, having displaced the law, Paul now returns to where he left off. He now focuses on the second part of his thesis statement in 4:13: the promise of Abraham inheriting the world, which comprises Judean and gentile Christians, comes by the trust in God that Abraham had. To do this, Paul brings in the critical role of trust via the statement οὗ δὲ οὐκ ἔστιν νόμος οὐδὲ παράβασις ("But where there is not law, there is no transgression [4:15b]). Most scholars view this statement as performing a subsidiary role of supporting the earlier statement that "the law produces wrath" (4:15a).[123] Byrne is perceptive when he opines that "it is not clear why Paul formulates this sentence in the negative.... [H]e might as well—and perhaps better—have said: 'because the law makes sin into transgression.'"[124] Unfortunately, he does not pursue this line of inquiry and construes it, like the majority of interpreters, as supporting what precedes it. I have grouped the last clause in 4:15b with what follows as introducing the pivotal role of trust rather than concluding what precedes it. This answers Byrne's query as to why the last clause in 4:15b is framed negatively. Specifically, it is where the argument that began in 4:13 is heading. At the same time, 4:15b prepares for the argument that follows.

2.3.2. Romans 4:16

At this point, Paul introduces wisdom rhetorolect, whose presence is indicated by the topos of Abraham being "the father of all of us" (4:16). After Paul has dissuaded the implied audience from relying on the law by the use of apocalyptic rhetorolect, he now uses wisdom rhetorolect, whose secondspace contains the conceptualization of God as father. The implied audience is thus urged to rely on God as a kind father who teaches wisdom (thirdspace).[125]

---

123. Dunn construes 4:15b as explaining "how the process of wrath works out" (*Romans 1–8*, 215). In a similar vein, see Godet, *Commentary on St. Paul's Epistle to the Romans*, 177; Moo, *Epistle to the Romans*, 277; Cranfield, *Epistle to the Romans*, 1:241; Schreiner, *Romans*, 230–31; more recently, see also Tom Holland, *Romans: The Divine Marriage* (Eugene, OR: Pickwick, 2011), 139; Matera, *Romans*, 114.

124. Byrne, *Romans*, 158.

125. See the secondspace of wisdom rhetorolect, where God is regarded as a father who teaches wisdom (Robbins, *Invention of Christian Discourse*, 109).

Before analyzing 4:16, several social intertextures need to be brought to light. First, 4:15b (the case) does not lead naturally to 4:16 (the result). An unstated rule in the form of social intertexture is required to bridge 4:15b and 4:16, namely, the rule that the law is antithetical to trust. That they are antithetical is clear. As explained above (4:15a), honor that comes by the law requires one to perform deeds that conform to the laws of the Roman world. Also, as discussed in 4:4–5, if deeds that earn (acquired honor) are not involved, the only way to gain (ascribed) honor is by trust in—that is, loyalty to—a patron. In this case, the honor is gained by becoming a descendant of Abraham. But how does trust realize becoming Abraham's descendant? This brings me to the second social and cultural intertexture. Adoption offers a way to forge a patron-client—or in the case of 4:16, a *pater*-son—relationship.[126] This validates Paul's myth of origins and thus creates ideological texture that prompts the audience to accept Abraham's worldwide fatherhood. The ideological texture is further strengthened by Erin M. Heim's observation that adoption is a metaphor, and metaphors, "as performative utterances, ... are active agents that create and structure their interpreter's perception of reality."[127] The perception of reality or the meaning created by the metaphor "results from the *interanimation* of the tenor and vehicle" and "occurs in the hypnotic dance between words and thoughts, in the midst of the somewhat mysterious interaction between its model, tenor, and vehicle."[128] Here, the tenor, "the subject upon which it is hoped light will be shed," is Paul's myth of origins that gentiles are descendants of Abraham.[129] The vehicle, "the subject to which allusion is made in order to

---

126. Peppard notes that Kunst has demonstrated that "the performance and social acceptance of various kinds of adoptive or quasi-adoptive relationships—other than those legalized according to the Roman codes—was much more common than previous scholarship acknowledged" (*Son of God*, 53). Similarly, Erin M. Heim, *Adoption in Galatians and Romans: Contemporary Metaphor Theories and the Pauline Huiothesia Metaphors*, BibInt 153 (Leiden: Brill, 2017), 121; see Christiane Kunst, *Römische Adoption: Zur Strategie einer Familienorganisation*, FAB 10 (Hennef: Clauss, 2005). Peppard also comments that "the status or 'social power' of the father was made real by the possession of clients gained through adoption" (*Son of God*, 55).

127. Heim, *Adoption in Galatians and Romans*, 80.

128. Ibid., 43, 44–45, emphasis original.

129. Gregory W. Dawes, *The Body in Question: Metaphor and Meaning in the Interpretation of Ephesians 5:21–33*, BibInt 30 (Leiden: Brill, 1998), 27.

shed that light," is adoption.[130] How the mind construes the meaning of a metaphor—in this case, adoption—depends on the model(s) that resides in the thoughts of the audience.[131] The model that Paul employs is that of the Roman practice of adoption.[132] Michael Peppard's investigation of the ancient Roman practice of adoption sheds light on this model.[133] I shall discuss some salient points of his essay in what follows.

Why is adoption a viable and desirable mode of securing an heir? The patron god or *pater* of the Roman Empire was Jupiter. J. Rufus Fears makes the important observation that the concept of *pater* was not about bringing forth descendants but about rule and dependence. The son looks to the *pater* for divine protection from the one who supplies the dependent's needs.[134] Jupiter's role as *pater* of the Roman Empire, however, was

---

130. Dawes, *Body in Question*, 27. Heim rightly rejects finding a single literal referent for the metaphor, for instance, by answering the question, "what is *X* a metaphor for?" Such an approach of identifying a paraphrase for the metaphor is reductionist, as it does not "evoke the same mental simulation as the original metaphor" (*Adoption in Galatians and Romans*, 46). This reductionist approach returns to comparison theories that scholars now regard as inadequate; see Janet Martin Soskice, *Metaphor and Religious Language* (Oxford: Clarendon, 1985), 10–15, 24–26.

131. Dawes explains that "a model is a consistent imaginative construct or (if one prefers) a consistent pattern of thought by means of which apparently isolated phenomenon may be seen to be related to one another" (*Body in Question*, 38). See also Heim, *Adoption in Galatians and Romans*, 43–45.

132. James M. Scott argues for a Judean understanding of adoption. See Scott, *Adoption as Sons of God: An Exegetical Investigation into the Background of* ΥΙΟΘΕΣΙΑ *in the Pauline Corpus*, WUNT 2/48 (Tübingen: Mohr Siebeck, 1992), 88–115, 269. Yigal Levin correctly retorts that adoption as a legal institution is undocumented in both ancient and modern Judean laws. As for biblical stories that contain adoption themes, they could not be shown to contain any legal consequences. See Levin, "Jesus: 'Son of God' and 'Son of David': The Adoption of Jesus into the Davidic Line," *JSNT* 28 (2006): 423. More correctly, Francis Lyall and Kyu Seop Kim maintain that adoption in the Letter to the Romans should be read in light of Roman law rather than Greek practice, as Christians in Rome were under Roman rule and might be familiar with the legal laws of adoption. Moreover, compared to Greek culture, Roman adoption was instituted primarily for inheritance reasons and is thus more compatible with the issue of inheritance in Rom 4. See Francis Lyall, *Slaves, Citizens, Sons: Legal Metaphors in the Epistles* (Grand Rapids: Academie, 1984), 98–99; Kyu Seop Kim, "Another Look at Adoption in Romans 8:15 in Light of Roman Social Practices and Legal Rules," *BTB* 44 (2014): 135.

133. Peppard, *Son of God*, 60–80.

134. J. Rufus Fears, "Jupiter and Roman Imperial Ideology," *ANRW* 17.1: 21.

taken over by Augustus after 27 BCE. Such a conceptualization of adoption probably influenced Paul's thoughts in Rom 4. This is corroborated by the fact that it was only during the reign of Emperor Domitian (81–96 CE) that a conscious effort was made to reinstate Jupiter's role as *pater*.[135] Thus, during this period, Augustus and his successors took on the role of *pater* of the Roman Empire. That the ideology of the Augustan dynasty as *pater* or patron of the Roman Empire permeated the fabric of Roman society is evident from several observations. As discussed above, Augustus took on an authentic role of *pater* when he (including his family) was involved extensively in performing public service.[136] Furthermore, the *genius* and *numen* of Augustus were worshiped in his lifetime and became a part of the official state cult.[137] Ittai Gradel maintains that the emperor as *pater familias* with the worship of his *genius* incorporated into the constitution of Rome took place for the first time during Claudius's reign.[138] Peppard sums up the matter: "The *genius Augusti*, the guardian spirit of the imperial *gens*, … filled the neighborhoods of Rome…. The provinces responded with loyalty to their new father, demonstrating the successful inculcation

---

135. Ibid., 89.

136. See above, chapter 4, §2.1, "Romans 4:13: Abraham and His Descendants Do Not Inherit the Promise by Means of the Mosaic Law but by Trust in God."

137. See Lily Ross Taylor, *The Divinity of the Roman Emperor* (Middletown: American Philological Association, 1931), 151–54, 182, 220, 227. Tiberius initially refused the title of *pater patriae*. James B. Rives observes that the "general tendency to treat imperial cult as a political phenomenon cloaked in religious dress" (see, e.g., Antonia Tripolitis, *Religions of the Hellenistic-Roman Age* [Grand Rapids: Eerdmans, 2002], 2–3) has been debunked. See Rives, "Graeco-Roman Religion in the Roman Empire: Old Assumptions and New Approaches," *CBR* 8 (2010): 252. Rather, the worship of the Augustan *genius* and *numen* should be regarded as a religious phenomenon. On the question of the extent of Augustus's deity, Simon Price pictures the Roman emperor as "between human and divine." See Price, *Rituals and Power: The Roman Imperial Cult in Asia Minor* (Cambridge: Cambridge University Press, 1984), 233. Ittai Gradel provides a more nuanced understanding that the reason why Roman emperors were regarded as divine was because they held immense power with regard to the well-being of the Roman populace (cf. Rives, "Graeco-Roman Religion," 254–55). See Gradel, *Emperor Worship and Roman Religion*, OCM (Oxford: Clarendon, 2002), 27–32. This understanding of Augustus's status of divinity reinforces his role as *pater familias*.

138. Gradel explains that this was the first time because prior to Augustus, the title of *pater patriae* was purely honorary with no practical consequences (*Emperor Worship*, 187).

of imperial ideology."[139] He had become the father of the whole human race.[140] In light of the benefaction that the Roman emperor brings to the Roman people, it is no wonder that the Roman populace was so concerned that someone suitable should inherit the throne.

The modes for choosing an heir were either by natural dynasty or adoption. Mason Hammond explains why adoption was desirable. He notes that from the Julio-Claudians through the Severans, adoption was a mode of transmitting imperial power. He assigns to it a determining role that secured the support of the army and the confirmation of the Senate.[141] Such support basically represented the choice of the Roman populace that lent ideological power to the mode of adoption. The Roman populace also believed that the adopted heir apparent was a foresight of the *providentia* of the reigning emperor.[142] Adoption, then, demonstrated to the Roman populace the Roman's emperor's concern for stability after his death for the Roman Empire.[143] These observations lent ideological power to securing an heir by adoption.

That being said, ascension to the Roman throne by adoption also contained tension.[144] Gaius and Lucius were sons of Agrippa and Julia and grandsons of Augustus. They died before they could ascend to imperial power. This led Augustus to begin his will in this way: "Since a cruel fate has bereft me of my sons Gaius and Lucius, be Tiberius Caesar heir to two-thirds of my estate" (Suetonius, *Tib.* 23 [Rolfe, LCL]). Suetonius interprets this will by saying that "these words in themselves added to the suspicion of those who believed that he had named Tiberius his successor from necessity rather than from choice, since he allowed himself to write such a preamble" (*Tib.* 23 [Rolfe, LCL]). The sentiment of the Romans corroborates this disparaging interpretation: "You are no knight. Why so? The hundred thousands are lacking. If you ask the whole tale, you were an exile at Rhodes" (*Tib.* 59 [Rolfe, LCL]). When Nero took the throne of

---

139. Peppard, *Son of God*, 66.

140. Ibid.

141. Mason Hammond, "The Transmission of Powers of the Roman Emperor from the Death of Nero in A.D. 68 to That of Alexander Severus in A.D. 235," *MAAR* 24 (1956): 67.

142. Arthur D. Nock, "A Diis Electa: A Chapter in the Religious History of the Third Century," in *Essays on Religion and the Ancient World*, ed. Zeph Stewart (Oxford: Clarendon, 1972), 264–65.

143. Ando, *Imperial Ideology*, 34.

144. Peppard, *Son of God*, 73–80.

Claudius, Tacitus called it a "ruinous adoption" and said that Claudius had destroyed the purity of his lineage (*Ann.* 13.2.2). The common people also disapproved of the adoption of Nero: "When the transaction [of adopting and designating Nero as the future heir] was over, no one was so devoid of pity as not to feel compunction for the lot of Britannicus" (*Ann.* 12.26.2 [Jackson, LCL). Peppard puts into proper perspective these two somewhat conflicting and yet complementary modes of assuming the throne:[145]

> In Roman culture, where political, economic, and social powers were governed by father-son relations, natural family lines were undoubtedly important. Family ideology was *so* important, in fact, that any successor to great paternal power ought to be construed as the son of that father. If the most powerful fathers in the cosmos—paradigmatic emperors such as Augustus and Trajan—did not have eligible natural sons, the adoption of sons would therefore be necessary and appropriate to the propagation of Roman power and ideology.... Whenever a man in the Roman world is the son of a powerful father, whether through decree or narrative characterization, his sonship can be interpreted anew in the pervasive light of Roman family ideology, which was concentrated in the imperial household. And the more powerful a father is—even all-powerful, as a god—the more relevant adoption becomes to understand that father's relationship to his son.[146]

Noteworthy is the observation that whether the Roman throne is taken up by an adopted son or a natural son, both modes highlight the importance Romans attach to a son ascending the throne. Several facets of this ideology are at work in 4:16. First, Judean Christians are natural sons of Abraham, while gentile Christians are his sons through adoption. Second, underlying trust in a patron is a social intertextural link to adoption. This link forges a father-son relationship between Abraham and gentiles. Third, in view of the fact that the relevance of adoption is proportional to the power of the father, Abraham's extensive fatherhood makes adoption relevant. Fourth, this adoption is realized by narrative characterization, or more precisely, by a construction of myths in 4:2–8, and defended in 4:9–12 and 4:13–16. That a myth of origins is implied is demonstrated by the prepositional phrase ἐκ πίστεως Ἀβραάμ ("of the trust of Abraham"). Hodge clarifies the prepositional phrase ἐκ πίστεως ("of trust"). She argues

---

145. Ibid., 67–85.
146. Ibid., 85.

that it can be translated in contexts of descent and kinship as "those whose line of descent springs from faithfulness."[147] Adoption is thus not only a legitimate mode by which gentile Christians become heirs of Abraham; more importantly, adoption is also desirable. This model of Roman adoption informs the metaphor of adoption and mobilizes ideological power in Paul's defense against the Mosaic law. It also lends support to Paul's construction of a myth of origins: by trust in God through adoption, not only Judeans but gentiles, whom Judeans cast as outsiders, can become heirs of Abraham.[148] This corroborates Heim's contention that "if the stability of a metaphor's meaning aids in creating boundaries around a particular group, then its elasticity of meaning permits group members to 'stretch' it to fit their individual differences while still speaking to the common ground of the collective."[149] I shall now analyze 4:16.

The causal διὰ τοῦτο ("for this reason") refers to the preceding argument in 4:13–15a. In view of the fact, however, that νόμος ("law") includes also the earlier discussed concepts ἔργον ("deed") and περιτομή ("circumcision"), 4:16 probably brings to a conclusion the foregoing argument in 4:2–16. That νόμος is an all-inclusive term is demonstrated by it being a centerpiece in the preceding argument of Rom 1–3 under which deeds of the Mosaic law and circumcision were subsumed (e.g., 2:25; 3:30). Thus, the reason indicated by διὰ τοῦτο refers to the inability of the deeds of the Mosaic law (4:2–8, 13–16) and circumcision (4:9–12) to realize the promise of the worldwide fatherhood of Abraham. The prepositional phrase ἐκ πίστεως, when read together with the causal phrase, means that the Mosaic law (including circumcision) has been rendered ineffective. Hence, trust is required. More precisely, the object of trust is a patron. In the Roman imperial system, the reigning emperor selects an heir. Constitutionally, however, the emperor's authority is vested in the Roman populace and approved by the Senate. Likewise, although one inherits Abraham's inheritance by becoming his descendant, God is the one who grants that favor (grace). Hence, the real patron is God. The

---

147. For a listing of ancient references that contain such a meaning, see Hodge, *If Sons, Then Heirs*, 79–91. These include Aristotle's discussion of the mechanics of procreation in *Gen. an.*; Plato, *Menex.*; the LXX; and Paul (Rom 11:1; 9:6; Gal 2:15; 1:15; 4:4; Phil 3:5; etc.).

148. On gentiles as outsiders, see above, chapter 2, §3.3, "Romans 3:21–31: Jesus Atones for the Sins of Both Judeans and Gentiles."

149. Heim, *Adoption in Galatians and Romans*, 107.

purpose (ἵνα) is to cause the clients, Judean and gentile Christians, to enter into a position of favor with the patron God. The final result is the procurement of the promise of inheriting the world given to all (παντί), Judean and gentile Christians alike (referring indirectly to the letter's major concern), as Abraham's descendants.[150] At this point, with an οὐ μόνον ... ἀλλὰ καί (not only ... but also) construction, Paul qualifies that this resulting promise is not given only to those who possess the Mosaic law. This not only recalls Paul's foregoing rhetoric in 4:2–15, but it also, more importantly, brings to the fore his major concern in Rom 1–4: to divest Judeans of their reliance on the Mosaic law. This promise is also granted to those who are descended from the trust of Abraham. The function of the dependent clause ὅς ἐστιν πατὴρ πάντων ἡμῶν ("who is the father of us all") should be read in light of the emphasis of 4:16—that trust in God is necessary because the Mosaic law has failed to realize the promise of making Abraham a father. This dependent clause reinforces the viability of receiving the promise by trust in God because Abraham was given the promise that he would inherit the world, that is, he would become the father of both Judean and gentile Christians. Romans 4:17–25 also bears out this observation.[151] Furthermore, important for our discussion is the observation that Abraham is described as πατὴρ ἡμῶν ("our father"). This contrasts the partitive description (Judeans/gentiles; circumcised/uncircumcised) that characterizes what precedes it. It indicates that Paul has finished removing Judean ethnic identity markers (the Mosaic law, including circumcision) as barriers that divide Judean and gentile Christians. At the same time, this final dependent clause of 4:16 introduces the main concern of the final section, 4:17–25, which seeks to instate the role of trust in realizing the worldwide fatherhood of Abraham.

3. Romans 4:17–25: Trust Realizes Abraham's Worldwide Fatherhood

After displacing the role of the Mosaic law (4:2–16), in this section Paul explains how trust in God realizes righteousness that will result in Abraham's worldwide fatherhood. Paul first spells out the object of Abraham's

---

150. Jewett notes that this "crucial" word has occurred nineteen times already (*Romans*, 330).

151. See below, chapter 4, §3, "Romans 4:17–25: Trust Realizes Abraham's Worldwide Fatherhood."

trust, namely, God who raises the dead (4:17). Then he emphasizes the degree of his trust (4:18–19a) by saying that Abraham trusted that God could do the impossible. Finally, he elaborates on the content of Abraham's trust (4:19b–22).

Topoi related to death (4:17, 19, 24, 25) and life (4:17, 24) and the reversal motif of death to life dominate this section. These inputs form the firstspace of miracle rhetorolect to create transforming power in the secondspace of God. The firstspace and secondspace will blend in the thirdspace to move the implied audience to seek after "a human body [that] is healed and amazingly transformed."[152] Thus, the objective of the rhetoric in 4:17–25 is to move the implied audience to seek after a body that is raised from the dead. By this argument, Paul seeks to arrive at the conclusion that Judeans and, especially, gentiles by trust in God become Abraham's descendants. Romans 4:17–25 offers a counterargument, and hence a conclusion to the implicit contention of the Judean interlocutor in 4:1 that Abraham became the forefather of Judeans by means of his human efforts. To understand the argument of 4:17–25, two social inter-textures that underlie death and life need to be explained. The first, death and pollution, holds that death contains spiritual pollution; the second, patrilineal descent, believes that a person is present in his father in seminal form.

3.1. Death and Pollution

Malina observes that human beings

> share in the basic human experience called the sacred. The sacred is that which is set apart to or for some person. It includes persons, places, things, and times that are symboled or filled with some sort of set-apartness that we and others recognize.... Some common synonyms for the sacred include *holy, saint,* and *sacral.*[153]

---

152. See the thirdspace of miracle rhetorolect in Robbins, *Invention of Christian Discourse,* 109. David A. deSilva sharpens the parameters for identifying miracle rhetorolect by noting that its presence is not denoted by every outward manifestation of divine intervention. Rather, miracle discourse should testify "to God's interventions in the past story of God's people, ... not expectations of how God will act in the future." See deSilva, "Toward a Socio-rhetorical Taxonomy of Divine Intervention," in Gowler, Bloomquist, and Watson, *Fabrics of Discourse,* 316.

153. Malina, *New Testament World,* 163, emphasis original.

The opposite of the "sacred" is the profane, whose synonyms include the unholy and the nonsacred.[154] Similarly, deSilva adds,

> People of a particular culture create a system that defines what is proper and improper to specific places, times, and people. This is part of a natural social process of creating order within the particular social entity and defining and defending the boundaries of that social entity.[155]

Judeans and gentiles in the ancient world were no exception: they also had their conceptualizations of what were sacred and profane. David deSilva also elaborates that gentile Christians would have no difficulty understanding the New Testament authors' reworking of Judean purity codes. This is due to the fact that the "meaning and significance of pure versus defiled, of sanctified versus profane, would already be deeply inscribed in his or her mind" due to Greek culture, which was pervaded with pollution taboos.[156] The same applies to Roman culture as well. In other words, gentile Christians would have been significantly influenced by the dominant Greek or Roman culture when reading New Testament letters, including the Letter to the Romans. The discussions below explain how Judeans and gentiles construe death as a religious pollution.

3.1.1. A Roman Perspective

As I have argued above, Roman culture, being the dominant culture of Rome and to a lesser extent Corinth, asserted its influence on a broad territorial region.[157] Its sphere of influence would include the majority of the Roman Christians, as they were gentiles living in Rome. Romans, including those who lived morally blameless lives, considered themselves ritually polluted by events of birth and death.[158] An ordinary ancient

---

154. Ibid.

155. David A. deSilva, *An Introduction to the New Testament: Contexts, Methods and Ministry Formation* (Downers Grove, IL: InterVarsity Press, 2004), 113.

156. Ibid., 114. See also deSilva's comments on how the pollution caused by murder and the required purification drive the Greek tragedy *Oedipus the King* (115–16). Such pollution taboos, as deSilva insists, would have influenced the ethics of gentiles.

157. See above, chapter 1, §2.2, "Intertexture," and chapter 4, §2.2.2, "Romans 4:15a."

158. Elaine Fantham, "Purification in Ancient Rome," in *Rome, Pollution and Pro-*

Roman understood "pollution/sin … [as] that sense of something (a person, an object, an activity) was amiss, or out of order, in relation to the gods."[159] They believed that a corpse had the ability to contaminate those who came close to it.[160] That ancient Romans regarded death as a religious pollution is shown by the way they viewed objects and people who had contact with a corpse.[161] The house of the deceased became a *familia funesta* ("unclean household") household, in contrast to a *familia pura* ("pure household"). Precautions were taken to guard against accidental exposure to the dead.[162] These include placing branches of cypress around the door to show that death had occurred in the household, playing flutes and horns to a distinctive tune that accompanied the corpse, and having family members cover their heads with ashes and wear a mourning gown (alternatively referred to as *toga pulla, atra,* or *toga sordida*). John Bodel comments that magistrates, high priests, the Pontifex Maximus, and the Flamen Dialis were the main people concerned, as their religious purity affected the welfare of the state.[163] The descriptions of funerary workers also imply the idea of religious pollution. A worker who cremated corpses was described as *sordidus*; a mortician was called a *pollinctor* since he was a "perfumer of the polluted"; a funeral director was *inquinatissimus* ("most foul"). These terms denote religious pollution.[164] Funerary workers at Puteoli were also refused entry into the town except on official business. The above observations show that ancient Romans attached to death the notion of religious pollution. Coupled with the fact that an average of 1,500 corpses were unclaimed and unwanted annually, the problem of death pollution must have weighed

---

priety, ed. Mark Bradley and Kenneth Stow (Cambridge: Cambridge University Press, 2012), 62.

159. So Roger Beck, "Rome," in *Religions of the Ancient World: A Guide*, ed. Sarah Iles Johnston (Cambridge: Harvard University Press, 2004), 509.

160. Hugh Lindsay, "Death-Pollution and Funerals in the City of Rome," in *Death and Disease in the Ancient City*, ed. Valerie M. Hope and Eireann Marshall (London: Routledge, 2000), 152.

161. John Bodel, "Dealing with the Dead: Undertakers, Executioners and Potter's Fields in Ancient Rome," in Hope and Marshall, *Death and Disease*, 141; Jack Lennon, "Carnal, Bloody and Unnatural Acts: Religious Pollution in Ancient Rome" (PhD diss., University of Nottingham, 2011), 27.

162. See Bodel, "Dealing with the Dead," 141.

163. Ibid.

164. Ibid.

on the minds of ancient Romans, including Paul and the real audience of Romans.[165] Furthermore, the life span in ancient Rome was generally very short. Valerie M. Hope estimates life expectancy in ancient Rome as a whole to be around twenty-five to thirty years. If a child survived infancy, a life span of about forty to fifty years was realistic. The risk of death for babies and children, however, was high.[166] In view of these short life spans, contact with dead bodies would certainly be a taboo for ancient Roman society.

The danger that pollution posed to the living included infertility. Jack Lennon's observation is helpful:

> Contact of any sort with death could be particularly damaging, especially with regard to the fertility of the bride, which we have already seen in the death-based pollution caused by menstrual blood whether against crops, animals which have consumed it, or even pregnant women who come into the slightest contact with it.[167]

Seneca the Elder believed that fertility in a marriage could be endangered if someone who was thinking of marriage or having a child met a man who had just returned from the graveyard (*Ex. con.* 4.1).[168]

---

165. For a conservative estimate in the period 100 BCE to 200 CE, see ibid., 129.

166. Valerie M. Hope, *Death in Ancient Rome: A Sourcebook* (London: Routledge, 2007), 10. Of the twelve children born to the mother of Tiberius and Gaius (as it was reputed), only three survived to adulthood. See also David S. Potter and David J. Mattingly, who estimates life expectancy to be in the lower twenties. See Potter and Mattingly, *Life, Death, and Entertainment in the Roman Empire* (Ann Arbor: University of Michigan Press, 1999), 88. Walter Scheidel, while doubting the validity of ages recorded on tombstones and high mortality life tables, nevertheless agrees that the general outlook was for a very short life expectancy. See Scheidel, "Disease and Death," in *The Cambridge Companion to Ancient Rome*, ed. Paul Erdkamp (Cambridge: Cambridge University Press, 2013), 45–52.

167. Lennon, "Carnal, Bloody and Unnatural Acts," 193. See also Pliny the Elder, *Nat.* 28.79–82.

168. *Ex. con.* 4.1: *Senex, orbus, infelix, hoc tantum inter miserias solatium capio quod miserior esse non possum. Cineres meorum in sepulchro uideo. Magnum solatium est saepius appellare liberorum non responsura nomina. Hic mihi uiuendum est ne cui de nuptiis, ne cui de liberis cogitanti dirum omen occurram.* See ibid., 193–94.

3.1.2. A Judean Perspective

Judeans also view death as containing religious pollution. Richard D. Nelson's observations are helpful. Leviticus 10:10, "You are to distinguish between the holy and the common, and between the unclean and the clean" (NRSV), introduces two pairs of terms that frame the purity system of ancient Israel.[169] The first pair is *clean* and *unclean*. An object is clean when it is confined to certain boundaries or is in its proper place. Its external boundaries are also complete and intact. The reverse is true for an object that becomes unclean: it is not in its proper place or classification, and the integrity of its external boundaries has been compromised in some ways.[170] It is capable of causing religious pollution.[171] Death makes a body unclean because the boundary between the living and dead is broken. The external boundary of a body is compromised, as a dead body is decaying from wholeness to the eventual state of bones.[172] Thus, anyone or anything that comes in contact with a dead body becomes unclean (Lev 11:31–32). The second pair is *common* and *holy*. The term common refers to the space in which human beings ordinarily function and live.[173] The corresponding term holy describes objects or spaces that have been set apart for God from the ordinary or common.[174] Places, times, people, and objects that belong to the common social space could become holy. For instance, common objects like vestments (worn by priests), the altar, and sacrifices, when set apart for God, become holy.[175]

For most of the time, an Israelite was clean and common. A woman who had a bloody bodily discharge would be unclean and common. Dead bodies were also unclean and common.[176] Food sold in the market was clean and common and could be eaten by the common lay Israelite. Tithes

---

169. Richard D. Nelson, *Raising Up a Faithful Priest: Community and Priesthood in Biblical Theology* (Louisville: Westminster John Knox, 1993), 20. Similarly, deSilva, *Introduction to the New Testament*, 118.

170. Nelson adds that "common" carries with it no negative connotations (*Raising Up a Faithful Priest*, 21–22). See also deSilva, *Introduction to the New Testament*, 118.

171. See deSilva, *Introduction to the New Testament*, 118; David P. Wright, "Holiness (OT)," *ABD* 3:246–47.

172. Nelson, *Raising Up a Faithful Priest*, 23.

173. Ibid., 25; deSilva, *Introduction to the New Testament*, 118.

174. See deSilva, *Introduction to the New Testament*, 118.

175. Nelson, *Raising Up a Faithful Priest*, 26.

176. See deSilva, *Introduction to the New Testament*, 118.

given to the priests would be clean and holy. In this case, only priests who have kept themselves holy could consume these tithes. Common Israelites were disallowed from eating these tithes. In other words, different permutations of the two pairs—clean and unclean, common and holy—were legitimate. The one combination that cannot be allowed is when holy and unclean come together.[177] David deSilva concludes,

> It was the duty of Israel to preserve the holy from being brought into contact with the impure (the unclean), so that the source of holiness, God, would continue to show favor toward Israel and would not be provoked either to withdraw from the people or consume them.[178]

In the case of Rom 4:17–25, such an antithesis between the unclean and holy exists: Abraham, who has a dead, and hence unclean, reproductive organ, attempts to seek the favor of Yahweh, the holy God, for descendants through his dead reproductive organ.[179]

3.2. Patrilineal Descent

It was well known in Mediterranean culture that a descendant is present in seminal form in the father.[180] Aristotle believed that the matter that makes up the physical body of a child was passed on from the mother to the child: "The female contribution ... contains all the parts of the body *potentially*, though none in actuality" (*Gen. an.* 2.4 [Peck, LCL], emphasis added). The father was thought to shape the body and the character of his child: "The male is that which has the power to generate ... out of which ... the generated offspring comes into being" (*Gen. an.* 1.20 [Peck, LCL]). In another ancient text, in an effort to spurn the teachings of his mentor, Macro, Gaius Julius Caesar argued that just as the actions of a man are preserved ἐν τοῖς σπερματικοῖς ("in the descendants"), so also is his aptitude to govern (Philo, *Legat.* 1.55). In the Hebrew Bible, when Rebecca asks God about the children who are struggling in her womb, God explains that

---

177. Nelson, *Raising Up a Faithful Priest*, 34.

178. See deSilva, *Introduction to the New Testament*, 118. Nelson cites Isa 6:3–5; 35:8; 52:1, 11; which illustrate the "antithesis between the holy and the unclean" (ibid.).

179. See the discussion below, chapter 4, §2.2.2, "Romans 4:15a."

180. Hodge points out several ancient texts that show that inhabitants of the Mediterranean world believed that a person was contained in the seeds of his ancestors (*If Sons, Then Heirs*, 94–103).

the two children represent two nations. In other words, "each twin is not only an individual but also a whole people (*ethnos* or *laos*). Thus, many descendants are contained in Rebecca's womb."[181] With these two social intertextures clarified, we shall investigate the rhetoric of 4:17–25.

3.3. Romans 4:17: Abraham Trusted in God Who Could Raise the Dead

Romans 4:17 spells out the object of Abraham's trust—God who is able to raise the dead to life. Paul begins by anchoring the preceding final dependent clause, ὅς ἐστιν πατὴρ πάντων ἡμῶν ("who is the father of us all"), upon Scripture by reciting verbatim Gen 17:5 LXX.[182] There is, however, a difference. Abraham's fatherhood as πατὴρ πάντων ἡμῶν ("Judean and gentile Christians") is now expanded to that of πολλῶν ἐθνῶν ("many nations"). The rationale of Paul's argument is to include the part (Judean and gentile Christians) in the whole (all nations).[183] The whole (the promise of Abraham's worldwide fatherhood) carries absolute value because it is founded upon Scripture.[184] If the whole promise is fulfilled, then a part of this whole promise will also be fulfilled. This makes Gen 17:5 LXX an apt recitation. The text, however, also poses a difficulty, as there is no mention in Gen 17 LXX that Abraham ἐπίστευσεν ("trusted"). One possible solution is to see ἐπίστευσεν as a reference to Gen 15:6, where the aorist tense signifies an event that took place before the account of Gen 17.[185] This solution, however, is untenable, as the nature of Abraham's trust in 4:17 is one that believes in God who raises the dead. Abraham's trust cannot be extricated from the setting of Gen 17, which centers on Abraham and Sarah's old age. A more probable solution is to see trust as encapsulated in the rite of circumcision that Abraham performed on his household. This way of construing circumcision is borne out by 4:9–12, where Paul argued that circumcision affirms a righteousness that comes by trust.

---

181. Hodge, *If Sons, Then Heirs*, 96–97.

182. In the other thirteen occurrences (not counting 4:17) of καθὼς γέγραπται, all refer to what immediately precedes them.

183. Perelman and Olbrechts-Tyteca, *New Rhetoric*, 231–41.

184. Dunn, *Romans 9–16*, 63; Perelman and Olbrechts-Tyteca, *New Rhetoric*, 77–79.

185. Dunn, *Romans 1–8*, 217. Jewett construes it as an extended midrash drawn from Gen 15:6 (*Romans*, 333).

The promise that Abraham would be the father of many nations is fulfilled by trust. Some scholars view the object of Abraham's trust as the promise.[186] Although they also include God in the object of trust, this interpretation misses Paul's point. This verse spells out clearly the object of trust. The direct object of ἐπίστευσεν is the relative pronoun οὗ. This pronoun refers to God, with its case being attracted to θεοῦ.[187] The aspect of trust is specific and is denoted by the parallel participial expressions τοῦ ζῳοποιοῦντος τοὺς νεκρούς ("who makes alive the dead") and καλοῦντος τὰ μὴ ὄντα ὡς ὄντα ("calls the things that do not exist as existing"). That these should be construed as parallel is evinced by two observations. First, syntactically, the one who makes alive and the one who calls are the same person.[188] Second, they are structurally similar, as both contain a substantive participle that takes on a direct object. Thus, the object of trust is God who makes alive the dead.[189]

When 4:17 is read together with the social intertexture underlying death as a form of religious pollution, God is construed as someone who can remove religious pollution. Furthermore, when 4:17 is read together with the social intertexture of patrilineal descent, God's ability to raise the dead to life also includes his ability to raise descendants from a person's dead body. In the case of Abraham, God's ability to bring life aids the fulfillment of the recitation of Gen 17:5 LXX, that is, Abraham's worldwide fatherhood. How Abraham's trust in God realizes the promise of his worldwide fatherhood is explained in what follows.

3.4. Romans 4:18–19a: Abraham's Great Trust Realized His Worldwide Fatherhood

Romans 4:18–19a is framed by the common motif of a high degree of trust: "hope against hope" (4:18) and "not having been weakened in trust"

---

186. E.g., Jewett, *Romans*, 333; Schreiner, *Romans*, 235; Moo, *Epistle to the Romans*, 280.

187. BDF §294.

188. For discussion on what constitutes a correct application and an abuse of Granville Sharp's rule, see Wallace, *Greek Grammar*, 271–72.

189. Various commentators (e.g., Moo, *Epistle to the Romans*, 279–80; Schreiner, *Romans*, 236–37) dismiss a reference to the tradition of *creatio ex nihilo*. Contra Dunn, "Salvation Proclaimed," 218; Cranfield, *Epistle to the Romans*, 1:244; Otfried Hofius, "Eine altjüdische Parallele zu Röm 4:17b," *NTS* 18 (1971): 93–94; Jonathan Worthington, "Creatio Ex Nihilo and Romans 4:17 in Context," *NTS* 62 (2016): 59.

(4:19). Thus, this section emphasizes the extent or degree of Abraham's trust in God.

The relative pronoun ὅς refers not simply to Abraham but to the subject of the preceding verb ἐπίστευσεν. This observation implies that what follows continues to delineate the content of Abraham's trust. Abraham's trust is further described as παρ' ἐλπίδα ἐπ' ἐλπίδι ("against hope on the basis of hope"). The meaning of the prepositional phrase παρ' ἐλπίδα is debated. It can mean either "beyond hope" or, more likely, "against hope."[190] First, this prepositional phrase should be read together with the adjoining ἐπ' ἐλπίδι, which means "on the basis of hope." These two prepositional phrases, when read together, form a polarity of Abraham's opposing views of his ability to have descendants. Such a polarity coheres with the repeated emphasis in 4:17–21 that he believes the hope given by God will be realized despite his "dead body," which does not carry any hope of having a descendant. The focus of παρ' ἐλπίδα ἐπ' ἐλπίδι teases out the nature of the trust: it is thoroughly focused on God. A social and cultural intertexture underlies the nature of trust that is described as παρ' ἐλπίδα ἐπ' ἐλπίδι: "pistis/fides ... are frequently marked, especially in literature, at moments of crisis or decision, or when an exceptional instance of the quality is called for."[191] This creates ideological texture that prompts the audience to imitate Abraham's trust.

More specifically, this hope in God is expressed by the infinitival purpose clause εἰς τὸ γενέσθαι αὐτὸν πατέρα πολλῶν ἐθνῶν ("with the result that he became the father of many nations" [NRSV]). Abraham's fatherhood is promised by God as it is warranted by Scripture. Unlike the earlier recitation in 4:17, which is introduced by καθὼς γέγραπται ("just as it has been written"), the recitation of Scripture in 4:18 is introduced by κατὰ τὸ

---

190. For "beyond hope," see Jewett, who bases this understanding on Philo, *Mos.* 1.250, where a king of Canaan obtained an easy victory that was παρ' ἐλπίδα, that is, better than what he had hoped for (*Romans*, 335); see, similarly, Cranfield, *Epistle to the Romans*, 1:245. Most commentators render this "against hope"; see, e.g., Christopher Bryan, *A Preface to Romans: Notes on the Epistle in Its Literary and Cultural Setting* (New York: Oxford University Press, 2000), 118; Dunn, *Romans 1–8*, 219; Moo, *Epistle to the Romans*, 283; more recently, see Matera, *Romans*, 116; Holland, *Divine Marriage*, 140.

191. Morgan, *Roman Faith and Christian Faith*, 74–75. See her examples of trust demonstrated in times of crisis or decision in various relationships in the early principate for family members and lovers (46–47), for masters and slaves (51–52), for patron and client (61–62), and for military relationships (77–85).

εἰρημένον ("according to what had been said").[192] As discussed in 4:1, by using the verb λέγειν ("to say"), Paul intimates that he is arguing against the Judean interlocutor's main contention in 4:1 that gives rise to the rhetoric of Rom 4, namely, that Abraham received fatherhood by his human efforts. The content of the recitation proves my point.

The oral-scribal recitation οὕτως ἔσται τὸ σπέρμα σου ("so shall your descendant be") is taken verbatim from Gen 15:5 LXX. The focus of this recitation is debated. Some scholars do not give much attention to the significance of this recitation.[193] This ignores Paul's emphatic use of λέγειν to introduce the recitation, which indicates that what follows seeks to refute the contention of the Judean interlocutor in 4:1. Others group it together with the promise of many descendants of Gen 17:5.[194] Such a construal fails to explain why Paul recites only the last clause of Gen 15:5 LXX. I contend that this recitation highlights the fact that Abraham's worldwide fatherhood is a result of God blessing Abraham personally, as the second singular person σου ("your") and the singular σπέρμα ("descendant") emphasize. In this way, Abraham's personal act of trust in God that realizes his fatherhood comes into sharp focus.

How the final participial clause καὶ μὴ ἀσθενήσας τῇ πίστει ("and he did not weaken in trust" [4:19a]) is related to the finite verb κατενόησεν ("considered") is controverted. Some position the finite verb κατενόησεν as being subordinate to the participle ἀσθενήσας ("weaken").[195] This amounts to the unlikely option of treating the participle ἀσθενήσας as an independent participle, an interpretation that should only be used as a last resort.[196] Some think that this participle substantiates (at least conceptually) the thought in 4:20.[197] This view, however, still fails to explain how the par-

---

192. Lenski notices the difference in the way this recitation is introduced, as compared to 4:17 (*Interpretation of St. Paul's Epistle to the Romans*, 323). Unfortunately, he does not pursue the otherwise critical difference.

193. So Barrett, *Epistle to the Romans*, 97; Bryan, *Preface to Romans*, 118; Fitzmyer, *Romans*, 387; Schreiner, *Romans*, 237.

194. So Cranfield, *Epistle to the Romans*, 1:246–47; Dunn, *Romans 1–8*, 219; Moo, *Epistle to the Romans*, 283; Jewett, *Romans*, 336; Matera, *Romans*, 116.

195. See Moo, *Epistle to the Romans*, 283, where he refers to Maximilian Zerwick, *Biblical Greek* (Rome: Pontifical Biblical Institute, 1963), 263, 376. See also Schreiner, *Romans*, 237.

196. James A. Brooks and Carlton L. Winbery, *Syntax of New Testament Greek* (Washington, DC: University Press of America, 1979), 152.

197. Cranfield thinks it is a causal participle whose main thought lies in the verb

ticiple qualifies the main verb κατενόησεν. I propose that this participle is related grammatically to, and hence qualifies, the preceding main verb, ἐπίστευσεν. Thus, 4:18–19a could be translated as "Hoping against hope, he trusted [ἐπίστευσεν] that he would become 'the father of many nations'.... He did not weaken [ἀσθενήσας] in trust." Not only is this grammatically legitimate, it is also contextually satisfying: it is similar in thought to the double prepositional phrase παρ᾽ ἐλπίδα ἐπ᾽ ἐλπίδι, which also qualifies ἐπίστευσεν. The similarity is that both emphasize Abraham as trusting God when it is seemingly impossible to do so. This participle also concludes the emphasis of the recitation of Gen 15:5 LXX—that Abraham's unflagging trust is instrumental to his worldwide fatherhood.

3.5. Romans 4:19b–21: Abraham Trusted God Who Could Remove Pollution from His and Sarah's Reproductive Organs

Against most interpreters, I contended above that the clause containing the participle ἀσθενήσας (4:19a) concludes the preceding thought. Thus, 4:19b begins a new thought by elaborating on some details of the content of Abraham's trust. The important question is how 4:19b and what follows, which describe in some detail Abraham's trust, mobilize ideological power.

Paul reconfigures Gen 17:17 LXX and describes Abraham's body as νενεκρωμένον ἑκατονταετής που ὑπάρχων. The word νεκροῦν can signify a state of impotency.[198] In a somewhat similar vein, several English Bible versions seem to regard this death as figurative: "as good as dead."[199] This perhaps stems from the explanatory "being about a hundred years old." The problems with this construal are several. Paul does not use any

---

διεκρίθη. Cranfield even considers the possibility of adopting a minor reading where a particle of negation is attached to κατενόησεν (Epistle to the Romans, 1:247). This reading (found in D F G Ψ and other late manuscripts) is correctly rejected in favor of the one without the particle of negation in view of the attestation of earlier manuscripts (א A B C) and the principle that the more difficult reading is the more likely reading. Jewett thinks this participle stands in antithesis to ἐνεδυναμώθη (Romans, 336).

198. BDAG, s.v. "νεκρόω."

199. So NRSV, NIV, ESV. Rodrigo J. Morales is one of the few commentators who shares my observation that "the Greek literally reads 'dead'" (" 'Promised through His Prophets in the Holy Scriptures': The Role of Scripture in the Letter to the Romans," in Sumney, Reading Paul's Letter to the Romans, 117).

particle of comparison.[200] Neither is there any clear indication from the context of Rom 4 that some kind of an analogy is involved. The explanatory note about Abraham being a hundred years old does not constitute evidence as it merely points to the cause of this death.[201] The contrary, however, is true. The immediate context of Rom 4 describes Abraham's trust as one that trusts God who is able to make alive τοὺς νεκρούς ("the dead" [4:17]). Also, in applying Rom 4 to the implied audience, God is described as the one who raised Jesus ἐκ νεκρῶν ("from the dead" [4:24]). Thus, when Abraham considers his body νενεκρωμένον ("dead"), it should also take on this meaning, namely, a σῶμα ("body") that is void of physical life. Several observations clarify the scope of νεκροῦν ("to die"). In Paul's major discussions on issues pertaining to sexuality (1 Cor 6 and 7), it is significant that he uses σῶμα (1 Cor 6:13, 15, 16, 18, 19; 7:4; also, Rom 1:24).[202] In these discussions, this word is viewed as the medium by which sexual intercourse is performed. Thus, Abraham's dead σῶμα refers to the inability of his body to provide the necessary semen for procreation. This conclusion ties in with the fact that dead sperm is often connected with death in antiquity.[203] Such a conceptualization coheres also with how Sarah is described: her μήτρα ("womb") is dead, and hence is unable to conceive. In other words, Abraham's and Sarah's reproductive organs are physically dead. When read in light of the social intertexture underlying death, Abraham's and Sarah's reproductive organs are dead and contain pollution. This implies also that the descendants present in Abraham's body in seminal form (according to the social intertexture of "patrilineal descent") are also dead, and hence polluted. Despite

---

200. On the uses of comparative conjunctions, see Wallace, *Greek Grammar*, 675.

201. Wallace (ibid., 631) notes that causal participles often precede the main controlling verb. He observes, however, that causal participles that come after the main verb are also attested, e.g., in John 4:6; 11:38.

202. See also Karl O. Sandnes (*Belly and Body in the Pauline Epistles*, SNTSMS 120 [Cambridge: Cambridge University Press, 2002], 14–60), who argues that presuppositions underlying the working of the belly are the same as those regarding the body. He also surveys Greco-Roman literature to show that the belly is often thought of as the medium by which sexual desires are experienced.

203. Bodel, "Dealing with the Dead," 137: "Artemidorus [1.78] comments on the case of a man who, having dreamed he had entered a house of prostitution and was unable to leave, died a few days later: 'it is reasonable that this place should resemble death, because a whore-house is known as a common place (koinos topos), like that which receives corpses, and much sperm perishes there.'"

Abraham's and Sarah's dead reproductive organs, however, Abraham demonstrates trust in God, as Paul says in the words εἰς δὲ τὴν ἐπαγγελίαν τοῦ θεοῦ οὐ διεκρίθη τῇ ἀπιστίᾳ. Here, the particle δέ is construed as an adversative that contrasts with the thought begun in 4:19b, where Abraham recognizes his and Sarah's dead reproductive organs (4:19a). Abraham does not dispute (οὐ διεκρίθη) because of ἀπιστία ("unbelief"), a label designed to shame one who is disloyal to one's friends.[204] Instead, he believes that God is able to realize the promise (τὴν ἐπαγγελίαν) for him.[205] The reappearance of ἐπαγγελία, after having dropped out of the

---

204. On οὐ διεκρίθη meaning "does not dispute," see Benjamin Schliesser, who convincingly argues against the usual translation with its attached meaning of "doubt." First, prior to the New Testament, the verb διακρίνεσθαι does not take on this meaning in classical/Hellenistic Greek. Second, the usual meanings attested in classical/Hellenistic Greek should be considered unless no suitable one fits the clause and literary context in which the deponent verb appears. Only then can the interpreter argue for a special New Testament meaning or a "semantic shift." See Peter Spitaler, "Διακρίνεσθαι in Mt. 21:21, Mk. 11:23, Acts 10:20, Rom. 4:20, 14:23, Jas. 1:6, and Jude 22—the 'Semantic Shift' That Went Unnoticed by Patristic Authors," NovT 49 (2007): 1–35. In the case of Rom 4:20, however, the usual meaning, "dispute" or "contend," which is attested in classical/Hellenistic Greek fits the context and should thus be adopted. Schliesser also observes that "the line of argument of the first chapters of Romans shows that the apostle is less concerned with the psychology of faith than with the question of how human beings position themselves before God. Do they hear and yield to his word or do they adopt a rebellious and disobedient attitude?" In other words, διακρίνεσθαι should be translated as "dispute" with an attitude of active rebellion against God. See Schliesser, " 'Abraham Did Not "Doubt" in Unbelief' (Rom 4:20): Faith, Doubt, and Dispute in Paul's Letter to the Romans," JTS 63 (2012): 497–522. F. C. Synge, by drawing a contrast between this deponent verb and faith, suggests the translation "to decide that a thing is impossible." See Synge, "Not Doubt but Discriminate," ExpT 89 (1978): 203. Michel also assigns a more active stance to the verb διεκρίθη: "Der Glaube überwindet den Unglauben, der die Verheißung in Zweifel auflösen will" (Der Brief an die Römer, 173). Contra most commentators, e.g., Moo, Epistle to the Romans, 284; Cranfield, Epistle to the Romans, 1:248; Godet, Commentary on St. Paul's Epistle to the Romans, 181; Stuhlmacher, Paul's Letter to the Romans, 75. For this use of ἀπιστία, see Morgan, Roman Faith and Christian Faith, 56. Cf. Dio Chrysostom, Rhod. 33. Plutarch, Mor. 53, assigns to the flatterer the characteristic of ἀπιστία. The dative phrase τῇ ἀπιστίᾳ here in Romans is instrumental (see Wallace, Greek Grammar, 162), as trust in 4:17–25 is thought of as that which brings about the promise of Abraham's worldwide fatherhood.

205. The preposition here should contain the same force as in the other εἰς-plus-accusative constructions in Rom 4 (4:3, 5, 9, 22). In these other occurrences, the construction εἰς δικαιοσύνην indicates a result where the client is ascribed honor by the

text since its earlier appearance in 4:13–16, is significant. In all probability, Paul, by using ἐπαγγελία, intends for the implied audience to recall not only the content of the promise (Abraham inheriting the world) but also the contrast between ἐπαγγελία and νόμος and the absence of wrath in 4:13–16.[206] Thus, that which Abraham does not dispute is not merely that God is able to make alive his dead body (σῶμα) and Sarah's dead womb. Abraham also trusts that God is able to remove any wrath that results from religious pollution that may hinder the fulfillment of the promise. That wrath is immediately in view is corroborated by the juxtaposition of transgression and righteousness in 4:25. This understanding also coheres with the social intertextures of the cognates of νεκρ-, where death is perceived as containing religious pollution. Specifically, death is a consequence of sin.[207]

Instead of disputing, Abraham does the opposite. He is ἐνεδυναμώθη ("strengthened") by means of trust.[208] Most commentators understand that that which is ἐνεδυναμώθη is trust, giving the sense of a growing trust. Such a construal goes against several observations. For one, to describe Abraham's trust in God in Rom 4 using incremental terms undermines Paul's rhetoric, as Paul builds his present rhetoric on Abraham's high degree of trust as signified by the expression παρ' ἐλπίδα ἐπ' ἐλπίδι ἐπίστευσεν. Also, describing Abraham's trust as being strengthened by trust seems redundant.[209] More likely, that which is ἐνεδυναμώθη is Abraham's σῶμα ("body"). This interpretation coheres with the usage of the verb elsewhere. In Pauline usage, the object that is strengthened is Paul himself so that he can accomplish a particular aspect of his ministry (see Phil 4:3; 1 Tim 1:12; 2 Tim 2:1; 4:17).[210] Similarly here, Abraham's body

---

patron. Righteousness, then, becomes a possession of the client. Likewise here, Abraham also possesses the promise.

206. Cranfield is one of the few commentators who comments on the "vitally important" occurrence of ἐπαγγελία at this point, although he fails to properly elicit its significance (*Epistle to the Romans*, 1:248; see also Jewett, *Romans*, 337, following Cranfield).

207. See below, chapter 4, §3.7.2, "Romans 4:24–25."

208. The dative phrase τῇ πίστει is instrumental, as it contrasts τῇ ἀπιστίᾳ.

209. Godet chooses to attach the verb ἐνεδυναμώθη to the participle δούς (*Commentary on St. Paul's Epistle to the Romans*, 182).

210. For instance, in Phil 4:13 Paul was strengthened by God giving him the secret (μεμύημαι) of eating to the fullest and going hungry. See Peter T. O'Brien, who refers to God's power that gave Paul contentment. See O'Brien, *The Epistle to the Philippians: A Commentary on the Greek Text*, NIGTC (Grand Rapids: Eerdmans, 1991),

is strengthened so that his reproductive organs can function normally, and hence procreate. Scholars take the aorist participle in the clause δοὺς δόξαν τῷ θεῷ ("gave glory to God") as being contemporaneous with the aorist verb ἐνεδυναμώθη. More likely, it should be construed as indicating the cause that gives rise to the main verb.[211] This agrees with a possible construal of the time of the verbal nature of an aorist participle, that its action took place before the action of the main verb. Thus the sense of the interpretation is that Abraham is strengthened because he gave glory to God. God strengthening Abraham contrasts with the label ἀπιστία, which is designed to shame a person who lacks trust or loyalty. It also fits the use of the verb δοξάζειν in 1:21, where the gentiles' refusal to give glory to God brought adverse consequences.[212] Here, in 4:20, Abraham was strengthened in his body by God because he gave God glory. In an honor-shame culture, this equates to Abraham giving honor to God the patron so that God gives Abraham strength to procreate. Paul has chosen the language of the honor-shame culture to impress on the implied audience the need for God's help, as they would look to their patrons for provision. This mobilizes ideological power to persuade the implied audience to imitate Abraham's trust, which is elaborated in what follows: καί plus πληροφορηθείς ("was fully convinced"). The connective καί is epexegetic. What follows in "because he was fully convinced that that which he has promised, he is able to do" (4:21) refers to the way that a client honors his patron by trusting in his patron's ability to provide for the client.[213] Paul accentuates the role of trust by using the verb πληροφορεῖν, which carries the basic meaning of "to be full of," in this case, trust in the patron. As in 4:20, the verb ἐπήγγελται ("he had promised") recalls the juxtaposition of wrath and promise in 4:13–16. Thus, Abraham trusts God to avert wrath so that the promise of his worldwide fatherhood can be realized. In light of the above mentioned social intertextures, pollution results in infertility. Hence, Abraham also trusts God to remove pollution in his reproductive

---

527. In 1 Tim 1:12, this strengthening empowers Paul for ministry so that Christ can demonstrate his patience to those who would believe. See Philip H. Towner, *The Letters to Timothy and Titus*, NICNT (Grand Rapids: Eerdmans, 2006), 137.

211. See BDF §339; Wallace, *Greek Grammar*, 631.

212. Adams is probably right to see in 4:20 an allusion to 1:21 ("Abraham's Faith," 47).

213. See deSilva, *Honor, Patronage, Kinship and Purity*, 115.

organs and pollution in his future descendants who are present with him in seminal form.

3.6. Romans 4:22: The Entire Preceding Argument Shows That Abraham Was Made Righteous by Trust

With an inferential διό, Paul starts to conclude the preceding section. Instead of concluding with a statement about Abraham's worldwide fatherhood, however, Paul returns once again to his recitation of Gen 15:6 LXX. Scholars who insist that the main rhetoric (rather than a supporting thesis) of Rom 4 is about justification by trust (faith) have not provided a satisfactory connection between 4:22 and what immediately precedes it. Moo, for example, acknowledges that 4:22 primarily concludes what immediately precedes it. He thinks that the recitation of Gen 15:6 LXX summarizes Abraham's demonstration of trust in Gen 17 and also in his later life.[214] Others in this camp contend that διό reaches back to the argument starting with 4:3.[215] These interpretations, however, ignore the focus of 4:13–21, which is about how Abraham's trust in God achieved his worldwide fatherhood and is not merely a demonstration of his trust in God (in general).

To understand how the recitation of Gen 15:6 concludes what immediately precedes it and yet also reaches back to the argument starting with 4:3, we need to recall my earlier point about Gen 15:6 LXX. I argued that the righteousness referred to in Gen 15:6 LXX is not primarily about forensic justification. Rather, it is a relational term that denotes a state of cordial relationship, that is, a relationship that is characterized by righteousness between a client (Abraham) and his patron (God). This cordial relationship that was realized by Abraham's trust in God culminated in God granting him many descendants, namely, a worldwide fatherhood. The close connection between 4:22, which contains the recitation of Gen 15:6 LXX, and what immediately precedes it (4:17–21), which discusses Abraham's worldwide fatherhood, confirms my earlier interpretation of Gen 15:6 LXX and its meaning in 4:3: the righteousness in Gen 15:6 LXX has to do with Abraham's worldwide fatherhood.

---

214. Moo, *Epistle to the Romans*, 286; in a similar vein, see Cranfield, *Epistle to the Romans*, 1:250.

215. E.g., Dunn, *Romans 1–8*, 221; Godet, *Commentary on St. Paul's Epistle to the Romans*, 183.

Why does Paul conclude with Gen 15:6 LXX? Scholars generally agree that this recitation concludes the entire rhetoric. The question is: in what way? I contend that Paul, by harking back to the beginning of the argument, is drawing the implied audience back to the point where he first used Gen 15:6 LXX. There, he used this recitation to refute the Judean interlocutor's contention in 4:1: "What shall we say? Have we found Abraham to be our forefather by his own human efforts?" In this introductory question in 4:1, the Judean interlocutor, whose question is articulated by Paul, is attempting to argue that Abraham became the forefather of Judeans by means of his human efforts, that is, deeds related to the Mosaic law. Starting with 4:3, Paul frames his entire argument with the recitation of Gen 15:6 LXX. He disproves the Judean interlocutor's contention and shows instead that Abraham became the Judeans' forefather by trust. Paul then concludes his rhetoric in 4:22 with the LXX text (Gen 15:6) that began his refutation in 4:3.

3.7. Romans 4:23–25: When We, Like Abraham, Trust God Who Raised Jesus from the Dead, Who Was Delivered over to Death, We Will Also Be Made Righteous

Scholars agree that this section applies the implications of the foregoing rhetoric to the implied audience.[216] What is unclear is how this application takes the argument of Romans to the next stage. In what follows I shall explain how it does so.

3.7.1. Romans 4:23

In 4:23, the verb ἐγράφη ("it was written") refers to the recitation of Gen 15:6 LXX. Paul, however, further abbreviates it to ἐλογίσθη αὐτῷ ("it was reckoned to him") so as to accentuate his point: "But it was not written because of him only." Scholars debate how Gen 15:6, which was addressed specifically to Abraham, could also be written for others. Explanations include Paul adopting a typological interpretation, viewing it as promise fulfillment, or applying a universal principle common to both Christians and Abraham.[217]

---

216. E.g., Dunn, *Romans 1–8*, 239; Fitzmyer, *Romans*, 388.

217. Typological interpretation: Goppelt, *Typos*, 127–29; Dunn, *Romans 1–8*, 222; see also Goppelt, "Paul and Heilsgeschichte: Conclusions from Romans 4 and 1 Corinthians 10:1–13," trans. Mathias Rissi, *Int* 21 (1967): 315–26. Promise fulfill-

As my discussion below will explain, 4:23 should be understood in light of the social intertexture of patrilineal descent.[218]

3.7.2. Romans 4:24–25

In light of the above discussed social intertexture of patrilineal descent, the phrase ἀλλὰ καὶ δι᾽ ἡμᾶς ("but also because of us") implies that the seminal form in Abraham includes a large group of people to whom God will reckon righteousness. In view of the emphasis on Abraham's world-wide fatherhood throughout 4:17–22, the pronoun ἡμᾶς ("us") must include both Judean and gentile Christians. As I have argued above, by the pronoun ἡμᾶς, Paul is no longer engaging the Judean interlocutor but is now addressing directly the implied audience.[219] Significant for our discussion are several points. First, this corroborates my proposal that Paul recites Gen 15:6 LXX not to prove justification by trust but to show that this righteousness so attained by Abraham obtains for him a worldwide fatherhood. Also, that Paul should, after this recitation of Gen 15:6 LXX, proceed to apply his rhetoric to the implied audience sharpens the focus of the purpose of this rhetoric, which is to prove the worldwide fatherhood of Abraham. Second, this social intertexture lends ideological power to Paul's use of the Scripture text, Gen 15:6 LXX: when God reckoned Abraham as righteous, Abraham's descendants were included because they were with Abraham in seminal form.

At this juncture, Paul has demonstrated by the foregoing rhetoric several pivotal points. He started the rhetoric by asking if Judean Christians had a case that Abraham obtained righteousness (which gained him worldwide fatherhood) by way of his human efforts (4:1). In response, Paul first undermines the role of the deeds of the Mosaic law (4:2–8), circumcision (4:9–12), and the Mosaic law itself (4:13–16). He then brings in the role of trust via the topoi death and life (4:17–25). These topoi offer Paul a gateway to introduce the topos of sin and the critical linchpin, "Jesus the Lord," who unites the dissenting factions of Judean and gentile Christians. How he does this is the subject of the discussion that follows.

---

ment: Schreiner, *Romans*, 241. Universal principle: Lenski, *Interpretation of St. Paul's Epistle to the Romans*, 326; Barrett, *Epistle to the Romans*, 98–99; Cranfield, *Epistle to the Romans*, 1:250; Matera, *Romans*, 117–18.

218. See above, chapter 4, §3.2, "Patrilineal Descent."

219. See above, chapter 3, §2.1.2, "The Referent of 'We' in 4:1."

First, as for Abraham, the Christian's object of trust is God. This is in keeping with the social intertexture of patrilineal descent that Paul utilizes to mobilize ideological power that Abraham's descendants must do as their ancestor Abraham did (4:12) since descendants bear resemblance to their ancestors.[220] A social and cultural texture also underlies God as the object of trust. Paul is using God as the superordinate prototype to unite the dissenting factions. Second, having stated earlier in 4:19 that Abraham's body is dead, and hence contains religious pollution, the descendants who are with him in seminal form are also ritually unclean. This implies that religious pollution, brought about by death, is present not only in gentiles but also in Judeans. Judean Christians do not possess righteousness just because they possess the law. In this way, ideological power is mobilized to diminish the boast of Judean Christians toward gentile Christians by delegitimating the Mosaic Law as an ethnic identity marker for Judeans. Hence, expiation is required for both groups. The social and cultural intertexture that underlies death and expiation, as explained below, shows that such a need weighs heavily on the minds of the ancient implied audience.

Upon death in a Roman house, a series of purification rites took place. These rites only seemed to have ceased around 200 CE.[221] After removing the corpse for burial, the *euerriator*, usually the heir to the family cult, was responsible for sweeping the house where death had occurred. An incomplete purification procedure had serious repercussions since it was thought that failure to do so would be expiated by death.[222] During the days of rest and mourning after death (*feriae denicales*), several meals were undertaken for purification purposes. At the tomb, a meal called *silicernium* was eaten.[223] On the ninth day, a meal called *novemdial sacrificium* was observed that concluded *feriae denicales*.[224] This meal required a sacrifice of a wether (a castrated ram) to the tutelary spirit Lar of the Roman household. A sacrifice (*porca praesentanea*) of a sow was also mandatory in

---

220. See above, chapter 4, §3.2, "Patrilineal Descent."

221. Lindsay, "Death-Pollution," 165–66.

222. Ibid., 166.

223. J. M. C. Toynbee, *Death and Burial in the Roman World* (Baltimore: Johns Hopkins University Press, 1996), 50; ibid.

224. Hugh Lindsay notes that this meal comprised two parts: a sacrifice and a subsequent banquet. See Lindsay, "Eating with the Dead: The Roman Funerary Banquet," in *Meals in a Social Context: Aspects of the Communal Meal in the Hellenistic and Roman World*, ed. Inge Nielsen and Hanne Sigismund Nielsen, ASMA 1 (Aarhus: Aarhus University Press, 1998), 73.

the presence of the corpse to cleanse pollution that resided in the Roman *familia*.[225] Upon return from the funeral, anyone who had participated in the interment had to go through a purification rite called the *suffitio*, in which a laurel branch was used to sprinkle water on the participant. He also had to go under a fire.[226]

Roman pontiffs chose inhumation over cremation as they were concerned that the deceased should receive a *locus religiosus*, that is, a respected place of burial. Thus, even after cremation, the *os resectum*, a small piece of the corpse, was retained for burial. This concern stemmed from the notion that if the dead were not properly buried, the ghost of the deceased would return to trouble the living. This was claimed to have happened in the case of Caligula, who was hurriedly buried. The caretakers of the garden of the Lamian family claimed to have seen frightening apparitions every night. It was thought that his ghost was only appeased after his sisters returned from exile to perform the necessary funeral rites to expiate the pollution (Suetonius, *Cal.* 59).

That religious pollution required expiation was also well known from public disasters. When Rome encountered military disasters inflicted by Hannibal at Lake Trasimene, the Sibylline Books (books guarded by the Roman senate that recorded prophecies) were consulted. It was revealed that the disasters were a result of an unfulfilled vow made to Mars, which was regarded as a religious pollution. Expiation took the form of a *lustratio*, a procession of animal sacrifices. Another example took place when the consul Marcus Licinius Crassus was preparing to leave Rome to attack the Parthians in 55 BCE. The consul was cursed by the tribune Gaius Ateius Capito because the war initiated by Crassus was considered to be unjust. Two years later, Crassus and his legions were destroyed. The whole of Rome suffered national guilt as they felt that they had been punished for impiety. These themes were taken up by the Augustan poets Vergil and Horace, who stressed the need for expiation of the impiety of Romans. Some say that the narratives composed by these poets were designed to promote Augustus's statesmanship. Whatever the reasons were, discourses on collective sin, divine punishment, and expiation were thus written.[227]

---

225. Lindsay, "Death-Pollution," 166.

226. Toynbee, *Death and Burial*, 50; Lindsay, "Death-Pollution," 167; cf. Fantham, who adds that the participant in the interment possibly had to leap across the fire while being sprinkled with laurel ("Purification in Ancient Rome," 65).

227. Beck, "Rome," 510.

The need for expiation as a result of pollution and sin, then, constitutes social intertexture underlying death and its resulting pollution.

Similar cultural intertexture also underlies a Judean's perception of religious pollution. Various rituals recorded in the Hebrew Bible provide for the expiation of sin. If someone dies in the presence of a Nazirite, and thus pollutes the "consecrated head," religious pollution is expiated by sacrificing two turtledoves or two young pigeons one as a sin offering and the other as a burnt offering (Lev 6:11). If someone dies in a tent, then everyone who comes into the tent or is in the tent becomes unclean. Religious pollution is expiated by being sprinkled with hyssop dipped in water that is mixed with the ashes of the purification offering. This expiation process applies to everyone who came into contact with objects related to the dead body, including the bones, the slain, the corpse, or the grave.

Hence, both Judeans and gentiles required the expiation of religious pollution. They needed, like Abraham, to trust God who could raise the dead to life. Scholars debate the similarity of the content of Abraham's and the implied audience's trust. That both trusts are parallel is evinced by similarities in the key words πιστεύειν ("to trust" [4:17, 24]) and λογίζεσθαι ("to be reckoned" [4:22, 24]) and the idea that both Abraham and the implied audience trust God who makes alive the dead (4:17, 24). But what God did for Abraham does not seem to be exactly parallel to what God will do for the implied audience. Whereas God raised to life Abraham's body, God raised to life Jesus and not the implied audience. This leads Jewett to conclude that "while the words 'trust' and 'reckon' link them to the Abraham story, the content of their trust differs substantially" since, unlike the implied audience's trust, Abraham's trust has to do with progeny.[228] Similarly, Moo agrees that while "the locus of faith has shifted…, the ultimate object of faith has always been the same." By that, he thinks that the promise given to Abraham finds fulfillment in Christ and the Christians.[229] These interpretations are not satisfactory, however, as they undermine Paul's rhetoric. Paul, by making clear a parallelism between the implied audience's trust in God and Abraham's trust in God, positions Abraham as the superordinate figure of all who trust God. In other words, Paul's persuasion is only as strong as the similarity between the trust of

---

228. So Jewett, *Romans*, 341.

229. So Cranfield, *Epistle to the Romans*, 1:251; Barrett, *Epistle to the Romans*, 24; Godet, *Commentary on St. Paul's Epistle to the Romans*, 183.

Abraham and that of the implied audience. If this parallelism is broken, the ideological power of Paul's rhetoric to persuade the implied audience of the viability of trust would also be undermined.

The trusts of both Abraham and that of the implied audience are the same. Several observations support my position. First, Paul explicitly states that Abraham's trust in God brings righteousness simultaneously to *both* Abraham and (proleptically) to the implied audience (4:23–24). Hence, the trust in God that the implied audience now needs to exercise cannot be different from that of Abraham. The difference is not in the content of the trust but in the effects brought about by trust. For Abraham, the result was fatherhood. For the implied audience, the result was sonship; that is, the implied audience became Abraham's descendants and heirs. The same idea is operative in 4:13. Whereas Abraham received the promise when he became the father of the world that comprised both Judean and gentile Christians, the Judean and gentile Christians receive the promise when they become Abraham's descendants. Second, that both trusts in God are the same is required by the need for Abraham's descendants to walk in the footsteps of the trust in God of their "father Abraham" (4:12). Third, Abraham's body was dead (4:19), and consequently those of his descendants are also, as they were present in Abraham seminally. Hence, both require a trust in God that can expiate them of religious pollution, that is, of sin. But how is God going to expiate religious pollution? We may expect that this question weighed heavily on the minds of the implied audience due to the above-discussed social and cultural intertextures underlying death, specifically, the need for expiation of religious pollution. At this point, Paul aptly introduces Jesus who can expiate their religious pollution. The religious pollution that affects the implied audience, however, does not appear to be the same as that of Abraham's: Abraham's problem was death; the implied audience's problem was trespasses (4:25). Death and trespasses, however, are clearly connected as Paul later makes clear in 6:23, when he claims that the wages of sin or trespasses is death. Several comments clarify this apparent incongruity. By making a parallel comparison between the trust of Abraham and that of the implied audience (4:23–25), Paul understands the religious pollution caused by death to be parallel in some way to that caused by trespasses. Paul's construal builds on a social intertexture in which death is a consequence of trespasses/sin (Rom 6:23). David deSilva notes that in Greco-Roman literature, such as the Oedipus Greek tragedy, murder, sacrilege, or other serious offenses must be prosecuted. If they are not, avenging gods will destroy entire families or even cities.[230] For example, the whole of Rome suffered national guilt after the Battle of Carrhae in 53 BCE, when Marcus Licinius Crassus and his legions were destroyed by the Parthians. Romans felt that they had been punished for impiety by this humiliating defeat.[231] The Letter to the Romans also sheds a similar light on the cultural intertexture of death. In Rom 6, the Greek word νεκρός ("dead") is contrasted with the new life that Christ experiences after his resurrection. This life describes one that has been freed from bondage to sin. A σῶμα ("body") is also νεκρόν ("dead") because of sin (8:10). Thus, in Romans, the word νεκρός denotes a state that is a consequence of sin. To remove the religious pollution caused by sin, the implied audience needs to trust their patron, God, to provide them someone who can expiate their sins. By this, I am also positing that Abraham's trust in God was the same as that of the present implied audience who lived centuries later. To what extent Abraham was aware of Jesus who would come to expiate his pollution is a moot point, since Paul does not make this clear. That being said, however, this point being moot does not undercut this interpretation, as Paul's persuasiveness is not compromised. In fact, the converse is true: by maintaining Jesus as the only one who can expiate sin, Paul mobilizes ideological power by holding up Jesus prominently as a superordinate figure to unite the dissenting factions. For religious pollution, understood as sin, to be expiated, the implied audience needs to trust God "who raised [τὸν ἐγείραντα] Jesus our Lord from the dead [νεκρῶν]" (4:24).

Important for a correct understanding is the point that Paul brings Jesus into his rhetoric as the solution to the deadness of Abraham's body and as the response of God to Abraham's trust (4:17–25). Jesus is also the solution to how Abraham was going to attain worldwide fatherhood. This role of Jesus is appropriately introduced into the rhetoric using a blend of apocalyptic and priestly rhetorolect.

The presence of apocalyptic rhetorolect is indicated by Paul's positioning of Abraham as the *pater patriae* of the Roman Empire, which fits the firstspace of a political empire.[232] Apocalyptic rhetorolect is detected in 4:24, where Jesus is described as being raised from the dead by God. According to 1:3, Jesus's status as the son of God was made explicit by his

---

230. See deSilva, *Introduction to the New Testament*, 115–16.
231. See above, chapter 4, §3.7.2, "Romans 4:24–25."
232. Robbins, *Invention of Christian Discourse*, 109.

resurrection from the dead.[233] By using this rhetorolect, Paul mobilizes ideological power to persuade the implied audience that Jesus is capable of helping the implied audience receive resurrection and eternal life.[234] Second, apocalyptic rhetorolect is also present, as the word resurrection contains eschatological overtones.[235] In using apocalyptic rhetorolect, Paul is aiming to create a new culture, and hence a new superordinate ethnic identity to unite both Judean and gentile Christians. Social and cultural texture is present where Jesus functions as a broker in the Mediterranean culture. This lends ideological power to Paul's rhetoric by persuading the implied audience of the need for someone to expiate religious pollution. Two things make Jesus a worthy broker between God and Christians.

First, Jesus was handed over (to death) for the trespasses of the implied audience. That the verb παρεδόθη should take on the unstated object νεκρός ("death") is apparent from the contrasting statement "and he was raised because of our righteousness." Jesus's dying for trespasses recalls the temple and altar. This provides the input for the firstspace of priestly rhetorolect. Here, Jesus functions as the priest-messiah in the secondspace to generate purity between God and humans in the thirdspace.[236] By using priestly rhetorolect, ideological power is generated to persuade the implied audience that the apocalyptic state, in which Abraham is the father of all nations, is achievable.

Second, Jesus "was raised because of our righteousness [δικαίωσιν]" (4:25). Several observations point in the direction that δικαίωσις ("righteousness") refers, minimally, to a life of ethical living. The underlying cultural intertexture often attaches resurrection with ethical living. This is prevalent in Romans. For example, in words similar to 4:24, Paul in 6:4 says that because Christ ἠγέρθη ἐκ νεκρῶν ("was raised from the dead"),

---

233. See also Phil 2:6–12. The inner-texture of Phil 2:6–12 comprises the opening (2:6), and the closing (2:9–12). The closing, 2:9–12, should be construed as the response to the opening, 2:6. This observation implies that the resurrection of Jesus Christ demonstrates what had not been previously obvious when Christ took the form of a slave (2:7): that Jesus Christ is equal with God. For scholars who view Phil 2:6–12 as presupposing a preexistent Christ, see, e.g., Gordon D. Fee, *Pauline Christology: An Exegetical-Theological Study* (Peabody, MA: Hendrickson, 2007), 375; O'Brien, *Epistle to the Philippians*, 236.

234. Robbins, *Invention of Christian Discourse*, 109.

235. So Dunn, who comments that God's making Jesus alive is "the eschatological counterpart of" his making Sarah's womb alive (*Romans 1–8*, 223).

236. Robbins, *Invention of Christian Discourse*, 109.

Christians, by being identified with Christ's death, are able to walk in newness of life. This refers to the ability to live an ethical life (cf. 6:9–10). In 7:4, because Christians have died to the law, they now belong to a new master, the one who was raised from the dead (τῷ ἐκ νεκρῶν ἐγερθέντι) in order that "we might bear fruit for God." Paul contends that because the Spirit of God τοῦ ἐγείραντος τὸν Ἰησοῦν ἐκ νεκρῶν ("who raised Jesus from the dead" [8:11]) dwells in Christians, God will give life to σώματα ὑμῶν ("your bodies"). This life is given by the Spirit.[237] But for the Spirit to give life, the Christian must put to death the deeds of the body (8:13) and live ethically according to the Spirit (8:5–6). In other words, the life that God raises from the dead manifests itself in ethical living. Romans 4:24–25 thus concludes that not only does Jesus expiate the pollution due to death so that the implied audience can become Abraham's descendants, but he also enables these descendants to live an ethical life. But since an ethical life in Romans is measured against the law of Moses (Rom 2; 7:7–8; 8:1–4), trust in God who raised Jesus from the dead enables Judean Christians and, in particular, gentile Christians to fulfill the requirements of the Mosaic law. By living an ethical life, Christians affirm their trust in and loyalty to God their patron. As a result, God the patron would regard such Christians as righteous.[238]

Thus, Paul's rhetoric of Abraham's trust (faith) has adequately responded to the twofold concern enunciated at the beginning of this section, that Judean Christians do not have an edge over gentile Christians. The reason is that both were formally dead in Abraham's body due to religious pollution from death and, more specifically, sin. Furthermore, gentile Christians are now able to live up to the ethical demands of the Mosaic law. Judean Christians and, in particular, gentile Christians are, therefore, righteous in their relationship with God. Also, Paul has made it clear that Judean Christians possessing the law of Moses no longer have a

---

237. My understanding about the significance of Jesus's resurrection as being necessary for Christians' ethical living finds support in Barclay, who observes that "the resurrection of Jesus is that explosive moment when the power of the Spirit was unleashed, creating the life from death on which the believers' faith is pinned (4:24–25) and out of which their identity is formed (6:1–12; 8:9–11). This trio—power, Spirit, resurrection—constitutes the mode by which the Christ-gift takes transformative effect in the human sphere" (*Paul and the Gift*, 461).

238. See above, chapter 2, §4.3, "Romans 7:1–6: Trust in God Frees Christians from Condemnation Due to Noncompliance with the Mosaic Law." See also chapter 2, n. 209, above.

reason to boast toward the gentile Christians of the Christian community in Rome.

5
SUMMARY AND CONCLUSION

1. Summary

Using a diatribe, Paul engages in an intra-Judean debate with a Judean interlocutor, with the implied audience, comprising Judean and gentile Christians, listening to the debate. Paul articulates a question posed by the Judean interlocutor: "What shall we say? Have we found Abraham to be our forefather by his own human efforts?" This question is directed at the implied audience, Judean Christians, who think that Abraham became the forefather of Judeans by his own human efforts. This is a rhetorical question that expects to be negated by the implied audience comprising Judean and gentile Christians. The question is asking if it is possible to argue for the case that Abraham acquired righteousness, and hence honor, so as to become the father of Judeans by means of his human efforts, namely, by observing the Mosaic law (4:1). Undergirding this question is the social and cultural intertexture that descendants resemble their ancestor(s). Thus, if the Judean interlocutor has a case, Abraham gained righteousness by deeds of the Mosaic law, and Judeans, then, can gain righteousness by doing likewise. Paul sets out to refute this contention in 4:1 in several stages.

First, Paul argues that doing the deeds of the Mosaic law did not earn Abraham a righteousness that gained him fatherhood (4:2–8). By dissimulation, Paul assumes the role of Judean sacred Scripture and recites Gen 15:6 LXX as a *chreia* to begin his refutation. This *chreia* is to the point, as it is about Abraham's fatherhood. Its implication is clarified by the social intertexture that favor and deeds are opposing concepts. In other words, a client who receives from the patron a benefaction, righteousness, by trust receives a favor. The patron does not expect to be reciprocated in kind. Rather, reciprocation takes the form of loyalty and trust. David, as patriarch of the messianic kingdom, whose nature is that of an extended household, is also invoked. This mobilizes ideological power to persuade the implied audience to do as David their patriarch did. To further his persuasion, Paul recites Ps 31:1–2a LXX. The sensory-aesthetic texture containing bless/blessing repetitions motivates the implied audience to attain righteousness by trust. This recitation also recalls the whole psalm. The rhetoric emphasizes that forgiveness of sins and a righteous relationship between the patron and client is attained by repentance from sin. Righteousness is hence not attained by doing the deeds of the Mosaic law.

Second, Paul refutes the role of circumcision in attaining a righteousness that achieves fatherhood for Abraham (4:9–12). This rite is chosen for discussion as it is the epitome of the deeds of the Mosaic law. He contends that Abraham was regarded by God, the patron, as being righteous when he was in a state of uncircumcision. This fits Abraham for the role of father of gentile Christians. Moreover, Abraham's trust was affirmed through circumcision. This suits him for the role of the father of Judeans. Thus, righteousness can be ascribed to both gentiles and Judeans. Paul's construal of Abraham's circumcision as a proof of righteousness also maintains the importance of circumcision, an ethnic identity marker of Judeans. This preserves the ethnic identity of Judeans and makes them favorably disposed to accepting righteousness that comes by trust. Hence, Abraham becomes a superordinate figure who unites Judean and gentile Christians. Unity is possible not only because they have a common ancestor; more importantly, this common ancestor ascribes to both Judeans and gentiles righteousness so that Judean Christians no longer have a reason to boast over gentile Christians, as they now satisfy purity rules through Christ.

Third, Paul argues against the role of the Mosaic law (4:13–16) from the perspective of promise in order to further undermine the role of circumcision (as circumcision is part of the Mosaic law). The gentile and the Judean interlocutors lost the series of challenge-riposte and counter-riposte games in 1:18–3:20, and hence are indicted for breaking the moral law. This forms the unstated case. Together with the rule that breaking the law leads to wrath, the consequence is that the Mosaic law results in wrath for both the gentile and the Judean interlocutors. Consequently, the promise would be abolished if one relies on the Mosaic law. Also, Paul's description of Abraham as "heir of the world" (4:13) positions him as the *pater patriae* of the Roman Empire. This allows Paul to bring into the argument the social and cultural intertexture that the Roman Emperor does not ascend the throne by the law. Instead, he needs to receive the favor of his patron, the general Roman populace. In this way, the role of the Mosaic law as contributing to righteousness is undermined.

Fourth, having undermined reliance on the Mosaic law and its deeds by the preceding argument in 4:2–16, Paul is now ready to bring in the role of Abraham's trust (4:17–25). The ideological power of the rhetoric of Abraham's trust builds on two social intertextures: death carries religious pollution and descendants are present in seminal form in their ancestors. The reason Abraham's trust in his patron, God, brought him worldwide fatherhood was because he trusted in God who was able to raise to life the dead. God's resurrection power entails removing religious pollution in Abraham's dead reproductive organs and in the descendants who were seminally present with Abraham. This religious pollution, sin, is removed via Jesus, who acts as a broker between God and humankind. Jesus's death expiates religious pollution. This results in Abraham becoming a father of many descendants and the implied audience becoming Abraham's descendants. Jesus's resurrection enables the implied audience to live an ethically righteous life and one that, minimally, satisfies the requirements set by the Mosaic law. In this way, not only Judean Christians but also gentile Christians can become righteous. The Judean Christians' boast towards the gentile Christians is thus removed.

2. Conclusion

In Romans, the dissension between Judean and gentile Christians is a deep-seated one because it occurs along the fault lines of Judean ethnic identity. It is deep seated because members who belong to an ethnic group will not allow their ethnic identity to be erased. In this letter, Judean Christians define their ethnic identity as a people who possesses the Mosaic law. Furthermore, Judeans are part of a society that is set within Mediterranean agonistic culture, where honor is the main core value, and hence the most sought-after good. Consequently, Judean Christians use the Mosaic law to gain honor from gentile Christians. The reason why the Mosaic law is a means to honor is because, from an emic perspective, Judeans construe possessing the Mosaic law as gaining them righteousness. This righteousness is not only a social marker, but more importantly, it is also an ethical construct. It is this resulting ethical righteousness, from the Judean emic viewpoint, that gains them honor in the eyes of the significant other, God. The consequence is that gentile Christians are considered inferior by

Judean Christians. To alleviate this dissension, Paul uses the rhetoric of Abraham's trust or faith.

Fortunately, ethnicity is not a primordial but a malleable construct. Romans 4 represents Paul's discursive strategy for reconstructing the ethnic identity of both Judean and gentile Christians so that both groups have equal honor. To achieve his objective, Paul first removes the Mosaic law as a means to acquiring honor. At the same time, he reconstructs the ethnic identity of Judean Christians without obliterating their present Judean identity, which is particularly associated with circumcision and the Mosaic law. The end of Paul's rhetoric is to make Judean Christians Abraham's descendants by trust in their patron, God. He also reconstructs the ethnic identity of gentile Christians, making them Abraham's descendants by trusting in the same patron, God. In this way, gentile Christians can receive honor by ascription.

Paul also explains why Abraham's trust in his patron, God, resulted in descendants. Abraham trusted a God who was able to raise the dead. God was able to make alive his dead body and the descendants who were present in Abraham in seminal form. Specifically, God's power enables him (God) to remove religious pollution—that is, sin—that inhibits life. God accomplishes removal of religious pollution by means of a broker, Jesus Christ, who expiates sin. Furthermore, Jesus's resurrection life also enables both Judean and gentile Christians to live an ethical life that results in a state of righteousness. Thus, both ethnic groups, Judean and gentile Christians, can fulfill the Mosaic law and be regarded as righteous before the significant other, God. In this way, gentile Christians gain honor so that Judean Christians no longer have a valid reason to consider them as inferior.

BIBLIOGRAPHY

Adams, Edward. "Abraham's Faith and Gentile Disobedience: Textual Links between Romans 1 and 4." *JSNT* 65 (1997): 47–66.

Adkins, Lesley, and Roy Adkins. *Handbook to Life in Ancient Rome.* New York: Infobase, 2004.

Alexander, Thomas D. "A Literary Analysis of the Abraham Narrative in Genesis." PhD diss., Queen's University of Belfast, 1982.

Allen, Amy. "Power, Subjectivity, and Agency: Between Arendt and Foucault." *IJPS* 10 (2002): 131–49.

Allen, David M. "Introduction: The Study of the Use of the Old Testament in the New." *JSNT* 38 (2015): 3–16.

Alter, Robert. *The Art of Biblical Narrative.* New York: Basic Books, 1981.

———. *The Five Books of Moses: A Translation with Commentary.* London: Norton, 2004.

Anbar, Moshé. *Les Tribus Amurrites de Mari.* OBO 108. Freiburg: Universitätsverlag; Göttingen: Vandenhoeck & Ruprecht, 1991.

Ando, Clifford. *Imperial Ideology and Provincial Loyalty in the Roman Empire.* Berkeley: University of California Press, 2000.

Arendt, Hannah. *On Violence.* London: Lane, 1970.

Aristotle. *Generation of Animals.* Translated by A. L. Peck. LCL 366. Cambridge: Harvard University Press, 1943.

Aune, David E. *The Westminster Dictionary of New Testament and Early Christian Literature and Rhetoric.* Louisville: Westminster John Knox Press, 2003.

Austin, J. L. *How to Do Things with Words.* 2nd ed. Cambridge: Harvard University Press, 1962.

Bakhtin, Mikhail M. *The Dialogic Imagination: Four Essays.* Edited by Michael Holquist. Translated by Caryl Emerson and Michael Holquist. Austin: University of Texas Press, 1981.

———. "The Problem of Speech Genres." Pages 60–102 in *Speech Genres and Other Late Essays*. Edited by Caryl Emerson and Michael Holquist. Translated by Vern W. McGee. Austin: University of Texas Press, 1986.

Baldwin, Joyce G. *1 and 2 Samuel: An Introduction and Commentary*. TOTC. Leicester: Inter-Varsity Press, 1988.

Barclay, John M. G. "'Do We Undermine the Law?' A Study of Romans 14:1–15:6." Pages 287–308 in *Paul and the Mosaic Law*. Edited by James D. G. Dunn. Tübingen: Mohr Siebeck, 1996.

———. *Paul and the Gift*. Grand Rapids: Eerdmans, 2015.

Barrett, C. K. *A Commentary on the First Epistle to the Corinthians*. BNTC. London: Black, 1971.

———. *The Epistle to the Romans*. BNTC. London: Black, 1957.

Barth, Fredrik. *Ethnic Groups and Boundaries: The Social Organization of Cultural Difference*. Oslo: Johansen & Nielsen, 1969.

Bates, Matthew W. "A Christology of Incarnation and Enthronement: Romans 1:3–4 as Unified, Nonadoptionist, and Nonconciliatory." *CBQ* 77 (2015): 107–27.

Baumann, Gerd. *The Multicultural Riddle: Rethinking National, Ethnic, and Religious Identities*. London: Routledge, 1999.

Beale, Gregory K. *Handbook on the New Testament Use of the Old Testament: Exegesis and Interpretation*. Grand Rapids: Baker Academic, 2012.

Beck, Roger. "Rome." Pages 509–11 in *Religions of the Ancient World: A Guide*. Edited by Sarah Iles Johnston. Cambridge: Harvard University Press, 2004.

Beker, J. Christiaan. *Paul the Apostle: The Triumph of God in Life and Thought*. Philadelphia: Fortress, 1984.

———. *Paul's Apocalyptic Gospel: The Coming Triumph of God*. Philadelphia: Fortress, 1982.

Bell, Catherine. *Ritual Theory, Ritual Practice*. New York: Oxford University Press, 1992.

Benveniste, Émile. *Problems in General Linguistics*. Translated by Mary Elizabeth Meek. Coral Gables: University of Miami Press, 1971.

Beresford, James M. "The Significance of the Fast in Acts 27:9." *NovT* 58 (2016): 155–66.

Berger, Klaus. "Abraham in den paulinischen Hauptbriefen." *MTZ* 17 (1966): 47–89.

Berger, Peter L., and Thomas Luckmann. *The Social Construction of Reality: A Treatise in the Sociology of Knowledge*. London: Penguin, 1967.

Berquist, Jon L. "Theories of Space and Construction of the Ancient World." Pages 151–76 in *Foundations for Sociorhetorical Exploration: A Rhetoric of Religious Antiquity Reader*. Edited by Vernon K. Robbins, Robert H. von Thaden Jr., and Bart B. Bruehler. RRA 4. Atlanta: SBL Press, 2016.

Best, Ernest. *The Letter of Paul to the Romans*. CBC. Cambridge: Cambridge University Press, 1967.

Bitzer, Lloyd. "The Rhetorical Situation." *PR* 1 (1968): 1–14.

Black, Matthew. *Romans*. NCBC. Grand Rapids: Eerdmans, 1989.

Bloomquist, L. Gregory. "Paul's Inclusive Language: The Ideological Texture of Romans 1." Pages 119–50 in *Foundations for Sociorhetorical Exploration: A Rhetoric of Religious Antiquity Reader*. Edited by Vernon K. Robbins, Robert H. von Thaden Jr., and Bart B. Bruehler. RRA 4. Atlanta: SBL Press, 2016.

Bodel, John. "Dealing with the Dead: Undertakers, Executioners and Potter's Fields in Ancient Rome." Pages 128–51 in *Death and Disease in the Ancient City*. Edited by Valerie M. Hope and Eireann Marshall. London: Routledge, 2000.

Borkowski, Andrew. *Textbook on Roman Law*. London: Blackstone, 1994.

Botha, Pieter J. J. "The Verbal Art of the Pauline Letters: Rhetoric, Performance and Presence." Pages 409–28 in *Rhetoric and the New Testament: Essays from the 1992 Heidelberg Conference*. Edited by Stanley E. Porter and Thomas H. Olbricht. JSNTSup 90. Sheffield: Sheffield Academic, 1993.

Bourdieu, Pierre. *The Logic of Practice*. Translated by Richard Nice. Stanford, CA: Stanford University Press, 1990.

———. *Outline of a Theory of Practice*. Translated by Richard Nice. Cambridge: Cambridge University Press, 1977.

Bowditch, Phebe Lowell. *Horace and the Gift Economy of Patronage*. CCT. Berkeley: University of California Press, 2001.

Brandt, William J. *The Rhetoric of Argumentation*. Indianapolis: Bobbs-Merrill, 1970.

Bratcher, Robert G., and William D. Reyburn. *A Handbook on Psalms*. New York: United Bible Societies, 1993.

Brenton, Lancelot C. L. *The Septuagint LXX: Greek and English*. London: Bagster & Sons, 1851.

Brooks, James A., and Carlton L. Winbery. *Syntax of New Testament Greek*. Washington, DC: University Press of America, 1979.

Bruce, Frederick Fyvie. *The Letter of Paul to the Romans: An Introduction and Commentary*. TNTC 6. Grand Rapids: Eerdmans, 1985.

Brueggemann, Walter. *Genesis*. IBC. Atlanta: John Knox, 1982.

Bruehler, Bart B. "From This Place: A Theoretical Framework for the Social-Spatial Analysis of Luke." Pages 197–235 in *Foundations for Sociorhetorical Exploration: A Rhetoric of Religious Antiquity Reader*. Edited by Vernon K. Robbins, Robert H. von Thaden Jr., and Bart B. Bruehler. RRA 4. Atlanta: SBL Press, 2016.

Bryan, Christopher. *A Preface to Romans: Notes on the Epistle in Its Literary and Cultural Setting*. New York: Oxford University Press, 2000.

Bumazhnov, Dmitrij F. Review of *The Impact of Yom Kippur*, by Daniel Stökl Ben Ezra. *SCJR* 1 (2006): R16–17. https://tinyurl.com/SBL4822a.

Burke, Kenneth. *A Rhetoric of Motives*. New York: Braziller, 1950.

Buswell, James O. *A Systematic Theology of the Christian Religion*. Grand Rapids: Zondervan, 1962.

Byrne, Brendan. *Romans*. SP 6. Collegeville, MN: Liturgical Press, 1996.

———. *"Sons of God"—"Seed of Abraham": A Study of the Idea of the Sonship of God of All Christians in Paul against the Jewish Background*. AnBib 83. Rome: Pontiff Biblical Institute Press, 1979.

Calderone, Salvatore. *Pistis-Fides: Ricerche di storia e diritto internazionale nell'antichità*. Messina: Università degli studi, 1964.

Calvert-Koyzis, Nancy. *Paul, Monotheism and the People of God: The Significance of Abraham Traditions for Early Judaism and Christianity*. JSNTSup 273. London: T&T Clark, 2004.

Cambier, Jules. *L'Évangile de Dieu selon l'Épître aux Romains: Exégèse et théologie biblique*. StudNeot 3. Bruges: de Brouwer, 1967.

Camp, Claudia V. "Storied Space, or Ben Sira 'Tells' a Temple." Pages 177–96 in *Foundations for Sociorhetorical Exploration: A Rhetoric of Religious Antiquity Reader*. Edited by Vernon K. Robbins, Robert H. von Thaden Jr., and Bart B. Bruehler. RRA 4. Atlanta: SBL Press, 2016.

Campbell, William S. "Covenant Theology and Participation in Christ: Pauline Perspectives on Transformation." Pages 41–60 in *Paul and Judaism: Crosscurrents in Pauline Exegesis and the Study of Jewish-Christian Relations*. Edited by Reimund Bieringer and Didier Pollefeyt. LNTS 463. London: Bloomsbury, 2012.

———. *Paul and the Creation of Christian Identity*. London: T&T Clark, 2008.

———. "Romans III as Key." Pages 251–64 in *The Romans Debate*. Edited by Karl P. Donfried. Rev. and exp. ed. Peabody, MA: Hendrickson, 1991.

———. "The Rule of Faith in Romans 12:1–15:13: The Obligation of Humble Obedience to Christ as the Only Adequate Response to the Mercies of God." Pages 259–86 in *Romans*. Vol. 3 of *Pauline Theology*. Edited by David M. Hay and E. Elizabeth Johnson. SBLSymS 23. Atlanta: Society of Biblical Literature, 2002.

Carson, D. A. Introduction to *The Complexities of Second Temple Judaism*. Vol. 1 of *Justification and Variegated Nomism*. Edited by D. A. Carson, Peter T. O'Brien, and Mark A. Seifrid. Grand Rapids: Baker Academic, 2001.

Chapple, Allan. "Getting Romans to the Right Romans: Phoebe and the Delivery of Paul's Letter." *TynBul* 62 (2011): 195–214.

Charland, Maurice. "Rehabilitating Rhetoric." Pages 464–73 in *Contemporary Rhetorical Theory: A Reader*. Edited by John L. Lucaites, Celeste M. Condit, and Sally Caudill. New York: Guilford, 1999.

Chatman, Seymour. *Story and Discourse: Narrative Structure in Fiction and Film*. New York: Cornell University Press, 1978.

Cicero. *Letters to Friends*. Edited and translated by D. R. Shackleton Bailey. Vol. 1. LCL 205. Cambridge: Harvard University Press, 2001.

———. *On Duties*. Translated by Walter Miller. LCL 30. Cambridge: Harvard University Press, 1913.

———. *On Invention; Best Kind of Orator; Topics*. Translated by H. M. Hubbell. LCL 386. Cambridge: Harvard University Press, 1949.

———. *On Old Age; On Friendship; On Divination*. Translated by William A. Falconer. LCL 154. Cambridge: Harvard University Press, 1923.

Cohen, Shaye J. D. *The Beginnings of Jewishness: Boundaries, Varieties, Uncertainties*. Berkeley: University of California Press, 1999.

Combrink, H. J. Bernard. "Shame on the Hypocritical Leaders in the Church." Pages 1–35 in *Fabrics of Discourse: Essays in Honor of Vernon K. Robbins*. Edited by David B. Gowler, L. Gregory Bloomquist, and Duane F. Watson. Harrisburg, PA: Trinity Press International, 2003.

Consigny, Scott. "Rhetoric and Its Situations." *PR* 7 (1974): 175–85.

Conzelmann, Hans. *An Outline of the Theology of the New Testament*. London: SCM, 1969.

Coote, Robert B. "Tribalism—Social Organization in the Biblical Israels." Pages 35–49 in *Ancient Israel: The Old Testament in Its Social Context*. Edited by Philip F. Esler. Minneapolis: Fortress, 2006.

Craigie, Peter C. *Psalms 1–50*. WBC. Waco, TX: Word, 1983.

Cranfield, C. E. B. *The Epistle to the Romans*. 2 vols. ICC. Edinburgh: T&T Clark, 1975–79.

———. "'The Works of the Law' in the Epistle to the Romans." *JSNT* 43 (1991): 89–101.

Cranford, Michael. "Abraham in Romans 4: The Father of All Who Believe." *NTS* 41 (1995): 71–88.

Cremer, Hermann. *Die Paulinische Rechtfertigungslehre*. Gütersloh: Bertelsmann, 1899.

Crenshaw, James L. *Old Testament Wisdom: An Introduction*. Atlanta: John Knox, 1981.

Crook, Zeba A. "Reciprocity: Covenantal Exchange." Pages 78–91 in *Ancient Israel: The Old Testament in Its Social Context*. Edited by Philip F. Esler. Minneapolis: Fortress, 2006.

Dahood, Mitchell S. J. *Psalms 1–50*. AB 16. New York: Doubleday, 1966.

Das, A. Andrew. *Solving the Romans Debate*. Minneapolis: Fortress, 2007.

Davies, William D. *The Gospel and the Land: Early Christianity and Jewish Territorial Doctrine*. Los Angeles: University of California Press, 1974.

Dawes, Gregory W. *The Body in Question: Metaphor and Meaning in the Interpretation of Ephesians 5:21–33*. BibInt 30. Leiden: Brill, 1998.

deSilva, David A. *Honor, Patronage, Kinship and Purity: Unlocking New Testament Culture*. Downers Grove, IL: InterVarsity Press, 2000.

———. *An Introduction to the New Testament: Contexts, Methods and Ministry Formation*. Downers Grove, IL: InterVarsity Press, 2004.

———. "Toward a Socio-rhetorical Taxonomy of Divine Intervention." Pages 303–16 in *Fabrics of Discourse: Essays in Honor of Vernon K. Robbins*. Edited by David B. Gowler, L. Gregory Bloomquist, and Duane F. Watson. Harrisburg, PA: Trinity Press International, 2003.

Dodd, C. H. *According to the Scriptures: The Sub-structure of New Testament Theology*. London: Nisbet, 1952.

Donaldson, Terence L. "'Gentile Christianity' as a Category in the Study of Christian Origins." *HTR* 106 (2013): 433–58.

Donfried, Karl P. "A Short Note on Romans 16." Pages 44–52 in *The Romans Debate*. Edited by Karl P. Donfried. Rev. and exp. ed. Peabody, MA: Hendrickson, 1991.

Douglas, Mary. *Natural Symbols*. New York: Random House, 1973.

Downs, David J. Review of *Solving the Romans Debate*, by A. Andrew Das. *RBL* 10 (2008): 468–72.

Drane, John W. "Why Did Paul Write Romans?" Pages 208–27 in *Pauline Studies: Essays Presented to Professor F. F. Bruce on His Seventieth Birthday.* Edited by Donald A. Hagner and Murray J. Harris. Grand Rapids: Eerdmans, 1980.

Du Toit, Andreas B. "Vilification as a Pragmatic Device in Early Christian Epistolography." *Bib* 75 (1994): 403–12.

Dudley, Donald. *The Romans.* London: Hutchinson, 1970.

Duncan, John. "The Hope of Creation: The Significance of ἐφ᾽ ἐλπίδι (Rom 8.20c) in Context." *NTS* 61 (2015): 411–27.

Dunn, James D. G. *Romans 1–8.* WBC. Waco, TX: Word, 1988.

———. *Romans 9–16.* WBC. Waco, TX: Word, 1988.

———. "Salvation Proclaimed: VI. Romans 6:1–11: Dead and Alive." *ExpTim* 93 (1982): 259–64.

Dunson, Ben C. *Individual and Community in Paul's Letter to the Romans.* WUNT 332. Tübingen: Mohr Siebeck, 2012.

Durkheim, Émile. *The Elementary Forms of the Religious Life.* Translated by Joseph Ward Swain. New York: Free Press, 1965.

Eagleton, Terry. *Literary Theory: An Introduction.* Oxford: Blackwell, 1983.

Eemeren, Frans H. van. "Argumentation Theory: An Overview of Approaches and Research Themes." Pages 9–26 in *Rhetorical Argumentation in Biblical Texts: Essays from the Lund 2000 Conference.* Edited by Anders Eriksson, Thomas H. Olbricht, and Walter Übelacker. Harrisburg, PA: Trinity Press International, 2002.

Ehrensperger, Kathy. "Paul and the Authority of Scripture." Pages 291–320 in *As It Is Written: Studying Paul's Use of Scripture.* Edited by Stanley E. Porter and Christopher D. Stanley. Atlanta: Society of Biblical Literature, 2008.

———. *Paul at the Crossroads of Cultures: Theologizing in the Space Between.* LNTS 456. London: Bloomsbury, 2013.

Eilers, Claude. *Roman Patrons of Greek Cities.* Oxford: Oxford University Press, 2002.

Elliott, John H. "Household/Family in the Gospel of Mark as a Core Symbol of Community." Pages 36–63 in *Fabrics of Discourse: Essays in Honor of Vernon K. Robbins.* Edited by David B. Gowler, L. Gregory Bloomquist, and Duane F. Watson. Harrisburg, PA: Trinity Press International, 2003.

———. *What Is Social-Scientific Criticism?* Minneapolis: Augsburg Fortress, 1993.

Elliott, Neil. *The Arrogance of Nations: Reading Romans in the Shadow of Empire*. Minneapolis: Fortress, 2008.

———. *The Rhetoric of Romans: Argumentative Constraint and Strategy and Paul's Dialogue with Judaism*. JSNTSup 45. Sheffield: Sheffield Academic, 1990.

Emerton, J. A. "The Riddle of Gen XIV." *VT* 21 (1971): 403–39.

Engberg-Pedersen, Troels. "Gift-Giving and Friendship: Seneca and Paul in Romans 1–8 on the Logic of God's Χάρις and Its Human Response." *HTR* 101 (2008): 15–44.

Eriksson, Anders. "Enthymemes in Pauline Argumentation: Reading between the Lines in 1 Corinthians." Pages 243–59 in *Rhetorical Argumentation in Biblical Texts: Essays from the 2002 Heidelberg Conference*. Edited by Anders Eriksson, Thomas H. Olbricht, and Walter Übelacker. Harrisburg, PA: Trinity Press International, 2002.

Esler, Philip F. *Community and Gospel in Luke-Acts: The Social and Political Motivations of Lucan Theology*. SNTSMS 57. Cambridge: Cambridge University Press, 1987.

———. *Conflict and Identity in Romans: The Social Setting of Paul's Letter*. Minneapolis: Fortress, 2003.

Estrada, Nelson P. *From Followers to Leaders: The Apostles in the Ritual of Status Transformation in Acts 1–2*. LNTS 255. London: Bloomsbury, 2004.

Fantham, Elaine. "Purification in Ancient Rome." Pages 59–66 in *Rome, Pollution and Propriety*. Edited by Mark Bradley and Kenneth Stow. Cambridge: Cambridge University Press, 2012.

Fauconnier, Gilles, and Mark Turner. *The Way We Think: Conceptual Blending and the Mind's Hidden Complexities*. New York: Basic Books, 2002.

Fears, J. Rufus. "Jupiter and Roman Imperial Ideology." *ANRW* 17.1: 3–141.

Fee, Gordon D. *God's Empowering Presence: The Holy Spirit in the Letters of Paul*. Peabody, MA: Hendrickson, 1994.

———. *Pauline Christology: An Exegetical-Theological Study*. Peabody, MA: Hendrickson, 2007.

Filson, Floyd V. "The Significance of the Early House Churches." *JBL* 58 (1939): 105–12.

Fisk, Bruce N. "Synagogue Influence and Scriptural Knowledge among the Christians of Rome." Pages 157–85 in *As It Is Written: Studying Paul's Use of Scripture*. Edited by Stanley E. Porter and Christopher D. Stanley. SymS 50. Atlanta: Society of Biblical Literature, 2008.

Fitzgerald, John T. "Paul and Friendship." Pages 319–43 in *Paul in the Greco-Roman World: A Handbook*. Edited by J. Paul Sampley. Harrisburg, PA: Trinity Press International, 2003.

Fitzmyer, Joseph A. *The Acts of the Apostles: A New Translation with Introduction and Commentary*. AB 31. New York: Doubleday, 1998.

———. *Romans: A New Translation with Introduction and Commentary*. AB 33. New York: Doubleday, 1993.

Flanagan, James W. "Chiefs in Israel." *JSOT* 20 (1981): 47–73.

Fokkelman, Jan P. *Reading Biblical Poetry: An Introductory Guide*. Translated by Ineke Smit. Louisville: Westminster John Knox, 2001.

Forman, Mark. *The Politics of Inheritance in Romans*. SNTSMS 18. Cambridge: Cambridge University Press, 2011.

Foster, Robert L. "The Justice of the Gentiles: Revisiting the Purpose of Romans." *CBQ* 76 (2014): 684–703.

Fowl, Stephen. "The Use of Scripture in Philippians." Pages 163–84 in *Paul and Scripture: Extending the Conversation*. Edited by Christopher D. Stanley. ECL 9. Atlanta: Society of Biblical Literature, 2012.

France, Richard T. "The Formula-Quotations of Matthew 2 and the Problem of Communications." *NTS* 27 (1980): 233–51.

Fredriksen, Paula. "Judaizing the Nations: The Ritual Demands of Paul's Gospel." *NTS* 56 (2010): 232–52.

———. "Paul's Letter to the Romans, the Ten Commandments, and Pagan 'Justification by Faith.'" *JBL* 4 (2014): 801–8.

Gadamer, Hans-Georg. *Truth and Method*. Translated by Garret Barden and John Cumming. 2nd ed. London: Sheed & Ward, 1975.

Gaertner, Samuel L., John F. Dovidio, Jason A. Nier, Brenda S. Banker, Christine M. Ward, Melissa Houlette, and Stephenie Loux. "The Common Ingroup Identity Model for Reducing Intergroup Bias: Progress and Challenges." Pages 133–48 in *Social Identity Processes: Trends in Theory and Research*. Edited by Dora Capozza and Rupert Brown. Thousand Oaks, CA: Sage, 2000.

Gardner, Jane F. *Family and Familia in Roman Law and Life*. Oxford: Clarendon, 1998.

Garroway, Joshua D. "The Circumcision of Christ: 15:7–13." *JSNT* 34 (2012): 303–22.

Gaston, Lloyd. *Paul and the Torah*. Vancouver: University of British Columbia Press, 1987.

Gathercole, Simon J. *Where Is Boasting? Early Jewish Soteriology and Paul's Response in Rom 1–5*. Grand Rapids: Eerdmans, 2002.

Geertz, Clifford. *The Interpretation of Cultures*. New York: Basic Books, 1973.

———. "Primordial Sentiments and Civil Politics in the New States." Pages 105–57 in *Old Societies and New States*. Edited by Clifford Geertz. London: Free Press of Glencoe, 1963.

Georgi, Dieter. *Remembering the Poor: The History of Paul's Collection for Jerusalem*. Nashville: Abingdon, 1992.

———. *Theocracy in Paul's Praxis and Theology*. Translated by David E. Green. Minneapolis: Fortress, 1991.

Gignac, Alain. "The Enunciative Device of Romans 1:18–4:25: A Succession of Discourses Attempting to Express the Multiple Dimensions of God's Justice." *CBQ* 77 (2015): 481–502.

Gil-White, Francisco J. "How Thick Is Blood? The Plot Thickens …: If Ethnic Actors Are Primordialists, What Remains of the Circumstantialist/Primordialist Controversy?" *ERS* 22 (1999): 789–820.

Gillman, Florence M. *A Study of Romans 6:5a: United to a Death like Christ's*. San Francisco: Mellen Research University, 1992.

Godet, Frederic L. *Commentary on St. Paul's Epistle to the Romans*. Grand Rapids: Kregel, 1977.

Goppelt, Leonhard. "Paul and Heilsgeschichte: Conclusions from Romans 4 and 1 Corinthians 10:1–13." Translated by Mathias Rissi. *Int* 21 (1967): 315–26.

———. *Typos: The Typological Interpretation of the Old Testament in the New*. Translated by Donald Madvig. Grand Rapids: Eerdmans, 1982.

Gottwald, Norman K. *The Tribes of Yahweh: A Sociology of the Religion of Liberated Israel, 1250–1050 B.C.E.* Maryknoll, NY: Orbis Books, 1979.

Goulder, Michael. *St. Paul versus St. Peter: A Tale of Two Missions*. Louisville: Westminster John Knox, 1995.

Gowler, David B. "Text, Culture, and Ideology in Luke 7:1–10." Pages 89–125 in *Fabrics of Discourse: Essays in Honor of Vernon K. Robbins*. Edited by David B. Gowler, L. Gregory Bloomquist, and Duane F. Watson. Harrisburg, PA: Trinity Press International, 2003.

Gradel, Ittai. *Emperor Worship and Roman Religion*. OCM. Oxford: Clarendon, 2002.

Granerød, Gard. *Abraham and Melchizedek: Scribal Activity of Second Temple Times in Genesis 14 and Psalm 110*. BZAW 406. Berlin: de Gruyter, 2010.

Grimes, Ronald L. *Beginnings in Ritual Studies*. Washington, DC: University Press of America, 1982.

———. *Ritual Criticism: Case Studies in Its Practice, Essays on Its Theory.* Waterloo, ON: Ritual Studies International, 2010.

Grubbs, Judith E. *Women and the Law in the Roman Empire: A Sourcebook on Marriage, Divorce and Widowhood.* London: Routledge, 2002.

Guerra, Anthony J. *Romans and the Apologetic Tradition.* Cambridge: Cambridge University Press, 1995.

Haacker, Klaus. *Der Brief des Paulus an die Römer.* THKNT 6. Leipzig: Evangelische Verlagsanstalt, 1999.

Habel, Norman C. "Yahweh, Maker of Heaven and Earth." *JBL* 91 (1972): 321–37.

Habermas, Jürgen. "Hannah Arendt's Communications Concept of Power." *SR* 44 (1977): 3–24.

Hahn, Ferdinand. "Das Gesetzesverständnis im Römer- und Galaterbrief." *ZNW* 67 (1976): 29.

Halbwachs, Maurice. *The Collective Memory.* Translated by Francis J. Ditter and Vida Yazdi Ditter. New York: Harper & Row, 1980.

Hall, Jonathan M. *Ethnic Identity in Greek Antiquity.* Cambridge: Cambridge University Press, 1997.

Hamilton, Victor P. *The Book of Genesis: Chapters 1–17.* NICOT. Grand Rapids: Eerdmans, 1990.

Hammond, Mason. *The Augustan Principate in Theory and Practice during the Julio-Claudian Period.* Cambridge: Harvard University Press, 1933.

———. "The Transmission of Powers of the Roman Emperor from the Death of Nero in A.D. 68 to That of Alexander Severus in A.D. 235." *MAAR* 24 (1956): 63–133.

Harris, Rendel J. *Testimonies.* Cambridge: Cambridge University Press, 1916–1920.

Harris, William V. "The Concept of Class in Roman History." Pages 598–690 in *Forms of Control and Subordination in Antiquity.* Edited by Toru Yuge and Masaoki Doi. Leiden: Brill, 1988.

———. "The Late Republic." Pages 511–39 in *The Cambridge Economic History of the Greco-Roman World.* Edited by Walter Scheidel, Ian Morris, and Richard Saller. Cambridge: Cambridge University Press, 2007.

Harrison, James R. *Paul's Language of Grace in Its Graeco-Roman Context.* WUNT 2/172. Tübingen: Mohr Siebeck, 2003.

Haslam, S. Alexander, John C. Turner, Penelope J. Oakes, Craig McGarty, and Katherine J. Reynolds. "The Group as the Basis for Emergent Stereotype Consensus." *ERSP* 8 (1998): 203–9.

Hays, Richard B. *The Conversion of the Imagination: Paul as Interpreter of Israel's Scripture*. Grand Rapids: Eerdmans, 2005.

———. " 'Have We Found Abraham to Be Our Forefather according to the Flesh?'A Reconsideration of Rom 4:1." *NovT* 27 (1985): 76–98.

Heim, Erin M. *Adoption in Galatians and Romans: Contemporary Metaphor Theories and the Pauline Huiothesia Metaphors*. BibInt 153. Leiden: Brill, 2017.

Hester, James D. "The Use and Influence of Rhetoric in Galatians 2:1–14." *TZ* 42 (1986): 386–408.

Hester (Amador), J. David. *Academic Constraints in Rhetorical Criticism of the New Testament*. JSNTSup 174. Sheffield: Sheffield Academic, 1999.

Hippocrates. *Ancient Medicine; Airs, Waters, Places; Epidemics 1 and 3; The Oath; Precepts; Nutriment*. Translated by W. H. S. Jones. LCL 147. Cambridge: Harvard University Press, 1923.

Hock, Ronald F., and Edward N. O'Neil, eds. *The Progymnasmata*. Vol. 1 of *The Chreia in Ancient Rhetoric*. SBLTT 27. Atlanta: Scholars Press, 1986.

Hodge, Caroline J. *If Sons, Then Heirs: A Study of Kinship and Ethnicity in the Letters of Paul*. New York: Oxford University Press, 2007.

Hoffman, Lawrence A. *Covenant of Blood: Circumcision and Gender in Rabbinic Judaism*. Chicago: University of Chicago Press, 1996.

Hofius, Otfried. "Eine altjüdische Parallele zu Röm 4:17b." *NTS* 18 (1971): 93–94.

Holland, Tom. *Romans: The Divine Marriage*. Eugene, OR: Pickwick, 2011.

Homer. *The Illiad of Homer*. Translated by Richmond Lattimore. Chciago: University of Chicago Press, 1951.

Hope, Valerie M. *Death in Ancient Rome: A Sourcebook*. London: Routledge, 2007.

Hopkins, Keith. "Rome, Taxes, Rents, and Trade." Pages 190–230 in *The Ancient Economy*. Edited by Walter Scheidel and Sitta von Reden. ERAW. Edinburgh: Edinburgh University Press, 2002.

Horsley, Richard A. *Galilee: History, Politics, People*. Valley Forge, PA: Trinity Press International, 1995.

Hubbard, Moyer V. *New Creation in Paul's Letters and Thought*. SNTSMS 119. Cambridge: Cambridge University Press, 2002.

Huber, Lynn R. "Knowing Is Seeing: Theories of Metaphor Ancient, Medieval, and Modern." Pages 235–84 in *Foundations for Sociorhetorical Exploration: A Rhetoric of Religious Antiquity Reader*. Edited by

Vernon K. Robbins, Robert H. von Thaden Jr., and Bart B. Bruehler. RRA 4. Atlanta: SBL Press, 2016.

Hübner, Hans. *Law in Paul's Thought*. Edited by John Riches. Translated by James C. G. Greig. SNTW. Edinburgh: T&T Clark, 1984.

Hughes, Everett C. *On Work, Race, and the Sociological Imagination*. Edited by Lewis A. Coser. Chicago: University of Chicago Press, 1994.

Hunsaker, David M., and Craig R. Smith. "The Nature of Issues: A Constructive Approach to Situational Rhetoric." *WSC* 40 (1976): 144–56.

Hunter, Archibald M. *Paul and His Predecessors*. Philadelphia: Westminster, 1961.

Hüsken, Ute. "Ritual Dynamics and Ritual Failure." Pages 337–66 in *When Rituals Go Wrong: Mistakes, Failure and the Dynamics of Ritual*. Edited by Ute Hüsken. Numen 115. Leiden: Brill, 2007.

Hutchinson, John, and Anthony D. Smith. *Ethnicity*. Oxford: Oxford University Press, 1996.

Jeal, Roy R. "Clothes Make the (Wo)Man." Pages 393–414 in *Foundations for Sociorhetorical Exploration: A Rhetoric of Religious Antiquity Reader*. Edited by Vernon K. Robbins, Robert H. von Thaden Jr., and Bart B. Bruehler. RRA 4. Atlanta: SBL Press, 2016.

Jenkins, Richard. *Rethinking Ethnicity: Arguments and Explorations*. London: Sage, 1997.

Jeremias, Joachim. *Jerusalem in the Time of Jesus: An Investigation into Economic and Social Conditions during the New Testament Period*. Philadelphia: Fortress, 1969.

Jervis, L. Ann. "Divine Retribution in Romans." *Int* 69 (2015): 323–37.

———. *The Purpose of Romans*. JSNTSup 55. Sheffield: Sheffield Academic, 1991.

———. "The Spirit Brings Christ's Life to Life." Pages 139–56 in *Reading Paul's Letter to the Romans*. Edited by Jerry L. Sumney. RBS 73. Atlanta: Society of Biblical Literature, 2012.

Jewett, Robert. "The Redaction and Use of an Early Christian Confession in Romans 1:3–4." Pages 99–122 in *The Living Text: Essays in Honor of Ernest W. Saunders*. Edited by Robert Jewett and Dennis E. Groh. Washington, DC: University Press of America, 1985.

———. *Romans: A Commentary*. Hermeneia. Minneapolis: Fortress, 2007.

Jipp, Joshua W. "Rereading the Story of Abraham, Isaac, and 'Us' in Romans 4." *JSNT* 32 (2009): 217–42.

Johnson, Lee A. "Paul's Letter Reheard: A Performance-Critical Examination of the Preparation, Transportation, and Delivery of Paul's Correspondence." *CBQ* 79 (2017): 60–76.

Josephus, Flavius. *Jewish Antiquities: Books 16–17.* Translated by R. Marcus and A. Wikgren. LCL 410. Cambridge: Harvard University Press, 1963.

Kaiser, Walter C. *The Uses of the Old Testament in the New.* Chicago: Moody Press, 1985.

Kaplan, Yehiel. "The Changing Profile of the Parent-Child Relationship in Jewish Law." Pages 21–80 in *The Jewish Law Annual.* Vol. 18. Edited by Berachyahu Lifshitz. London: Routledge, 2009.

Karris, Robert T. "Rom 14:1–15:13 and the Occasion of Romans." *CBQ* 35 (1973): 155–78.

Käsemann, Ernst. *Commentary on Romans.* Translated by Geoffrey W. Bromiley. Grand Rapids: Eerdmans, 1973.

———. *Perspectives on Paul.* London: SCM, 1971.

Keesmaat, Sylvia C. "Reading Romans in the Capital of the Empire." Pages 47–64 in *Reading Paul's Letter to the Romans.* Edited by Jerry L. Sumney. RBS 73. Atlanta: Society of Biblical Literature, 2012.

Kennedy, George A., trans. *Aristotle on Rhetoric: A Theory of Civic Discourse.* Oxford: Oxford University Press, 1991.

———. *New Testament Interpretation through Rhetorical Criticism.* Chapel Hill: University of North Carolina Press, 1984.

———, trans. and ed. *Progymnasmata: Greek Textbooks of Prose Composition and Rhetoric.* WGRW 10. Atlanta: Society of Biblical Literature, 2003.

———. "Reworking Aristotle's *Rhetoric.*" Pages 77–94 in *Foundations for Sociorhetorical Exploration: A Rhetoric of Religious Antiquity Reader.* Edited by Vernon K. Robbins, Robert H. von Thaden Jr., and Bart B. Bruehler. RRA 4. Atlanta: SBL Press, 2016.

Kertzer, David I. *Ritual Politics and Power.* New Haven: Yale University Press, 1988.

Kim, Johann D. *God, Israel, and the Gentiles: Rhetoric and Situation in Romans 9–11.* SBLDS 176. Atlanta: Society of Biblical Literature, 2000.

Kim, Kyu Seop. "Another Look at Adoption in Romans 8:15 in Light of Roman Social Practices and Legal Rules." *BTB* 44 (2014): 133–43.

Kirk, J. R. Daniel. *Unlocking Romans: Resurrection and the Justification of God.* Grand Rapids: Eerdmans, 2008.

Klein, Günter. "Exegetische Probleme in Römer 3,21–4,25: Antwort an Ulrich Wilckens." *EvT* 24 (1964): 676–83.

———. "Paul's Purpose in Writing the Epistle to the Romans." Pages 29–43 in *The Romans Debate*. Edited by Karl P. Donfried. Rev. and exp. ed. Peabody, MA: Hendrickson, 1991.

———. "Römer 4 und die Idee der Heilsgeschichte." *EvT* 23 (1963): 424–47.

Kloppenborg, John S. "Ideological Texture in the Parable of the Tenants." Pages 64–88 in *Fabrics of Discourse: Essays in Honor of Vernon K. Robbins*. Edited by David B. Gowler, L. Gregory Bloomquist, and Duane F. Watson. Harrisburg, PA: Trinity Press International, 2003.

Knauf-Belleri, Ernst A. "Edom: The Social and Economic History." Pages 93–117 in *You Shall Not Abhor an Edomite for He Is Your Brother: Edom and Seir in History and Tradition*. Edited by Diana V. Edelman. ABS 3. Atlanta: Scholars Press, 1995.

Koch, Dietrich-Alex. *Die Schrift als Zeuge des Evangeliums: Untersuchungen zur Verwendung und zum Verständnis der Schrift bei Paulus*. BHT 69. Tübingen: Mohr Siebeck, 1986.

Kugel, James L. *The Idea of Biblical Poetry: Parallelism and Its History*. New Haven: Yale University Press, 1981.

Kunst, Christiane. *Römische Adoption: Zur Strategie einer Familienorganisation*. FAB 10. Hennef: Clauss, 2005.

La Piana, George. "Foreign Groups in Rome during the First Centuries of the Empire." *HTR* 20 (1927): 183–403.

Lagrange, Marie-Joseph. *Saint Paul: Épître aux Romains*. Paris: Gabalda, 1916.

Lakoff, George. *Women, Fire, and Dangerous Things: What Categories Reveal about the Mind*. Chicago: University of Chicago Press, 1987.

Lambrecht, Jan. "Romans 4: A Critique of N. T. Wright." *JSNT* 36 (2013): 189–94.

Lampe, Peter. *Christians at Rome in the First Two Centuries: From Paul to Valentinus*. Translated by Michael Steinhauser. Minneapolis: Fortress, 2003.

———. "The Roman Christians of Romans 16." Pages 216–30 in *The Romans Debate*. Edited by Karl P. Donfried. Rev. and exp. ed. Peabody, MA: Hendrickson, 1991.

Lane, Crystal. *The Rites of Rulers: Ritual in Industrial Society—the Soviet Case*. Cambridge: Cambridge University Press, 1981.

Lausberg, Heinrich. *Handbook of Literary Rhetoric: A Foundation for Literary Study*. Edited by Davide E. Orton and R. Dean Anderson. Translated by Matthew T. Bliss, Annemiek Jansen, and David E. Orton. Leiden: Brill, 1998.

Leff, Michael C. "The Uses of Aristotle's Rhetoric in Contemporary American Scholarship." *Argumentation* 7 (1993): 313–27.

Lemche, Niels P. "Justice in Western Asia in Antiquity, or: Why No Laws Were Needed!" *CKLR* 70 (1995): 1695–716.

———. "Kings and Clients: On Loyalty between the Ruler and the Ruled in Ancient Israel." *Semeia* 66 (1995): 119–32.

Lennon, Jack. "Carnal, Bloody and Unnatural Acts: Religious Pollution in Ancient Rome." PhD diss., University of Nottingham, 2011.

Lenski, R. C. H. *The Interpretation of St. Paul's Epistle to the Romans*. Minneapolis: Augsburg, 1936.

Lévi-Strauss, Claude. *The Naked Man: Introduction to a Science of Mythology*. Translated by John Weightman and Doreen Weightman. New York: Harper & Row, 1981.

Levin, Yigal. "Jesus: 'Son of God' and 'Son of David': The Adoption of Jesus into the Davidic Line." *JSNT* 28 (2006): 415–42.

Levine, Lee I. *The Ancient Synagogue: The First Thousand Years*. 2nd ed. New Haven: Yale University Press, 2005.

———. *Judaism and Hellenism in Antiquity: Conflict or Confluence?* Seattle: University of Washington Press, 1998.

———. "The Second Temple Synagogue: The Formative Years." Pages 7–31 in *The Synagogue in Late Antiquity*. Edited by Lee I. Levine. Philadelphia: American Schools of Oriental Research, 1987.

Lieu, Judith M. "Letters and the Topography of Early Christianity." *NTS* 62 (2016): 167–82.

Lincoln, Andrew T. "The Stories of Predecessors and Inheritors in Galatians and Romans." Pages 172–203 in *Narrative Dynamics in Paul*. Edited by Bruce W. Longenecker. Louisville: Westminster John Knox, 2002.

Lincoln, Bruce. *Theorizing Myth: Narrative, Ideology, and Scholarship*. Chicago: University of Chicago Press, 1999.

Lindsay, Hugh. "Death-Pollution and Funerals in the City of Rome." Pages 152–72 in *Death and Disease in the Ancient City*. Edited by Valerie M. Hope and Eireann Marshall. London: Routledge, 2000.

———. "Eating with the Dead: The Roman Funerary Banquet." Pages 67–80 in *Meals in a Social Context: Aspects of the Communal Meal in the Hellenistic and Roman World*. Edited by Inge Nielsen and Hanne Sigismund Nielsen. ASMA 1. Aarhus: Aarhus University Press, 1998.

Liverani, Mario. "Pharaoh's Letters to Rib-Adda." Pages 3–13 in *Three Amarna Essays*. Malibu, CA: Undena, 1979.

———. "Political Lexicon and Political Ideologies in the Amarna Letters." *Berytus* 31 (1983): 41–56.

Loader, William. *The Septuagint, Sexuality, and the New Testament: Case Studies on the Impact of the LXX in Philo and the New Testament.* Grand Rapids: Eerdmans, 2004.

Lohse, E. "Ὁ νόμος τοῦ πνεύματος τῆς ζωῆς: Exegetische Anmerkungen zu Röm 8,2." Pages 279–87 in *Neues Testament und christliche Existenz: Festschrift für Herbert Braun zum 70. Geburtstag am 4. Mai 1973.* Edited by Hans Dieter Betz, Herbert Braun, and Luise Schottroff. Tübingen: Mohr, 1973.

Longenecker, Bruce W. *Eschatology and the Covenant: A Comparison of 4 Ezra and Romans 1–11.* JSNTSup 57. Sheffield: JSOT Press, 1991.

Longenecker, Richard N. *The Epistle to the Romans.* NIGTC. Grand Rapids: Eerdmans, 2016.

Lopez, Davina C. "Visual Perspectives: Imag(in)Ing the Big Pauline Picture." Pages 93–116 in *Studying Paul's Letters: Contemporary Perspectives and Methods.* Edited by Joseph A. Marchal. Minneapolis: Fortress, 2012.

Lowe, Bruce A. "Paul, Patronage and Benefaction: A 'Semiotic' Reconsideration." Pages 57–84 in *Paul and His Social Relations.* Edited by Stanley E. Porter and Christopher D. Land. Pauline Studies 7. Leiden: Brill, 2013.

Lucas, Alec J. "Reorienting the Structural Paradigm and Social Significance of Romans 1:18–32." *JBL* 131 (2012): 121–41.

Luz, Ulrich. *Das Geschichtsverständnis des Paulus.* BEvT 49. Munich: Kaiser, 1968.

Lyall, Francis. *Slaves, Citizens, Sons: Legal Metaphors in the Epistles.* Grand Rapids: Academie, 1984.

Mack, Burton L. *The Christian Myth: Origins, Logic, and Legacy.* New York: Continuum, 2001.

Malina, Bruce J. "Communicativeness (Mouth-Ears)." Pages 27–30 in *Handbook of Biblical Social Values.* Edited by John J. Pilch and Bruce J. Malina. Peabody, MA: Hendrickson, 1998.

———. "Eyes-Heart." Pages 68–72 in *Handbook of Biblical Social Values.* Edited by John J. Pilch and Bruce J. Malina. Peabody, MA: Hendrickson, 1998.

———. "Faith/Faithfulness." Pages 72–75 in *Handbook of Biblical Social Values.* Edited by John J. Pilch and Bruce J. Malina. Peabody, MA: Hendrickson, 1998.

————. "Fate." Pages 79–81 in *Handbook of Biblical Social Values*. Edited by John J. Pilch and Bruce J. Malina. Peabody, MA: Hendrickson, 1998.

————. "Love." Pages 127–30 in *Handbook of Biblical Social Values*. Edited by John J. Pilch and Bruce J. Malina. Peabody, MA: Hendrickson, 1998.

————. *The New Testament World: Insights from Cultural Anthropology*. Louisville: Westminster John Knox, 2001.

————. "Patronage." Pages 151–55 in *Handbook of Biblical Social Values*. Edited by John J. Pilch and Bruce J. Malina. Peabody, MA: Hendrickson, 1998.

Malina, Bruce J., and John J. Pilch. *Social-Science Commentary on the Book of Revelation*. Minneapolis: Fortress, 2000.

Malina, Bruce J., and Richard L. Rohrbaugh. *Social-Science Commentary on the Gospel of John*. Minneapolis: Fortress, 1998.

Marcus, Joel. "The Circumcision and Uncircumcision in Rome." *NTS* 35 (1989): 67–81.

Marshall, I. Howard. *The Acts of the Apostles*. TNTC. Leicester: Inter-Varsity Press, 1980.

Marshall, Peter. *Enmity in Corinth: Social Conventions in Paul's Relations with the Corinthians*. WUNT 2/23. Tübingen: Mohr Siebeck, 1987.

Martin, Brice L. *Christ and the Law in Paul*. NovTSup 62. Leiden: Brill, 1989.

Mason, Steve. "Jews, Judeans, Judaizing, Judaism: Problems of Categorization in Ancient History." *JSJ* 38 (2007): 457–512.

Matera, Frank J. *Romans*. Paideia. Grand Rapids: Baker Academic, 2010.

Matthews, Victor H. *Pastoral Nomadism in the Mari Kingdom (ca. 1830–1760 B.C.)*. ASORDS 3. Cambridge: American Schools of Oriental Research, 1978.

McBride, S. Dean, Jr. "Polity of the Covenant People: The Book of Deuteronomy." Pages 17–34 in *Constituting the Community: Studies on the Polity of Ancient Israel in Honor of S. Dean McBride, Jr.* Edited by John T. Strong and Steven S. Tuell. Winona Lake, IN: Eisenbrauns, 2005.

McFadden, Kevin W. "The Fulfillment of the Law's Dikaiōma: Another Look at Rom 8:1–4." *JETS* 52 (2009): 483–97.

McGinn, Thomas A. J. *Prostitution, Sexuality, and the Law in Ancient Rome*. New York: Oxford University Press, 2003.

McNutt, Paula M. *Reconstructing the Society of Ancient Israel*. Louisville: Westminster John Knox, 1999.

Meeks, Wayne A. *The First Urban Christians: The Social World of the Apostle Paul*. New Haven: Yale University Press, 1983.

———. "Judgment and the Brother: Romans 14:1–15:13." Pages 290–300 in *Tradition and Interpretation in the New Testament: Essays in Honor of E. Earle Ellis for His Sixtieth Birthday*. Edited by Gerald F. Hawthorne and Otto Betz. Grand Rapids: Eerdmans, 1987.

———. *The Moral World of the First Christians*. LEC 6. Philadelphia: Westminster, 1986.

Mendenhall, George E. "Covenant Forms in Israelite Tradition." *BA* 17.3 (1954): 50–76.

Metzger, Bruce M. *A Textual Commentary On The Greek New Testament*. 2nd ed. Stuttgart: Deutsche Bibelgesellschaft, 1994.

Michel, Otto. *Der Brief an die Römer*. Göttingen: Vandenhoeck & Ruprecht, 1978.

Miller, Arthur B. "Rhetorical Exigence." *PR* 5 (1972): 111–18.

Miller, Carolyn R. "The Aristotelian Topos: Hunting for Novelty." Pages 95–118 in *Foundations for Sociorhetorical Exploration: A Rhetoric of Religious Antiquity Reader*. Edited by Vernon K. Robbins, Robert H. von Thaden Jr., and Bart B. Bruehler. RRA 4. Atlanta: SBL Press, 2016.

Miller, David M. "Ethnicity, Religion and the Meaning of Ioudaios in Ancient 'Judaism.'" *CBR* 12 (2014): 216–65.

Minear, Paul S. *The Obedience of Faith: The Purposes of Paul in the Epistle to the Romans*. London: SCM, 1971.

Mommsen, Theodor. *A History of Rome under the Emperors*. Translated by Clare Krojzl. London: Routledge, 1996.

Moo, Douglas J. *The Epistle to the Romans*. NICNT. Grand Rapids: Eerdmans, 1996.

Morales, Rodrigo J. "'Promised through His Prophets in the Holy Scriptures': The Role of Scripture in the Letter to the Romans." Pages 109–24 in *Reading Paul's Letter to the Romans*. Edited by Jerry L. Sumney. RBS 73. Atlanta: Society of Biblical Literature, 2012.

Morgan, Teresa. *Roman Faith and Christian Faith: Pistis and Fides in the Early Roman Empire and Early Churches*. Oxford: Oxford University Press, 2015.

Morris, Pam, ed. *The Bakhtin Reader: Selected Writings of Bakhtin, Medvedev, and Voloshinov*. London: Arnold, 1994.

Moxnes, Halvor. "Honour and Righteousness in Romans." *JSNT* 32 (1988): 61–77.

———. *Theology in Conflict: Studies in Paul's Understanding of God in Romans*. NovTSup 53. Leiden: Brill, 1980.

Munck, Johannes. *Paul and the Salvation of Mankind*. Translated by Frank Clarke. London: SCM, 1959.

Murphy-O'Connor, Jerome. "Corinth." *ABD* 1:1135–39.

———. *St. Paul's Corinth: Texts and Archaeology*. Wilmington: Glazier, 1983.

Murray, John. *The Epistle to the Romans*. Grand Rapids: Eerdmans, 1997.

Nanos, Mark D. "The Jewish Context of the Gentile Audience Addressed in Paul's Letter to the Romans." *CBQ* 61 (1999): 283–304.

———. *The Mystery of Romans: The Jewish Context of Paul's Letter*. Minneapolis: Fortress, 1996.

Nelson, Richard D. *Raising Up a Faithful Priest: Community and Priesthood in Biblical Theology*. Louisville: Westminster John Knox, 1993.

Neubrand, Maria. *Abraham, Vater von Juden und Nichtjuden: Eine exegetische Studie zu Röm 4*. FB 85. Würzburg: Echter, 1997.

Neyrey, Jerome H. "Equivocation." Pages 63–68 in *Handbook of Biblical Social Values*. Edited by John J. Pilch and Bruce J. Malina. Peabody, MA: Hendrickson, 1998.

———. "Limited Good." Pages 122–27 in *Handbook of Biblical Social Values*. Edited by John J. Pilch and Bruce J. Malina. Peabody, MA: Hendrickson, 1998.

Nickelsburg, George W. E. "Response to Sarah Tanzer." Pages 51–54 in *Conflicted Boundaries in Wisdom and Apocalypticism*. Edited by Benjamin G. Wright III and Lawrence M. Wills. SymS 35. Atlanta: Society of Biblical Literature, 2005.

Nock, Arthur D. "A Diis Electa: A Chapter in the Religious History of the Third Century." Pages 252–70 in *Essays on Religion and the Ancient World*. Edited by Zeph Stewart. Oxford: Clarendon, 1972.

Norden, Christopher G. "Paul's Use of the Psalms in Romans: A Critical Analysis." *EvQ* 88 (2016): 71–88.

O'Brien, Peter T. *The Epistle to the Philippians: A Commentary on the Greek Text*. NIGTC. Grand Rapids: Eerdmans, 1991.

Okamura, Jonathan. "Situational Ethnicity." *ERS* 4 (1981): 452–65.

Oropeza, B. J. *Jews, Gentiles, and the Opponents of Paul: Apostasy in the New Testament Communities*. Eugene, OR: Cascade, 2012.

Osiek, Carolyn, and David L. Balch. *Families in the New Testament World: Households and House Churches*. Louisville: Westminster John Knox, 1997.

Paden, John N. "Urban Pluralism, Integration and Adaptation of Communal Identity in Kano, Nigeria." Pages 242–70 in *Front Tribe to Nation in Africa: Studies in Incorporation Processes*. Edited by R. Cohen and J. Middleton. Scranton, NJ: Chandler Publishing, 1970.

Pareto, Vilfredo. *The Mind and Society*. London: Cape, 1935.

Patton, John H. "Causation and Creativity in Rhetorical Situations: Distinctions and Implications." *QJS* 65 (1979): 36–55.

Pearson, Brook W. R. "Baptism and Initiation in the Cult of Isis and Sarapis." Pages 42–62 in *Baptism, the New Testament and the Church: Historical and Contemporary Studies in Honour of R. E. O. White*. Edited by Stanley E. Porter and Anthony R. Cross. JSNTSup 171. Sheffield: Sheffield Academic, 1999.

Peppard, Michael. *The Son of God in the Roman World: Divine Sonship in Its Social and Political Context*. Oxford: Oxford University Press, 2011.

Perelman, Chaim, and Lucie Olbrechts-Tyteca. *The New Rhetoric: Treatise on Argumentation*. Translated by John Wilkinson and Purcell Weaver. Notre Dame, IN: University of Notre Dame Press, 1969.

———. *On the Embassy to Gaius; General Indexes*. Translated by F. H. Colson. LCL 379. Cambridge: Harvard University Press, 1962.

———. *On the Special Laws, Book 4; On the Virtues; On Rewards and Punishments*. Translated by F. H. Colson. LCL 341. Cambridge: Harvard University Press, 1939.

Philo. *On the Embassy to Gaius; General Indexes*. Translated by F. H. Colson. Index by J. W. Earp. LCL. Cambridge: Harvard University Press, 1962.

———. *On the Special Laws, Book 4; On the Virtues; On Rewards and Punishments*. Translated by F. H. Colson. LCL. Cambridge: Harvard University Press, 1939.

Pilch, John J. "Are There Jews and Christians in the Bible?" *HvTSt* 53 (1997): 119–25.

———. "Domination Orientation." Pages 48–50 in *Handbook of Biblical Social Values*. Edited by John J. Pilch and Bruce J. Malina. Peabody, MA: Hendrickson, 1998.

———. "Trust (Personal and Group)." Pages 201–4 in *Handbook of Biblical Social Values*. Edited by John J. Pilch and Bruce J. Malina. Peabody, MA: Hendrickson, 1998.

Piper, John. *The Justification of God: An Exegetical and Theological Study of Romans 9:1–23*. Grand Rapids: Baker, 1993.

Plevnik, Joseph. "Honor/Shame." Pages 89–92 in *Handbook of Biblical Social Values*. Edited by John J. Pilch and Bruce J. Malina. Peabody, MA: Hendrickson, 1998.

Plutarch. *Can Virtue Be Taught?; On Moral Virtue; On the Control of Anger; On Tranquility of Mind; On Brotherly Love; On Affection for Offspring. Whether Vice Be Sufficient to Cause Unhappiness; Whether the Affections of the Soul are Worse Than Those of the Body; Concerning Talkativeness; On Being a Busybody.* Vol. 6 of *Moralia.* Translated by W. C. Helmbold. LCL. Cambridge: Harvard University Press, 1939.

——. *Demosthenes and Cicero; Alexander and Caesar.* Vol. 7 of *Lives.* Translated by Bernadotte Perrin. LCL. Cambridge: Harvard University Press, 1919.

——. *Lives: Demosthenes and Cicero; Alexander and Caesar.* Translated by Bernadotte Perrin. LCL 99. Cambridge: Harvard University Press, 1919.

——. *Moralia.* Translated by W. C. Helmbold. Vol. 6. LCL 337. Cambridge: Harvard University Press, 1939.

Porter, Stanley E. "Did Paul Have Opponents in Rome and What Were They Opposing?" Pages 149–68 in *Paul and His Opponents.* Edited by Stanley E. Porter. Pauline Studies 2. Leiden: Brill, 2005.

Post, Edwin. *Selected Epigrams of Martial: Edited, with Introduction and Notes.* Boston: Ginn, 1908.

Potter, David S., and David J. Mattingly. *Life, Death, and Entertainment in the Roman Empire.* Ann Arbor: University of Michigan Press, 1999.

Price, Simon. *Rituals and Power: The Roman Imperial Cult in Asia Minor.* Cambridge: Cambridge University Press, 1984.

Rad, Gerhard von. *Genesis.* Translated by John H. Marks. Philadelphia: Westminster, 1955.

——. *Old Testament Theology.* Translated by D. M. G. Stalker. New York: Harper, 1962.

Räisänen, Heikki. *Paul and the Law.* Philadelphia: Fortress, 1986.

Reasoner, Mark. *The Strong and the Weak: Romans 14.1–15:13 in Context.* SNTSMS 103. Cambridge: Cambridge University Press, 1998.

——. "The Theology of Romans 12:1–15:13." Pages 287–300 in *Romans.* Vol. 3 of *Pauline Theology.* Edited by David M. Hay and E. Elizabeth Johnson. SBLSymS 23. Atlanta: Society of Biblical Literature, 2002.

Rendall, Robert. "Quotation in Scripture as an Index of Wider Reference." *EvQ* 36 (1964): 214–21.

Rengstorf, Karl H. "ἀποστελλω κτλ." *TDNT* 1:398.

Rhyne, Thomas C. *Faith Establishes the Law.* SBLDS 55. Chico, CA: Scholars Press, 1981.

Richards, E. Randolph. *Paul and First-Century Letter Writing: Secretaries, Composition and Collection*. Downers Grove, IL: InterVarsity Press, 2004.

———. *The Secretary in the Letters of Paul*. WUNT 2/42. Tübingen: Mohr Siebeck, 1991.

Richards, Kent H. "Bless/Blessing." *ABD* 1:753–56.

Richardson, Neil. *Paul's Language about God*. JSNTSup 99. Sheffield: Sheffield Academic, 1994.

Ridderbos, Herman N. *Paul: Outline of His Theology*. Grand Rapids: Eerdmans, 1975.

Rimmon-Kenan, Shlomith. *Narrative Fiction: Contemporary Poetics*. London: Methuen, 1983.

Rives, James B. "Graeco-Roman Religion in the Roman Empire: Old Assumptions and New Approaches." *CBR* 8 (2010): 240–99.

Robbins, Vernon K. "The Chreia." Pages 1–23 in *Greco-Roman Literature and the New Testament: Selected Forms and Genres*. Edited by David E. Aune. SBLSBS 21. Atlanta: Scholars Press, 1988.

———. "Conceptual Blending and Early Christian Imagination." Pages 161–98 in *Explaining Christian Origins and Early Judaism: Contributions from Cognitive and Social Science*. Edited by Petri Luomanen and Ilkka Pyysiainen Uro. BibInt 89. Leiden: Brill, 2007.

———. *Exploring the Texture of Texts*. Harrisburg, PA: Trinity Press International, 1996.

———. *The Invention of Christian Discourse*. RRA 1. Dorset: Deo, 2009.

———. "Rhetography: A New Way of Seeing the Familiar Text." Pages 367–92 in *Foundations for Sociorhetorical Exploration: A Rhetoric of Religious Antiquity Reader*. Edited by Vernon K. Robbins, Robert H. von Thaden Jr., and Bart B. Bruehler. RRA 4. Atlanta: SBL Press, 2016.

———. "Sociorhetorical Criticism: Mary, Elizabeth, and the Magnificat as a Test Case." Pages 29–76 in *Foundations for Sociorhetorical Exploration: A Rhetoric of Religious Antiquity Reader*. Edited by Vernon K. Robbins, Robert H. von Thaden Jr., and Bart B. Bruehler. RRA 4. Atlanta: SBL Press, 2016.

———. *The Tapestry of Early Christian Discourse*. London: Routledge, 1996.

Robbins, Vernon K., Robert H. von Thaden Jr., and Bart B. Bruehler. Introduction to *Foundations for Sociorhetorical Exploration: A Rhetoric of Religious Antiquity Reader*. Edited by Vernon K. Robbins, Robert H. von Thaden Jr., and Bart B. Bruehler. RRA 4. Atlanta: SBL Press, 2016.

Rock, Ian E. *Paul's Letter to the Romans and Roman Imperialism: An Ideological Analysis of the Exordium (Romans 1:1–17)*. Eugene, OR: Pickwick, 2012.

Rohrbaugh, Richard L. "Honor: Core Value in the Biblical World." Pages 109–25 in *Understanding the Social World of the New Testament*. Edited by Dietmar Neufeld and Richard E. DeMaris. London: Routledge, 2010.

Roosen, A. "Le Genre Littéraire de l'Épître Aux Romains." Pages 465–71 in *Studia Evangelica*. Edited by Frank L. Cross. Vol. 2. TU 87. Berlin: Akademie, 1964.

Rouwhorst, G. "The Origins and Evolution of Early Christian Pentecost." *StPatr* 35 (2001): 309–22.

Safrai, Shmuel. "Home and Family." Pages 728–92 in *The Jewish People in the First Century*. Edited by Shmuel Safrai and Menachem Stern. CRINT 1.2. Philadelphia: Fortress, 1976.

Saller, Richard P. *Personal Patronage under the Early Empire*. Cambridge: Cambridge University Press, 1982.

Sampley, J. Paul. "Romans in a Different Light: A Response to Robert Jewett." Pages 109–29 in *Romans*. Vol. 3 of *Pauline Theology*. Edited by David M. Hay and E. Elizabeth Johnson. SBLSymS 23. Atlanta: Society of Biblical Literature, 2002.

Sanday, William, and Arthur C. Headlam. *A Critical and Exegetical Commentary on the Epistle to the Romans*. ICC. Edinburgh: T&T Clark, 1895.

Sanders, E. P. *Paul and Palestinian Judaism: A Comparison of Patterns of Religion*. Philadelphia: Fortress, 1977.

———. *Paul, the Law, and the Jewish People*. Minneapolis: Fortress, 1983.

Sandnes, Karl O. *Belly and Body in the Pauline Epistles*. SNTSMS 120. Cambridge: Cambridge University Press, 2002.

Scharbert, Josef. "'Gesegnet sei Abraham vom Höchsten Gott'? Zu Gen 14,19 und ähnlichen Stellen im Alten Testament.'" Pages 387–401 in *Text, Methode und Grammatik: Wolfgang Richter zum 65. Geburtstag*. Edited by Walter Gross, Hubert Irsigler, and Theodor Seidl. St. Ottilien: EOS, 1991.

Scheidel, Walter. "Disease and Death." Pages 45–69 in *The Cambridge Companion to Ancient Rome*. Edited by Paul Erdkamp. Cambridge: Cambridge University Press, 2013.

Schlier, Heinrich. *Der Römerbrief*. HThKNT 6. Freiburg: Herder, 1977.

Schliesser, Benjamin. "'Abraham Did Not "Doubt" in Unbelief' (Rom 4:20): Faith, Doubt, and Dispute in Paul's Letter to the Romans." *JTS* 63 (2012): 492–522.

———. *Abraham's Faith in Romans 4: Paul's Concept of Faith in Light of the History of Reception of Genesis 15:6*. WUNT 2/224. Tubingen: Mohr Siebeck, 2007.

Schreiner, Thomas. *Romans*. BECNT. Grand Rapids: Baker, 1998.

Schrenk, Gottlob. "πατήρ κτλ." *TDNT* 6:697.

Schwartz, Seth. *Were the Jews a Mediterranean Society? Reciprocity and Solidarity in Ancient Judaism*. Princeton: Princeton University Press, 2010.

Scott, George M., Jr. "A Resynthesis of the Primordial and Circumstantial Approaches to Ethnic Group Solidarity: Towards an Explanatory Model." *ERS* 13 (1990): 147–71.

Scott, James M. *Adoption as Sons of God: An Exegetical Investigation into the Background of ΥΙΟΘΕΣΙΑ in the Pauline Corpus*. WUNT 2/48. Tübingen: Mohr Siebeck, 1992.

Seneca the Elder. *Declamations*. Translated by M. Winterbottom. Vol. 1. LCL 463. Cambridge: Harvard University Press, 1974.

Seneca. *Epistles 66–92*. Translated by Richard M. Gummere. LCL 76. Cambridge: Harvard University Press, 1920.

Severy, Beth. *Augustus and the Family at the Birth of the Roman Empire*. New York: Routledge, 2003.

Sherwin-White, A. N. Review of *Personal Patronage under the Early Empire*, by Richard P. Saller. *CR* 33 (1983): 271–73.

Shils, Edward. "Ritual and Crisis." Page 723 in *The Religious Situation*. Edited by Donald R. Cutler. Boston: Beacon, 1968.

Singer, Milton. *Traditional India: Structure and Change*. Philadelphia: American Folklore Society, 1959.

Sisson, Russell B. "A Common Agōn." Pages 242–63 in *Fabrics of Discourse: Essays in Honor of Vernon K. Robbins*. Edited by David B. Gowler, L. Gregory Bloomquist, and Duane F. Watson. Harrisburg, PA: Trinity Press International, 2003.

Smit, Peter-Ben. "Ritual Failure in Romans 6." *HvTSt* 72 (2016): art. 3237. doi: 10.4102/hts.v72i4.3237.

Smith, Anthony D. *The Ethnic Origins of Nations*. Oxford: Blackwell, 1986.

———. *The Ethnic Revival*. Cambridge: Cambridge University Press, 1981.

Snodgrass, Klyne R. "Spheres of Influence: A Possible Solution to the Problem of Paul and the Law." *JSNT* 32 (1988): 93–113.

Soskice, Janet Martin. *Metaphor and Religious Language*. Oxford: Clarendon, 1985.

Sparks, Kenton L. *Ethnicity and Identity in Ancient Israel: Prolegomena to the Study of Ethnic Sentiments and Their Expression in the Hebrew Bible*. Winona Lake, IN: Eisenbrauns, 1998.

Spitaler, Peter. "Διαχρίνεσθαι in Mt. 21:21, Mk. 11:23, Acts 10:20, Rom. 4:20, 14:23, Jas. 1:6, and Jude 22—the 'Semantic Shift' That Went Unnoticed by Patristic Authors." *NovT* 49 (2007): 1–35.

Stamps, Dennis L. "Rethinking the Rhetorical Situation: The Entextualization of the Situation in the New Testament Epistles." Pages 193–290 in *Rhetoric and the New Testament: Essays from the 1992 Heidelberg Conference*. Edited by Stanley E. Porter and Thomas H. Olbricht. Sheffield: JSOT Press, 1993.

Stanley, Christopher D., ed. *Arguing with Scripture: The Rhetoric of Quotations in the Letters of Paul*. New York: T&T Clark International, 2004.

———. "'Neither Jew nor Greek': Ethnic Conflict in Graeco-Roman Society." *JSNT* 64 (1996): 101–24.

———. *Paul and the Language of Scripture: Citation Technique in the Pauline Epistles and Contemporary Literature*. SNTSMS 74. Cambridge: Cambridge University, 1992.

———. "What We Learned and What We Didn't." Pages 321–30 in *Paul and Scripture: Extending the Conversation*. Edited by Christopher D. Stanley. ECL 9. Atlanta: Society of Biblical Literature, 2012.

Stansell, Gary. "Wealth: How Abraham Became Rich." Pages 92–110 in *Ancient Israel: The Old Testament in Its Social Context*. Edited by Philip F. Esler. Minneapolis: Fortress, 2006.

Stark, Rodney. *The Rise of Christianity: A Sociologist Reconsiders History*. Princeton: Princeton University Press, 1996.

Ste. Croix, G. E. M. de. *The Class Struggle in the Ancient Greek World: From the Archaic Age to the Arab Conquests*. Ithaca: Cornell University Press, 1981.

Stendahl, Krister. "The Apostle Paul and the Introspective Conscience of the West." *HTR* 56 (1963): 199–215.

Stowers, Stanley K. *The Diatribe and Paul's Letter to the Romans*. SBLDS 57. Chico, CA: Scholars Press, 1981.

———. *A Rereading of Romans: Justice, Jews, and Gentiles*. New Haven: Yale University Press, 1994.

Stökl Ben Ezra, Daniel. "'Christians' Observing 'Jewish' Festivals of Autumn." Pages 51–73 in *The Image of the Judaeo-Christians in Ancient*

Jewish and Christian Literature. Edited by Peter J. Tomson and Doris Lambers-Petry. WUNT 158. Tübingen: Mohr Siebeck, 2003.

———. "Fasting with Jews, Thinking with Scapegoats: Some Remarks on Yom Kippur in Early Judaism and Christianity, in Particular 4Q541, Barnabus 7, Matthew 27 and Acts 27." Pages 163–87 in *The Day of Atonement: Its Interpretations in Early Jewish and Christian Traditions.* Edited by Thomas Hieke and Tobias Nicklas. TBN 15. Leiden: Brill, 2012.

———. *The Impact of Yom Kippur on Early Christianity: The Day of Atonement from Second Temple Judaism to the Fifth Century.* WUNT 163. Tübingen: Mohr Siebeck, 2003.

Strack, Hermann, and Paul Billerbeck. *Kommentar zum Neuen Testament aus Talmud und Midrasch.* 6 vols. Munich: Beck, 1922–1961.

Strange, James F. "Ancient Texts, Archaeology as Text, and the Problem of the First-Century Synagogue." Pages 27–45 in *Evolution of the Synagogue: Problems and Progress.* Edited by Howard Clark Kee and Lynn H. Cohick. Harrisburg, PA: Trinity Press International, 1999.

Stuhlmacher, Peter. "N. T. Wright's Understanding of Justification and Redemption." Pages 359–74 in *God and the Faithfulness of Paul: A Critical Examination of the Pauline Theology of N. T. Wright.* Edited by Christoph Heilig, J. Thomas Hewitt, and Michael F. Bird. WUNT 2/413. Tübingen: Mohr Siebeck, 2016.

———. *Paul's Letter to the Romans: A Commentary.* Louisville: Westminster John Knox, 1994.

———. "The Purpose of Romans." Pages 230–45 in *The Romans Debate.* Edited by Karl P. Donfried. Rev. and exp. ed. Peabody, MA: Hendrickson, 1991.

Suetonius. *Lives of the* Caesars. Translated by J. C. Rolfe. Vol. 1. LCL 31. Cambridge: Harvard University Press, 1914.

Swetnam, James. "The Curious Crux at Romans 4,12." *Bib* 61 (1980): 110–15.

Synge, F. C. "Not Doubt but Discriminate." *ExpTim* 89 (1978): 203–4.

Tacitus. *Annals: Books 4–6, 11–12.* Translated by John Jackson. LCL 312. Cambridge: Harvard University Press, 1937.

Tajfel, Henri, ed. *Differentiation between Social Groups: Studies in the Social Psychology of Intergroup Relations.* London: Academic Press, 1978.

Tajfel, Henri, and John C. Turner. "The Social Identity Theory of Intergroup Behavior." Pages 7–24 in *Psychology of Intergroup Relations.*

Edited by Stephen Worchel and William G. Austin. Chicago: Nelson-Hall, 1986.

Tajfel, Henri, M. G. Billig, R. P. Bundy, and Claude Flament. "Social Categorization and Intergroup Behavior." *European Journal of Social Psychology* 1 (1971): 149–77.

Tambiah, Stanley J. "The Magical Words of Power." *Man* 3 (1968): 175–208.

Taylor, Lily Ross. *The Divinity of the Roman Emperor*. Middletown: American Philological Association, 1931.

Thaden, Robert H. von, Jr. "A Cognitive Turn: Conceptual Blending within a Sociorhetorical Framework." Pages 285–328 in *Foundations for Sociorhetorical Exploration: A Rhetoric of Religious Antiquity Reader*. Edited by Vernon K. Robbins, Robert H. von Thaden Jr., and Bart B. Bruehler. RRA 4. Atlanta: SBL Press, 2016.

Thiselton, Anthony C. *The First Epistle to the Corinthians*. NIGTC. Grand Rapids: Eerdmans, 2000.

Thom, Johan C. "'The Mind Is Its Own Place': Defining the Topos." Pages 555–73 in *Early Christianity and Classical Culture: Comparative Studies in Honor of Abraham J. Malherbe*. Edited by John T. Fitzgerald, Thomas H. Olbricht, and L. Michael White. NovTSup 110. Leiden: Brill, 2003.

Thompson, John B. *Ideology and Modern Culture: Critical Social Theory in the Era of Mass Communication*. Stanford, CA: Stanford University Press, 1990.

———. *Studies in the Theory of Ideology*. Berkeley: University of California Press, 1984.

Thurén, Lauri. *Derhetorizing Paul: A Dynamic Perspective on Pauline Theology and the Law*. Repr. ed. Harrisburg, PA: Trinity Press International, 2002.

———. *The Rhetorical Strategy of 1 Peter with Special Regard to Ambiguous Expressions*. Åbo: Åbo Academy, 1990.

Tiwald, Markus. "Christ as Hilasterion (Rom 3:25): Pauline Theology on the Day of Atonement in the Mirror of Early Jewish Thought." Pages 189–209 in *The Day of Atonement: Its Interpretations in Early Jewish and Christian Traditions*. Edited by Thomas Hieke and Tobias Nicklas. TBN 15. Leiden: Brill, 2012.

Tobin, Thomas H. *Paul's Rhetoric in Its Contexts: The Argument of Romans*. Peabody, MA: Hendrickson, 2004.

———. "What Shall We Say Abraham Found? The Controversy behind Romans 4." *HTR* 88 (1995): 437–52.

Todorov, Tzvetan. *Symbolism and Interpretation*. Translated by Catherine Porter. Ithaca: Cornell University Press, 1982.

Toney, Carl N. *Paul's Inclusive Ethic: Resolving Community Conflicts and Promoting Mission in Romans 14–15*. WUNT 2/252. Tübingen: Mohr Siebeck, 2008.

Tov, Emmanuel. "Jewish Greek Scriptures." Pages 223–37 in *Early Judaism and Its Modern Interpreters*. Edited by Robert A. Kraft and George W. E. Nickelsburg. BMI 2. Atlanta: Scholars Press, 1986.

Towner, Philip H. *The Letters to Timothy and Titus*. NICNT. Grand Rapids: Eerdmans, 2006.

Toynbee, J. M. C. *Death and Burial in the Roman World*. Baltimore: Johns Hopkins University Press, 1996.

Tripolitis, Antonia. *Religions of the Hellenistic-Roman Age*. Grand Rapids: Eerdmans, 2002.

Turner, John C., ed. *Rediscovering the Social Group: A Self-Categorization Theory*. Oxford: Blackwell, 1987.

Turner, Mark. *The Literary Mind*. New York: Oxford University Press, 1996.

Turner, Victor W. *From Ritual to Theater: The Human Seriousness of Play*. New York: Performing Arts Journal Publications, 1982.

Vatz, Richard E. "The Myth of the Rhetorical Situation." *PR* 6 (1975): 154–61.

Vermes, Geza, ed. and trans. *The Complete Dead Sea Scrolls in English*. Rev. ed. London: Penguin, 2004.

Vida, G. Levi Della. "El 'Elyon in Gen 14:18–20." *JBL* 63 (1944): 1–9.

Waetjen, Herman C. *The Letter to the Romans: Salvation as Justice and the Deconstruction of Law*. New Testament Monographs 32. Sheffield: Sheffield Phoenix, 2011.

Wallace, Daniel B. *Greek Grammar beyond the Basics: An Exegetical Syntax of the New Testament*. Grand Rapids: Zondervan, 1996.

Wallace, Karl R. "The Substance of Rhetoric: Good Reasons." *QJS* 49 (1963): 239–49.

Wallace-Hadrill, Andrew. "Patronage in Roman Society." Pages 63–87 in *Patronage in Ancient Society*. Edited by Andrew Wallace-Hadrill. LNSAS 1. London: Routledge, 1989.

Walters, James C. "Paul, Adoption, and Inheritance." Pages 42–76 in *Paul in the Greco-Roman World: A Handbook*. Edited by J. Paul Sampley. Harrisburg, PA: Trinity Press International, 2003.

Waltke, Bruce K. *The Book of Proverbs*. NICOT. Grand Rapids: Eerdmans, 2004.

Waltke, Bruce K., and Cathi J. Fredricks. *Genesis: A Commentary*. Grand Rapids: Zondervan, 2001.

Waltke, Bruce K., and M. O'Connor. *An Introduction to Biblical Hebrew Syntax*. Winona Lake, IN: Eisenbrauns, 1990.

Wanamaker, Charles A. "'By the Power of God': Rhetoric and Ideology in 2 Corinthians 10–13." Pages 194–221 in *Fabrics of Discourse: Essays in Honor of Vernon K. Robbins*. Edited by David B. Gowler, L. Gregory Bloomquist, and Duane F. Watson. Harrisburg, PA: Trinity Press International, 2003.

———. "Epistolary vs. Rhetorical Analysis: Is a Synthesis Possible?" Pages 255–86 in *The Thessalonians Debate: Methodological Discord or Methodological Synthesis*. Edited by Karl P. Donfried and Johannes Beutler. Grand Rapids: Eerdmans, 2000.

Wartenberg, Thomas E. *The Forms of Power: From Domination to Transformation*. Philadelphia: Temple University Press, 1990.

Watson, Duane F. "Keep Yourselves from Idols: A Socio-rhetorical Analysis of the Exordium and Peroratio of 1 John." Pages 281–302 in *Fabrics of Discourse: Essays in Honor of Vernon K. Robbins*. Edited by David B. Gowler, L. Gregory Bloomquist, and Duane F. Watson. Harrisburg, PA: Trinity Press International, 2003.

Watson, Francis. *Paul, Judaism and the Gentiles*. SNTSMS 56. Cambridge: Cambridge University Press, 1986.

———. "The Two Roman Congregations." Pages 203–15 in *The Romans Debate*. Edited by Karl P. Donfried. Rev. and exp. ed. Peabody, MA: Hendrickson, 1991.

Weber, Max. *Economy and Society: An Outline of Interpretive Sociology*. Edited by Guenther Roth and Claus Wittich. Translated by Ephraim Fischoff. Berkeley: University of California Press, 1978.

Wedderburn, A. J. M. "The Purpose and Occasion of Romans Again." Pages 195–202 in *The Romans Debate*. Edited by Karl P. Donfried. Rev. and exp. ed. Peabody, MA: Hendrickson, 1991.

Weima, Jeffrey A. D. *Neglected Endings: The Significance of the Pauline Letter Closings*. JSNTSup 101. Sheffield: Sheffield Academic, 1994.

Weinfeld, Moshe. *Deuteronomy 1–11*. AB 5. New York: Doubleday, 1991.

Wenham, Gordon J. *The Book of Leviticus*. NICOT. Grand Rapids: Eerdmans, 1979.

———. *Genesis 1–15*. WBC. Dallas: Word, 1987.

White, Eugene E. *The Context of Human Discourse: A Configurational Criticism of Rhetoric.* Columbia: University of South Carolina Press, 1992.

White, John L. *Light from Ancient Letters.* Philadelphia: Fortress, 1986.

Whitsett, Christopher G. "Son of God, Seed of David: Paul's Messianic Exegesis in Romans 1:3–4." *JBL* 119 (2000): 661–81.

Whittle, Sarah. *Covenant Renewal and the Consecration of the Gentiles in Romans.* SNTSMS 161. New York: Cambridge University Press, 2015.

Wilckens, Ulrich. "Die Rechtfertigung Abrahams nach Römer 4." Pages 111–27 in *Studien zur Theologie der Alttestamentlichen Überlieferungen: Festschrift für Gerhard von Rad.* Edited by Rolf Rendtorff and Klaus Koch. Neukirchen-Vluyn: Neukirchener Verlag, 1961.

———. "Zu Römer 3,21–4,25: Antwort an G. Klein." *EvT* 24 (1964): 586–610.

Wilder, Amos N. *Early Christian Rhetoric: The Language of the Gospel.* Cambridge: Harvard University Press, 1964.

Williamson, Paul R. *Abraham, Israel, and the Nations: The Patriarchal Promise and Its Covenantal Development in Genesis.* JSOTSup 315. Sheffield: Sheffield Academic, 2000.

Wilson, James P. "Romans Viii, 28: Text and Interpretation." *ExpTim* 60 (1948–1949): 110–11.

Wilson, Robert R. "Deuteronomy, Ethnicity, and Reform: Reflecting on the Social Setting of Deuteronomy." Pages 107–24 in *Constituting the Community: Studies on the Polity of Ancient Israel in Honor of S. Dean McBride, Jr.* Edited by John T. Strong and Steven S. Tuell. Winona Lake, IN: Eisenbrauns, 2005.

Wissowa, Georg. *Religion und Kultus der Römer.* Munich: Beck, 1912.

Witherington, Ben, III. *The Acts of the Apostles.* Grand Rapids: Eerdmans, 1998.

Worthington, Jonathan. "Creatio Ex Nihilo and Romans 4:17 in Context." *NTS* 62 (2016): 49–59.

Wright, David P. "Holiness (OT)." *ABD* 3:246–47.

Wright, N. T. "Justification by (Covenantal) Faith to the (Covenantal) Doers: Romans 2 within the Argument of the Letter." *CovQ* 72 (2014): 98–108.

———. *The Kingdom New Testament: A Contemporary Translation of the New Testament.* New York: HarperOne, 2011.

———. "Paul and the Patriarch: The Role of Abraham in Romans 4." *JSNT* 35 (2013): 207–41.

———. "Romans and the Theology of Paul." Pages 3–67 in *Romans.* Vol. 3 of *Pauline Theology.* Edited by David M. Hay and E. Elizabeth Johnson. SBLSymS 23. Atlanta: Society of Biblical Literature, 2002.

Wuellner, Wilhelm. "Paul's Rhetoric of Argumentation in Romans." *CBQ* 38 (1976): 330–51.

———. "Where Is Rhetorical Criticism Taking Us?" *CBQ* 49 (1987): 448–63.

Young, Norman H. "Romans 14:5–6 in Its Social Setting." *AUSS* 54 (2016): 51–70.

Young, Stephen L. "Paul's Ethnic Discourse on 'Faith': Christ's Faithfulness and Gentile Access to the Judean God in Romans 3:21–5:1." *HTR* 108 (2015): 30–51.

Zahn, Theodor. *Der Brief des Paulus an die Römer.* Leipzig: Deichert, 1910.

Zerwick, Maximilian. *Biblical Greek.* Rome: Pontifical Biblical Institute, 1963.

Ancient Sources Index

Hebrew Bible/Septuagint

Genesis

11:27–12:9	172
12	159
12–14	171
12–22	222
12–24	126
14	166–68, 170–72, 174
14–15	166
14:17	169
14:17–21	166, 170, 172, 174
14:17–24	166–68, 170–72
14:18	169
14:18–20	169
14:18–24	168, 172
14:19	169
14:19–20	169
14:20	170
14:21	169
14:22	170
14:22–24	170
15	113, 149, 159, 165–66, 171–72, 174, 206
15:1	166, 172–73, 175
15:1–2	171–72, 176
15:1–6	175
15:1–21	166
15:3	173
15:3–17	171, 173
15:4	174
15:5	113, 159, 165, 173, 222, 254–55
15:6	71, 156–60, 165–66, 173–74, 176–78, 187, 195, 204–5, 229, 251, 260–62, 271

15:7	175
15:7–21	175
15:8	175
15:9–17	175
15:9–21	175
15:12	171
15:13–16	165
15:13–17	171
15:18–21	171, 176
16:16	206
17	113, 165, 251, 260
17:5	113, 251–52, 254
17:9–14	127
17:11	208
17:17	255
17:24	206
18	165–66
18:16–33	173
22	165

Leviticus

4	199
5	199
6:11	265
10:10	106, 249
11:31–32	249
16	199
16:21–22	200
16:33	199
18:5	99

Numbers

20:29	173
25:10–13	208
25:12	208

Deuteronomy	
6:1–5	137
6:6–7	137
6:6–9	137
6:25	145
14:19	61
15:4–5	61
15:10	61
16:18–20	167
17:8–13	152
17:9	152
17:18	152
17:18–20	152–53
21:18–21	137
24:19	61
30:11–14	152
32:6	144
32:6–14	145
Judges	
21:6	191
1 Samuel	
13:14	191
24:17	174
2 Samuel	
2:4	189–90
2:7	189
2:10	189
3:1	189
5:1	191
5:1–3	190
5:11	189
5:16	189
7	43
7:1–17	191
7:14	145
12:19	189
12:20	189
14:18	189
17:21	189
Psalms	
1:1	189

1:1–2a	195
2	43
2:12	189
31	113, 188, 196, 198, 200, 202
31:1	189, 196
31:1–2	113, 191, 193–95
31:1–2a	71, 193–95, 199, 272
31:2	196
31:2b	193, 195
31:3	193
31:3–5	193, 195
31:3–7	194
31:6–7	194
31:8–9	194
31:8–11	194
31:10–11	194
31:11	194
32	196, 198
32:1–2a	198
32:1–2	202
32:8–9	194
78:35	169
105:20	64
105:31	208
143:1	174
143:2	174
Isaiah	
6:3–5	250
11	189
11:1	189
35:8	250
51:1	250
51:11	250
Jeremiah	
23:5–6	189
Ezekiel	
22:26	106
34:23–31	189
37:24–28	189
44:23	106

Deuterocanonical Books

Tobit
   3:6   61
   4:7   61
   4:9   61
   4:14   61

Additions to Esther
   14:15   210
   14:17   106

Wisdom of Solomon
   13:1–9   62
   14:22–31   62

Sirach (or Ecclesiasticus)
   14:1   189
   14:2   189
   14:20   189
   25:8   189
   25:9   189
   44:19–21   147
   45:25–26   188
   47:1–11   191
   47:2–11   188
   47:22   189
   48:11   189
   50:28   189

Baruch
   57:1–2   4

1 Maccabees
   1:15   204
   1:62–63   106
   2:51–52   177
   2:52   147
   2:57   191

2 Maccabees
   6:18–31   106
   16:24   186

4 Maccabees
   4–18   106
   8:5–7   186
   13   214
   13:13   214
   13:18   214
   13:19   214
   16:18–22   185
   16:20–21   186
   16:22   186
   16:24   186

Pseudepigrapha

Apocalypse of Abraham
   2.1–9   138
   4.3   138
   6.6–7   138
   7.7–12   138

2 Baruch
   48:22–24   145

Joseph and Aseneth
   8:5   106

Jubilees
   11:16–17   138
   15:26, 27   210
   16:25–28   4
   19:8–9   147
   24:11   4

Letter of Aristeas
   128–71   62
   158   152
   168   152

Psalms of Solomon
   17.23–51   189

Sibylline Oracles
   3.8–45   62

Testament of Judah
  15:4   106

Testament of Reuben
  1:10   106

Dead Sea Scrolls

Damascus Document, Cairo Genizah
  3:2   4
  3:2–4   147
  6:17   106
  12:20   106
  16:4–6   210

Florilegium
  1:10–13   189

Pesher Genesis
  49   189

Ancient Jewish Writers

Josephus, *Against Apion*
  1.179   121
  2.282   196
  9.359   153

Josephus, *Jewish Antiquities*
  2.11   138
  4.176–331   152
  11   121
  13.257   210
  13.257–258   221
  17.14   82
  20.17–96   122

Josephus, *Jewish War*
  5.380   127

Philo, *De Abrahamo*
  1.130   138

Philo, *De virtutibus*
  189–200   135

  195   135

Philo, *De vita Mosis*
  1.250   253
  2.84   152
  2.20–25   196

Philo, *Legatio ad Gaium*
  1.55   250
  361   106

New Testament

Matthew
  2   160
  2:8   125
  7:7   125
  12:43   125
  21:21   257
  27   197

Mark   227
  7:2   106
  10:17–22   137
  11:23   257

Luke
  1:3   38
  1:70   43
  7:1–10   17
  11:9   125
  18:11–12   143

John
  4:6   256
  11:38   256

Acts
  1:1   38
  2:1   198
  2:5   38
  2:9–11   120
  2:46   198
  3:1   198
  3:18   38

5:20	198
8:1	36
8:27–35	37
10:1–2	37
10:2	37
10:20	257
11:1	46
11:19–21	36
11:25–26	125
12:3	198
13:5	36
13:14	36
13:16–22	36
14:1	36
17:1	36
17:1–4	36
17:10	36
17:17	36
18:2	36–38, 40
18:3	37
18:4	36
18:19	36
18:26	36
19:8	36
20:6	198
21:26	198
27	197
27:9	197

Romans

1	49
1–3	75, 83, 95, 221–22, 229, 231, 243
1–4	244
1–8	181
1–11	103
1:1	41–43, 55, 230
1:1–4	216
1:1–5	47, 57
1:1–5a	57
1:1–7	26, 42, 47, 57
1:1–12	52
1:1–15	31, 40–41, 55, 59, 128, 156
1:1–17	56
1:2	43, 151
1:2–3	56

1:2–4	43
1:3	55, 189
1:3–4	43, 69, 226
1:4	55, 59
1:5	41, 43, 45, 55–57
1:5–6	46, 51
1:7	57
1:8	41, 223, 227
1:8–12	41
1:8–15	26, 47, 50, 59, 61
1:9	41, 59
1:9–10	47
1:10	41, 56
1:10–11	59
1:10–15	49
1:11	41, 45, 48–52, 56, 61, 69
1:11–12	48, 52
1:11–13	49
1:11–15	49–50
1:12	47, 51–53, 57, 61
1:12b	41
1:12–13	48
1:13	41, 47–49, 51, 53, 56–57, 69
1:13b	47
1:13–14	51
1:14	41, 49, 59, 62–63
1:14–15	42, 49–50
1:15	42, 49
1:16	49, 59–60, 65
1:16–17	41–42, 49, 56–57, 59, 61, 73
1:16–3:31	58
1:16–4:25	58, 143–44, 221
1:16–8:39	74
1:16–11:36	56
1:16–15:13	51, 69, 73
1:17	60, 62, 68, 73
1:18	60–62, 73
1:18–32	60, 62, 68, 231
1:18–3:8	143
1:18–3:20	56, 58, 60–62, 64, 67, 229–31, 272
1:18–3:31	68, 112
1:18–4:25	131
1:18–8:39	95
1:18–11:36	42, 49, 58

Romans (cont.)

1:18–15:13	61, 72
1:20	223
1:21	259
1:21–24	63
1:23	8, 64
1:24	62, 231, 256
1:28	231
1:28–31	64
1:28–32	63
1:29–31	63–64
1:32	216
2	8, 10, 269
2:1	62–64, 91
2:1–11	64
2:1–16	62, 65
2:1–29	58, 60, 68
2:1–3:30	63
2:2	63, 231
2:3	63
2:6	94
2:7	77
2:9	49, 63, 66
2:10	49, 66
2:14–15	230
2:17	58, 67, 221
2:17–20	65
2:17–22	64
2:17–23	231
2:17–24	65
2:17–25	145
2:17–29	62, 64–65, 207
2:19	65
2:21–22	143
2:22	65
2:23	65, 67
2:24–29	143
2:25	127, 204, 207, 217, 243
2:25–27	220–21
2:25–29	204, 211, 217
2:26	127
2:27	127
2:28	217, 221
2:28–29	204, 217
2:29	127

3–4	8
3:1	127
3:1–4	216
3:5	124, 129–31, 231
3:6	223
3:6–8	124
3:7–31	112
3:9	49, 64–66
3:9–10	56
3:9–20	65, 143
3:10	69
3:10–18	69
3:13–18	143
3:19	65, 223, 227
3:19–20	64
3:20	61, 65, 70, 134, 143
3:21	62, 66, 70, 73–74, 134, 216
3:21–22	5
3:21–26	4
3:21–28	134
3:21–31	22, 28, 66, 200, 243
3:21–4:25	58
3:21–5:1	129
3:22–26	66
3:23	66
3:24–26	66
3:25	66, 197, 200
3:26	66, 74
3:27	5, 8, 66–67, 113
3:27–28	8, 67, 70, 143
3:27–30	112
3:27–31	4–6, 66–68, 75, 219
3:28	67
3:29–30	67, 204
3:30	66–68, 127, 243
3:31	5
4	1–9, 12–15, 29, 31–32, 58, 69–70, 72, 74, 76–78, 84, 87, 91, 93, 95, 101–2, 104, 106, 108–14, 116, 124–26, 134, 138, 143, 155–56, 158, 165–66, 186–87, 200–201, 207, 210, 214, 219, 222, 254, 256–58, 260
4:16	70, 72, 111, 114–16, 124–28, 130–36, 139–40, 149–50, 187, 189, 202, 205, 245, 254, 261–62, 271

4:1a 116
4:1–2 124
4:1–3 6
4:1–8 10–11, 111, 124
4:1–22 11
4:1–25 69
4:28 70, 116, 132–34, 140–42, 158–59, 219
4:2a 71, 141, 143–44, 146, 148
4:2b 141, 148–49
4:2c 141, 149
4:2–4 8
4:2–5 114, 196, 202
4:2–8 6, 71, 112, 115, 124, 140–42, 146, 149, 202–6, 214, 242–43, 262, 271
4:2–15 244
4:2–16 111, 244, 273
4:2–22 114
4:3 115–16, 141–42, 150, 158–60, 177, 187, 189, 191, 205, 219, 260–61
4:3–5 158
4:3–8 142, 149, 159
4:4 12, 141, 181, 216
4:4–5 71, 113, 158–60, 165–66, 176–78, 184, 187–89, 206, 238
4:4–6 70, 134
4:4–8 124
4:5 141, 165, 187, 204–5, 257
4:6 115–16, 141, 189, 194, 203
4:6–7 12
4:6–8 114, 188–89, 194, 202–3
4:7–8 141
4:9 11, 115–16, 141, 156, 202–6, 219, 257
4:9a 205, 224
4:9b 205
4:9–10 8, 113
4:9–11 211
4:9–12 10–11, 71, 112, 114–15, 127, 201–2, 217, 219–20, 223, 229, 242, 251, 262, 272
4:9–21 124
4:9–25 111

4:10 71, 206, 210, 213
4:10–11 205
4:10–12 127
4:11 206–8, 213–14
4:11a 71, 206–7, 218
4:11b 71, 112, 212
4:11b–12 207
4:11–12 8–9, 106, 127, 203, 205, 211, 224
4:11–22 124
4:12 106, 112, 127, 213, 215, 217–18, 263, 266
4:13 8, 9, 218–19, 222–23, 227–28, 237, 240, 272
4:13a 218
4:13–14 8, 113
4:13–15 224
4:13–15a 243
4:13–16 11, 71, 112, 114–15, 218–20, 242–43, 258–59, 262, 272
4:13–21 260
4:13–22 11
4:14 218–19, 228
4:14a 228
4:14b 228, 231
4:14b–15 10
4:14–15 232
4:14–15a 219, 228
4:14–16 227, 228
4:14–24 222
4:15 218–19, 221, 229
4:15a 228–29, 233, 237–38, 246, 250
4:15b 236–38
4:15b–16 236
4:16 113, 132, 216, 218–19, 236–38, 242–44
4:16–18 8–9
4:17 8, 12, 113, 245, 251–53, 256, 265
4:17–21 253, 260
4:17–22 11, 114, 262
4:17–25 28, 71–72, 111–12, 115, 244–45, 250–51, 257, 262, 267, 273
4:18 115–16, 165, 187, 224
4:18–19a 245, 252, 255
4:19 245, 253, 263, 266

Romans (cont.)

4:19–20	186
4:19a	254–55, 257
4:19b	255, 257
4:19b–21	255
4:19b–22	245
4:20	113, 254, 257, 259
4:21	259
4:22	62, 156, 257, 260–61, 265
4:23	112, 128, 156, 261–62
4:23–24	113, 266
4:23–25	72, 74, 76–80, 82–84, 87, 90–91, 94–97, 103–4, 108, 110, 114, 124, 128, 261, 266
4:24	75–76, 91, 245, 256, 265, 267–68
4:24–25	76–77, 101, 112, 114, 258, 262, 267, 269
4:25	101, 245, 258, 266, 268
5	74–75, 78, 101
5–8	95
5–15	70
5:1	75, 110
5:1a	75
5:1–2	76
5:1–11	76
5:1–21	27, 74–75
5:1–15:13	72, 74
5:2	75
5:2a	75
5:2b	75
5:3	75
5:3–4	75
5:3–5	92
5:4	75
5:5	53
5:6–8	76
5:9	74, 76
5:10	76
5:10a	76
5:10b	76
5:10–11	216
5:11	74
5:12	77, 223
5:12–14	76
5:12–17	76–77
5:12–21	76
5:13	77, 223
5:14	77
5:15	76–77
5:15–17	76
5:16	77
5:17	76–77
5:18	77
5:18–21	76
5:20	76–77
5:20–21	80
5:21	75, 77
6	77, 83, 101, 103, 267
6–7	83
6–8	108
6:1	77–79, 124, 129–31
6:2	77
6:1–4	77
6:1–11	77, 79
6:1–12	269
6:1–14	77–78, 104, 108–9
6:1–23	77
6:2	78
6:3	79
6:3b	79
6:3–5	78
6:3–14	78
6:4	77, 79, 268
6:5	79
6:5–14	79
6:6	80
6:6–10	80
6:7	80
6:9–10	269
6:10	77
6:11	77, 90
6:11–13	103
6:11–14	80
6:13	77
6:14	81, 84
6:15	77
6:15–23	77, 80
6:19	74, 103
6:21	74
6:21–22	49

6:22	74	8:1–11	91
6:23	90, 266	8:1–17	91, 94
7	81, 89, 93, 104	8:1–27	93
7:1	84	8:1–39	87
7:1–3	82–83	8:2	83, 88–90
7:1–6	80–82, 84, 269	8:3	81, 90, 94
7:2	91	8:4	89–90, 98
7:3	82	8:5–6	98, 269
7:4	82–83, 269	8:5–8	89
7:5	83–84	8:6	90
7:5–6	83	8:7	98
7:6	74, 83–84, 97	8:7–8	90
7:6a	84	8:9	90
7:6b	84	8:9–11	269
7:7	124, 129–31	8:10	91, 104, 267
7:7a	85	8:10a	90
7:7b	85	8:10b	90
7:7–8	269	8:10–11	94
7:7–11	86	8:11	91, 104, 269
7:7–24	88	8:13	269
7:7–25	84–88	8:14	91
7:8	85	8:15	91
7:10	86	8:15–16	91
7:11	85	8:17	91
7:12	85	8:18	74, 92–93
7:13	85	8:18–30	91–92, 94
7:14	52	8:18–39	92
7:14–25	89	8:19–21	92
7:15–22	81	8:22	74
7:16	85	8:23	92
7:17	74	8:26–27	92
7:18	86	8:28	92–93
7:21	86	8:30	92, 94
7:22	86	8:31	94, 124, 129, 131
7:23	86, 107, 206	8:31–39	94
7:23a	86	8:32	216
7:24	86–88, 104	8:33a	94
7:24–25	85, 101	8:33b	94
7:25	84, 86–88, 91, 94, 107	8:34a	94
7:25a	86	8:34b	94
7:25b	86, 92	8:39	90, 95
8	69, 73–74, 83, 87, 91, 95, 101, 104, 109	9–11	95–96, 101, 217
8:1	74, 90, 94	9:1	90
8:1–4	269	9:1–7	216
		9:1–10:21	96

Romans (*cont.*)

9:1–11:36	96
9:3	40
9:6	96, 243
9:7	126
9:10	127
9:14	124, 129–31
9:17	151–52
9:20	96
9:22	96
9:28–29	96
9:30	96–97, 124
9:30–31	98, 129, 131
9:30–32	216
9:30–33	96, 98–100
9:30–10:13	95–96, 98, 101, 193
9:31	97
9:32–33	99
9:32b	97
9:32b–33	97
9:33	97
10:1	97–98
10:1–4	97–98
10:1–13	100
10:4	98–99
10:5	99
10:5–13	99
10:6	99
10:6–7	99
10:6–8	152
10:6–9	99
10:6–17	96
10:7	96
10:8–11	99
10:9	96, 99–101
10:9b	101
10:10	101
10:11	101, 152
10:18	96
11:1	126, 216, 243
11:1–12	96
11:2	152
11:5	74
11:9	189
11:12	101, 223
11:13	96, 101
11:13–16	102
11:13–24	56
11:13–25	95–96
11:14	102
11:15	96, 101–2, 223
11:16	102
11:17	54
11:17–32	56, 102
11:18	102, 107
11:18–20	103
11:19–24	102
11:20	54, 96
11:23	96
11:24	48
11:25	48
11:25–29	102
11:30–31	74
11:30–32	102
11:33–35	102
12–15(16)	56
12:1	103
12:1–2	102–3
12:1–13:14	103
12:1–15:13	57, 102–3
12:3	206
12:16	54
13:5	62
13:11	74
14–15	39
14:1	54, 103–4, 107, 109–10
14:1–3	107
14:1–5	54
14:1–15:6	105
14:1–15:13	56, 58, 103–4, 106, 208
14:3	104, 107
14:4	107
14:4–6	57
14:4–12	105
14:5	104, 107–8
14:5–6	107, 198
14:6	104
14:6b	104
14:6–9	108
14:9	57

14:10	54	15:25–31	52
14:10–12	108	15:26	49
14:13	54, 108	15:27	52
14:14	90	15:30	51, 53
14:14–15	104	15:30–16:23	51
14:14–16:23	50	15:32	51–52
14:15	54	16	39, 47, 54, 58
14:16	108	16:1–16	40
14:17	104, 108–9	16:2	90, 153, 163–64
14:18–21	109	16:3–16	40, 54
14:19	54, 108	16:5	38
14:20–21	108	16:7	40
14:20–23	104	16:11	40
14:22	109	16:11–13	90
14:22–23	109	16:11–14	38
14:23	257	16:13	40
15	49	16:14	51
15:1	104, 109	16:16	40
15:1–3	109	16:17	40, 51, 54–55
15:1–16:27	31	16:17–20	54, 56
15:4	109, 152	16:17a–20	50
15:4–6	110	16:18	54
15:5	57, 109	16:22	164
15:6	46	16:25–27	50
15:7	62	16:26	74, 151–52
15:7–9	110		
15:7–13	73, 105	1 Corinthians	
15:8–9	105	1:23	8
15:10–12	110	4:2	132
15:12	73, 189	4:21	132
15:12–13	73	6	256
15:13	108, 110	6:12	92
15:14	51	6:13	256
15:14–15	51	6:15	256
15:14–16	51	6:16	92, 256
15:14–16:24	50	6:18	256
15:14–16:27	40–50, 55–56	6:19	256
15:15	51, 56	7	256
15:15–16	56	7:4	256
15:16	51	8–10	104
15:16–29	51	10:1–13	261
15:17	90	10:13	92
15:22	62	15:15	132
15:23–24	50–52	16:8	198
15:24	52–53		

2 Corinthians   156
  3–4   54
  5:3   132
  6:1   92
  7:1   44
  9:4   132
  10–13   22
  11:22   126
  12:20   132

Galatians   54, 89, 126, 156
  1:15   243
  2:1–14   164
  2:7   106
  2:15   243
  2:17   132
  3:6   158
  3:10–14   127
  4:1–5   127
  4:4   243
  4:13   192
  4:13–14   192
  4:15   192

Philippians
  2:6–12   268
  3:5   243
  4:3   258
  4:13   258

1 Thessalonians
  3:2   45
  3:13   44–45

2 Thessalonians
  2:17   45
  3:5   45

1 Timothy
  1:12   258–59

2 Timothy
  2:1   258
  4:17   258

Philemon
  1   153
  7   153
  17   107

James
  1:6   257
  2:23   158

Jude
  22   257

Revelation
  5:5   189
  22:16   189

Greco-Roman Literature

Aelius Theon, *Progymnasmata*
  96–97   157

Aristotle, *Athēnaiōn politeia*
  27.2   183

Aristotle, *De generatione animalium*
  1.2   250
  2.4   243, 250

Aristotle, *Politica*
  4.11   182

Aristotle, *Rhetorica*
  3.12.1–3   146

Cicero, *De amicitia*
  65   188

Cicero, *Epistulae ad familiares*
  1.8.1   163
  2.6.1–2   13
  3.1.1   163
  3.5.1   163
  4.2.1   163
  10.7.1   163

Cicero, *De inventione rhetorica*
  1.15.20   41
  3.54   164

Cicero, *De natura deorum*
  2.154   174

Cicero, *De officiis*
  1.47   180
  2.69   185
  2.69–71   185
  3.69–70   231

Cicero, *Topica*
  74   186

Columbia Papyri (P.Col.)
  3.6   163

Demetrius, *De elocutione*
  224   50

Dio Cassius, *Historia romana*
  44.4.4   224

Dio Chrysostom, *Rhodiaca*
  33   257

Diodorus, *Bibliotheca historica*
  40.3   121

Herodotus, *Historiae*
  7.150–152   120

Hesiod, *Catalogue of Women*
  frag. 4   119

Hippocrates, *Jusj.*
  5–10   136

Justinian, *Institutiones*
  1.2.23.1   232

Juvenal, *Satirae*
  14.96–106   37

Plato, *Menexenus*   243

Plautus, *Menaechmi*
  571–572   185

Pliny the Elder, *Naturalis historia*
  28.79–82   248
  29.17   186

Pliny the Younger, *Epistulae*
  2.13   180
  2.13.5   185
  3.2.1–3   185
  10.4.3–4   185
  10.51   13

Plutarch, *Alexander*
  329   136

Plutarch, *De fraterno amore*
  1 (478b)   230

Plutarch, *Moralia*
  53   257

Quintilian, *Institutio oratoria*
  6.1.1   41
  6.1.52   41

Rhetorica ad Herennium
  2.30.47   41
  4.34   25

Seneca, *De beneficiis*
  1.10.5   76
  2.17.3   181
  2.32.1   181
  2.34–35   181
  4.18.1–4   181
  7.18.1   181

Seneca, *De clementia*
  1.14   225

Seneca, *Epistulae morales*
   81.27   185

Seneca the Elder, *Ex. con.*
   4.1   248

Strabo, *Geographica*
   1.2.32   183

Suetonius, *Gaius Caligula*
   59   264

Suetonius, *Divus Claudius*
   25.4   27

Suetonius, *Divus Julius*
   6.1   135
   42.3   38
   76   224

Suetonius, *Tiberius*
   23   241
   24.1   233
   59   241

Tacitus, *Annales*
   1.12   225
   12.26.2   242
   13.2.2   242

Tacitus, *Historiae*
   5.4.2   106

Modern Authors Index

Adams, Edward 62, 259
Adkins, Lesley 82
Adkins, Roy 82
Alexander, Thomas D. 172
Allen, Amy 154
Allen, David M. 160
Alter, Robert 172–73, 175
Anbar, Moshé 190
Ando, Clifford 224–26, 241
Arendt, Hannah 154
Aune, David E. 33, 50, 63, 158
Austin, J. L. 192
Bakhtin, Mikhail M. 3, 32
Balch, David L. 223
Baldwin, Joyce G. 191
Banker, Brenda S. 139
Barclay, John M. G. 179–84, 225, 269
Barrett, C. K. 44, 106–7, 143, 155, 160, 177, 213, 219, 229, 254, 262, 265
Barth, Fredrik 74, 117–18, 121
Bates, Matthew W. 43–44
Baumann, Gerd 136–37
Beale, Gregory K. 160
Beck, Roger 247, 264
Beker, J. Christiaan 31–32, 73, 135
Bell, Catherine 209, 211–12
Benveniste, Émile 131
Beresford, James M. 197–98
Berger, Klaus 1
Berger, Peter L. 9–10
Berquist, Jon L. 26
Best, Ernest 43–44
Billerbeck, Paul 196
Billig, M. G. 68
Bitzer, Lloyd 32–36, 55, 58, 160

Black, Matthew 93
Bloomquist, L. Gregory 16–17, 21–22, 62, 73–74, 227, 234, 245
Bodel, John 247–48, 256
Borkowski, Andrew 223
Botha, Pieter J. J. 164
Bourdieu, Pierre 151, 212, 226
Bowditch, Phebe Lowell 185
Brandt, William J. 41
Bratcher, Robert G. 193–94
Brenton, Lancelot C. L. 170, 208
Brooks, James A. 254
Bruce, Frederick Fyvie 93
Brueggemann, Walter 175
Bruehler, Bart B. 16, 28, 42
Bryan, Christopher 253–54
Bumazhnov, Dmitrij F. 197
Bundy, R. P. 68
Burke, Kenneth 15, 150
Buswell, James O. 94
Byrne, Brendan 5–6, 89, 219, 222, 237
Calderone, Salvatore 184
Calvert-Koyzis, Nancy 111, 138
Cambier, Jules 215
Camp, Claudia V. 28
Campbell, William S. 39, 56–57, 106–7, 134
Carson, D. A. 1
Chapple, Allan 163
Charland, Maurice 15
Chatman, Seymour 17
Cohen, Shaye J. D. 121–22
Combrink, H. J. Bernard 17
Consigny, Scott 35
Conzelmann, Hans 5

Coote, Robert B.   190–91

Craigie, Peter C.   145, 193, 195

Cranfield, C. E. B.   3, 5, 44, 48–49, 54, 61, 67, 74, 80, 83, 88–89, 103, 107, 109, 111, 125, 133, 160, 177, 207, 212–13, 215, 219, 222, 229, 237, 252–55, 257–58, 260, 262, 265

Cranford, Michael   4, 6, 128

Cremer, Hermann   174

Crenshaw, James L.   70

Crook, Zeba A.   178

Dahood, Mitchell   194

Das, A. Andrew   37, 39–40, 45, 105

Davies, William D   223

Dawes, Gregory W.   238–39

deSilva, David A.   179, 184, 230, 245–46, 249–50, 259, 266–67

Dodd, C. H.   160

Donaldson, Terence L.   2, 46, 144

Donfried, Karl P.   54

Douglas, Mary   212

Dovidio, John F.   139

Downs, David J.   40

Drane, John W.   104

Du Toit, Andreas B.   90

Dudley, Donald   224–25

Duncan, John   92

Dunn, James D. G.   2, 6, 36–37, 39, 43–45, 50, 53–55, 59, 62–63, 73–75, 78–79, 83, 86–87, 89–90, 92, 98, 100–103, 107, 111, 124–28, 132–33, 143–45, 152–53, 159, 165, 196, 207, 213, 219–22, 229, 237, 251–54, 260–61, 268

Dunson, Ben C.   111

Durkheim, Émile   79, 209

Eagleton, Terry   15, 21–22

Eemeren, Frans H. van   17

Ehrensperger, Kathy   44–45, 59–60, 154–55, 184

Eilers, Claude   179

Elliott, John H.   7, 227

Elliott, Neil   41, 46, 49, 111, 117, 123, 225–26

Emerton, J. A.   168

Engberg-Pedersen, Troels   181

Eriksson, Anders   17

Esler, Philip F.   9–12, 36–37, 39–41, 45–46, 54–55, 63, 67–68, 75, 103, 105, 108, 116–23, 138–39, 154, 207, 217, 222, 227

Estrada, Nelson P.   100

Fantham, Elaine   246, 264

Fauconnier, Gilles   24–25, 196, 200, 203, 220, 236

Fears, J. Rufus   239–40

Fee, Gordon D.   44, 81, 88, 90, 92–93, 268

Filson, Floyd V.   136

Fisk, Bruce N.   38, 162

Fitzgerald, John T.   52–53

Fitzmyer, Joseph A.   5, 44, 54, 107, 197, 254, 261

Flament, Claude   68

Flanagan, James W.   190

Fokkelman, Jan P.   194–95

Forman, Mark   227

Foster, Robert L.   48–49

Fowl, Stephen   166

France, Richard T.   160

Fredricks, Cathi J.   171–72

Fredriksen, Paula   93

Gadamer, Hans-Georg   211

Gaertner, Samuel L.   139

Gardner, Jane F.   223

Garroway, Joshua D.   106

Gaston, Lloyd   4, 219

Gathercole, Simon J.   2, 64, 67, 146–47

Geertz, Clifford   19–20, 118, 151, 209

Georgi, Dieter   46, 226

Gignac, Alain   131

Gil-White, Francisco J.   121

Gillman, Florence M.   79

Godet, Frederic L.   44, 47, 144, 165, 229, 237, 257–58, 260, 265

Goppelt, Leonhard   1, 261

Gottwald, Norman K.   190–91

Goulder, Michael   89

Gowler, David B.   17

Gradel, Ittai   240

Granerød, Gard 172
Grimes, Ronald L. 210–11
Grubbs, Judith E. 82
Guerra, Anthony J. 68
Haacker, Klaus 227
Habel, Norman C. 169
Habermas, Jürgen 154
Hahn, Ferdinand 89
Halbwachs, Maurice 153
Hall, Jonathan M. 118, 120
Hamilton, Victor P. 170, 172, 175
Hammond, Mason 232–33, 241
Harris, Rendel J. 157
Harris, William V. 182–83
Harrison, James R. 179–80, 182
Haslam, S. Alexander 139
Hays, Richard B. 2, 4, 6, 125, 128–33
Headlam, Arthur C. 44, 82–83, 104
Heim, Erin M. 238–39, 243
Hester (Amador), J. David 3, 151
Hester, James D. 164
Hock, Ronald F. 157
Hodge, Caroline J. 87–88, 122–23,
    135–37, 209, 214–15, 242–43, 250–51
Hoffman, Lawrence A. 201
Hofius, Otfried 252
Holland, Tom 237, 253
Hope, Valerie M. 248
Hopkins, Keith 182
Horsley, Richard A. 117
Houlette, Melissa 139
Hubbard, Moyer V. 77
Huber, Lynn R. 24–25, 169
Hübner, Hans 5, 89
Hughes, Everett C. 117
Hunsaker, David M. 35–36
Hunter, Archibald M. 43
Hüsken, Ute 210–11
Hutchinson, John 118
Jeal, Roy R. 21
Jenkins, Richard 74, 118
Jeremias, Joachim 146
Jervis, L. Ann 42, 44, 89
Jewett, Robert 2, 5–6,
    12, 36, 38–39, 41, 43–45, 50–52, 54,
60, 62–63, 70, 74–75, 78, 83, 86, 89,
92–93, 98–103, 107, 109, 111, 125–27,
129–30, 132–33, 143–44, 159, 162–64,
177, 202, 207, 213, 216, 219, 227, 244,
251–55, 258, 265
Jipp, Joshua W. 128–29, 202
Johnson, Lee A. 164
Kaiser, Walter C. 74, 160
Kaplan, Yehiel 223–24
Karris, Robert T. 104
Käsemann, Ernst 1, 3–5, 44, 63, 81–
    82, 86–87, 92, 98, 100, 106, 109, 125,
    187, 202, 213, 219, 222
Keesmaat, Sylvia C. 226
Kennedy, George A. 13, 23–24, 34,
    157, 178, 233–34
Kertzer, David I. 212
Kim, Johann D. 96
Kim, Kyu Seop 239
Kirk, J. R. Daniel 128, 130
Klein, Günter 1, 49
Kloppenborg, John S. 22
Knauf-Belleri, Ernst A. 190
Koch, Dietrich-Alex 157
Kugel, James L. 195
Kunst, Christiane 238
La Piana, George 39
Lagrange, Marie-Joseph 83, 93
Lakoff, George 24, 29
Lambrecht, Jan 132
Lampe, Peter 36–40
Lane, Crystal 209
Lausberg, Heinrich 41, 50
Leff, Michael C. 115
Lemche, Niels P. 167
Lennon, Jack 247–48
Lenski, R. C. H. 229, 254, 262
Lévi-Strauss, Claude 212
Levin, Yigal 239
Levine, Lee I. 162, 198, 201
Lieu, Judith M. 50
Lincoln, Andrew T. 126
Lincoln, Bruce 136
Lindsay, Hugh 247, 263–64
Liverani, Mario 168

Loader, William 137
Lohse, E. 86
Longenecker, Bruce W. 86
Longenecker, Richard N. 90, 127, 204, 208, 222
Lopez, Davina C. 234
Loux, Stephenie 139
Lowe, Bruce A. 179–80
Lucas, Alec J. 64
Luckmann, Thomas 9–10
Luz, Ulrich 74, 133
Lyall, Francis 239
Mack, Burton L. 136
Malina, Bruce J. 27, 76, 93, 95, 99, 112, 115–17, 142, 145–46, 148, 178, 188, 193, 245–46
Marcus, Joel 105
Marshall, I. Howard 197
Marshall, Peter 53
Martin, Brice L. 86
Mason, Steve 116, 122–23
Matera, Frank J. 229, 237, 253–54, 262
Matthews, Victor H. 190
Mattingly, David J. 248
McBride, S. Dean, Jr. 152–53
McFadden, Kevin W. 94
McGarty, Craig 139
McGinn, Thomas A. J. 82
McNutt, Paula M. 190
Meeks, Wayne A. 18–19, 104
Mendenhall, George E. 167
Metzger, Bruce M. 126
Michel, Otto 124, 133, 213, 257
Miller, Arthur B. 35
Miller, Carolyn R. 115
Miller, David M. 116, 121–22
Minear, Paul S. 41
Mommsen, Theodor 232–33
Moo, Douglas J. 3, 5, 35, 45, 49, 50, 54–55, 61–63, 73–75, 78, 80, 89, 101–3, 107–9, 124–25, 127, 133, 143, 144, 158–59, 165, 202, 205, 207, 213, 215, 222, 229, 237, 252–54, 257, 260, 265
Morales, Rodrigo J. 255

Morgan, Teresa 14, 20, 45, 100, 174–76, 184–86, 232, 253, 257
Morris, Pam 3
Moxnes, Halvor 1, 7–9, 43, 56, 65, 67, 142
Munck, Johannes 46
Murphy-O'Connor, Jerome 231
Murray, John 229
Nanos, Mark D. 38, 57
Nelson, Richard D. 249, 250
Neubrand, Maria 12, 128, 216
Neyrey, Jerome H. 67, 100
Nickelsburg, George W. E. 70
Nier, Jason A. 139
Nock, Arthur D. 241
Norden, Christopher G. 193
O'Brien, Peter T. 258, 268
O'Connor, Michael P. 171
O'Neil, Edward N. 157
Oakes, Penelope J. 139
Okamura, Jonathan 119
Olbrechts-Tyteca, Lucie 150–51, 161, 192, 221, 229, 234, 236, 251
Oropeza, B. J. 40, 55
Osiek, Carolyn 223
Paden, John N. 119
Pareto, Vilfredo 151
Patton, John H. 34
Pearson, Brook W. R. 79
Peppard, Michael 233, 238–42
Perelman, Chaim 150–51, 161, 192, 221, 229, 234, 236, 251
Pilch, John J. 89, 109, 117
Piper, John 174
Plevnik, Joseph 67
Porter, Stanley E. 54–55
Post, Edwin 100
Potter, David S. 248
Price, Simon 240
Rad, Gerhard von 169–70, 174
Räisänen, Heikki 89, 98, 112
Reasoner, Mark 57, 104–5
Rendall, Robert 160
Rengstorf, Karl H. 42
Reyburn, William D. 193–94

Reynolds, Katherine J. 139
Rhyne, Thomas C. 5
Richards, E. Randolph 163–64
Richards, Kent H. 192
Richardson, Neil 149
Ridderbos, Herman N. 89
Rimmon–Kenan, Shlomith 17
Rives, James B. 240
Robbins, Vernon K. vii, 14–28, 42, 69–
70, 73–74, 77–78, 81, 85, 87–88, 96,
103, 113–15, 124, 137, 140, 142, 157,
168, 171, 188–89, 192, 196, 199, 201,
203, 218–20, 231, 233–34, 236–37,
245, 267–68
Rock, Ian E. 43
Rohrbaugh, Richard L. 116–17, 230
Roosen, A. 49
Rouwhorst, G. 198
Safrai, Shmuel 201
Saller, Richard P. 179
Sampley, J. Paul 50
Sanday, William 44, 82–83, 104
Sanders, E. P. 1, 81
Scharbert, Josef 169
Scheidel, Walter 248
Schlier, Heinrich 5, 52
Schliesser, Benjamin 158, 257
Schreiner, Thomas 4, 6, 73, 75, 87, 89,
107, 125, 133, 145, 202, 213, 229, 237,
252, 254, 262
Schrenk, Gottlob 126
Schwartz, Seth 61
Scott, George M. 118
Scott, James M. 239
Severy, Beth 42, 224–25
Sherwin-White, A. N. 179
Shils, Edward 209
Singer, Milton 211
Sisson, Russell B. 22
Smit, Peter–Ben 210
Smith, Anthony D. 118, 121–22
Smith, Craig R. 35–36
Snodgrass, Klyne R. 86, 89
Soskice, Janet Martin 239
Sparks, Kenton L. 153

Spitaler, Peter 257
Stamps, Dennis L. 31–33, 36
Stanley, Christopher D. 144, 154, 157–
58, 160–61
Stansell, Gary 170
Stark, Rodney 216
Ste. Croix, G. E. M. de 182
Stendahl, Krister 144
Stökl Ben Ezra, Daniel 196–98
Stowers, Stanley K. 2, 63–64, 70, 84–
85, 95–96, 98, 104–5, 111, 125, 127–
30, 133–34, 214
Strack, Hermann 196
Strange, James F. 162
Stuhlmacher, Peter 1, 49, 125, 143, 257
Swetnam, James 216
Synge, F. C. 257
Tajfel, Henri 68, 138
Tambiah, Stanley J. 212
Taylor, Lily Ross 240
Thaden, Robert H. von, Jr. 16, 21, 25, 42
Thiselton, Anthony C. 155
Thom, Johan C. 42
Thompson, John B. 22, 151–56, 199
Thurén, Lauri 33, 89, 120, 126, 143
Tiwald, Markus 197
Tobin, Thomas H. 6, 36, 39–40, 61,
62, 78, 107, 132
Todorov, Tzvetan 32
Toney, Carl N. 104–7
Tov, Emmanuel 157
Towner, Philip H. 259
Toynbee, J. M. C. 263–64
Tripolitis, Antonia 240
Turner, John C. 68, 138
Turner, Mark 24–25, 196, 200, 203,
220, 236
Turner, Victor W. 211, 226
Vatz, Richard E. 34–35
Vermes, Geza 147
Vida, G. Levi Della 153, 169
Waetjen, Herman C. 159
Wallace-Hadrill, Andrew 185
Wallace, Daniel B. 169, 217, 228, 252,
256–57, 259

Wallace, Karl R.   15
Walters, James C.   223
Waltke, Bruce K.   171–72, 195
Wanamaker, Charles A.   vii, 22–23, 156
Ward, Christine M.   139
Wartenberg, Thomas E.   154
Watson, Duane F.   16
Watson, Francis   2, 9–10, 106, 144
Weber, Max   117
Wedderburn, A. J. M.   51
Weima, Jeffrey A. D.   54
Weinfeld, Moshe   145
Wenham, Gordon J.   168–72, 175, 199
White, Eugene E.   161
White, John L.   164–65
Whitsett, Christopher G.   43–44
Whittle, Sarah   152
Wilckens, Ulrich   1, 4
Wilder, Amos N.   158
Williamson, Paul R.   175
Wilson, James P.   93
Wilson, Robert R.   152–53
Winbery, Carlton L.   254
Wissowa, Georg   176
Witherington, Ben, III   197
Worthington, Jonathan   252
Wright, David P.   249
Wright, N. T.   2, 94, 129–30, 132, 165,
    187, 208
Wuellner, Wilhelm   23, 33, 50–51
Young, Norman H.   107
Young, Stephen L.   129
Zahn, Theodor   128
Zerwick, Maximilian   254

Subject Index

Abraham, v–vi, 1–7, 9–14, 19, 27–28, 42,
53, 62, 69–72, 84, 89, 106, 111–14,
124–42, 144, 146–50, 156–59, 161,
165, 168–77, 186–88, 196, 200, 202,
204–10, 212–20, 222–28, 230, 232–33,
236–38, 240, 242–45, 250–63, 265–68,
271–78, 280, 284, 286–87, 294, 298,
300, 302, 304–5
    father, forefather, fatherhood, 1–2, 4,
        6, 8–9, 12, 19, 26–28, 69–72, 106,
        112–14, 124–29, 131–37, 139–40,
        145–49, 159, 167, 190, 202, 205–7,
        212–20, 223–25, 233, 236–38,
        240–45, 250–55, 257, 259–62,
        266–68, 271–73, 280, 286
    fictive kinship, 135–36
    model par excellence, 3
    myth of origins. See myth of origins
    pater familias. See pater familias
    pater patriae. See pater patriae
    superordinate. See superordinate
adoption, 44, 223, 238–43, 276, 286, 288–
    90, 299, 303
Augustus, 42, 82, 224–25, 232–33, 235,
    240–42, 264, 299
    heir, 8–9, 88, 123, 135, 136–37, 172–
        73, 209, 214, 222–23, 227–28, 233,
        239, 241–43, 250–51, 263, 266,
        272, 286
    practice, 239, 288
    metaphor, 167, 238–39, 243, 280, 286,
        291, 299
    natural dynasty, 241
    Nero, 225, 233, 241–42, 285
    pater familias. See pater familias

    providential, 241
    Roman populace, 219, 233–34, 240–
        41, 243, 273
    Tiberius, 225, 233–34, 240–41, 248
audience
    implied, 17, 33, 42–4, 47–8, 50, 52–60,
        62, 66, 69–72, 74–6, 78–81, 84–5,
        88, 93, 96–8, 101, 103, 108, 111–
        12, 114, 124, 127–8, 131–32, 135,
        137, 140–41, 149, 154, 156, 162,
        165–66, 179, 208, 210, 212, 218–
        20, 231, 234, 236–37, 242, 245, 256,
        258–59, 261–63, 265–69, 271–73
    real, 21, 29, 36, 43, 47, 50, 57–8, 64,
        82, 123, 156, 160–62, 165, 196, 207,
        248
blessedness, blessing. See David
boast, boasting, 2, 5, 8, 56, 58, 64–8, 70,
    72, 75–7, 84, 91, 95, 102, 107, 111–12,
    132, 141–44, 147–50, 159, 192, 196,
    214, 222, 263, 270, 272–73, 283
broker, 14, 66, 75, 77, 91, 93–101, 193,
    225, 268, 273–74
challenge. See honor
chreia, 157–58, 165, 177–78, 187, 271,
    286, 297
circumcision, 8, 10–11, 19, 66, 71, 105–
    06, 110, 112, 114–15, 126–27, 133,
    138, 141, 143, 201–13, 215–18, 220–
    22, 229, 243–44, 251, 262, 272, 274,
    283, 286, 292
    imagined world, 209
    lived world, 209
    performance theorists, 211
    ritual failure, 210, 211, 299

circumcision (cont.)
 ritual, rite, 78–79, 106, 143, 201, 205–6, 210–12, 251, 272, 276, 282–85, 287, 299, 303
 seal of righteousness, 207–8, 212
 successful ritual, 209–10
citation, 18–19, 71, 101, 113, 156–58, 160–61, 165–66, 177–78, 187–89, 193–96, 198, 200, 204–5, 208, 251–55, 260–62, 271–72, 300
 carrier of the letter, delivery, 162–65, 279, 288
 context, 160–61, 165–66, 187, 193, 222
 literacy rate, 161, 164–65, 234
 synagogues, 162, 198, 282, 290, 301
 translations, translate, 157, 162
Claudius's edict. *See* rhetorical situation
conflict. *See* ideological
culture, 7, 8, 11–12, 15, 17–21, 29, 42, 45, 58–59, 64–66, 74–75, 82, 89, 91, 93, 95, 99–100, 118–19, 136–37, 140, 144, 148–49, 151, 153–55, 176–80, 182–84, 188, 191, 209, 211, 230–31, 239, 242, 246, 250, 259, 268, 273, 280–81, 284, 302
 capital, 151–53
 dominant, conquering, 20, 231, 246
 fields of interaction, 151–54
 Hellenistic, Greek, 2, 19–20, 46, 49–50, 57, 59–60, 63, 118–120, 122, 136, 144, 179, 183. 239–40, 246, 257, 263, 285, 300, 303
 Judean, 2, 4–5, 8, 10, 13, 20–21, 36, 45–46, 53, 56, 59–61, 65, 67–68, 105–7, 112, 121, 126, 137, 142–43, 146, 148, 198, 204, 207–8, 249, 265
 Mediterranean, 7, 11, 13, 18–22, 27, 58, 64–66, 89, 91, 93, 95, 99–100, 116, 142–45, 148–49, 153, 183, 188, 191, 193, 230, 250, 268, 273
 Roman, 8, 12–14, 19–20, 45, 52–53, 59–60, 78, 100–1, 106–7, 135, 144, 148, 174–80, 183–86, 219, 223–26, 230–32, 238–43, 246–48, 253, 256,

culture, Roman (cont.)
 263–64, 266, 272–73, 275, 277, 281–85, 288, 290, 293, 295–96, 300–3
 subculture, 20
 symbolic form, 151–52, 154, 209
David, 19, 42, 44, 141, 174, 188–91, 196, 199–200, 239, 271–72, 290, 304
 blessing, blessedness, 71, 113–14, 141, 188, 192–95, 199–200, 202–4, 206, 272, 296
 patriarch, patriarchal, 11, 72, 121, 129–30, 132, 136–37, 165, 175, 187, 190–91, 208, 271–72, 305
 putative, fictive kinship, 21, 135–36, 191
 repentance, 193, 195, 272
death. *See* pollution
deeds, 3, 5, 8, 13, 65–67, 70–71, 77, 89–90, 94–95, 99, 101, 103, 112, 114, 133–35, 140–44, 146, 148–49, 159, 176–77, 187–89, 191–96, 200, 202–3, 238, 243, 261–62, 271–73
diatribe, 60, 63, 70, 111, 127, 130–31, 271, 300
ethical life, 14, 44, 56–57, 60, 68–69, 72, 77, 80, 108, 181, 268–69, 273–74
ethnicity, ethnic, 2, 4, 10, 13, 21, 44–46, 579, 67, 70, 74, 88, 105–6, 113, 116–23, 126–27, 129, 136–37, 144–45, 153, 187, 204, 207–8, 210–11, 216–17, 222, 244, 263, 268, 272–74, 276, 284–87, 293–94, 299–300, 305
 primordialism, primordial, 118–21, 274, 284, 298
 situational, 119–20, 139, 294
 cultural features, 74, 117–19
expiate, expiation. *See* pollution
faith, faithfulness. *See also* patron-client, trust
favor. *See* patron-client
glory, glorification. *See* resurrection
Godfearers. *See* rhetorical situation
grace. *See* favor
heir, 8–9, 172–73, 222–23, 227, 233, 239, 241–43, 263, 272

Holy Spirit, 44, 51, 53, 56–57, 81, 83–84, 87–94, 98–99, 104, 108–9, 269, 282, 287

honor, 7–9, 12–14, 21, 58, 64–69, 72, 74–77, 85, 89, 91–95, 97, 99–100, 102, 112, 116, 142–43, 146–49, 176–78, 182, 184, 191–93, 198, 202, 206, 230–31, 238, 257–59, 271, 274, 280, 295, 297
  ascribed, 13, 68, 71, 142, 191, 206, 214–15, 230, 238, 257, 272
  challenge, riposte, 21, 64–65, 95, 102, 116, 189, 202, 230–31, 272
  inherited, 13, 112, 142, 145, 202, 214–15, 220
  limited good, 67, 93, 100, 145, 294
  shame, 7–8, 12, 17, 21, 64–67, 75, 92, 97, 142–43, 148–49, 191–92, 214, 230, 257, 259, 279, 295

ideological power, texture, ideology, 3, 9, 14–17, 19, 21–22, 29, 42–44, 60, 62, 67, 69, 74, 78–81, 84, 88, 93, 96–97, 134–37, 140, 150–51, 153–56, 171, 176, 191–92, 199, 209, 211–12, 215, 217–18, 224, 226, 233, 236, 238, 240–43, 255, 259, 262–63, 266–68, 272–73, 275, 277, 282, 284, 289–90, 302–3
  conflict, 1, 7–10, 22, 37, 55, 104, 106, 109, 119, 138–39, 282, 293, 300, 302
  domination, dominance, 89, 154, 155, 224, 295, 304
  institution, institutional, 22–23, 153–54, 199, 224, 239

inner texture, 14, 16–18, 114–15, 168, 171, 192, 205, 268
  argumentative, 17, 141–42, 144, 146, 205, 228, 236
  narrational, 168, 169
  opening-middle-closing, 17, 114, 171
  progressive, 17, 114–15, 205
  repetitive, 17, 114–15, 205
  sensory-aesthetic, 17–18, 25, 54, 115, 192–93, 272

interlocutor, 58, 60, 62–65, 70, 77–78, 80, 111–12, 116, 127–28, 130–32,

interlocutor (cont.)
  134, 140, 148–49, 159, 254, 261–62, 271–72

intertexture
  cultural, 18, 19, 42, 76, 80, 87, 134, 137, 140, 144, 146, 182–83, 189, 204, 217, 220, 223, 226, 233, 238, 253, 263, 266–68, 272
  historical, 18–19, 79, 156, 199
  oral-scribal, 18, 43, 97, 99, 208
  social, 19, 78–82, 88, 135, 176–78, 184, 214, 219, 230–34, 238, 245, 251–52, 256, 258–59, 262–63, 265–66, 217, 273

Ioudaios. See Judean
Jew. See Judean
Judean
  homeland, territory, 119–20, 122, 139, 294
  ethnicity. See ethnicity

law
  annulment, 80–82, 85, 98
  condemn, indict, 60–64, 65–66, 69, 76–77, 80–84, 86–91, 94, 97, 104, 143, 196, 227, 231, 269, 272
  of sin, 86–89, 92
  of the Spirit, 88
  fulfill, 81, 85, 87–88, 90–91, 93, 97–99, 108, 269, 274

limited good. See honor
loyalty. See patron-client, trust
Mediterranean culture. See culture
metaphor, metaphorical, 24–25, 78, 89, 156, 238–39, 243, 280, 286, 299
myth of origins, v, 13, 112, 136, 201–8, 212, 215–16, 220, 238, 242–43
  adoption. See adoption
  essentialist, 136–37
  malleable, 119, 135–36, 274
  narrative characterization, 242
  natural, 136, 241–42
  processual, 136–37

pater familias, 223–24, 227, 240
  Augustus. See Augustus
  genius, 240

pater familias (*cont.*)
    Jupiter, 239–40
    pater patriae. See pater patriae
pater patriae, 218, 224, 225–27, 240, 267, 272
    cultural scripts, 226
    public service, 224–25, 240
    Roman Emperor cult, 226
patrilineal descent, 218, 224–27, 240, 267, 272
    ancestors, 119, 134, 137, 177, 215, 218, 250, 263, 271, 273
    resemblance, 134, 171, 214–15, 217, 263, 271
    seminal form, 72, 137, 245, 250, 256, 260, 262, 266, 273–74
patron-client, 14, 21, 53, 69, 145, 148, 153, 167–68, 170, 172–74, 178–79, 185, 206, 212, 224–25
    favor, 12, 14, 53, 75, 76–78, 80, 94, 99, 112, 130, 132, 141, 146, 148, 166, 173–74, 177–82, 184–85, 187, 192, 206, 214, 221, 228, 236, 243–44, 250, 271–72
    fides, 14, 45, 101, 176, 184–86, 188, 231–32, 253, 278, 293
    trust, v–vi, 13–14, 45–47, 48, 51–53, 56–58, 60, 66–67, 69, 71–72, 74–77, 80, 84, 88, 95–102, 104, 108–9, 111–13, 132, 134–35, 138, 141–42, 145, 149–50, 156, 158–59, 165–66, 173–74, 176–78, 184–88, 192, 200, 202, 204–8, 212–220, 224–25, 227–29, 231–33, 236–38, 240, 242–45, 251–63, 265–67, 269, 271–74, 295
pollution, 13–14, 72, 245–49, 252, 255–56, 258–60, 263–69, 273–74, 282, 290
    dead, death, 7, 13, 19, 27, 72, 74–80, 83–90, 92, 94, 96, 101–2, 104, 112, 114, 137, 186, 188, 245–53, 255–58, 261, 263–69, 273–274, 277, 281, 286, 290, 296, 298, 302
    expiate, expiation, 66, 263–69
    infertility, 248, 259

pollution (*cont.*)
    profane, 246
    purity, 21, 77–78, 85, 105–6, 115, 144–48, 179, 196, 199, 201, 246–47, 249, 268, 272, 280
    sacred, 245–46
promise, vi, 4, 53, 71–72, 96, 112, 114–15, 132, 134, 166, 171, 173, 175, 214, 218–20, 222–23, 226–31, 236–37, 240, 243–44, 251–52, 254, 257–59, 261, 265, 266, 272, 305
    heir. *See* adoption
    law. *See* law
    pater familias. See pater familias
    pater patriae. See Abraham
    trust. *See* patron-client, trust; patron-client, *fides*
    world, 8–9, 12, 218, 220, 222–28, 232–33, 237, 244, 258, 266, 272
recategorization. *See* superordinate
resurrection, 14, 44, 72–73, 74–90, 82–84, 87–88, 91, 94–96, 101–3, 128, 219, 267–69, 273–74, 288
    ethical life. *See* ethical life
    glory, glorification, 69, 73, 75–76, 91–92, 94–95
    reproductive organs, 250, 255–57, 259, 273
rhetography, 24, 200, 234
rhetorical situation, v, 14, 31–36, 40–41, 51, 53–55, 57–58, 144, 160, 277, 295, 299, 303
    Claudius's edict, 36, 38–39, 58, 105, 162
    constraints, 33–35
    ethos, 32, 41–43, 47, 57, 60, 181
    exigence, 34–36, 48, 50, 54–56, 95–96, 111, 113, 295
    exordium, 16, 31–32, 40–43, 45, 47, 51, 53, 55, 57, 156, 297, 304
    Godfearers, 37, 39, 162, 196, 198
    historical situation, 32, 36, 39–40, 144
    implied, entextualized, rhetorical situation, v, 14, 31–33
    literacy rate. *See* citation

rhetorical situation (cont.)
    names, 39, 40, 57, 120
    pathos, 32, 47, 51, 53–54, 60, 62, 76,
        85, 97–98, 103
    peroratio, 16, 31–32, 40–41, 50–51,
        55–56, 73, 304
    strong, weak, 4, 9, 56–58, 61, 104–9,
        208, 296
rhetorolect
    apolocalyptic, 23, 25–27, 69–70,
        72–74, 81, 85, 87–88, 96, 115, 218–
        20, 236–37, 267–68
    conceptual blending theory, 24
    critical spatiality theory, 24
    ICM (Idealized Cognitive Model), 24,
        28
    miracle, 23, 27, 115, 245
    precreation, 23, 27, 70
    priestly, 23, 28, 66, 77–78, 115, 196,
        201, 203, 212, 218, 220, 267–68
    prophetic, 23, 26, 42, 44, 47, 60, 66,
        69–70, 114, 188, 196, 212
    two-dimensional matrix, 28
    wisdom, 23, 25–26, 47, 51, 70, 89, 90,
        103, 113–115, 124, 140, 142, 158,
        188–89, 196, 203, 212, 218, 237
righteousness
    deeds. *See* deeds
    ethical life, living. *See* ethical life
    favor. *See* patron-client
    gift. *See* patron-client, favor
    Mosaic law. *See* law
    relationship, 181, 186, 200, 206, 210,
        214, 228, 260, 272
    Spirit. *See* Holy Spirit
    trust. *See* patron-client
riposte. *See* patron-client, challenge, ri-
    poste
ritual, rite. *See* circumcision
salvation, 1, 4–5, 13, 46, 59–61, 69, 73, 76,
    79, 85, 87–88, 91, 97, 102, 104, 109,
    126, 144, 159, 252, 281, 294, 303
shame. *See* honor
significant other, 8, 13–14, 72, 75, 102,
    176, 230, 273–74

sin
    condemnation. *See* law
    expiation. *See* pollution
    indictment. *See* law, condemn, indict
    Mosaic law. *See* law
    pollution. *See* pollution
social and cultural texture, 14, 16, 21, 67,
    69, 93, 99–100, 134–35, 137–38, 144,
    151, 176, 204, 209, 216, 226, 263, 268,
    271
    anthropological, 21
sociological, 9, 16, 21–22, 26, 117, 287
social identity theory. *See* superordinate
sociorhetorical interpretation (SRI), 14–
    16, 18, 25–26, 29, 115, 140, 150, 189,
    205
spaces
    firstspace (experienced), 25–28, 47,
        96, 103, 113, 115, 137, 140, 196,
        199, 201, 212, 218–20, 236, 245,
        267, 268
    generic (conceptual mental), 25, 203
    secondspace (conceptualized), 25–28,
        44, 75, 85, 96, 196, 199, 212, 220,
        236, 239, 245, 268
    thirdspace (of blending), 25, 29,
        69–70, 72, 75, 77, 81, 85, 87, 96,
        103, 114, 124, 140, 188, 196, 200,
        203, 212, 218–19, 237, 245, 268
superordinate, 10–11, 53, 139–40, 215–
    16, 227, 263, 265, 267–68, 272
    recategorization, 10, 139
    social identity theory, 10–12, 68, 138–
        39, 301
weak and strong. *See* rhetorical situation
works. *See* deeds

CPSIA information can be obtained
at www.ICGtesting.com
Printed in the USA
BVHW03*1709290318
511957BV00001B/1/P